JOINT PARENTAL AUTHORITY

EUROPEAN FAMILY LAW SERIES

JOINT PARENTAL AUTHORITY

A comparative legal study on the continuation of joint parental authority after divorce and the breakup of a relationship in Dutch and Danish law and the CEFL principles

C.G. JEPPESEN DE BOER

intersentia

Antwerpen – Oxford – Portland

Distribution for the UK:
Hart Publishing Ltd.
16C Worcester Place
Oxford OX1 2JW
UK
Tel: + 44 1865 51 75 30
Fax: + 44 1865 51 07 10

Distribution for Switzerland and Germany:
Stämpfli Verlag AG
Wölflistrasse 1
CH-3001 Bern
Switzerland
Tel: + 41 (0)31 300 63 18
Fax: + 41 (0)31 300 66 88

Distribution for the USA and Canada:
International Specialized Book Services
920 NE 58th Ave Suite 300
Portland, OR 97213
USA
Tel: + 1 800 944 6190 (toll free)
Tel: +1 503 287 3093
Fax: + 1 503 280 8832
email: info@ isbs.com

Distribution for other countries:
Intersentia Publishers
Groenstraat 31
BE-2640 Mortsel
Belgium
Tel: + 32 3 680 15 50
Fax: + 32 3 658 71 21

This volume is based on the dissertation defended by the author at Utrecht University on 23 May 2008.

Typesetting: G.J. Wiarda Institute for Legal Research, Boothstraat 6, 3512 BW Utrecht.

Christina Gyldenløve Jeppesen
Joint parental authority. A comparative legal study on the continuation of joint parental authority after divorce and the breakup of a relationship in Dutch and Danish law and the CEFL principles

ISBN 978-90-5095-800-4
D/2008/7849/44
NUR 822

ACKNOWLEDGEMENTS

First and foremost, I would like to thank my supervisor at the Molengraaff Institute, Katharina Boele-Woelki, for providing me with the possibility of writing a PhD thesis on an enticing topic which sent me on a journey into not just law, but also the social sciences. You were the perfect supervisor: supportive, sometimes demanding, but always fair and your comments were always useful.

Secondly, I wish to thank a Lecturer at the University of Copenhagen, Annette Kronborg, for inspiration and support. Without you, I might have lingered on in search of an understanding of the best interests principle. You always knew how to steer me in the direction of responsibility towards the law.

The Molengraaff Institute was an inspiring place to carry out the research and I have missed the discussions with my colleagues during the last year when I was not present very often. Thank you to all my direct colleagues in the Section on Private International Law, Comparative Law and Family Law: Bente, Ellen, Merel, Nora, Richard, Vesna, Wendy and Trix who in various ways have contributed to this book. A special thank you to Ian Curry-Sumner with whom I shared an office during the initial years of our research and further shared many spectacular moments. You have helped and supported me in so many ways. Further, a special thank you to Machteld Vonk who provided me with both practical and academic advice.

Furthermore, I wish to thank Corrie van Rooijen and Mila Putters at the Wiarda Institute for advice and support throughout the years of research and to thank the Netherlands Organisation for Scientific Research (NWO) for financing the research. Further, thank you to Peter Morris for editing the English and to Titia Kloos and Willemien Vreekamp at the Wiarda Institute for editing the manuscript for publication.

Finally, I wish to thank the members of the reading committee: Professor Antokolskaia, Professor Giesen, Professor Godsk-Pedersen, Professor Goldschmidt, Dr Punselie and Dr Spruijt.

The last phase of writing a PhD was not an easy task. The many recent and pending changes to the law meant that the manuscript for this book remained open-ended during the final phase. The combination of a PhD thesis and caring for two young children is a challenge. I thank my husband, Dennis de Boer, for not losing faith in the project, even when times were tough, and our children Oscar and Erik for not losing faith in me during all the hours spent 'upstairs' working on 'the book'.

The book would not have been completed at this stage or perhaps ever if I had not had as much help from my parents-in-law Hans and Inneke de Boer and my mother Ruth Jeppesen who for long periods stayed with us in Haarlem. Thank you for the love and care that you give to our boys and for all the practical help that you have provided.

TABLE OF CONTENTS

Chapter II.
Past present and future 31

LIST OF ABBREVIATIONS

CEFL	Commission on European Family Law
CRC	UN Convention on the rights of the child
DCC	Dutch Civil Code
ECHR	European Convention on Human Rights
ECtHR	European Court of Human Rights
LJN	Landelijke jurisprudentienummer
NJ	Nederlandse Jurisprudentie
TFA	Tidsskrift for familie- og arveret
UFR	Ugeskrift for Retsvæsen
WPNR	Weekblad voor Privaatrecht, Notariaat en Registratie

PART I
THE LAW IN CONTEXT

CHAPTER I
INTRODUCTION

PROLOGUE

At a time when the notion of fault is generally viewed as an irrelevant factor in the procedures pertaining to the dissolution of a failed marriage,[1] it is an interesting phenomenon that fault pertaining to the failure of continued parenting is increasingly viewed as a relevant factor in procedures concerning the division of powers and responsibilities concerning children.

It is possible to view the development as a transfer of legal norms from the marriage to parenting. The pertinent question which arises is whether the determination of fault in relation to failed parenting is any less dubious than when fault was taken into consideration in relation to a failed marriage?[2]

I.1. INTRODUCTION

I.1.1. THE SUBJECT-MATTER

This study provides a comparative legal study of the concept and content of joint parental authority after divorce and the breakup of a relationship in Dutch and Danish law and the recently drafted Principles on parental responsibilities by the Commission on European Family Law.[3]

---

1. K. Boele-Woelki, F. Ferrand, C. González Beilfuss, M. Jäntera-Jareborg, N. Lowe, D. Martiny, W. Pintens, *Principles of European Family Law Regarding Divorce and Maintenance Between Former Spouses*, Antwerp-Oxford: Intersentia, 2004, p. 26, 54 and p. 75-76.
2. A. Kronborg, *Forældremyndighed og Menneskelig Integritet*, Copenhagen: Jurist- og Økonomforbundets Forlag, 2007, p. 99-100 with reference to K. Illum, 'Skyld og Skilsmisse', *UFR, Section B*, 1932, p. 265-274 and Dutch Parliamentary proceedings 1968/1969 (*Kamerstukken*), 10 213, No. 3, p. 14: 'It is after all frequently not possible to ascertain which spouse carries the most blame for the break down of the marriage'.
3. The subject-matter and purpose is further elaborated in more detail below, Section I.2.1.

I.1.2. NATIONAL DEVELOPMENTS

In the Netherlands, a joint request procedure was given a legislative basis allowing unmarried parents to obtain and ex-spouses to retain joint parental authority in 1995.[4] Only three years later the legislature amended the Dutch Civil Code in favour of an automatic continuation of joint parental authority after divorce. After the amendment joint parental authority after divorce has become the legal norm also in cases where the parent with whom the child resides opposes such an allocation.[5] This dramatic change may be illustrated by some statistics. Before the amendment (1997) 34% of parents opted for joint parental authority after divorce. After the change (1998) joint parental authority continued in 74% (1999) and 93% (2001) of divorces.[6] The change spurred intense debate amongst academics and left a whole set of questions unanswered. Is joint parental authority a time bomb, an empty gesture or a means to enhance relationships?[7]

There is currently a proposed Act to facilitate 'Continued Parenting' after a divorce or the breakup of a relationship by requiring parents to agree on a 'parenting plan' which would substantiate how the parents are to divide care and responsibilities after a divorce or the breakup of a relationship. The possibility to make use of mediation is an inherent element in the proposed Act. The proposal also aims to establish a set of minimum norms for the division of 'care and responsibilities'. Among these norms is the fact that it should not in principle be possible to agree that there should be no contact between the parent (who does not reside with the child) and the child. The primary aim of this proposal is to implement *a child's right to be cared for by both parents.*

In Denmark, a joint request procedure was introduced in 1986 allowing unmarried parents to obtain and ex-spouses to retain joint parental authority. After 2002 it continued after divorce unless a request for sole parental authority was

4 The term 'parental authority' rather than 'parental responsibilities/responsibility' has been chosen in respect of the law of the Netherlands and Denmark, See below Section I.5. of this Chapter.

5 In cases where joint parental authority was established by unmarried parents (primarily based upon parental agreement) the development after the breakup of a relationship is similar, Chapters II and V, Sections II.2.4. and V.4.1.2.

6 Dutch Statistical Authority, CBS on www.statline.nl.

7 P. van Teffelen: 'Gezamenlijke gezag na scheiding: tijdbom, lege huls of groeimodel', *FJR* 2000, p. 26-29.

made by one or both of the parents.[8] The new Danish Act on Parental Responsibility (2007) abandons the principle that a parent has a right to request the allocation of sole parental authority when the parents do not live together or intend to dissolve their relationship. The primary aim of the Act is to establish the principle that *a child has the right to two parents.* Notwithstanding the fact that the Act was supported by the entire Danish Parliament, the Act and in particular the possibility to establish joint parental authority, when one parent requests sole parental authority, has been debated. The Act must be viewed in connection with the recently enacted Structural reform (of family law procedures), which provides one administrative venue for divorce petitions and cases on parental authority and contact. One of the main purposes of this reform was to achieve negotiated solutions by offering access to counselling and mediation.

I.1.3. EUROPEAN DEVELOPMENTS

The national developments in Dutch and Danish law providing a shift from a joint request procedure to an automatic continuation of joint parental authority, even when the parent with whom the child resides opposes this, is clearly the trend in most European countries.[9] This shift is also clearly expressed in the policy of the Council of Europe. While the 1984 Recommendation on Parental Responsibilities provided for the possibility of a joint exercise of parental responsibilities after divorce and in respect of unmarried parents where the parents consented or agreed, the 2002 White Paper provides that a divorce or the break up of a relationship should not as such affect the rights of parents to exercise parental responsibilities. Furthermore, the agreement between the parents should not be a condition for the joint exercise of parental responsibilities.[10]

The recent non-binding principles of the Commission on European Family Law (CEFL) take a complete step forward and provide for joint parental responsibili-

---

8 At the time of enactment it was considered that approximately 90% of parents opted for joint parental authority after divorce. Explanatory notes to L 198, 2000, Forslag til ændring af retsplejeloven og forskellige andre love, p. 11. Joint parental authority also continues after relationship break-up.

9 K. Boele-Woelki, B. Braat, I. Curry-Sumner (Eds), *European Family Law in Action, Volume III: Parental Responsibilities*, Antwerp-Oxford: Intersentia, 2005, p. 77-104 and p. 275-297.

10 Council of Europe: Recommendation No. R(84)4 of 28.02.1984 on Parental Responsibilities, principle 6 and *White Paper on Principles concerning the Establishment and Legal Consequences of Parentage*, 2002, Principle 22 with Explanation No. 66.

ties *ex lege* for all legal parents irrespective of their marital status or co-habitation.[11]

The underlying idea is that the joint exercise of parental responsibilities is in the best interests of the child irrespective of the marital and relationship status and that the parents' consent or agreement is not decisive. Further, as depicted in the National Developments, the endorsement of alternative dispute resolution emerges as a common approach.[12]

I.1.4. COMMON PERSPECTIVES

The principle of the best interests of the child is the leading principle in cases concerning the allocation of parental authority and contact. This general principle, which is most often associated with Article 3 of the UN Convention on the Rights of the Child (CRC), also has a longer legislative history in the Netherlands and Denmark in relation to disputes concerning the allocation of parental authority after divorce. In fact, the principle came to replace paternal supremacy and fault, in relation to the dissolution of the parents' marriage, as the determining principle for the allocation of parental authority after divorce.[13]

The principle may, however, be described as unclear in comparison with other legal principles.[14] The content of the principle is generally left undefined, but with the acknowledgement, that it is a changing notion depending on prevailing societal values and the individual child.[15] As such, it does not discern the abstract from the concrete and consequently may be described as concealing a paradox. The tendency towards an upgrading from 'a primary consideration' as contained in the CRC to 'the primary consideration' that is the deciding or paramount consideration reinforces rather than relieves the paradox of this principle,

11 K. Boele-Woelki, F. Ferrand, C. González Beilfuss, M. Jänterä-Jareborg, N. Lowe, D. Martiny, W. Pintens, *Principles of European Family Law Regarding Parental Responsibilties*, Antwerp-Oxford: Intersentia, 2007, Principle 3:10, p. 79 hereafter referred to as *Principles*.

12 Principles, principle 3:36, p. 231, Comparative overview p. 232-233, Council of Europe, Recommendation No. R(98)1 of 21.01.1998 on Family Mediation.

13 Chapter II.

14 J.B.M. Franken, *Mr. C. Asser's Handleiding tot de Beoefening van het Nederlands Burgerlijk Recht, Algemeen Deel, Een Vervolg*, Deventer: Kluwer, 2005, p. 56.

15 Principles, principle 3:3, Comment 1, p. 38, Lov om Forældreansvar, L 133, Comment to § 4.

because it stresses that all decisions must be based upon this indeterminable principle.[16]

In her article REECE[17] articulates this paradox when she shows how the paramountcy principle, the 'determining principle', is used to promote normality to the detriment of those who do not fit the standard of the nuclear family (in this case homosexual parents). REECE concludes her analysis with the following statement:

> 'We have come full circle. We began by discussing the paramountcy principle at the social level, searching for a justification for it in the importance of children or of childhood. We then realised that the principle had been reduced to the level of the individual. We now find that the paramountcy principle has been replaced by the policy of promoting the nuclear family, which is indeed a policy of relevance to society, not the individual.'

Currently the predominant discourse within the researched jurisdictions seems to be that parents should continue to share parental authority when they do not live together and also in situations when they do not agree on such an allocation. This discourse is construed, as depicted above in the National Developments, as the right of the child to two parents. CANTWELL has criticised the use of aims in a rights terminology in relation to a child's right to a 'family' considering that:

> 'Whether the right to a family be cited as a shorthand version of the facts designed for rapid public understanding, the result of wishful thinking, or a deliberately manipulative misinterpretation of the CRC, it constitutes an extremely dangerous lack of rigour over use of the term right. Children, in that case, could have the right to be loved, the right to live in peace and other desirable things that no State or other entity could ever commit itself to delivering. Confusing a right with a claim or an aim, however, legitimate the motivation may seem to some, simply brings us

---

16 Principles, principle 3:3, Danish Act on Parental Responsibility, Art. 4, Dutch law does not contain a general best interests principle but it has been considered that the best interests of the child constitute the primary consideration, Dutch Parliamentary proceedings 1992/1993 (*Kamerstukken*), 22 855, No. 3, p. 15. Art. 3, CRC has direct effect in Dutch law, G.C.A.M. Ruitenberg, *Het Internationaal Kinderrechtenverdrag in de Nederlandse rechtspraak*, Amsterdam: SWP, 2003, p. 61-87.

17 H. Reece, 'The Paramountcy Principle, Consensus or Construct', *Current Legal Problems*, 1996, p. 267-304.

> back to the pre-CRC days, when all sorts of rights were being invented and unilaterally proclaimed at whim; it completely undermines the significance of genuine children's rights as set out in the CRC.'[18]

This study addresses an area of the law where the regulation may be viewed as representing a balancing of current societal values, such as the equality principle, and an ascertainment of the individual child's autonomy and protection rights. It should be noted, however, also at this early stage, that the use of an aim such as 'a child's right to two parents' as a basis for regulation in this field of law raises pertinent questions with regard to the understanding of the best interests principle. With REECE'S articulation of the paradox in mind, it is appropriate to consider whether the promotion of a post-divorce and relationship break-up ideal is detrimental to those children who come from families who do not fit the standard of the amicable post-divorce family.

I.2. THE RESEARCH

I.2.1. PURPOSES, SUBJECT-MATTER AND STRUCTURE

This study has two main purposes. In the first place it is a comparative legal study of Dutch and Danish law concerning the following legal construction; joint parental authority seen in the context of a shift from a joint request procedure to the automatic continuation and the stipulated aim that a child has the right to two parents. The study covers the current law on the allocation and exercise of joint parental authority, as well as related rights such as contact rights and procedural perspectives.[19] The comparison also includes the conceptual choices made by the Commission on European Family Law (CEFL) in its recently developed non-binding *Principles* concerning parental responsibilities for the harmonisation of family law in Europe.

---

18 N. Cantwell, 'An uncharacteristically concise comment' in: '*Liber Amicorum*', Defence for Children International, 2007, p. 3.

19 In national laws the aim of promoting joint parenting entails more than the allocation of joint parental authority, for example the change or transfer of sole parental authority in cases of contact frustration. While the focus in this study is on the legal construction of joint parental authority, this construction must also be viewed and understood in the context of the aim of promoting joint parenting in relation to the allocation of sole parental authority and the exercise of contact rights.

In the second place the purpose is to provide an understanding of this development in a comparative perspective, thereby assessing the main causes of this development, the effects upon the law and critically assessing this development. The foundations for the critical assessment are deliberated separately below.[20]

There are two aspects which are particularly worth considering in relation to the subject-matter of this study. In the first place, it will be considered whether the law pertaining to the core subject-matter of this study of one country may be characterised as being more individualised.

It should be noted that the individualised family is an unclear concept, which is associated with both negative and positive consequences. A common feature is the emphasis on *individual choice*. In a family law context, the process of individualisation is most often associated with the development towards individual rights as opposed to rights and duties which existed primarily in the context of the legitimate family, which was based upon marriage.[21] In this study the law is seen as being more individualised when it emphasises personal choice, and less so when general legal norms are given priority.

In the second place, it is worth considering whether the law pertaining to the core subject-matter of this study of one country may be characterised as providing more of a *child protection function* than a private dispute settlement function. MNOOKIN describes the distinction between 'private dispute settlement' and 'child protection' as follows:

> 'The private-dispute-settlement function is involved when the court must choose between two or more private individuals, each of whom claims an associational interest with the child. (…) The second function, child-protection, involves the judicial enforcement of standards of parental behaviour believed necessary to protect the child. This function is consistent with the well established principle that the *parens patriae* power of

[20] Section I.2.3.

[21] M. Antokolskaia, *Harmonisation of Family Law in Europe: A historical perspective*, Antwerp-Oxford: Intersentia, 2006, p. 25 has described the development as moving from a transpersonalistic way of thinking; 'the individual was subservient to the family, and the family was subservient to society at large' to an interpersonalistic perspective, which can be phrased as 'family is made for man not man for the family'.

the state empowers courts to remove children from parental custody if that is necessary for their protection.'[22]

This book is divided into three main parts:

1. The law in context (Chapters II-IV).
2. The comparison between Dutch and Danish law and the CEFL principles (Chapters V-VIII).
3. Development (Chapter IX).

The first part aims to place the subject-matter in relation to Dutch and Danish law in a broader legal and sociological perspective. Chapter II describes the conceptual development of parental authority and contact in a historic perspective and Chapter III focuses on the influence of human rights upon this development.[23] Chapter IV primarily describes national research results of a socio-legal nature in respect of parental authority and contact.[24]

The second part contains the core comparative research between Dutch and Danish law and the CEFL principles. This part is divided into four Chapters which to a large extent reflect the law of the chosen jurisdictions; the allocation of parental authority (Chapter V), the establishment of residence and relocation (Chapter VI), the exercise of parental authority (Chapter VII) and, finally, the related perspectives, contact and procedures (Chapter VIII).

The structure of this book is consequently the following:

Part I: The law in context

1. An initial mapping of the jurisdictional characteristics and the main concepts (Chapter I).
2. The main conceptual development of parental authority and contact from the beginning of the last century until the present pending reforms (Chapter II).

---

22 R.H. Mnookin, 'Child Custody Adjudication: Judicial functions in the Face of Indeterminacy', *Law and Contemporary Problems*, No. 39, 1975, p. 229 derived from J. Graversen, 'Fælles forældremyndighed ved separation og skilsmisse', Copenhagen: Socialforskningsinstituttet No. 43, 1984, p. 20.

23 These Chapters also serve as a referential framework for the comparison contained in Chapters V-VIII.

24 The content of this Chapter also serves as a yardstick for the critical assessment, see below Section I.2.2.

3. A description and analysis of the influence of the European Convention on Human Rights and the United Nations Convention on the Rights of the Child upon, in particular, the concept of joint parental authority (Chapter III).
4. A mapping of the relevant Dutch and Danish statistical and socio-legal research data concerning joint parental authority and contact (Chapter IV).

Part II: The comparison between Dutch and Danish law and the CEFL principles

5. A description and comparison of the current law regulating the initial allocation of sole/joint parental authority, the allocation after divorce and the breakup of a relationship as well as subsequent changes. Further, it describes and compares the possibility to share parental authority with a non-parent and the allocation of parental authority after a parent's death (Chapter V).
6. A description and comparison of the current law regulating the establishment of residence after divorce and the breakup of a relationship as well as the regulation of a parent's relocation (Chapter VI).
7. A description and comparison of the current law regulating the content and exercise of joint parental authority (Chapter VII).
8. A description and comparison of the current law regulating contact rights of parents and children. Further, a deliberation of some main features of the procedural system pertaining to divorce and procedures concerning parental authority and contact. Here there is a comparison of the right and/or obligation to participate in alternative dispute resolution and the procedural rights of the child. Finally, this Chapter describes and compares the enforcement of contact and parental authority (Chapter VIII).

Part III: Development

9. The main conclusions, an analysis and a critical assessment (Chapter IX).

I.2.2. CRITICAL ASSESSMENT

The critical assessment contained in Chapter IX will consider the developments in the continuation of joint parental authority in a socio-legal and legal context. Particular attention is directed towards the distinction between the main rule (joint parental authority) and the exception (sole parental authority) and the way this distinction operates within the law.

It is important to note that the operation of joint parental authority within the law has distinct procedural perspectives. An example thereof is provided by the

Danish legislature which in the Explanatory notes to the Structural reform of 2005 (concerning family law procedures) qualified three different parent groups according to their ability to negotiate a solution. The Explanatory notes read as follows:

> 'In cases involving children, the parents may overall be divided into three main groups. The first group consists of parents who – possibly with assistance from family or other persons from their network – are capable of making agreements concerning their continued care for the children after they have broken up. An unknown number of parents, who initially disagree, reach a negotiated settlement without necessarily initiating a judicial procedure – in some cases after consulting an attorney or others. The next group is in need of guidance in the form of counselling or mediation in order to reach agreement on the children's future. (...). A small number of parents, the third group, start a judicial procedure and go all the way or part of the way.'[25]

The Danish approach based on reaching negotiated solutions clearly considers that the approach will work for the second group of parents but is nonetheless applied across the board.

The Dutch legislature has not made a similar distinction, but considerations of a similar nature may be found in the pending proposal concerning 'Continued Parenting'.[26] In this proposal which implements the obligation to submit a 'parenting plan' together with the divorce petition (whether contentious or non-contentious) the Dutch Minister of Justice relies upon the rising number of uncontested divorce procedures (52%) at the same time acknowledging that the measures contained in the Act will not work for everybody. The requirement placed upon all parents to submit a parenting plan is justified as follows:

> 'In a number of cases it will not be reasonably possible to achieve agreement upon a parenting plan or to draft such a plan. This may be the case in situations where there is no (longer any) communication between the parents, the mother has moved to a safe house or a parent is in an institution due to a psychiatric disorder. As a result the parenting plan will be incomplete or even non-existent.

---

25 Explanatory notes to Proposal, L 28 presented on 24.02.2005, p. 17.

26 Parliamentary proceedings 2004/2005 (*Kamerstukken*), 30 145, No. 3, p. 1-5

> The situation in which no (complete) parenting plan can be submitted is more likely to arise in the case of a unilateral request for divorce. Even so, there is still an obligation to submit a parenting plan also in cases of a unilateral request. Alongside the principal reason why all parents are requested to submit a parenting plan, there is another reason to retain the obligation to submit a parenting plan in all situations, which is to prevent the creation of an escape route. Spouses would be able to agree that one of them would submit a unilateral request which the other parent would then consent to. This is already undesirable because it does not contribute to making both parents aware of their individual responsibility also after the divorce.'[27]

As can be deduced from this statement, the reason for upholding the requirement to submit a parenting plan even in situations where such a plan cannot reasonably be expected is to prevent the creation of an escape route for other groups of parents. As such, it pays little attention to the consequences of the requirement for this group of parents (and children).

Finally, the assessment draws upon criticism of a more fundamental character raised against the conceptual developments in joint parental authority in Dutch and Danish law. In Dutch law the development has been criticised, in particular, from a care/ethical perspective.[28] In Danish case law there has been criticism of the evolvement of 'the negotiated family' (*aftalefamilien*)[29] based upon an analysis of the dispositives of law and governmentality.[30]

I.2.3. FURTHER LIMITATION OF THE RESEARCH

The study takes into account the developments up until 1 October 2007. This means that the recently adopted Danish Act on Parental Responsibility, which entered into force on 1 October 2007, forms the starting point for the comparison and that the main changes deriving from the pending Dutch reform of

---

27 Parliamentary proceedings 2004/2005 (*Kamerstukken*), 30 145, No. 3, p. 5.

28 For example, C. van Wamelen, 'De eerbiediging van een zorgrelatie', *NEMESIS*, 1996, p. 76-82.

29 See also C. Jeppesen and A. Kronborg, 'Danish Regulation of the Parent-Child Relationship', in I. Schwenzer (Ed.), *Tensions Between Legal, Biological and Social Conceptions of Parentage*, Antwerp-Oxford: Intersentia, 2007, p. 141-157.

30 A. Kronborg, 2007, supra. Dispositive in the sense of 'the mode of power' (*magtformer*). This analysis uses methodology which is based upon the doctoral thesis by S. Rafffnsøe, *Sameksistens uden common sense. En elliptisk arabesk*, Volume I-III, Copenhagen: Akademisk Forlag A/S, 2002 concerning the authorship of M. Faucault.

'Continued Parenting', which was adopted in June 2007 by the Dutch Parliament's Second Chamber, are considered.[31]

The research is limited to issues of a private law nature.[32] While the research pays attention to some systemic features of the law relating to parental authority and further considers the child protection function inherent in the core subject-matter of this study,[33] it does not address the law relating to child protection measures. Further, it does not take into account the law relating to child abduction, which for both countries is based upon the Hague Convention.[34]

The study addresses the continuance of joint parental authority and contact after divorce[35] and *after the breakup of a relationship*. Since the allocation of joint parental authority to unmarried parents is not subject to a condition of co-habitation in Dutch or Danish law, the study will address the allocation and exercise of joint parental authority for unmarried parents without a specified requirement of previous co-habitation.[36] The relevant research subject may consequently also be described as joint parental authority for parents who (no longer) live together, but focussing, however, upon the situation after divorce and the breakup of a relationship.[37]

---

31 The Act must still be adopted by the First Chamber. Pending proposal, Parliamentary proceedings (*Kamerstukken I*) 2006/2007, 30 145 A.

32 It includes only a brief inventory of the law relating to child maintenance in respect of access to dispute settlement. Currently M. Jonker, a researcher at the University of Utrecht, is working on a project covering Dutch and Scandinavian child maintenance law.

33 Above, Section I.2.1.

34 Convention on the Civil Aspects of International Child Abduction, 25.10.1980. Further, both countries are signatories to the Convention on Jurisdiction, Applicable Law, Recognition, Enforcement and Co-operation in Respect of Parental Responsibility and Measures for the Protection of Children, 19.10.1996.

35 This study does not address the special implications for Dutch law when a marriage is converted into a registered partnership and is thereby dissolved in a non-judicial procedure. This possibility is likely to be removed with the pending proposal concerning 'Continued Parenting', Parliamentary proceedings 2007/2008 (*Kamerstukken* I), 30 145, A.

36 The numbers of children born to unmarried parents who do not co-habit at the time of birth form a minority (4%) in Denmark. There are no precise statistics for the Netherlands, below, Section I.4.2.

37 Recent years have brought pluriformity to the concept of legal parentage and joint parental authority. Two parents of the same sex can be the child's legal parents through adoption and consequently hold joint parental authority. Further, joint parental authority may come into place by operation of law when a child is born during a couople's marriage or registered partnership in the Netherlands. This study does not address pluriform parentage. New forms of parentage in Dutch and English law have been the subject of an earlier doctoral thesis (PhD) by M. Vonk, *Children and their Parents, A comparative study of the legal position of children with regard to their intentional and biological parents in English and Dutch law*, Antwerp-

The law on parentage concerns the establishment of parentage, the possibility to contest parentage and the regulation of parentage when modern reproductive techniques are used. The legal institution of adoption also establishes parentage. Considering that parental authority in most cases is based upon established parentage, the rules relating to the positive establishment of parentage are relevant for the law regulating the allocation of parental authority.

For married parents the positive establishment of parentage, in most cases, is relatively uncomplicated in Dutch and Danish law. The mother is the woman who gives birth to the child. The father is the mother's husband. Complications occur when paternity is contested and may also occur in relation to the use of modern reproductive techniques.

For unmarried parents, the situation is more complicated. The mother, according to the present law in the Netherlands and Denmark, is the woman who gives birth to the child. The positive establishment of paternity is, however, not as automatic as for married parents. It would provide an incomplete picture of the legal situation in respect of the allocation of parental authority to unmarried parents if no consideration was given to the establishment of parentage in this situation.

For this reason the main elements of the law concerning the positive establishment of parentage *in relation to unmarried parents* is included in Chapter II. Contesting paternity, complications relating to the use of modern reproductive techniques and the consequence of uncertainty concerning one or more possible father's paternity will not be addressed.

Oxford: Intersentia, 2007 and has also been addressed in a doctoral thesis (PhD) by I. Curry-Sumner, *All's well that ends registered? The substantive and private international law aspects of non-marital registered relationships in Europe*, Antwerp-Oxford, Intersentia, 2005. This study also does not address the special implications, which arise when a child is born to two opposite-sex parents in a registered partnership in the Netherlands (pertaining to the lack of a paternity presumption and the possibility to make use of a consensual non-judicial divorce procedure), see for more K. Boele-Woelki, I. Curry-Sumner, M. Jansen, W. Schrama, *Huwelijk of Geregistreerd Partnerschap?*, Deventer: Kluwer, 2007.

I.3. COMPARATIVE APPROACH

I.3.1. PURPOSES

The study has, as mentioned above, two main purposes.[38] In the first place it is a comparative legal study in respect of the law regulating the continuation of joint parental authority. Secondly, the aim is to provide an understanding of this development, thereby assessing its main causes, its effects upon the law and critically assessing this development.

The knowledge provided by this study may serve various purposes. Firstly, it may have added value in relation to the ongoing debate concerning the convergence of family law in Europe and the related discussions concerning the desirability and feasibility of the harmonisation of family law in Europe.[39] Secondly, it may provide inspiration for the national debates concerning the construction of joint parental authority and contact.

Further, it provides a micro-comparative study of the family law of two countries, which as far as is known has never been the subject of direct comparison.[40] Finally, the inclusion of the conceptual choices of the CEFL serves to provide an in-depth comparison of the national law of the Netherlands and Denmark concerning the continuance of joint parental authority in relation to the conceptual choices contained in these principles.

I.3.2. JURISDICTIONAL ACCOUNTABILITY

The choice of countries has been dominated by two considerations. In the first place, the selection should include countries where the developments in the continuation of joint parental authority and the related perspectives contain enough common elements, to justify the two main purposes. The question posed in relation to the comparative study and the critical assessment requires a

---

38 Section I.2.1.

39 The convergence/divergence and harmonisation debate has been extensively addressed by M. Antokolskaia, 2006, supra.

40 Although from a Dutch perspective research has been conducted into Danish law, for example H. Lenters, *De rol van de rechter in de echtscheidingsprocedure*, Doctoral thesis (PhD), Arnhem: Gouda Quint, 1993 and P.J.P. Tak, J.P.S. Fiselier, *Denemarken – Nederland, De rechtspleging vergeleken*, Nijmegen: Wolf Legal Publishers, 2004 with a contribution by this author.

qualified *tertium comparationis*,[41] which the laws of the Netherlands and Denmark provide.[42]

Secondly, it was important that the research could be conducted directly without relying upon translated sources and that the knowledge of each system was sufficient for a direct comparison. For this reason the laws of the Netherlands and Denmark were natural choices considering that the author is a qualified Danish lawyer with experience in family law cases, but has lived in the Netherlands and has worked with Dutch law for the past eight years.

I.3.3. THE CEFL PRINCIPLES ON PARENTAL RESPONSIBILITIES

The Commission on European Family Law (CEFL) was established in Utrecht in September 2001. The CEFL has as its main objective; the development of non-binding principles which may serve as an inspiration for the harmonisation of family law in Europe. While the harmonisation of private law in Europe has been the subject of several harmonisation projects, the harmonisation of family law had been considered, prior to the CEFL initiative, to be outside the scope of harmonisation based upon the notion that family law reflects national culture to a greater extent than private law in general.[43]

The drafting of principles must be seen, according to the Principles themselves, in the context of a growing convergence of national family law in Europe, reflecting common European values, and the desirability and necessity of the harmonisation of family law in Europe in order to facilitate the free movement of persons in Europe. The Principles also aim, however, to contribute to common European values regarding the child's rights and welfare.[44]

The Principles on parental responsibilities in many repects resemble the principles contained in the Council of Europe White Paper from 2002 on Principles concerning the Establishment and Legal Consequences of Parentage. The Principles, however, are based more explicitly upon comparative law[45] and are more

---

41 D. Kokkini-Iatridou, 'Some methodological aspects of comparative law', *NILR*, 1986, p. 159.

42 Above in Section I.1.2. The described development has many common elements. The aim 'continued parenting' and 'the right to two parents' and the means of continuing parental authority as well as the conceptual framework of parental authority and contact are similar.

43 The cultural constraints argument is extensively analysed by M. Antokolskaia, 2006, supra.

44 Principles, preamble, p. 7 and Comments 1-4, p. 8-9.

45 See for the working method of the CEFL www.2.law.uu/priv/cefl and K. Boele-Woelki, 'The working method of the Commission on European Family law', in K. Boele-Woelki (Ed.): *Common Core and Better law in European Family law*, Antwerp-Oxford: Intersentia, 2005, p. 15.

substantiated in respect of the choices which have been made between different solutions.[46] It has therefore been a natural choice to include a comparison of Dutch and Danish law with the CEFL principles which are relevant to the subject-matter of this study. It should be noted that the purpose of this comparison must be viewed in the context of the two main purposes deliberated above.[47] It is not the intention to generally assess whether harmonisation is possible or whether the principles represent *better law*.

I.3.4. METHOD OF COMPARATIVE RESEARCH

The subject-matter of this research concerns specific legal concepts and regulations and may as such be described as pertaining to a comparison of *legal institutions*. The aforementioned does not imply that the research is based only upon traditional sources of law. The intention is also to include non-legal sources, in particular national socio-legal research results concerning parental authority and contact.[48] The legal institutional approach is moreover supplemented with a *problem or fact approach*[49] in relation to the divisions and subdivisions of the Chapters. The study thus uses pluriform comparative methods with, however, a strong emphasis upon the *form and content* of the law. The division and subdivision of the main comparative Chapters (Chapters V-IX) reflect this choice.

Two methods that can be used in comparative research may be distinguished: the simultaneous or the successive method. The first method aims to describe the law of the chosen jurisdictions per legal question or problem/fact situation and the second method aims to describe the law in an individual report.[50] In this study the simultaneous method is generally utilised, although it is presented in individual Sections. At the end of each section the findings are compared and similarities and differences are identified and explained.[51] Chapter IX contains the integrated main comparative conclusions and the critical assessment.

46 The principles are based upon both the concept of a *common core* and the concept of *better law* and may also leave a choice to national law, supra, p. 31-32.

47 Sections I.2.1. and I.3.1.

48 Chapter IV. The content of Chapter IV does not amount to a multi-disciplinary approach. This Chapter merely makes use of available statistical data and socio-legal research results.

49 D. Kokkini-Iatridou, *Een inleiding tot het rechtvergelijkende onderzoek*, Deventer: Kluwer, 1988, p. 187-188.

50 D. Kokkini-Iatridou, 1988, supra, p. 187-188.

51 Chapters II, 'Past, Present and Future', III, 'The influence of Human Rights' and IV, 'Socio-legal Data' extract some main comparative features rather than making a complete comparison. Chapter VIII 'Contact, Procedures and enforcement' contains only a limited comparison.

I.4. SOME JURISDICTIONAL CHARACTERISTICS

I.4.1. LEGAL CHARACTERISTICS

The Netherlands and Denmark are both EU member states[52] and belong to the Western legal culture.[53] To a great extent, they are both parties to the same international conventions which are relevant for the subject-matter of this study.[54] In traditional comparative law the Netherlands and Denmark are concurrently described as belonging to the same or different, yet related, legal families.[55]

The evident difference is that Dutch civil law is regulated in a Civil Code (*Burgerlijke Wetboek*) while Danish civil law is regulated in hundreds of singular acts. Dutch family law is primarily contained in the Dutch Civil Code, Book 1, and the law on parental authority and contact may be found in Book 1, Titles 14 and 15.[56] The Danish law on parental authority may be found in the Act on Parental Responsibility.[57]

This study is presented in English but concerns the law of two jurisdictions where the vast majority of legal and non-legal materials are only available in the national languages. For the Netherlands use has been made of the existing

52 Denmark has made a reservation, pursuant to the Maastricht Treaty of 1992, concerning legal co-operation, Chapter IV of the EC Treaty. The result is that, amongst other things, EC Council regulation No. 1347/2000 of 29.05.2000 on jurisdiction and the recognition and enforcement of judgments in matrimonial matters and in matters of parental responsibility for children of both spouses (Brussels II Regulation) replaced by No. 2201/2003 of 27.11.2003 concerning jurisdiction and the recognition and enforcement of judgments in matrimonial matters and the matters of parental responsibility (Brussels II bis Regulation) are not applicable in Denmark.

53 J. Husa, 'Classification of Legal Families Today - Is It Time for a Memorial Hymn?' *Revue Internationale de Droit Comparé*, 2004, p. 11-38.

54 In particular, the European Convention on Human Rights (ECHR) and the UN Convention on the Rights of the Child (CRC). See a complete overview of relevant Conventions and other international documents, Principles, Appendices p. 278-280.

55 Zweigert and Kötz, *An introduction to Comparative Law*, Oxford: Clarington Press, 1995 classifies the Netherlands as belonging to the Romanistic-Germanic civil code family, p. 101-102 and Denmark to the Nordic family p. 276-285. R. David, considers both to belong to the Romanistic-Germanic family, R. David, *Les Grands systëmes de droit contemporains*, Paris: Dalloz, 1974, p. 110.

56 Unless otherwise stated all references to the Dutch Civil Code refer to Book 1.

57 Lov om forældreansvar, Act No. 499 of 06.06.2007.

translation of Book 1 of the Dutch Civil Code.[58] For Danish law there are no official or unofficial translations of the Danish Act on Parental Responsibility or other relevant sources of law. The consequence is that this book contains many translations of legal provisions, parliamentary proceedings, case law and literature which have all been translated by this author, unless otherwise stated.

Finally, it should be noted that the study concerns Danish law as it applies to the territory of Denmark excluding the law applicable in Greenland and the Faeroe Islands and Dutch law as it applies to the territory in Europe, thus excluding the law applicable in Aruba and the Dutch Antilles.

I.4.2. FAMILY CHARACTERISTICS

Common phenomena, such as an increase in female work participation, increasing divorce rates and an increase in the number of children born outside of marriage, have characterised the development of the family at the empirical level in Europe and in Western countries. These developments, however, have not taken place at the same pace or to the same degree. In respect of the Netherlands and Denmark it is characteristic that these developments have taken place at an earlier stage and been more prominent in Denmark than in the Netherlands. The intention here is to provide a rough description of the three following factors; work participation, divorce and the breakup of a relationship and the number of children affected and, finally, the numbers of children born outside of marriage.

Work participation

The general increase in female work participation in Western countries has led to a profound interest by sociologists in the causes and effects of women's work.[59] In the context of this study, the level of female work participation in the Netherlands and Denmark warrants mentioning primarily due to the notable difference between the Netherlands and Denmark. While in Denmark (2006)

---

58 I. Sumner and H. Warendorf, *Family Law Legislation of the Netherlands, A translation including Book 1 of the Dutch Civil Code procedural and transitional provisions and private international law legislation*, Antwerp-Oxford-New York: Intersentia, 2003, hereafter referred to as Book 1 translation.

59 T. van der Lippe, L. Dijk, 'Comparative Research on Women's Employment', *Annu. Rev. Sociol.*, 2002, p. 221. In this article the following various approaches to the study of female work participation is discussed: the macro approach (institutional approach), the micro approach and a combination of the two. The macro approach often makes use of the typology of the welfare regimes of G. Esping-Andersen, *The Three Worlds of Welfare Capitalism*, Princeton, Princeton University Press, 1990.

women's participation has almost reached the level of men's participation,[60] women continue to participate at a substantially lower level than men in the Netherlands.[61] This should not be taken to mean that women and men in Denmark also participate at an equal level in respect of household work and the caring of children. Women in Denmark continue to provide more care and take substantially more parental leave than men.[62] If viewed in the context of a gendered welfare state typology the Netherlands and Denmark have been characterised, in a Western perspective,[63] as follows:

60 Danmarks Statistik (Statistics Denmark). The work participation of respectively men and women was 75,8% versus 69,3% (2006). Further 23,6% of women and 16,6% of men worked part time (2006).

61 CBS (Statistics Netherlands), Emancipatiemonitor 2006. From this information it may be deduced that 52% (2000) and 54,1% (2005) of women participate in paid work of 12 hours or more and that men's participation was 76% (2002) and 72% (2005). The majority (68%) of women work part time (2005) and the average working hours of all working women was 24,9 hours per week.

62 See for more detailed information in respect of Denmark, for example, Facts on Gender Equality, Minister for Gender Equality (2006), available on www.lige.dk (English version).

63 A.S. Orloff, 'Women's Employment and Welfare Regimes: Globalization, Export Orientation and Social Policy in Europe and North America', Social Policy and Development Programme, Geneva: United Nations Research Institute for Social Development, Paper No. 12, June 2002, included in C. Webner and P. Abrahamson, 'Individualisation of family life and family discourses', ESPAnet conference, Oxford 2004, p. 3, available on www.apsoc.ox.ac.uk. It should be noted that the position of the Netherlands in the welfare typology is subject to debate, see, for example, the aforementioned p. 3 and T. Knijn, 'Social and Family Policy, the case of the Netherlands,' 2002, p. 2-3 available on www.york.ac.uk. The concept of de-familialisation refers to the degree to which welfare state or market provisions ease the burden of caring responsibilities for families, T. van der Lippe, L. Dijk, 2002, supra, p. 226-227.

Table 1: A summary of gendered regime characteristics

Name	Alias	Empirical examples in this study	Characteristics
Dual earner	• Lewis' weak male breadwinner/dual earner regimes • Esping-Andersen's Scandinavian regime	**Denmark**, Finland, Norway and Sweden	• Extensive public services • Generous transfers to families • Extensive de-familialisation
General family support	• Lewis' strong breadwinner model • Esping-Andersen's Continental regime	Austria, Belgium, France, Germany, Ireland, Italy, **the Netherlands** and Spain	• Moderate to generous transfers • Some tax breaks for housewives • Lacks public services • Little de-familialisation
Market-orientated	Esping-Andersen's liberal regime	Australia, Canada, Japan, New Zealand, Switzerland, United Kingdom and United States	• Few state services • Residual transfers • De-familialisation through markets

Divorce and the breakup of a relationship

Denmark presently (2005) has a higher percentage of divorces per 1000 inhabitants (2,8) than the Netherlands (2,1).[64]

In the Netherlands the number of divorces steadily increased from approximately 32,000 in 1998 to almost 38,000 in 2001. In the period 2001-2005 the number levelled out at 37,000-38,000 per year.[65] The percentage of divorces where there are minor children rose from 46% in 1996 to 57% in 2004.[66] It is estimated that approximately 1 in 6 children will experience their parents divorcing before they reach the age of majority. It is further estimated that there

64 For the Netherlands, see E. Spruijt, *Scheidingskinderen*, Amsterdam: SWP, 2007, p. 14. For Denmark the percentage has been calculated according to the number of divorces in relation to the population size (2005) based upon numbers derived from Statistics Denmark.

65 Since 2001 this number includes the number of 'lightning divorces' (the transformation of a marriage into a registered partnership after which a non-judicial termination procedure is possible).

66 E. Spruijt, 2007, supra, p. 16 based upon statistics from the CBS.

are approximately 18,000 children who experience the termination of their parents' relationship per year.[67]

In Denmark the number of divorces has been declining for two consecutive years and this is the first time in eight years that it has done so. In 2000 there were 14,394 divorces, in 2004 there was a record high number of 15,774 divorces and in 2005 and 2006, respectively, 15,300 and 14,343 divorces. In Denmark research shows that one in three children will experience their parents divorcing or their relationship breaking down before these children reach the age of majority.[68]

Children born outside of marriage

The number of children born outside of marriage is rising steadily in the Netherlands. In 1981, 5% were born outside marriage. In 1995, 16% and in 2006 37% of children were born outside of marriage.[69] There are no statistics or research providing information on how many of these children are born to unmarried co-habitating parents. It is also not known for how many of these children paternity has been established. It seems to be generally assumed that the majority of co-habitating unmarried parents will marry after the birth of the child.[70]

The number of children born outside of marriage has stabilised at approximately 45% during the past 20 years in Denmark. In 1981 36% of children were born outside of marriage, in 1987 45% and in 2006 46%.[71] Research has established that the majority of these children are born to co-habitating parents; only 4% of children are born to single mothers.[72] A relatively small number of children born to single mothers have no legal father. The Children Commission[73] considered that approximately 1% of children in this situation have no legal father. A search in Statistics Denmark confirms this approximation; for example, if a search is made for the number of children aged two in 2006 who have no legal father, the result is 861 which amounts to approximately 1,3% of the total number of children born in 2004.

---

67 E. Spruijt, 2007, supra, p. 16, A. de Graaf, 'Scheiden: motieven, verhuisgedrag en aard van de contacten', Voorburg: CBS, Bevolkingstrends 53, 2005, p. 39-47.

68 *Barnets perspektiv, Forældremyndighed, Barnets bopæl, Samvær, Tvangsfuldbyrdelse*, Commission report No. 1475/2006, p. 247.

69 CBS (Statistics Netherlands) on www.statline.nl.

70 Spruijt, 2007, supra, p. 16. However, Spruijt places a question mark after this consideration.

71 Danmarks Statistik (Statistics Denmark).

72 M. Heide Ottosen, *Samboskab, Ægteskab og Forældrebrud*, Copenhagen: Socialforskningsinstituttet, 2000, p. 43.

73 *Betænkning om børns retsstilling*, Commission report No. 1350/1997, p. 21.

I.4.3. FAMILY PROCEDURAL SYSTEMS

The Dutch and Danish family procedural systems are very different, in particular because of the widespread use of administrative procedures in Danish law. A further and more extensive description will be provided in Chapter VIII. The descriptions contained in this Chapter apply to a dispute concerning parental authority and contact, whether or not it is part of a divorce procedure.[74]

The Dutch family law procedural system

The Dutch family procedural system is based upon judicial procedures. A case concerning parental authority and contact must be brought before the courts of first instance, the district courts. There are 19 district courts. Most often in family law cases the court is presided over by a single judge. A number of district courts have a separate sector for family and juvenile cases. Furthermore, some cases are heard by the sub-district court, also referred to as the cantonal section of the district court (*kantongerechten*).[75]

A decision by the district courts may be appealed to one of the five courts of appeal. The court of appeal is presided over by a bench of three judges. The decision of the Court of Appeal may be appealed in cassation to the Supreme Court. The Supreme Court is a court of cassation, which means that only questions relating to the law are reviewed. The facts of the case established by the lower court are not reviewed. This distinction is often considered to be arbitrary. The result of this distinction is that it serves to limit the number of cases appealed in cassation.[76] The Supreme Court sits with five or three judges.[77] The Supreme Court may either dismiss the appeal or annul the decision of the lower court. If a decision is annulled the Supreme Court must decide the case, thereby rendering a final decision, or remit the case to a court of appeal, (most often to a different court of appeal than the one which delivered the decision which has been dismissed). This appeal court then tries the case in full. The Supreme Court has a Procurator General (Procureur-Generaal) who advises it on how to decide the case and, furthermore, he has the competence to seek a dismissal of a decision delivered by the lower courts. If such a decision is dismissed it only has relevance for future decisions. It does not influence the decision in relation to the parties.

---

74 This description does not pertain to enforcement measures and interim decisions.

75 Since 01.05.2007 the sub-district court only hears cases concerning financial matters.

76 A.F.M. Brenninkmeijer, 'Judicial Organization', in J. Chorus, P. Gerver, E. Hondius, *Introduction to Dutch law*', Alphen aan den Rijn: Kluwer, 2006, p. 58.

77 The court decides as a panel and a judge cannot give a dissenting judgment.

Table 2: Dutch Family law procedcural system

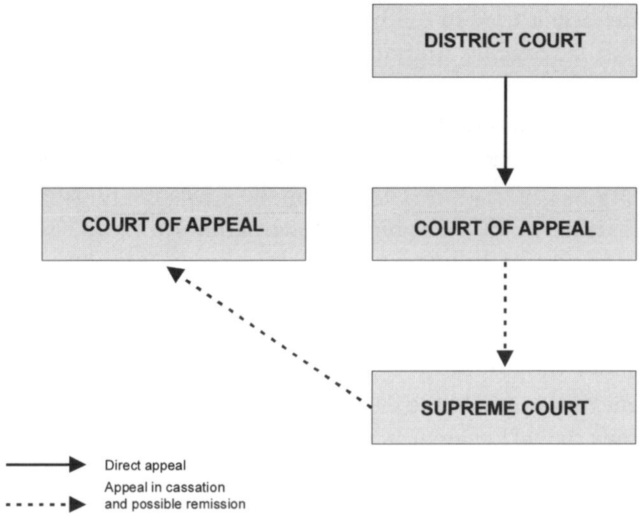

The Danish family law procedural system

Danish Family law procedures were reformed in the 2005 Structural reform. These changes came into effect on 1 January 2007.[78] Pursuant to the 2005 Structural reform (concerning the structure of family law procedures) all cases concerning parental authority and contact must be submitted to the regional state administration (an administrative authority).[79] There are five regional state administrations. If the parents cannot reach a negotiated agreement on the allocation of parental authority and the exercise of contact rights, for example through counselling, mediation or by the use of child expertise services, the regional state administration may, upon the request of one or both of the parties, submit the case to the district court (the court of first instance). There are 24 district courts. The district courts are normally presided over by one judge. There are formally no specialised family judges.

The decision of the district court may be appealed to the High Court. There are two High Courts, the Eastern High Court and the Western High Court. The High Court is a court presided over by three judges. The decision of the High Court may only be appealed to the Danish Supreme Court (the final court of appeal) if

78 Further, a general court reform has come into effect on 1 January 2007.

79 Before 01.01.2007 the general system was that disputes concerning parental authority were heard by the courts while the administrative authorities had sole competence in contact cases.

leave to appeal is granted by the Appeals Permission Board. Such leave is currently only granted if the case raises issues of principle or public interest. If leave is granted the case is tried in full by the Supreme Court. The Supreme Court is normally presided over by minimum 5 judges.[80]

An important exception to the above-mentioned procedure concerns a case on contact. The district courts only have competence to decide a dispute on contact as an ancillary matter in a case concerning the allocation of parental authority (only from 1 January 2007). The regional state administrations have sole competence to decide contact disputes. A complaint concerning a decision on contact may be submitted to the Regional State Administration which then submits the case to the Family Agency (*Familiestyrelsen*), which is also an administrative authority under the Danish Ministry for Family and Consumer Affairs. The Family Agency may uphold the decision, amend it or dismiss it. If a decision is dismissed, the original Regional State Administration is required to deliver a new decision. A decision by the Family Agency can be brought before the High Court for a limited review based upon Article 63 of the Danish Constitution. In this case the parties to the case are the person who brings the case to court and the Family Agency (The Ministry of Family and Consumer Affairs).

Table 3: Danish family law procedural system

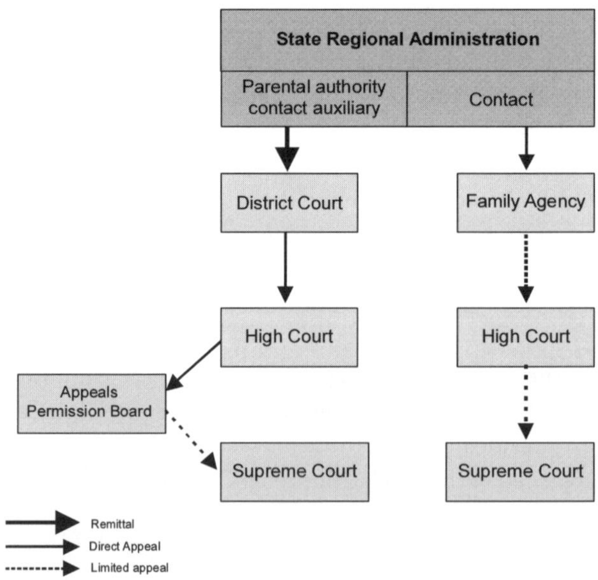

80 One or more judges may deliver a dissenting judgment.

I.5. INITIAL MAP OF CONCEPTS

Parental authority/parental responsibilities

The term parental authority has been chosen as the term, which describes powers and duties in respect of children, corresponding to the Dutch concept of *ouderlijk gezag*[81] and the Danish concept of *forældremyndighed*.[82] The historical conceptual development is further deliberated in Chapter II.[83] The CEFL principles use the term parental responsibilities, referring to, in particular, the general adoption of this term in international instruments.[84]

Guardianship

The term guardianship is the most direct translation of the Dutch concept *voogdij*[85] and the Danish concept *værgemål*.[86] These two concepts are distinctly different, however. In Dutch law it refers to the powers and duties which may be exercised by third persons (persons who are not legal parents). As such it refers to powers and duties resembling parental authority. In Danish law it only refers to the powers and duties in respect of the child's property. Powers and duties in respect of the child's property are normally held by the holder(s) of parental authority. The historic conceptual development is deliberated in Chapter II. In contrast the CEFL principles do not make use of the term guardianship. Third persons may hold *parental responsibilities*.[87] Further, the

---

81 The choice of the term parental authority in respect of Dutch law is derived from the Book 1 translation, supra, p. V. The Dutch report on parental responsibilities to the CEFL used the term parental responsibilities, http://www2.law.uu.nl/priv/cefl/.

82 The Danish CEFL report, which was co-authored by this author, used this term, http://www2.law.uu.nl/priv/cefl/. It is the most direct translation of the Danish concept. Two other concepts, custody and parental responsibility, are often used in unofficial translations, see, for example, http://www.juraportal.dk and http://familiestyrelsen.dk.

83 In both countries it has been considered whether to replace this concept with a concept that would place emphasis on the responsibilities of the parents rather than their authority. In the Netherlands it was considered whether to use the term 'parental care' (*ouderlijk zorg*). This concept, however, was not considered to cover the content of powers which are legal in nature, Parliamentary documents 1992/1993 (*Kamerstukken*), 23 012, No. 3, p. 5. In Denmark it has been considered on several occasions whether to change the concept to parental responsibility (*forældreansvar*). This did not occur, however, on the one hand because the concept of parental authority (*forældremyndighed*) has been viewed as having been generally adopted in society. On the other hand, because it is viewed as an incorrect signal to divest a parent of 'responsibility' in a procedure concerning the allocation of sole parental authority, Commission report No. 1475/2006, p. 270.

84 Principles, principle 3:1, p. 26-27.

85 Book 1 translation, supra, p. V.

86 Danish CEFL report, http://www2.law.uu.nl/priv/cefl/.

87 Principles, principle 3:9, International Instruments, p. 66-69 and Comments, p. 76-78.

administration of the child's property and legal representation are considered to form a part of parental responsibilities.[88]

Allocation

The term allocation is generally used to describe an appointment *ex lege* and a decision and/or agreement appointing one or two parents as the holder(s) of parental authority. The Dutch Civil Code generally uses the term *exercise* of parental authority to describe an allocation of parental authority. Such exercise may depend upon an *ex lege* allocation or a decision of the court or in the case of unmarried parents upon the registration of a joint request in the Custody Register. Danish law generally uses the term *have* parental authority, which is better translated with the term *hold*, concerning the initial allocation of parental authority (ex lege or pursuant to an agreement). The term reallocation is generally used to describe a subsequent change in the allocation of parental authority.[89]

The CEFL principles use the term *have* parental responsibilities in respect of parents[90] and the term *attribution* mainly to describe an allocation of parental responsibilities to third persons.[91] The term attribution is, however, generally used to indicate an allocation of parental responsibilities whether this is based on an agreement or a decision by a competent authority.

Residence

The term (main) residence is generally used to describe the situation where the parents hold or exercise joint parental authority and where the child's residence with one of them is determined by a decision of the court or pursuant to a parental agreement. The Dutch Civil Code does not currently expressly provide this possibility, but it has been established in case law where it is referred to as the main residence (*hoofdverblijf*). In Danish law the new Act on Parental Responsibility (2007) has created this possibility using the term *bopæl*, which is best translated as residence.[92]

88 Principles, principle 3:22, p. 143, Comment 1, p. 150 and principle 3:24, Comment 2, p. 163.

89 The Dutch Civil Code uses the term '*change of decision*', Art. 253o(1) and the Danish Act on Parental responsibility uses the term '*transfer*'.

90 Principles, principle 3:8, p. 59.

91 Principles, principle 3:9, p. 66.

92 Art. 17, Act on Parental Responsibility.

Parent

The term parent is generally used in the meaning *legal parent* unless otherwise stated.[93]

Resident parent

The term resident parent is used to indicate that the child factually resides primarily with this parent.

Shared residence

The term shared residence is used to indicate that the child more or less resides equally with both parents pursuant to an agreement or a court decision. The main term used in Dutch law is *co-ouderschap* (co-parentage) and in Danish law *deleordning* (share arrangement). The term alternate residence is used to describe more unusual share arrangements such as rotating residence every other year. The CEFL principles use the term alternating residence to describe a shared residence.[94]

Contact

The term contact has been chosen as the most direct translation of the Dutch concept *omgang*[95] and the Danish concept *samvær*.[96] The term has a dual meaning because it refers to a legal concept as well as a factual event. The meaning will be substantiated in the text. The historic conceptual development is deliberated in Chapter II. The CEFL principles also use the term contact.[97]

Divorce and judicial separation

In both the Netherlands and Denmark a divorce and judicial separation are available. Divorce constitutes the termination of the marriage while judicial separation terminates certain legal effects of the marriage although the marriage is not dissolved. In both countries judicial separation may be utilised by spouses who for religious or other reasons do not wish to terminate the marriage, but only certain effects thereof. In Danish law, however, judicial separation also has a different function which is to provide (the main) reason for a divorce.[98] The

---

93 Taken to mean the parent whose legal parentage has been established. Chapter II, Sections II.2.4. and II.3.4. deliberates the development in the establishment of parentage for unmarried parents corresponding to the general limitation in this study, above Section I.2.3.

94 Principles, principle 3:20, p. 130.

95 Book 1 translation, supra, p. 152.

96 Danish CEFL report concerning parental responsibilities, http://www2.law.uu.nl/priv/cefl/.

97 Principles, principle 3:25, p. 164 and principle 3:26, p. 176.

98 K. Boele-Woelki, B. Braat, I. Sumner (Eds.), *European Family Law in Action, Volume I: Grounds for Divorce*, Antwerp-Oxford-New York: Intersentia, 2003, p. 102.

relevance of judicial separation is only considered in relation to the allocation of parental authority to separated parents in Chapter V. Generally this study will use the term divorce covering both situations.[99]

[99] Chapter II, providing the historical background, also pays no special attention to a judicial separation in relation to parental authority, notwithstanding the fact that, historically, it was a more important legal institution than it is today (save for the function of providing the main reason for a divorce in Denmark).

CHAPTER II
PAST, PRESENT AND FUTURE

II.1. INTRODUCTION

The aim of this Chapter is to place the development of certain concepts of the law on parental authority and contact in a historical context.[1] The main points to be looked at are the sources of law (law reform/case law) and the main reasoning for any main changes. This development is described taking the law as it was at the beginning of the previous century as a starting point. This is not an arbitrary choice. The previous century brought immense changes to the law regulating the parent/child relationship. While the present regulation of parental rights is perhaps best understood as a response to a general development towards individualisation where individual rights of parents (and children) replace regulation where rights were based primarily upon an existing marriage, it is nonetheless relevant to examine the historic origins.

Sections II.2. (the Netherlands) and II.3. (Denmark) describe the historical developments concerning, respectively, married and unmarried parents. The sections are subdivided into six sections with the following themes: parental authority during marriage, parental authority after divorce, contact after divorce, parentage and parental authority for unmarried parents, contact with an unmarried parent and pending legislation.[2]

In Section II.4. the findings are compared in relation to a number of themes which are the following: the developments in the law, dispute settlement – a national characteristic?, the post-divorce regulation of parental rights, the divorce procedure, the unmarried father's rights and the right to have two parents. The aim is to extract some main comparative features of the law and its *development*.

---

1 Further, this Chapter serves as a referential framework for the comparison contained in Chapters V-VIII where the use of the simultaneous method of comparison does not support an extensive deliberation of the historical developments.

2 Parentage for married parents is not deliberated, corresponding to the general demarcation laid down in Chapter I, Section I.2.4.

II.2. THE PARENT-CHILD RELATIONSHIP: THE NETHERLANDS

The Dutch Civil Code contained a sharp distinction between parental power and guardianship from the enactment of the Civil Children Act of 1901 in the Dutch Civil Code up until the reform of parental authority in 1995. Parental power was only associated with a joint exercise of parental rights by married parents *during their marriage*. When the marriage was dissolved by divorce or death, parental power ceased to exist. Single parents exercised guardianship. The rights and duties associated with parental power and guardianship were largely similar. The implication, however, was that parental power was exercised by two parents and guardianship by one parent (or a third person).

In 1995 the above-mentioned distinction between parental power linked only to marriage and guardianship linked to single parents and third persons was abandoned. Currently, the main rule is that legal parents (whether married, divorced or single) exercise parental authority and third persons exercise guardianship. The term custody (*gezag*) is the general term to describe both.

II.2.1. PARENTAL AUTHORITY DURING MARRIAGE

At the turn of the previous century the Dutch Civil Code from 1838, Book 1, titles 14 and 15 contained detailed provisions on the content, allocation and exercise of parental authority. Parental authority was alternatively referred to as parental power (*ouderlijke magt*) and paternal power (*vaderlijke magt*).[3] Parental power contained powers and duties in respect of the child's person.[4] These powers were vested in the parents but were exercised by the father. The powers and duties in respect of the child's property and the usufruct (paternal power) belonged to the father.[5] If the father was incapacitated, the mother could replace him in the exercise of parental power, but not formally in respect of paternal power.[6]

---

3 A.D.W. de Vries and F.J.G. van Tricht, *Geschiedenis der wet op de ouderlijke macht en de voogdij*, Groningen: J.B. Wolters, part II, 1905 p. 342.

4 Art. 353-361 old, DCC.

5 Art. 362-373 old, DCC.

6 Parental authority prior to the 1901 Civil Children Act is often described only in the context of paternal power (*vaderlijke magt*). The system was, as described, somewhat more complex containing a distinction between parental and paternal power, see also J.E. Doek, *Omgangsrecht*, 's-Gravenhage: VUGA, 1984, p. 14 and p. 173, footnote 6.

The 1901 Civil Children Act contained changes to the provisions on parental and paternal power in the Dutch Civil Code.[7] The term parental power now described the powers and duties in respect of the child's person, the administration of the child's property and the usufruct. Parental power was vested in the parents together, but was exercised by the father provided that he had not been discharged from parental power or was incapacitated. In these cases the mother exercised parental power. The difference between the mother's position compared to the position she had before the 1901 Children Act was slight. It did have the consequence, however, that the mother could exercise parental power in her own right and not just as a replacement. The implication of this was, for example, that the father could no longer assign a supervising guardian (*raadsman*) to supervise the mother's exercise of parental power after his death.

The mother's legal position in relation to the exercise of parental power was an important issue in the parliamentary procedures concerning the 1901 Civil Children Act. There was an increasing conviction that 'women were not incapable of taking care of and arranging for themselves and others'.[8] The relevant chapter of the explanatory notes to the Act was called 'equality between the spouses'. While actual equality between the parents was not pursued in this Act, it is clear that the increasing importance of the mother's legal position was considered beneficial. The draft act contained the proposal that both parents should consent to a minor's marriage and that parents should agree on the education and occupation of the minor. In the case of a dispute between them the court could decide. However, this proposed dispute-settlement procedure was rejected in the parliamentary debate on the act. It was considered to be 'contrary to the law and the nature of a Christian marriage'. Furthermore, court interference was considered to be 'adverse to family harmony' and more importantly 'the husband and wife would thereby be seen as members of a company with equal rights'.[9] A compromise was reached regarding the mother's consent to a minor's marriage. The mother's consent was necessary and the court could not settle a dispute on the matter. The result was that the mother was granted a right of veto in this respect.[10]

---

7 Burgerlijke Kinderwet of 06.02.1901, Stb. 62.

8 A.D.W. de Vries and F.J.G. van Tricht, *Geschiedenis der wet op de ouderlijke macht en de voogdij*, part I, Haarlem: Tjeenk Willinck & Zoon, 1910, p. 56.

9 A.D.W. de Vries and F.J.G. van Tricht, part I, supra, p. 57 and M. Braun: *De prijs van de liefde, De eerste feministische golf, het huwelijksrecht en de vaderlandse geschiedenis*, Doctoral thesis (PhD), Amsterdam: Het Spinhuis, 1992, p. 193.

10 M. Braun, 1992, supra, p. 194.

The joint exercise of parental power became law in 1947.[11] If there was a dispute, however, the father's will was decisive.[12] The powers and duties in respect of the administration of the child's property and legal representation continued to be exercised solely by the father.[13] Following an amendment[14] to the act the mother could ask the court to annul the father's decision if it was clearly contrary to or resulted in serious harm to the moral and mental interests or health of the minor.[15]

Equality for married parents in the exercise of parental power became law in 1984.[16] The parents now had an equal say in matters relating to the child's person, the administration of the child's property and legal representation. Casting paternal supremacy aside in favour of equality between the spouses necessitated a dispute-settlement mechanism according to the legislature and this was introduced in the Dutch Civil Code in Article 246(2) old (now Article 253a). This provision provides that in case of a dispute between the parents, either parent can request the court to decide on the disputed issue. In its decision the court is not bound by the requests of the parents, but may base its decision on what it considers to be desirable in the interest of the child.

II.2.2. PARENTAL AUTHORITY AFTER DIVORCE

According to the Dutch Civil Code of 1838 the father continued to exercise parental power after divorce.[17] However, the court could determine with whom the children should reside. The main rule was that the children should reside with the spouse who had requested the divorce (the innocent party). The court could, however, deviate from this rule and decide that the child should reside with the other spouse or a third person when this was in the child's best interests.[18]

---

11 Act of 10.07.1947, Stb. 232.

12 Art. 246(2) old, DCC.

13 Both parents had an equal right to the usufruct, but the father administered it, G. Delfos and J. Doek, *Kinderrecht, Civilrechterlijk deel*, Zwolle: Tjeenk Willinck, 1974, p. 113.

14 Parliamentary discussions 1946-1947 (*Kamerstukken*), p. 1524/1526 and p. 1544-1556 and G. Delfos and J. Doek, 1974, supra, p. 123-124.

15 Art. 246(3) old, DCC.

16 Act of 30.08.1984, Stb. 404, Parliamentary proceedings (*Kamerstukken)* 16 247. The Act did not contain a general revision of the provisions on parental authority. It was an Act which sought to dispense with the unequal trestment of men and women in various areas of family law.

17 Art. 285 old, DCC.

18 Art. 284 old, DCC.

The Civil Children Act of 1901 linked parental power solely with marriage. Consequently a divorce resulted in the appointment of one of the parents as the child's guardian. The court was free to allocate guardianship to either parent in the interests of the children.[19] Guardianship was always supplemented with supervisory guardianship by the other parent or a third person. Supervisory guardianship was primarily directed at supervising the child's property. It did not confer any right to intervene in the guardian's decisions concerning the child's person or contain a right to have personal contact with the child.[20] When this institution was abandoned in 1995 the role of the supervising guardian was considered to be very modest.[21]

II.2.2.1. Case law on joint parental power 1984-1995

The system which linked the joint exercise of parental power solely with marriage was successfully challenged before the Dutch Supreme Court in 1984. In its decision the Supreme Court allowed two parents to continue jointly exercising parental power after divorce on the basis of Article 8 of the ECHR.[22] This decision led to great uncertainty as to the scope of the right to exercise joint parental power after divorce.

In two decisions by the Supreme Court in 1986,[23] forming part of the so-called spring decisions,[24] the Supreme Court substantiated the conditions for continuing to exercise joint parental power after divorce and laid down the procedure to be followed. Joint parental power after divorce could continue or be re-established[25] after a request to the court if (a) both parents wanted to continue exercising joint parental power, (b) it was probable that, despite the divorce, a good mutual understanding, which is necessary for the exercise of joint parental power, would exist between the parents and they agreed on and provided for the costs of raising the child and, finally, (c) that joint parental power was not contrary to the best interests of the child.[26]

---

19 Art. 284 old, DCC.

20 G. Delfos and J. Doek, 1974, supra, p. 218-221.

21 Parliamentary proceedings 1992/1993 (*Kamerstukken*), 23 012, No. 3, p. 15.

22 Hoge Raad, 04.05.1984, *NJ* 1985, 510, annotated E.A.A. Luijten, E.A. Alkema.

23 Hoge Raad 21.03.1986, *NJ* 1986, 585, 586.

24 Hoge Raad 21.03.1986, *NJ* 1986, 585, 586, 587, 588, annotated by E.A.A. Luijten and E.A. Alkema, *NJ* 1986, 588. These developments in the case law and the reasoning of the Supreme Court based upon the ECHR are elaborated and analysed in Chapter III, Sections III.4.2. and III.4.6.

25 If guardianship had already been allocated upon divorce.

26 Hoge Raad 21.03.1986, *NJ* 1986, 586.

The possibility of exercising joint parental power as developed by the Supreme Court was thus based upon a high degree of consensus between the parents. The parents should both desire to exercise joint parental power and agree on all the terms, such as residence arrangements, contact between the non-resident parent and the child and the payment of child maintenance. Parental agreement was not enough, however. The court should also be satisfied that there was a 'good mutual understanding' between the parents and it should ascertain that the best interests of the child were not contrary to such an allocation of parental power, thereby implying that the allocation of joint parental power could not be viewed only in the context of a simple agreement between the parents.

While the spring decisions concerned primarily the allocation of joint parental power, the Supreme Court also considered how a subsequent request to retract the decision allocating the continuance of joint parental power should be addressed. The Supreme Court considered that 'the allocation can (...) be retracted' and replaced with an allocation of guardianship. The use of the term 'can' in connection with the Supreme Court's consideration in one of the decisions concerning unmarried parents[27] raised the point that a retraction of the decision establishing joint parental authority could not be viewed only in relation to one or both parents' wishes to have the decision overturned, but that such a retraction was also subject to a review in relation to the stipulated conditions concerning good mutual understanding and the best interests of the child (conditions (b) and (c)).

The system of joint parental power after divorce as developed by the Supreme Court co-existed with the legislative system of the post-divorce allocation of guardianship and supervising guardianship up until the reform of the Dutch Civil Code's provisions on parental authority and contact in 1995. The Dutch Minister of Justice had already announced his intention to propose a reform in 1986,[28] but a proposal did not emerge until 1993.[29]

27 Hoge Raad 21.03.1986, NJ 1986, 585 'Both parents can request, on the basis of Art. 291 of the old DCC, that the decision which establishes joint parental power be retracted. The Court will comply with this request if it appears that the conditions mentioned under (c) and (d) (corresponding to (b) and (c) for married parents) are no longer satisfied'.

28 Such an intention had also been announced earlier in the course of the parliamentary proceedings concerning the reform of divorce procedures and the right to contact after divorce, Parliamentary discussions 1980/1981 (*Handelingen*), 15 638, p. 4487.

29 Parliamentary proceedings 1992/1993 (*Kamerstukken*), 23 012, No. 3, p. 1. Although a proposal had been circulated for comments in 1986.

Meanwhile, developments in the case law somewhat weakened the intended review of a 'good mutual understanding' as a precondition for the allocation of joint parental authority. It appeared that district courts did not investigate whether a good mutual understanding existed between the parents. Rather, the courts relied upon a joint request from the parents as evidence of a good mutual understanding.[30] Furthermore the Supreme Court decided in a decision of 19 November 1993 that:

> 'the simple fact that a dispute has arisen between the parents concerning the costs of raising the child is not a sufficient reason to retract the decision to continue joint parental power after divorce'.[31]

These developments indicated that, on the one hand, a judicial review of a parental agreement concerning the allocation of joint parental power was limited, but, on the other, it became more substantial in a subsequent case concerning the termination of joint parental power. An investigation of the decisions delivered by the Arnhem District Court in 1992-1993 showed, however, that a subsequent request for the allocation of guardianship was granted in most cases. Rejections were generally associated with the fact that a minor, who had reached the age where he/she could be heard in the procedure (12+), wanted joint parental power to continue.[32]

II.2.2.2. Reforming the law on joint parental authority 1995-1998

Judicial activity in this field of law was subsequently replaced with legislative reform. Two Acts with an inherently different content in respect of the post-divorce allocation of parental authority were enacted in a very short time frame. The first, which came into force on 2 November 1995, contained a complete revision of the provisions on parental authority and contact.[33] The second enactment was introduced as an amendment to a proposed Act which was aimed at regulating the possibility for a social parent to exercise joint parental authority together with a parent. The amendment was introduced in the parliamentary proceedings in 1995/1996[34] and it entered into force on 1 January 1998.

---

30 C. van Wamelen, 'Eenhoofdig gezag na scheiding', *NEMESIS*, 2000, p. 59.

31 Hoge Raad, 19.11.1993, *NJ* 1994, 241, annotated by W. Hammerstein-Schoonderwoerd.

32 W.J.P. Kweens, 1998, supra, p. 283.

33 Wet tot nadere regeling van het gezag over en van de omgang met minderjarige kinderen, Act of 06.04.1995, Stb. 240.

34 Parliamentary proceedings 1995/1996 (*Kamerstukken*), 23 714, No. 7, p. 2.

The 1995 Act provided a legislative basis for joint parental authority after divorce based upon parental agreement. Article 251(2) of the old Dutch Civil Code now provided that the parents could continue to exercise joint parental authority after divorce upon a joint request. The court could deny this request if there was reason to believe that such allocation would be detrimental to the best interests of the child. According to the explanatory report a joint request indicated that a 'good mutual understanding' between the parents existed. A joint request was, however, not decisive in cases where it was doubtful that joint parental authority would be 'properly exercised'. Two elements were here at issue. In the first case it involved an assessment of a factual agreement on the care and upbringing of the child and, secondly, an assessment as to whether the request was real and not the result of undue influence by one parent.[35]

Joint parental authority could be changed into sole parental authority at the request of one or both parents, if the circumstances had changed since the allocation or if the decision had been based on incorrect or insufficient facts.[36] According to the notes on the act 'changed circumstances' were present, for example, 'if the relationship between the parents after divorce had worsened so that regular contact between the parents, which is necessary for the exercise of joint parental authority, no longer takes place or runs smoothly'. Changed circumstances also meant that 'the interests of the child would not be served by a continuation of joint parental authority in such a case'.[37]

The 1995 Act expressly provided that court access for dispute settlement, as laid down in 1984,[38] also applied to the situation where joint parental authority was exercised after divorce. The notes on the Act stated that 'the content of Article 253a does not provide a reason to change the allocation of parental authority in the sense that one parent is then allocated sole parental authority'.[39] Furthermore, the 1995 Act provided in Article 377h of the Dutch Civil Code that a contact order could be made in respect of a parent who shares parental authority. A certain political party[40] raised the question why it should be necessary to allow the Courts to decide on contact and financial questions considering that this would 'demonstrate that the parents evidently were unsuited to exercising joint parental authority'. The State Secretary's response to the question centred

35 Parliamentary proceedings 1992/1993 (*Kamerstukken*), 23 012, No. 3, p. 17-18.
36 Art. 253o, DCC.
37 Supra, p. 19.
38 Above Section II.2.1. of this Chapter.
39 Parliamentary proceedings 1992/1993 (*Kamerstukken*), 23 012, No. 3, p. 19.
40 CDA, a Christian liberal party.

on the advantages that a judicial decision provided in terms of executorial title.[41] In his answer the State Secretary did not differentiate between parents who have made agreements and wished these to be included in the divorce decree and parents who require a judicial decision.[42] A more elaborate balance concerning the limits of joint exercise based upon 'good mutual understanding' cannot be derived from the legislative history.

Only six months after joint parental authority based upon parental agreement had come into force, the matter of the automatic continuation of joint parental authority after divorce emerged in the legislative proceedings concerning another proposal.[43] This proposal was intended to create the possibility for a social parent to exercise joint parental authority together with a (legal) parent. The question of an automatic continuation of joint parental authority had already been debated in the course of the 1995 reform but was then rejected.[44] The proposed change was based upon a perceived societal need for change[45] and further reasoned on the basis of Article 8 of the ECHR, where a continuation was considered less interventionist in respect of the right to respect for family life. Further, the proposed change indicated to parents that they were responsible for their children.[46] In the parliamentary proceedings it was further argued that 25% of parents requested joint parental authority under the existing law (the 1995 reform). Joint parental authority was seen as generally accepted in society.[47] The new Article 251(2) of the Dutch Civil Code[48] provided that joint

41 Parliamentary proceedings 1993/1994 (*Kamerstukken*), 23 012, No. 5, p. 13-14.

42 Critical of this approach and indicating that a parental agreement could have been included in the divorce decree without Art. 377h, is C. van Wamelen, 2000, supra, p. 59.

43 Parliamentary proceedings 1995/1996 (*Kamerstukken*) 23 714, No. 7, *Wijziging van, onder meer, Boek 1 van het Burgelijk Wetboek in verband met invoering van medevoogdij en gezamenlijk voogdij*).

44 The Dutch Family Council (*Nederlandse Gezinsraad*) had suggested this solution and several political parties had expressed sympathy for it in the course of the parliamentary proceedings.

45 The State Secretary mentioned the opinions of the Dutch Family Council, the Dutch Child Protection Board and the Report of the De Ruyter Commission, *Anders Scheiden*, Rapport van de Commissie Herziennning scheidingsprocedure, 02.10.1996. The last-mentioned report had considered positive and negative aspects of the automatic continuation of joint parental authority and had concluded that an automatic continuation was favourable in the light of an alternative divorce procedure, which would be based upon mediation, although it would not be a prerequisite. Parliamentary proceedings 1995/1996 (*Kamerstukken*) 23 714, No. 11, p. 12.

46 Parliamentary proceedings 1995/1996 (*Kamerstukken*), 23 714. No. 7, p. 7, No. 11, p. 12.

47 It later appeared that the percentage was only 17%, C.G.M. van Wamelen, 'Nieuw Gezagsrecht', *FJR*, 1997, p. 272 and W.J.P. Kweens, 1998, supra, p. 278.

48 Act of 30.10.1997, Stb. 507 *Wet tot wijziging van onder meer, Boek 1 van het Burgerlijk Wetboek in verband met invoering van gezamenlijk gezag voor een ouder en zijn partner en van gezamenlijk voogdij.*

parental authority continues after divorce, unless the parents or one of the parents request the court in the best interest of the child to decide that parental authority (...) is allocated to one parent only.[49] The State Secretary was of the opinion that after some time joint parental authority would become the primary option.[50] The inherent question of under what conditions one parent could be allocated with sole parental authority was not entirely clear from the parliamentary proceedings. The underlying question was not if, but rather to what extent 'good mutual understanding' continued to play a role in the allocation of sole parental authority. From the parliamentary discussions it may be deduced that such an allocation should not be subject to a strict judicial review. A certain member of parliament[51] raised the issue as follows:

> 'Good mutual understanding is very essential. In the parliamentary discussions you (the State Secretary) have specifically mentioned this point. You have stated that when one of the partners says that 'good mutual understanding' no longer exists this is sufficient evidence that (joint parental authority) is no longer considered to be in the best interest of the child. Can you still confirm this position?' (Added)

The State Secretary confirmed this position and added:

> 'A simple reason (why the man or woman no longer wants to exercise joint parental authority) is sufficient and it is not necessary to enumerate reasons; sole parental authority must, however, be in the best interest of the child. That remains the main consideration.'[52]

The system adopted can be described as an exact mirror image[53] of the system enacted only two years earlier. The Act came as a surprise and received a mixed response in the literature.[54]

---

49 The criterion 'best interest of the child' was introduced as an amendment in the parliamentary proceedings 1996/1997, (*Kamerstukken*), 23 714, No. 14.

50 Parliamentary discussions 1996/1997 (*Handelingen*), 23 714, 62, p. 4517.

51 Ms. van der Burg from the PvdA, a social democratic party.

52 Parliamentary discussions 1996/1997 (*Handelingen*), 23 714, 62, p. 4530.

53 W.J.P. Kweens, 1998, supra, p. 278.

54 C.G.M. van Wamelen, 'Nieuw gezagsrecht', *FJR*, 1997, p. 264-274, W.J.P. Kweens, 'Nieuwe wetgeving inzake het ouderlijk gezag na echtscheiding', *FJR*, 1998, p. 278-284, F.W.J.M. Schols, 'Gezamenlijk gezag en gezamenlijke voogdij, een goed begin van het nieuwe jaar', *WPNR*, 1998, p. 1-5, E.J. Nicolai, 'De juridische positie van de niet-verzorgende ouder na echtscheiding', *NJB*, 1998, p. 695-699, A. Henstra, 'Kroniek van het personen- en familierecht', *NEMESIS*, 1998, p. 186-X, S. van Gestel, 'Beëindiging gezamenlijk gezag', *Advocatenblad*, 1998,

A case study of the judicial decisions on the allocation of parental authority in divorce cases at the Amsterdam District Court in the period following this enactment[55] showed that the Court initially allocated sole parental authority to one parent at the request of this parent because of 'poor mutual understanding' between the parents, regardless of whether this 'poor mutual understanding' gave rise to immediate communication problems or was based upon a fear that this would emerge later on.[56] Soon afterwards, however, the Court adopted a different approach – 'poor mutual understanding' or 'poor communication' were no longer sufficient for the allocation of sole parental authority. A history of violence or mental problems on the part of the non-resident parent was also not necessarily sufficient for the allocation of sole parental authority.[57]

The findings of the above-mentioned study were confirmed and further deliberated in a case study conducted at the District Court of s-Hertogenbosch in the period from 2001-2002.[58] This research showed that joint parental authority remained in place in 96.8 % of cases.[59] Further, it showed that a request for the allocation of sole parental authority was mostly based upon reasons such as drug abuse by the other parent, physical violence against the requesting parent and/or the child, serious cases of poor or no communication between the parents or the fact that the non-resident parent had never provided actual care for the child.[60]

In particular three decisions of the Dutch Supreme Court have further substantiated the post-divorce allocation of parental authority. Two decisions concerned the 'good mutual understanding' criterion. The third decision concerned a dispute between the parents regarding the child's primary residence.

---

p. 899-900, M. van Moorsel, 'Het gezamenlijk gezag na echtscheiding', *Rechtshulp*, 2000, No. 3, p. 1-10, B.E.L.A.M. de Groot, 'Ex-partner, maar niet ex-ouder', *FJR*, 1999, p. 90-96, P. van Teffelen, 'Gezamenlijk gezag na scheiding: tijdbom, lege huls of groeimodel?, *FJR*, 2000, p. 26-29.

55 M. van Moorsel, Gezamenlijk Gezag, *Een onderzoek naar de positie van de zorgouder na echtscheiding*, Utrecht: Wetenschapswinkel Rechten, University of Utrecht, 2000, pertaining to 150 divorce cases.

56 Supra, p. 24-25.

57 Supra, p. 25-28.

58 E. Benen and P. Vlaardingerbroek, 'Doorlopend ouderlijk gezag in de praktijk', *FJR*, 2004, p. 36-40 pertaining to a total amount of 3186 divorces.

59 In the vast majority of these cases the parents or one of them had not requested sole parental authority, supra, p. 37.

60 Supra, p. 39-40.

The question in the last-mentioned case[61] was whether a dispute over residence concerned the allocation of parental authority thus necessitating an allocation of sole parental authority to one of the parents or whether it concerned the exercise of parental authority implying that the court could decide on the child's residence pursuant to Article 253a of the Dutch Civil Code. The Supreme Court decided that 'the Court may allocate sole parental authority in this situation but is not restricted to such a decision, the relevant criterion is the best interest of the child' thereby upholding the decision of the Appeal Court to allocate joint parental authority and determine the child's main residence.

In the first decision by the Supreme Court[62] concerning the 'good mutual understanding' criterion the Supreme Court upheld the decision of the Appeal Court allocating sole parental authority to the mother based upon the facts of the case: the poor communication between the parents (the parents communicated only by post) and the acknowledged difficulties (by both parents) regarding joint decision making. The Supreme Court did, however, rephrase the reasoning of the Appeal Court considering that:

> 'it is not an incorrect perception of the law that the Court would allocate parental authority to one parent in the interests of the children considering the serious nature of the communication problems between the parents which brings about the unacceptable risk that *the children are torn or lost between the parents and where sufficient improvement could not be expected within a reasonable time.*' (Emphasis added).

This 'torn or lost between the parents' (*klem of verloren*) criterion has become the leading criterion to be considered in cases where there is a dispute concerning the allocation of joint or sole parental authority.

In a subsequent decision the Supreme Court confirmed this position and upheld the Appeal Court's decision to allocate joint parental authority (also determining the child's main residence) in a case where the problems concerning communication and joint decision making were more substantiated than in the previous case and where there was expert evidence strongly recommending the allocation of sole parental authority.[63]

---

61 Hoge Raad, 15.12.2000, *NJ* 2001, 123 annotated S.F.M. Wortmann.

62 Hoge Raad, 10.09.1999, *NJ* 2000, 20 annotated S.F.M. Wortmann.

63 Hoge Raad 19.04.2002, *NJ* 2002, 458.

These developments in the case law show that the courts' review is limited to ascertaining whether there is such a lack of co-operation that joint parental authority would be against the best interests of the child. This will only rarely be the case, however. The review based upon the criterion 'torn or lost' relates not just to what *is* but also to what may be expected in the future.[64]

The development in the case law where a decision on sole parental authority is often substituted with a decision on joint parental authority and a decision concerning the child's main residence has led to a general acknowledgement in the literature of the 'hollow or formal nature' of joint parental authority.[65] In this case the allocation of joint parental authority to the non-resident parent has been considered as 'a rag to wipe off the blood'.[66]

II.2.3. CONTACT AFTER DIVORCE

The question of a right to personal contact[67] for the parent who was not allocated parental guardianship was debated in relation to the 1901 Civil Children Act and rejected.[68] The parent who was not awarded guardianship could be appointed as the supervising guardian but, as mentioned above,[69] supervising guardianship did not entail a right to have personal contact. Decisions of lower courts acknowledging either parental agreement concerning contact or entailing a decision on a limited right to contact were set aside by the Supreme Court.[70] In a decision of 28 August 1939[71] the Supreme Court considered that the issue was not whether a positive obligation rested with the parent who was the child's guardian to facilitate contact with the other parent. Rather, the parent guardian had a general obligation to facilitate the general interests of the child (including in

64 The Court of Appeal stated that 'the parties, with sufficient effort, are considered to be able to deal with joint parental authority in a manner which will not be detrimental to (the child)', *NJ* 2002, 458.

65 P. van Teffelen, 2000, supra, p. 26-29, A. Heida, 'Gezamenlijk ouderlijk gezag na scheiding', *EB*, 2000, 7/8, p. 1-6.

66 'Een doekje voor het bloeden', S.F.M. Woortman in her annotation to the Supreme Court case, Hoge Raad 15.12.2000, *NJ* 2001, 123.

67 The terminology was then visitation right (*bezoekrecht*). The term contact (*omgang*) has been generally adopted since the report of the Wiarda Commission, *Jeugdbeschermingsrecht*, 26.01.1971.

68 A.D.W. de Vries and F.J.G. van Tricht I, supra, p. 217-218, p. 222. The matter was further raised in relation to the Children Act of 1947 and in the course of preparing the new Book 1, DCC; G. Delfos and J. Doek, 1974, supra, p. 254.

69 Section II.2.2.

70 J.E. Doek, 1984, supra, p. 19-28.

71 *NJ* 1939, 948 annotated P. Scholten.

most cases to insure that contact between the child and the other parent was not completely broken off). Consequently, a parent guardian who, without good reason, rejected any contact could be considered to be a poor guardian and a reallocation of guardianship to the other parent could be considered if this was generally in the best interests of the child.

In connection with the reform of divorce law in 1971[72] a provision granting the judiciary a discretionary power in relation to contact was introduced in the old Dutch Civil Code as Article 161(5). Article 161(5) provided that the court, at the request of both or one of the parents, could issue a contact order regarding contact between the child and the parent who had not been or would not be awarded custody (parental guardianship). The provision was meant to constitute a preliminary provision on contact to be deliberated later. It did, however, take twenty years before this provision was replaced under the 1990 reform of contact. Meanwhile developments in case law construed contact within human rights' terminology based upon Article 8 of the ECHR.[73]

In 1990 the present regulation of contact after divorce was formally adopted.[74] The old Article 161a, now Article 377a,[75] provides that the parent who does not have parental authority and the child have a right to contact. Contact may only be discharged due to four limiting reasons.[76]

With the 1995 reform,[77] which provided a legislative basis for joint parental authority after divorce, the right of the parent who shared parental authority to contact was seen as an element of parental authority. Consequently Article 377a applies only to parents who do not have parental authority. The court can issue a contact order in respect of a parent who has joint parental authority when this

---

72 Act of 06.05.1971, Stb. 290.

73 J. de Boer, 'Omgangsrecht als mensenrecht', *NJB* 1982, p. 1125, J.E. Doek, 1984, supra, p. 82-103.

74 Wet houdende nadere regeling van de omgang in verband met scheiding, Act of 01.12.1990, Stb. 482.

75 With the Act of 06.04.1995, Stb. 240, above Section II.2.2.2. this provision was placed in Title 15, DCC.

76 The reasons are that (a) contact would cause a serious detriment to the mental or physical development of the child, or (b) the parent is manifestly unfit or clearly must be considered not to be in a position to have contact, or (c) a child aged twelve or older while being heard has demonstrated to seriously object against contact with the parent, or (d) contact is otherwise contrary to the paramount interests of the child.

77 Section II.2.2. of this Chapter.

parent does not live with the child, Article 377h of the Dutch Civil Code. The consequence is that contact cannot be discharged pursuant to Article 377a.[78]

II.2.4. PARENTAGE AND PARENTAL AUTHORITY: UNMARRIED PARENTS

Historically and currently parental authority (previously parental guardianship) was based upon established parentage in the Netherlands.[79] Inherent in the Dutch law on the establishment of parentage up until the reform of parentage in 1998 were two notions. On the one hand, that the unmarried father could not recognise a child without the consent of the mother. On the other hand, that paternity could not be established against the wishes of the father.

At the turn of the previous century children born outside of marriage had no legal ties with the mother or the father before recognition (*erkenning*) had taken place.[80] If the child had been recognised it could obtain some of the status and the rights pertaining to legitimate children. A father could only recognise his child if the mother consented to such recognition.[81] However, if he did recognise the child, he became the child's guardian.

The position of the unmarried mother who had recognised the child, as opposed to the father who had also recognised the child,[82] was improved with the 1901 Civil Children Act. Firstly, it was no longer the father who was the guardian, but the parent who had recognised the child first. Secondly, in respect of simulta-

---

78 Contact may, however, be temporarily discontinued, Hoge Raad (Supreme Court), 18.11.2005, *NJ* 2005, 574.

79 This continues to be the case today with two specific exceptions. A non-parent may exercise joint authority together with a parent, Art. 253t, DCC and joint parental authority may come into play when a child is born during a registered partnership or marriage between two partners of the same (two female partners) or opposite sexes where one of the partners is not the legal parent and where the child has no legal ties with another parent, Art. 253sa.

80 'Erkenning' was then seen as a declaration of biological fact or evidence. Later it was seen as a declaration of intent, P. Vlaardingerbroek, K. Blankman, A.P. van der Linden, E.C.C. Punselie, C.G.M. van Wamelen, *Het hedendaagse personen- en familierecht*, Deventer: Tjeenk Willinck, 2002, p. 176, J. Wiarda, *Handleiding tot de beoefening van het Nederlands burgerlijk recht*, part 1, Zwolle: Tjeenk-Willinck, 1957, p. 497 (hereafter referred to as ASSER-WIARDA, 1957).

81 ASSER-DE-BOER, *Handleiding tot de beoefening van het Nederlands burgerlijk recht*, part 1, Zwolle: Tjeenk-Willinck, 2002, p. 519. The condition of consent was introduced in the Dutch Civil Code from 1838.

82 Children who were the result of an incestuous relationship or the result of adultery could not be recognised, ASSER-WIARDA, 1957, supra, p. 496.

neous recognition, the mother had the means to ensure that her recognition came first with the result that she became the child's guardian.[83] The possibility existed that the father who had recognised the child could request the court that he be assigned as the guardian of the child to the exclusion of the mother when this was deemed favourable to the child.[84]

Enforced establishment of paternity was not possible until the 1998 reform of parentage. The 1909 Act did, however, establish the possibility to claim maintenance from the father who had not recognised the child.[85]

From 1947 onwards the mother no longer had to recognise the child born outside of marriage.[86] Legal affiliation was established automatically at birth following the principle of *mater semper certa est*. This principle did not apply, however, to children who were born as a result of an incestuous relationship or as a result of adultery. These children were considered to be not only 'conceived outside the order but also contrary to the order' of marriage.[87] It also remained impossible for the father to recognise such children.

The unfavourable position of children born outside of marriage was increasingly considered to be unsustainable.[88] Their position in relation to the mother and the mother's family remained unfavourable until 1982. In 1982, following the Marcx decision,[89] legislation was enacted with retrospective effect to the date of the Marcx decision granting such children an equal position to children born within marriage in relation to the mother and the mother's family.[90] In relation to a general reform of the law of parentage, which would regulate, in particular, the establishment of paternity, the legislature began this process in 1980, a process which was to take 18 years before legislation was finally enacted.

---

83 ASSER-WIARDA, 1957, supra, p. 670.

84 Art. 290 old DCC.

85 Act of 16.11.1909, Stb. 363.

86 Act of 10.07.1947, Stb. 232.

87 Parliamentary discussions 1947 (*Handelingen*), p. 1538. The unfavourable position of children born as a result of an incestuous relationship or of adultery in relation to the establishment of maternal parentage were maintained until the new Book 1 of the DCC came into force in 1970, Act of 03.04.1969, Stb. 167. The fact that a child was born as a result of an incestuous relationship or adultery was often not revealed so that recognition by the mother was unnecessary and the position of the child was better than the position granted by law.

88 M. Rood-de Boer, *Ouders en Kinderen, aspecten van het familierecht*, Amsterdam: Becht, 1962, Doctoral thesis (PhD).

89 ECtHR, 13.06.1979 Paula Marcx v. Belgium.

90 Act of 27.10.1982, Stb. 608.

In its spring decisions of 1986 the Supreme Court made it possible for unmarried parents to exercise joint parental power upon request to the sub-district court based upon an interpretation of Article 8 of the ECHR.[91] The conditions laid down by the Supreme Court were the same as for married parents with the additional condition that joint parental power could only be exercised by unmarried parents when parentage was established.[92]

The exercise of (now) joint parental authority was given a legislative basis in 1995. Unmarried parents could now register an agreement on joint parental authority with the court's public custody register pursuant to Article 252 of the Dutch Civil Code.[93] Such registration is not subject to substantive review. The legislature chose this solution by analogy to the situation for married parents where joint parental authority arises *ex lege* and not by way of a court decision.[94]

II.2.4.1. Law reform of parentage 1998

With the 1998 reform of parentage the distinction between legitimate/illegitimate children was abandoned in favour of a distinction based upon the existence or non-existence of legal ties between the parent and child.[95] The mother is the woman who has given birth to the child based upon the principle of *mater cemper certa est.*[96] The establishment of paternity is more complicated. Dutch law operates with a distinction between the legal father, the biological father and the begetter. The biological father is the man who has provided the sperm which results in conception and the begetter is the man who together with the

---

91 Hoge Raad 21.03.1986, *NJ* 1986, 585, 586, 587, 588, annotated by E.A.A. Luijten and E.A. Alkema, *NJ* 1986, 588. These developments in the case law and the reasoning of the Supreme Court, based upon the ECHR, are elaborated in Chapter III, Section III.3.2.

92 The conditions were that: (a) both parents had legal ties with the child and hadve the capacity to exercise parental power, (b) both parents wanted to be allocated with joint parental powerpower, (c) it iswas probable that the parents hadve a good mutual understanding which is required for the exercise of joint parental power as well as an agreement on the division of the costs relating to the care forof the child and (d) that the interest of the child was not contrary to such allocation, *NJ* 1986, 585.

93 A recent development is that the courts are willing to hear a sole request for joint parental authority by an unmarried parent (typically the father). In Chapter III, Sections III.3.3., III.3.4. and III.3.5. this development based upon Art. 8, ECHR is discussed in detail. A legislative proposal is also pending, see below Chapter II.2.6.

94 Parliamentary proceedings 1992/1993 (*Kamerstukken*), 23 012, No. 3, p. 22-25.

95 Act of 24.12.1997, Stb. 722, Parliamentary documents (*Kamerstukken*) 24 649. See a general overview of this reform in English by M. Antokolskaia, 'The Recent Developments in Dutch Filiation, Adoption and Joint Custody Law', *Rivista di Diritto della familia e della Successioni in Europa*, No. 3, p. 791-804.

96 Art. 198, DCC.

mother has conceived the child in a natural way. From this it can be determined that the begetter is always the biological father, but the biological father is not always the begetter. This distinction is essential for the establishment of paternity in Dutch law.

While the 1998 reform abandoned the distinction between legitimate and illegitimate children, there remains a distinct difference in establishing the paternity of a child conceived within and outside marriage.[97] For a child born within marriage there is a presumption that the husband is the begetter of a child conceived during the marriage.[98] For a child born outside marriage paternity may be established through voluntary recognition or a judicial determination of paternity.[99] Both require that positive steps are taken by the parties involved (the father, mother, child).[100] Recognition by the father still requires consent from the mother if the child is under sixteen years of age (and from a child older than twelve), but such consent may be replaced by the consent of the court, if the recognition does not prejudice the interests of the mother in an undisturbed relationship with the child or the interests of the child and the man is the begetter of the child.[101]

Recognition cannot take place if the child already has two parents.[102] Reminiscent of the notion of the protection of an individual marriage, there are still limitations in respect of recognition. A married man can only recognise a child born outside this marriage if he has ties with the mother similar to those which exist in marriage or has a close personal relationship with the child. In this case the interests of the child in establishing paternity are weighed against the

---

97 W.M. Schrama provides an analysis of the compability of Dutch law in respect of unmarried cohabiting partners with the equality principle and concludes that Dutch law does not contravene the equality principle, but this is still inadequately regulated, M.H. Schrama, 'Is het Nederlandse afstammingsrecht in strijd met het gelijkheidsbeginsel? Over kinderen en badwater', *RM Themis*, 2007, No. 3, p. 86-94.

98 Art. 199, DCC.

99 Art. 199(b),(c) and (d), DCC.

100 The legal effects of recognition and enforced establishment are not completely equal. Enforced establishment has retrospective effect but recognition does not, Art. 202(1) and 203(2) DCC.

101 Art. 204, DCC. Prior to the 1998 reform a more limited form of replaced consent by the court had developed in case law, J. de Boer, *Handleiding tot de beoefening van het Nederlands burgerlijk recht*, part 1, Zwolle: Tjeenk-Willinck, 2002, p. 522-524 (hereafter referred to as ASSER-DE BOER, 2002) and P. Vlaardingerbroek et al., 2002, supra, p. 186-187. One of the intrinsic problems concerning replaced consent was that upon recognition the child would take the father's name. Since the 1998 reform of names the child retains the mother's name unless a choice for the father's name is made, ASSER-DE BOER, 2002, supra, p. 39-40.

102 Art. 204(f), DCC.

protection of the father's marriage.[103] A judicial determination of paternity may be requested by the mother (unless the child has reached the age of sixteen) and the child.[104] The judicial determination of paternity is only possible in respect of the begetter or the life companion of the mother who has agreed to an act which could have resulted in the begetting of the child.[105]

II.2.4.2. The biological father in Dutch law

The situations where, among others, the initiative for the establishment of paternity rests with the parties involved, where recognition requires the consent of the mother or the replaced consent of the court and where married men may only recognise a child born outside of their marriage under certain conditions give rise to a special category of fathers in Dutch law, namely the *biological father*. This category of fathers is incoherent. It may comprise biological fathers who are not the begetter of the child, for example, a known donor. Further, it may comprise fathers whose only bond with the mother and child consists of a fleeting relationship with the mother. It may also consist of fathers who have had or continue to have a longer relationship with the mother and/or have established a relationship with the child, but where the mother denies consent and where the consent of the court is not sought or is not awarded. Dutch law recognises certain rights and duties of biological fathers. A biological father who is the begetter of a child may be liable for the payment of child maintenance.[106] Further, the biological father may have a right to contact if he has a close personal relationship with the child.[107]

II.2.5. UNMARRIED PARENTS' RIGHT OF CONTACT

The rights of a parent who does not have parental authority[108] (typically the unmarried father) were given a legislative basis in 1995 in Article 377a of the Dutch Civil Code.[109] This provision applies to the legal parent. While the provision does not contain a distinction based upon the manner in which paternity is established (by recognition or judicial determination) or the previous rela-

103 B.E. Reinhartz, 'Afstamming' in *De familie geregeld*, Lelystad: Koniklijke Vermande, 2000 p. 81-82 advocates stronger protection for the biological father's spouse.
104 Art. 207(1), DCC.
105 Art. 207(1), DCC.
106 Art. 394, DCC.
107 Art. 377(f), DCC.
108 The right to contact of a parent who exercises parental authority is an inherent part of parental authority, see above Section II.2.3 of this Chapter.
109 Act of 06.04.1995, Stb. 240.

tionship with the mother and/or child, the Explanatory report to the Act stated that the intention of this provision related to, in particular, 'the non-marital relationship where the father has recognised the child'.[110]

Prior to this enactment, case law had established the possibility to issue a contact order in respect of a father who had recognised the child, or a mother who did not have parental authority (then parental guardianship) when the parents' family relationship had been comparable to a marriage by analogy to Article 161(5) of the old Dutch Civil Code.[111]

The 1995 enactment also provided a discretionary power for the court to issue a contact order in respect of a non-parent who has a close personal relationship with the child.[112] A father who is the begetter of the child (paternity has not been established) may fall within the scope of this provision depending on the bond with the child.[113]

II.2.6. PENDING LEGISLATION

There are presently two pending legislative proposals pertaining to the subject-matter of this study. The first proposal concerns the possibility for a parent to make a request for joint parental authority after an allocation of sole parental authority to one parent *ex lege* or upon a decision of the court. This development was preceded by developments in case law based upon Article 8 of the ECHR. The proposal is briefly discussed below and the preceding developments in relation to Art. 8 of the ECHR and the proposal are dealt with in detail in Chapter III.[114]

The second proposal concerning 'Continued Parenting' introduced a so-called parenting plan ('*ouderschapsplan*') as a precondition for requesting a divorce and

---

110 Parliamentary proceedings 1992/1993 (*Kamerstukken*), 23 012, No. 3, p. 25-26.

111 Supreme Court, 26.05.1997, *NJ* 1978, 417, 418, J.E. Doek, 1984, supra, p. 96-101, and in relation to Art. 161(5) old DCC Section II.2.3. of this Chapter.

112 Art. 377f, DCC.

113 Parliamentary proceedings 1992/1993 (*Kamerstukken*) 23 012, No. 3, p. 26-27. The Supreme Court had already considered that such a right existed on the basis of art. 8, ECHR, Hoge Raad 22.02.1985, *NJ* 1986, 3 annotated by W. Hammerstein-Schoonderwoerd. In a decision of 10.05.1985 the Supreme Court considered that the begetter could also rely upon such a right, Hoge Raad 10.05.1985, *NJ* 1986, 5. The Supreme Court retracted this position in its decision of 10.11.1989 where it considerd that supplementary factors of 'family life' were warranted, Hoge Raad, *NJ* 1990, 628 annotated by E.A.A. Luijten.

114 Section III.3.3.-III.3.5.

further contains other substantive changes to the law on parental authority. This proposal was adopted by the Dutch Parliament's Second Chamber on 12 June 2007 and is thus currently pending before the First Chamber of Parliament.[115] This proposal is discussed below.

II.2.6.1. Sole request for joint parental authority

This proposal aims to remove the necessity of making a joint request for the allocation of joint parental authority in all situations where one parent exercises sole parental authority. The initial proposal was aimed only at the situation where sole parental authority had been allocated to one parent pursuant to a court decision and was thus aimed at the possibility of re-allocating joint parental authority.[116] At a later stage the possibility to request joint parental authority in situations where the mother exercised sole parental authority *ex lege* was added.[117]

These proposals are justified in the light of the ECHR and preceding case law[118] and must be viewed in the light of the developments in the allocation of joint parental authority after divorce where sole parental authority is only allocated where there is a risk that the child will become 'torn or lost' between both parents with the understanding that it should always be possible to ascertain whether this risk continues to be present. The Council for the Judiciary reacted positively to the proposed amendments considering that in practice it is seen:

> 'As an illogical impediment that the court in the course of the divorce procedure can make a decision regarding the allocation of joint parental authority, but thereafter only upon a joint request. This impediment sometimes makes it difficult to allocate sole parental authority in the divorce procedure, when it can be expected that after a while the factual situation may change to allow for the exercise of joint parental authority'.[119]

It may be derived from this comment that the possibility to require a reallocation of joint parental authority at a later stage is considered beneficial not only

115 Parliamentary proceedings 2006/2007 (*Kamerstukken I*), 30145, A.
116 Parliamentary proceedings 2003/2004 (*Kamerstukken*), 29353, No. 1, p. 2, No. 3, p. 3-4.
117 Parliamentary proceedings 2004/2005 (*Kamerstukken*), 29353, No. 8, p. 1-3.
118 Analysed in detail in Chapter III, Sections III.3.3., III.3.4. and III.3.5.
119 Parliamentary proceedings 2003/2004 (*Kamerstukken*), 29 353, No. 3, p. 3-4.

because of a preference for joint parental authority, but also to facilitate a decision on sole parental authority.

II.2.6.2. Continued parenting

The present proposal concerning a parenting plan has a long legislative history. It is rooted in the ongoing debate in the Netherlands concerning the feasibility of introducing an administrative divorce procedure as well as the ongoing debate concerning the enforcement and facilitation of contact after divorce between a non-resident parent and a child.[120]

In 2004 a member of the Dutch Parliament's Second Chamber (LUCHTENVELD) presented a legislative proposal concerning a non-judicial divorce procedure (administrative divorce) which would create a new route to divorce while maintaining the existing judicial procedure (contentious and non-contentious).[121] The primary goal was to leave responsibility for the divorce and the care of the children to the spouses and to reduce the judicial aspects of divorce.[122]

The proposed administrative divorce procedure had several consequences for the allocation and exercise of parental authority after divorce. The main points were the following:

1. The administrative route and the non-contentious judicial divorce would be contingent upon making agreements in a so-called parenting plan concerning the exercise of joint parental authority.[123]
2. Joint parental authority would continue after divorce. The possibility to be allocated sole parental authority would only be open in the situation where the other parent requested such an allocation, thus eliminating the possibility for a request for sole parental authority.[124]

---

120 Parliamentary proceedings, 2003/2004 (*Kamerstukken*), 29 520.

121 Parliamentary discussions 2003/2004 (*Kamerstukken*) , 29676, No. 2, *Voorstel van wet tot wijziging van Boek 1 van het Burgerlijk Wetboek en van het Wetboek van Burgerlijke Rechtsvordering in verband met de invoering van de mogelijkheid van beëindiging van het huwelijk zonder rechterlijke tussenkomst alsmede van een gewijzigde vaststelling en effectieve handhaving van de afspraken en rechterlijke beslissingen die in verband met de ontbinding van het huwelijk of nadien tot stand zijn gekomen over de wijze waarop door beide ouders vorm wordt gegeven aan het voortgezet ouderschap (beëindiging huwelijk zonder rechterlijke tussenkomst en vormgeving voortgezet ouderschap).*

122 Parliamentary proceedings 2003/2004 (*Kamerstukken*), 29 676, No. 3, p. 1.

123 Parliamentary proceedings 2003/2004 (*Kamerstukken*), 29 676, No. 3, p. 8-10.

124 Parliamentary proceedings 2003/2004 (*Kamerstukken*), 29 676, No. 3, p. 11.

3. A child would have the right to equal care by both parents after divorce, thereby implying a 50/50 norm (shared residence) except in situations where practical circumstances prevented this and then only for the duration they were present.[125]
4. The introduction of a minimum standard of contact in cases where one parent has sole parental authority.
5. The introduction of a simple judicial petition procedure (without the requirement of legal representation) for the settlement of conflicts concerning the care of and responsibility for raising the child (the exercise of joint parental authority).[126]

The Dutch Minister of Justice opposed the introduction of an administrative divorce procedure and introduced a competing proposal which would implement the precondition of submitting a parenting plan for obtaining a judicial divorce. LUCHTENVELD'S proposal was however favoured by the Dutch Parliament's Second Chamber. After being amended a number of times, it was finally adopted by Parliament on 29 December 2005. The adopted proposal differed substantially from the initial proposal. The main differences were the following: In the first place, the administrative divorce procedure would not be open to parents with minor children. Consequently the parenting plan would be a precondition for requesting a judicial divorce (contentious or non-contentious). Furthermore, the 50/50 norm was weakened substantially in that consideration should be given to the care arrangements in place before the divorce and the standard for contact in cases where one parent exercises sole parental authority was omitted. Finally, the possibility to request sole parental authority was maintained.[127]

The LUCHTENVELD proposal met with substantial criticism[128] and it was soon clear that the majority of the First Chamber of Parliament was not in favour of the proposal. On 20 June 2006 the proposal was rejected.[129] The main opposition was directed towards the consequences regarding parental authority and contact and in particular the simple judicial procedure regarding disputes concerning the exercise of parental authority rather than the administrative divorce procedu-

---

125 Parliamentary proceedings 2003/2004 (*Kamerstukken*), 29 676, No. 3, p. 5 and 12.

126 Parliamentary proceedings 2003/2004 (*Kamerstukken*), 29 676, No. 3, p. 11-12.

127 Parliamentary proceedings, 2005/2006 (*Kamerstukken I*), 29 676 A.

128 Including at a seminar held at the Free University of Amsterdam in August 2005. The contributions are contained in M. Antokolskaia (ed.), *Herziening van het echtscheidingsrecht, Administratieve echtscheiding, mediation, voortgezet ouderschap*, Amsterdam: SWP, 2006.

129 Parliamentary discussions 2006 (*Handelingen I*) 32-1483.

re.[130] There was general trepidation that the courts would become overloaded with petitions concerning the exercise of parental authority.

The present proposal[131] is deemed to promote 'Continued Parenting' and pursues the aim of a child's right 'to be cared for by two parents' after divorce and after a relationship has broken up.[132] The main aim is to implement the parenting plan as a precondition for a judicial divorce (contentious and non-contentious) so that, prior to divorce, parents will consider how the care and upbringing will be divided between them. Unmarried parents are also required to agree on a parenting plan if their relationship comes to an end. In the case of a dispute between unmarried parents concerning the exercise of parental authority, the court may stay the proceedings until the requirement has been met.[133] Furthermore, the proposal concerns the enactment of several changes to the Dutch Civil Code. Some of the proposals put forward provide a shift in terminology. Others are directed at providing a normative content for 'Continued Parenting' after divorce and the obligation of parents to make 'verifiable agreements'. Finally, some concern the enactment of principles which have already been established in case law. These distinctions do not follow from the proposal and are therefore not sharp enough. They are intended to provide an overall overview of the proposal. The main proposals put forward by the Dutch Minister of Justice which provide a shift in terminology are:

---

130 Parliamentary discussions 2006 (*Handelingen I*) 32-1371-1441.

131 Parliamentary proceedings 2005/2006/2007 (*Kamerstukken*) 30 145, pending before the Dutch Parliament's First Chamber as 30 145, Concerning proceedings No. 1-9, 11-14, 16-17, 19, 21-22, 24, 26 *Wijziging van Boek 1 van het Burgerlijk Wetboek en het Wetboek van Burgerlijke Rechtsvordering in verband met het bevorderen van voortgezet ouderschap na scheiding en het afschaffen van de mogelijkheid tot het omzetten van een huwelijk in een geregistreerd partnerschap (Wet bevordering voortgezet ouderschap en zorgvuldige scheiding)*.

132 In the course of the parliamentary process in the Second Chamber, private members of parliament put forward a number of proposals aimed at reintroducing certain parts of the Luchtenveld proposal: the administrative divorce procedure, an equality norm and the simple judicial procedure concerning disputes over the exercise of parental authority. Further, a proposal aimed at introducing a minimum fine in cases concerning the frustration of contact was put forward. Most of the amendments were not adopted by the Second Chamber. One important exception concerns the norm for equal parenting, Parliamentary proceedings (Kamerstukken) 2006/2007 30 145, No. 11, 26. The following amendments were not adopted, Parliamentary proceedings 2006/2007 (*Kamerstukken*), 30 145, No. 10, 13, 15, 18, 20, 23 and 25.

133 By an amendment to the initial proposal, Parliamentary proceedings 2006/2007 (*Kamerstukken*) 30 145, No. 14.

1. The term contact is reserved for parents who do not exercise joint parental authority. For parents who exercise joint parental authority, the terminology to be used is the 'division of care and responsibilities for raising the child'.[134]
2. The provisions granting legal parents and non-parents who do not share parental authority and children a right to contact are merged into one provision.[135]

The main proposals pertaining to 'Continued Parenting' and the making of 'verifiable agreements', except for the parenting plan which is discussed below, are the following:

1. An explicit norm concerning the obligation of a parent with parental authority to facilitate the child's bonding with the other parent (whether or not this parent exercises parental authority).[136]
2. An explicit norm for equal (value) parenting.[137]
3. Introducing an enforceable obligation to ensure contact for the non-resident parent.[138]
4. The establishment of minimum norms to be included in the parenting plan; here it is included that contact cannot be reduced to nil.[139]
5. The possibility for the court to establish a shared residence.[140]

---

134 Pertaining to Arts 251, 253a, 377a and 377h, DCC, Parliamentary proceedings 2004/2005 (*Kamerstukken*), 30 145, No. 3, p. 5 and p. 14.

135 Pertaining to Arts 377a and 377f, DCC, Parliamentary proceedings 2004/2005 (*Kamerstukken*), 30 145, No. 3, p. 15-16.

136 Pertaining to Art. 247, DCC, Parliamentary proceedings 2004/2005 (*Kamerstukken*), 30 145, No. 3, p. 13.

137 Pertaining to Art. 247, DCC, Parliamentary proceedings 2006/2007 (Kamerstukken), 30 145, Nos. 13 and 26.

138 Pertaining to Art. 377a, Parliamentary proceedings 2004/2005 (*Kamerstukken*), 30 145, No. 3, p. 15.

139 To be derived from the Explanatory Report: '*In respect of the division of care and the responsibility for raising (the child) it is in principle not possible for the parents to determine that the child should have no contact with one of its parents. This does not adhere to the provided norm*', Parliamentary proceedings 2004/2005 (*Kamerstukken*), 30 145, No. 3, p. 6.

140 To be derived from the Explanatory Report: '*The court can divide the care and responsibilities (the care arrangement) so that they are in the best interests of the child. The care (...) may be divided equally between the parents (each parent: 50%) but a division of 12 days with one parent and two days with the other parent is also possible*', Parliamentary proceedings 2004/2005 (*Kamerstukken*), 30 145, No. 3, p. 14. The Explanatory Report assumes that this is in accordance with the present Art. 377h, DCC. The question of court-ordered shared residence was, however, not discussed in the course of the legislative proceedings regarding this provision (the 1998 reform). The concept of shared residence is deliberated in detail in Chapter VI, Section VI.3.1.

6. The possibility for the court to refer parents to mediation and a temporary payment of Euro 200 to cover the costs and the possibility for parents with low incomes to make use of mediation within the system of legal aid.[141]

The main proposals for the enactment of principles which have already been established in case law are:

1. The enactment of the possibility to establish a main residence.[142]
2. The enactment of the 'torn or lost' criterion and the introduction of a secondary general criterion for the allocation of sole parental authority.[143]
3. The possibility of temporarily discontinuing contact.[144]
4. An explicit mention of (existing) enforcement measures in the Dutch Civil Code.[145]

The justification for the proposal is distinctly different from that in the 1998 reform. While the main intention of the 1998 reform was to be non-interventionist based upon article 8 of the ECHR, thereby allowing joint parental authority to continue unaffected by divorce, the present proposal aims to oblige parents to make agreements upon divorce, strongly favouring continued *de facto* parenting, which may be described as an interventionist policy. Indeed Article 8 of the ECHR remains unmentioned.[146]

The proposal is ambiguous in its distinction or rather its lack of distinction between joint parental authority and 'Continued Parenting'. On the one hand, it is evident that the proposal aims to provide joint parental authority with a de facto content of parenting for both parents, which has not been achieved through the 1998 legislation. On the other hand, the development in the allocation of joint parental authority (from 34% in 1997 to 92% in 2003) is seen as a positive development in favour of the present proposal.

---

141 Parliamentary proceedings 2004/2005 (*Kamerstukken*), 30 145, No. 3, p. 2-3.

142 Pertaining to Art. 253a, DCC, Parliamentary proceedings 2004/2005 (*Kamerstukken*), 30 145, No. 3, p. 14.

143 Pertaining to Art. 251a, DCC, Parliamentary proceedings 2004/2005 (*Kamerstukken*), 30 145, No. 3, p. 14. The 'torn or lost' criterion is analysed in detail in Chapter V.4.3.

144 Pertaining to Art 251a, DCC, Parliamentary proceedings 2004/2005, 30 145, No. 2, p. 3.

145 By an amendment to the initial proposal, Parliamentary proceedings 2006/2007 (*Kamerstukken*), 30 145, No. 7, p. 2 and 4. This proposal probably does increase the possibility of using enforcement measures, in particular the physical fetching of the child. Enforcement measures are deliberated in Chapter VIII.5.1.

146 Art. 8, ECHR is mentioned in relation to the positive obligation to facilitate contact, Parliamentary proceedings 2004/2005 (*Kamerstukken*), 30145, No. 3, p. 4.

The parenting plan is constructed so that it is a precondition for requesting a divorce and it is irrelevant whether the divorce is contentious or non-contentious or indeed whether the allocation and exercise of parental authority is a matter of dispute. The consequence of submitting a unilateral or joint request for divorce which does not contain a parenting plan or contains an incomplete parenting plan is nullity. In this respect the parenting plan provides the 'portal' for divorce. The proposal does contain a certain escape route in situations where it is not possible to submit a parenting plan. This escape route is, however, not to be utilized simply because an agreement cannot be reached or the parties have no communication. In this case the parent requesting the divorce must present his or her own vision concerning the shaping of 'continued parenting'.[147] The Dutch Minster of Justice justifies the obligation to submit a parenting plan as follows:

> 'In a number of cases it will not be reasonably possible to achieve agreement upon a parenting plan or be possible to draft such a plan. This may be the case in situations where there is no (longer any) communication between the parents, the mother has resorted to a safe house or a parent, or because of a psychiatric disorder is staying in an institution. As a result the parenting plan will be incomplete or even lacking.
>
> The situation in which no (complete) parenting plan can be submitted is more likely to arise in the case of a unilateral request for divorce. Even so, the obligation to submit a parenting plan also still applies in the case of a unilateral request. Alongside the principal reason, there is another reason to retain the obligation to submit a parenting plan in all situations, which is to prevent the creation of an escape route. Spouses would be able to agree that one of them would submit a unilateral request to which the other parent would then consent.[148] This is undesirable because it does not contribute to making both parents aware of their individual responsibility also after the divorce'.[149]

---

147 Parliamentary proceedings 2004/2005 (*Kamerstukken*), 30 145, No. 3, p. 5-6.

148 Rather than submitting a joint request for divorce in which case a parenting plan would be obligatory. The distinction between a unilateral or joint request is somewhat obscure considering that a joint request for divorce currently doe not need to be supplemented by an agreement concerning the consequences of divorce (hereunder the allocation and exercise of parental authority). Critical of the procedural aspects concerning the obligation to submit a parenting plan is L.M. Coenraad, 'Procederen over het voortgezet ouderschap', in: M.V. Antokolskaia, 2006, supra, p. 69-98.

149 Parliamentary proceedings 2004/2005 (*Kamerstukken*), 30 145, No. 3, p. 5.

As a minimum, the contents of the parenting plan must include:

1. The manner in which the parents divide the care and responsibilities for raising the children or shaping the right and the obligation to have contact.
2. The manner in which the parents inform and consult each other concerning important matters related to the child and the child's property.
3. The costs of caring for the minor children (child maintenance).[150]

II.3. THE PARENT-CHILD RELATIONSHIP: DENMARK

The first Danish Act which contained a set of provisions on parental rights and duties was the Act on Incapacity and Guardianship in 1922.[151] Before then matters of parental rights referred to as parental power (*forældremagten*) or parental authority (*forældremyndighed*) were regulated by certain provisions in the Danish Act,[152] jurisprudence and case law.

The Act on Incapacity and Guardianship regulated the incapacity of minors as well as adults and parental authority in respect of minors. The Act was the result of the Family Law Commission's work. This Commission was established in 1910 and it embarked on extensive reform preparations in the area of family law. The work was done in close co-operation with similarly established commissions in Norway and Sweden and resulted in similar legislation regarding marriage and parental authority/guardianship in the three Nordic countries.[153]

According to the 1922 Act children born within and outside marriage were subject to parental authority (*forældremyndighed*) and guardianship (*værgemål*).

---

150 Parliamentary proceedings 2004/2005 (*Kamerstukken*), 30 145, No. 3, p. 5.

151 Lov om umyndighed og værgemål, Act No. 277 of 30.06.1922.

152 *Danske lov* from 1683 consisting of 6 books, which formed the foundation of Danish legislation. While most provisions have been replaced by new legislation the Act itself still remains in force.

153 The co-operation was strongest in the field of marriage law. Co-operation was not systematically continued and the three countries today have quite different rules in the field of marriage and parental authority. Some common features remain, for example, in respect of the distinction between parental authority and guardianship, see Chapter V, Section V.2.3.4. and in respect of access to dispute settlement, see below Section II.4.2. note 221 of this Chapter. Recently, an initiative has been taken by the Nordic Council to compare and analyse the scope for harmonisation in respect of different aspects of family law, amongst others, parental authority. This has resulted in several books, for example, S. Danielsen: *Nordisk Børneret* (Nordic child law) II, Copenhagen: Nord, 2003.

Parental authority relates to the duty to care for the child and the power to make decisions concerning that child, while guardianship relates to the power to administer the child's property and legal representation in respect thereof.

The 1922 Act was amended on a number of occasions, notably in 1986, but it survived intact up until 1996 when the Act on Parental Authority and Contact was enacted.[154] The 1922 Act still remained in force except for the provisions on parental authority and so did the division between parental authority and guardianship. Now, however, the rules were to be found in two separate acts.[155]

On 1 October 2007 the Act on Parental Responsibility[156] replaced the Act on Parental Authority and Contact. The division between parental authority and guardianship remains the same.

II.3.1. PARENTAL AUTHORITY DURING MARRIAGE

Before the 1922 Act married parents, who lived together, held parental power. The father was, however, supreme and could decide where the wife and the children should live according to the so-called law of the principal (*husbond-retten*).[157]

The main feature of the 1922 Act on Incapacity and Guardianship was equality between the spouses in their relationship with the children. Married parents held joint parental authority. Guardianship continued to be held by the father alone. The Commission suggested that parents should be able to bring a dispute before a public authority which would then decide on the disputed issue. The measure was proposed in order to fill the void that would occur when paternal supremacy was abandoned. The suggestion was not adopted, primarily due to resistance in Parliament, but also considering the aim of unity in the Nordic co-operation. Joint parental authority between married parents was thus based on agreement; no instrument to solve disputes between the holders of this authority

154 Lov om forældremyndighed og samvær, Act No. 416, 10.06.1997.

155 The 1922 Act was finally revoked with effect from 1 January 1997 when the new Act on Guardianship came into force, Værgemålsloven, Act No. 388, 14.06.1995.

156 Lov om forældreansvar, Act No. 499 of 06.06.2007.

157 V. Benzon, *Familieretten II, Ægteskabets retsvirkninger*, Copenhagen: G.E.C. Gad, 1926, p. 8 and I.H. Deuntzer: *Den Nordiske familie- og arveret*, 1878, p. 53.

was provided. If, however, the parents had ceased to live together sole parental authority could be allocated to one parent upon request.[158]

In 1957 the father ceased to be the sole guardian of the child and guardianship was held jointly. In the case of a dispute concerning guardianship an administrative authority was granted competence to decide on such disputes.[159]

II.3.2. PARENTAL AUTHORITY AFTER DIVORCE

Before the 1922 Act joint parental power was replaced with sole parental power after divorce. A divorce could be administratively granted where the parents agreed upon divorce. In such a case the parents would agree upon the allocation of sole parental power to one parent. If a divorce was granted based upon fault, sole parental power was generally granted to the other parent.[160]

According to the 1922 Act either parent could request that joint parental authority be replaced with sole parental authority, if they had ceased to live together because of a dispute. In the case of divorce or judicial separation the decree contained a decision or agreement on the allocation of sole parental authority to one of the parents. In case agreement on the allocation was not reached, the court allocated sole parental authority according to a 'just' principle, supplemented by a fault criterion. The text of the provision[161] read as follows:

> 'What especially with respect to the children's well-being is just. If it has been established that one parent is essentially to blame for the break-up of the marriage and they are equally capable of raising the children, the other parent shall be more inclined to obtain parental authority. Children under two years of age should only be exceptionally removed from the mother.'

The criteria for granting sole parental authority to one parent was thus a 'just' criterion referring to the well-beeing of the children, and only where both parents were equally capable of raising the child was a fault criterion applied

---

158 This only applied in cases where the parents had ceased to live together or intended to do so because of a dispute.

159 Act No. 17 of 06.02.1957.

160 V. Benzon: *Familieretten*, Copenhagen, C.E.G. Gad, 1924, p. 249, Danske lov 3-16-16-8. On the contrary I. Deuntzer considered that this point was not expresly contained in the legislative provisions, I. Deuntzer, 1878, supra, p. 53.

161 Art. 24, Lov om umyndighed og værgemål.

giving parental authority to the parent who was not to blame for the break-up of the marriage.[162] This fault criterion was removed in 1970 and so was the preference for the mother in obtaining parental authority over a child under the age of two.[163]

In the period from 1970-1980 an established Marriage Commission published eight reports reviewing the law relating to marriage, co-habitation and parental authority. These reports contained deliberations, discussions and suggestions rather than factual legislative proposals.[164] In 1981 the Children Commission was established to review all legislation relating to children. The Commission suggested, amongst other things, that married parents should be able to retain joint parental authority upon judicial separation and divorce and that unmarried parents should be able to make an agreement on joint parental authority. The Commission's suggestions did not contain an actual legislative proposal, but part of its deliberations and suggestions were included in the 1983 report by the working group established by the Justice Department, which contained a revised draft of the 1922 Act.[165]

II.3.2.1. Law reform concerning joint parental authority 1983-2007

The Danish law on parental authority has been revised, in particular, by means of three reforms in 1986, 1996 and 2007, all prepared by established Commissions. An important change – the automatic continuation of joint parental authority – was, however, enacted in 2001 pursuant to the Children Act which provided a substantive revision of the law on parentage.

---

162 The Commission stressed that the fault crieterion should not be used automatically, but only as a guiding criterion, Commission report 1913, p. 258.

163 Act No. 256 of 04.06.1969. The Commission report of 1964 stated the following: 'whoever is to blame for the breakdown of the marriage is in this connection completely irrelevant', p. 102. The Commission suggested that preference for the mother should be manintained as the practical main rule, but the provision was removed in the course of the parliamentary discussions on the act, Parliamentary news, *FTB* 1968-69, p. 1898.

164 Three reports dealt with parental authority. Commission report 4, No. 719/1974 concerning the conditions for judicial separation and divorce did not recommend that joint parental authority should become an option after divorce considering in particular that there was no real need for such an option when parents who agreed upon joint care were free to do so and further stressing the practical difficulties which could arise. Commission report 7, No. 796/ 1977 considered the judicial separation/divorce procedures, in particular the division of competence between the ordinary courts and the administrative authorities. Commission report 8, No. 91571980 considered non-marital cohabitation and the possibility for unmarried parents to make an agreement on joint parental authority.

165 Commission report No. 918/1981.

Two recent general reforms concerning 'rule simplification' in family law and a new structural reform concerning family law procedures have also made substantive changes to the procedural system regulating the allocation of parental authority after divorce. Although joint parental authority after divorce increasingly became the norm, Danish law maintained the principle that joint parental authority must be replaced with sole parental authority at the request of one parent up until 2007. The new complete revision of the law on parental authority (now the Act on Parental Responsibility) now abandons this principle making joint parental authority the general rule. An intrinsic element of the reforms of 1986, 1996 and the structural reform of 2005 has been the simultaneous enactment or strengthening of the right/duty to participate in alternative dispute resolution.

The 1983 report[166] on parental authority and contact contained a revised draft of the 1922 Act in respect of the provisions on parental authority, contact, and guardianship (of minors). The Act was adopted with a few non-substantial changes and came into force on 1 January 1986.[167] The Act contained the possibility for married parents, upon request, to retain joint parental authority after divorce and for unmarried parents to obtain joint parental authority upon request, subject to approval. In the case of a judicial separation or divorce an agreement or decision in respect of parental authority had to be made, but this also remained possible in the situation where the parents had ceased to live together or intended to do so because of a dispute. Joint parental authority was consequently based upon parental agreement and a joint request. An agreement would generally be approved unless it was considered to be against the best interests of the child. The essential feature of approval as a condition lay more in ensuring that an agreement between the parents was real and the possibility to advise the parents of the consequences of such an allocation than in a factual evaluation of the best interests of the child.[168]

The content of joint parental authority pursuant to the 1986 reform was based entirely upon parental agreement and it was left to the parents to determine the substantive content. This could amount to an agreement according to which the child should reside equally with both parents (shared residence), but the principle of joint parental authority did not contain any obligations as to how the parents should divide the care of the child.[169]

166 Commission Report No. 985/1983.
167 Act No. 230 (231) of 20.06.1985.
168 Commission Report No. 985/1983 p. 75, p. 32.
169 Commission Report 985/1983 p. 31.

Disputes of any kind, such as disputes concerning residence, contact or all other issues concerning the child's person could not be brought before an authority/ court.[170] In this respect joint parental authority outside of marriage was given the same form as joint parental authority within marriage. No access to a dispute settlement system was provided. The reason for this was that it was not considered appropriate to allow 'outsiders to decide on disputes'.[171] On the other hand, parents with joint parental authority, whether married or divorced, could always apply for the termination of joint parental authority when they did not live together or intended to end the relationship. Such a termination was not subject to any test considering the seriousness of the differences or whether termination was in the best interests of the child.

In the course of the parliamentary proceedings a provision providing that the administrative authorities should offer parents and children free counselling in cases where there was a dispute concerning parental authority and contact was adopted.[172]

In 1993 the Justice Department, following a request by the Danish Parliament, set up a Commission which was asked to analyse the current law on joint parental authority, counselling and contact and, if necessary, make proposals for change. The Commission published its report entitled 'joint parental authority, contact difficulties and child expert counselling' containing a draft act in 1994.[173] The Commission had considered whether joint parental authority should continue automatically after divorce and whether it should be possible for the courts to establish joint parental authority against the wishes of one parent. The Commission rejected both notions. The fact that an agreement or decision concerning parental authority must be made in the divorce procedure was considered to be part and parcel of the divorce procedure and was thus left for future consideration. The establishment of joint parental authority against the wishes of one parent was rejected on the following grounds:

170 Except for a dispute concerning child maintenance payments. The reason for this being that the Children Act of 1960 which regulated the obligation to pay maintenance was and remains (since the Children Act of 2001) based upon the principle that the parent who does not reside with the child has an obligation to pay maintenance. The obligation is thus independent of marital status and parental authority.

171 Report No. 985/1983 p. 35.

172 Act No. 230 (231) of 20.06.1985.

173 Commission Report 1279/1994, *Fælles forældremyndighed samværsvanskeligheder børnesagkyndig rådgivning.*

> 'Without research, a new system with such far-reaching consequences for children should not be introduced. On the present basis the Commission considers that joint parental authority only works if both parents remain positive. Enforced parental authority would require fundamental changes to the construction of parental authority and society would acquire an active role in determining the child's everyday life'.[174]

While enforced joint parental authority was rejected, the scope for joint parental authority was increased considerably with the introduction of the possibility to render a contact decision where the parents have joint parental authority. Furthermore, the preference for joint parental authority was demonstrated by the fact that a parental agreement on joint parental authority was now no longer subject to review, but became valid upon notification to the administrative authorities. A parental agreement allocating sole parental authority to one parent continued to be subject to approval.

Following the Children Commission's proposal in 2000, which included a proposal for the amendment of the Children Act in respect of the establishment of parentage,[175] the Justice Department suggested that joint parental authority should continue automatically after divorce with the following reasoning:

> 'The Justice Department has in that connection stressed that for unmarried cohabiting parents there is no requirement to decide on the issue of parental authority in case the relationship breaks up. In the light of the general principle of equality between married couples and unmarried cohabitating couples, which is the basis of the Children Act Proposal, it may seem less appropriate to uphold a requirement to make a decision for married couples. Furthermore, it is a fact that a considerable number of married couples divorcing or legally separating agree on joint parental authority'.[176]

---

174 Commission report 1279/1994 p. 14. The role of 'society' was seen as involving 'public parenting' which would inherently necessitate access to dispute settlement, p. 70. The Commission further considered that 'legislation is not a means to curb existing differences between parents and create co-operation which is not already present and which cannot be brought about voluntarily', p. 71.

175 See for more Section II.3.4. of this Chapter.

176 Notes to Proposal No. 198, Proposal for a change to the Procedural Act and various other acts, 2000, p. 11. It was estimated at the time that approximately 90% of parents agreed on joint parental authority upon judicial separation or divorce.

From the 1 January 2005 agreements on the allocation of parental authority (sole/joint) between the parents are no longer subject to a review but gain validity upon notification to the Regional State Administration.[177] The change was made in connection with many other changes in family law with the purpose of simplifying the rules. The reasoning of the legislature was partly ideological in nature as a review was considered to be 'paternalistic and outdated' and partly pragmatic: only a few agreements did not gain approval and the reasons for non-approval lay on the borderline of family law considerations such as an agreement on sole parental authority specifically made to render a decision concerning placing the child in care unenforceable.[178]

The Danish procedural system has been changed substantially from 1 January 2007. All cases concerning judicial separation, divorce, parental authority and contact must now begin at the administrative authorities and only when a solution cannot be found is the case, under certain conditions, submitted to the court by the Regional State Administration.[179] An inherent element of the administrative procedure is the use of counselling/mediation and child expertise.

II.3.2.2. The Act on Parental Responsibility 2007

Parental authority is currently regulated in the Act on Parental Responsibility. A Commission established in March 2005 was to consider the need for reform concerning, amongst other things, a stronger child-centred perspective in decisions on parental authority and contact, the possibility of establishing joint parental authority against the wishes of one parent and the possibility of establishing shared residence against the wishes of one parent.[180]

177 Act No. 446 of 09.06.2004.

178 *Regelforenkling på det familieretlige område*, Report given by a working group under the Justice Department, December 2003, p. 26-28. See for more information in Dutch: C. Jeppesen: 'Administratieve echtscheiding in Denemarken', *FJR*, October 2005, p. 174-181.

179 Act No. 525 of 24.06.2005. For more information on the entire reform in Dutch see also; C. Jeppesen: 2005, supra and C. Jeppesen.: 'Administratieve echtscheiding in Denemarken' in: M.V. Antokolskaia, *Herzienning van het echtscheidingsrecht*, 2006, supra.

180 The Commission had 14 members, mainly legal experts from the State Administration and external legal experts as well as (for the first time) representatives from private interest organisations: from a fathers' rights organisation (*Foreningen Far*), from a childrens' rights organisation (*Børns Vilkår*) and from a support organisation for women (*Mødrehjælpen*) as well as a child expert (one of the leading sociologists in this field, Mai Heide Ottosen).

The Commission published its report in May 2006 and it contained a draft proposal for a revised act on parental authority and contact.[181] The majority of the Commission proposed a limited possibility to establish joint parental authority against the wishes of one parent. The proposal did not contain the possibility to establish shared residence against one parent's wishes.

One of the main disputed elements in the recent reform has been the establishment of joint parental authority against the wishes of one parent. This aspect had been looked at in the light of Nordic experiences, in particular the laws of Sweden and Norway which both contain this possibility. The 2006 Commission was divided on this point. The majority proposed a limited possibility to establish joint parental authority against the wishes of one parent. The majority of the Commission proposed:

> 'That it should be possible to establish joint parental authority in exceptional cases even if one of the parents does not want this to be established. (...) It is the majority's perception that it should not be decisive for the allocation of joint parental authority that one parent does not wish the other parent to share parental authority. The possibility to enforce joint parental authority (...) may bring potential co-operation to light and it must be assumed that more cases will be settled by the parents.'

Futher, the majority reasoned:

> 'Such a possibility (...) must be viewed in connection with the possibilities which parents have after 1 January 2007.[182] Such access (...) will have a motivating effect in relation to the possibility of achieving a negotiated settlement at the administrative authorities. The possibility that a parent 'risks' the fact that the continuation of joint parental authority will be enforced might lead to a decrease in the number of court cases pertaining to the termination of joint parental authority which are not reasoned in relation to the child. (...) It is the majority's perception that it is easier to keep focusing upon the child at the administrative authorities where a negotiated solution is sought than in a court of law where a legal decision must be rendered.'

---

181 Commission Report No. 1475/2006, *Betænkning om Barnets perspektiv, Forældremyndighed, Barnets bopæl, Samvær og tvangsfuldbyrdelse.*

182 The date of the Structural reform, according to which all divorce petitions and matters relating to the allocation of parental authority and contact must begin at the (administrative) state administration.

The minority[183] were against the establishment of joint parental authority against the wishes of one parent considering that this is not in the interests of the child and they further reasoned:

> 'That the construction 'joint parental authority' presupposes that parents can co-operate in important matters concerning the child. To force reluctant parents to exercise parental authority undermines the fundamental idea of the potential for parental co-operation and is contrary to existing knowledge and experience on what is best for a child. When parents argue as to parental authority, this is a reflection of a lost ability to co-operate.
>
> The minority consider that disputes concerning parental authority rarely arise as a result of minor controversies. Before a case is initiated, there have often been controversies for a longer period of time. Experience shows that resident parents wait for a considerable time before a case is initiated, because such a case is stressful, costly and involves the risk of losing (sole parental authority to the other parent).[184] In families where there has been a history of violence, a tendency on the part of the resident parent to postpone a case concerning parental authority (to the detriment of the child) has been observed.'[185]

In December 2006, however, the Danish Minister of Family and Consumer Affairs released a press statement stating that political agreement had been reached on drafting a new proposal which would go further than the Commission's proposal. This proposal should contain the principle that joint parental authority is the general rule and that shared residence orders should be possible. The new proposal contained a completely rewritten Act (now the Act on Parental Responsibility) and a new Explanatory Report.[186] The proposal was published in December 2006, adopted on the 10 May 2007 and it entered into force on 1 October 2007. The new Act and the Explanatory notes incorporate many of the suggestions and deliberations of the 2006 Commission, but it also goes further.

---

183 The child expert sociologist Mai Heide Ottosen, the representatives of the womens' interests organisation (*Mødrehjælpen*) and the children's interests organisation (*Børns Vilkår*).

184 (Added).

185 Commission Report No. 1475/2006, p. 144-154.

186 Forslag til lov om forældreansvar, 2006/2007, L 133 presented 31.01.2007.

The main changes concerning parental authority are that joint parental authority becomes the main rule in all cases.[187] The court can only allocate sole parental authority to one parent (in all cases where there is joint parental authority) when there are 'weighty grounds' for such an allocation.[188] An alternative to the allocation of sole parental authority is the establishment of residence with one parent. This legal concept is new in Danish law. The Explanatory Report considers that most disputes concerning parental authority are in reality disputes concerning the child's primary residence. Further, the Act makes it possible to establish a contact arrangement, which amounts to shared residence in repect of the allocation of time.

The purpose of the Act on Parental Responsibility and the reason for the change in the title of the Act is justified in the Explanatory Report as follows:

> 'The title'Act on parental authority and contact' is no longer adequate when separate decisions concerning residence are introduced. At the same time the proposal contains substantial changes to the law on parental authority and implements an important principle, which is: that a child has the right to two parents. This fundamental principle means that the parents, regardless of the fact that they no longer live together, must take responsibility for the child, on the one hand by caring for the child, on the other by co-operating on important issues concerning the child. It is also the responsibility of both parents that there is contact with the parent with whom the child does not live. The title of the Act is consequently an illustration of its purpose – that the parents have and take responsibility for the child by co-operating on parental authority and contact'.[189]

---

187 The Act is completely revised and contains a number of changes. These changes will not be deliberated in detail considering that this Act forms the starting point for the deliberations contained in Chapters V-VIII.

188 According to the Explanatory notes referring to the law of Sweden 'it is not required that the parents agree upon all matters concerning the child. (...) It is relevant whether the parents can deal with the disagreements and co-operate in spite of these differences considering that the disagreements may be temporary.' Weighty grounds are present when there are severe and insurmountable differences or conditions pertaining to one of the parents such as violence, large-scale abuse, serious mental conditions or a lack of interest in the child, L 133, Comment to § 11. While the Explanatory Report refers to Swedish law it does not expressly consider the point raised by the Commission Report that Swedish law on this issue is being reconsidered, because more recent research has shown that serious parental conflicts affect the child more when there is joint parental authority than when there is sole parental authority, Explanatory Report 2006, Comments to § 11.

189 L 133, Comments to § 11.

II.3.3. CONTACT AFTER DIVORCE

Prior to the 1922 Act contact[190] between a parent, who had not been allocated sole parental authority after divorce, and his/her child was unregulated. It was not possible for the courts or administrative authorities to decide on contact. If the parents had made an agreement on contact such an agreement was valid and it was generally assumed that such an agreement could be enforced by the courts.[191]

The initial proposal for the 1922 Act did not contain a right for the parent who had not been allocated parental authority to have contact with the child. Article 70 of the proposal provided that a separation or divorce decree contained a decision concerning the allocation of sole parental authority and further that 'parental authority concerning each child *should be allocated undivided to one parent* '(emphasis added). The underlying reason for this was that contact was considered to be deeply problematic when it was not based upon (continued) parental agreement.[192] The final Act did, however, contain a right to contact based on considerations of Nordic unity.[193] The Commission considered the following in relation to the right to contact:

> 'All things considered, it would be harsh towards the parent who is deprived of normal contact with the children – because naturally they cannot stay with both parents when their co-habitation is terminated – to deprive this parent of all contact with the children. In the circumstances such a separation from one of the parents will undoubtedly be unnatural and damaging for the children. The Commission had also not intended that this should be the actual consequence of the suggested provision (...). Renewed consideration has led to the conclusion that the well-being of the children can also be protected even if the natural visitation right of both parents is recognised when this right is subject to control in cases of parental disagreement.'[194]

---

190 The term then used was *samkvemsret* which may be translated as a visitation right. The term *samværsret* (contact right) was used pursuant to the 1986 reform. The 1996 reform introduced the present term *samvær* (contact).

191 A. Bille, 'Samvær og forældremyndighed i historisk belysning', *UFR*, 1997B, p. 408-409.

192 Commission report, *Udkast til lov om ægteskabs indgåelse og opløsning*, 1913, p. 260.

193 Because Sweden and Norway wanted such a right included in their acts.

194 Commission report, Udkast til lov om ægteskabets retsvirkninger, 1918, p. 50.

Article 27 of the 1922 Act thus gave the parent who had not been allocated parental authority a right to contact unless special circumstances were present. Administrative case law on contact pursuant to the 1922 Act was limited considering the relatively small number of divorces. The administrative authorities concentrated their efforts on bringing about parental agreement. When there were serious conflicts, it was most likely that contact would be terminated. With the increase in divorce rates at the beginning of the 1970s more structure and uniformity was brought about concerning the criteria for and the amount of contact contained in a decision on contact although the starting point continued to be that of an individual assessment.[195]

Pursuant to the 1996 Act on Parental Authority and Contact, Article 16 provided that: 'the child's connection with both (legal) parents is sought and this is maintained by allowing the parent who does not live with the child to have a right to contact.' A contact decision could thus also be issued in respect of a parent who held joint parental authority.

The general purpose of the 1996 reform was to downgrade contact as a right by changing the concept from a 'contact right' to merely contact. It was considered by the 1994 Commission that the existing administrative case law had become too strict with regard to the possibility of rejecting or discharging contact in relation to the welfare of the child. The Commission considered that the scope for discharging contact should be increased.[196] Article 17(3) came to provide that contact may be rejected or that established contact may be terminated if this is necessary for the child.

The obstruction of contact was inserted in the provision concerning the reallocation of parental authority in the 1996 Act as the only consideration[197] to be

---

195 A. Bille, 1997, supra, p. 409-412.

196 Commission report 1279/1994, p. 137. It is generally acknowledged that pursuant to the 1996 reform the possibility to discharge a parent from the right to contact actually decreased rather than increased, A. Kronborg, *Forældremyndighed & Menneskelig Integritet*, Copenhagen: Jurist- og Økonomforbundets Forlag, 2007, p. 109-110. The 2007 reform again aims to increase the possibility of terminating the right to contact by adopting '*a child-centred perspective*' and the strengthening of the procedures in difficult cases, Explanatory notes, L 133, p. 52-53.

197 This consideration was not contained in the Commission's 1994 draft act, although it was mentioned amongst other considerations in the report, p. 145. The consideration was added in the course of the parliamentary proceedings. It is popularly recognised as the trade mark of the fathers' rights movement.

mentioned. The general criterion of the provisions on the reallocation of parental authority was what is best for the child.[198]

Pursuant to the new Act on Parental Responsibility (2007) the court may establish a contact arrangement which, time-wise, amounts to shared residence.

II.3.4. PARENTAGE AND PARENTAL AUTHORITY: UNMARRIED PARENTS

At the turn of the previous century children born within marriage were referred to as legitimate (*ægte*) children and children born outside marriage as illegitimate (*uægte*) children in Danish law. The illegitimate child was a full member of the mother's family on equal terms with legitimate children based on the principle *mater semper certa est*, but was not part of the father's family. The father's obligations towards an illegitimate child were reduced to an obligation to pay child maintenance. Paternity could not be established and the possibility for the father to recognise a child born outside marriage did not establish full legal ties between the father and the child, but only an obligation to pay maintenance and the possibility for the father to allow the child to bear his name. The father could not claim any parental rights; these belonged solely to the mother.[199]

In 1908 an unmarried mother who applied for public aid to support a child was put under an obligation to state who the child's father was so that a maintenance claim could be made in order to minimise the State's liability.[200] This forms the start of the obligation for a mother to state the father's identity in Danish law.

With the 1922 Act on Incapacity and Guardianship the unmarried mother retained sole parental authority and guardianship of a child born outside marriage.[201] It was not possible for the father to obtain parental authority, except for the possibility of a voluntary transfer of parental authority from the mother to the father.[202]

---

198 Articles 12 and 13, Lov om forældremyndighed og samvær.

199 J. Graversen, S. Beck, N. Munck, M. Højgaard Pedersen, P. Vesterdorf, *Familieret*, Copenhagen: Juristforbundets Forlag, 1986, p. 26.

200 Act No. 130 of 27.05.1908.

201 Art. 28(1), Act No. 277 of 30.06.1922.

202 The father who had recognised the child (*kuldlysning*) had a limited possibility to obtain parental authority in the case of the mother's death, Art. 28(2), 1922 Act.

The Children Act of 1937[203] had as its main goal to equate children born outside marriage with children born within marriage in relation to their parents. The Justice Department stated the following in relation to equality:

> 'The inequality which exists between children born outside marriage and legitimate children is an injustice to the former. The institution of marriage is no longer threatened by loose sexual relationships. This institution is so deeply rooted in our society that it does not need (...) protection. Children born outside marriage should be able to claim the same from their parents as legitimate children. The source of their rights in relation to their parents is the same as for legitimate children; the natural relationship created upon conception and societal interests cannot justify depriving children of these rights (...). In relation to the parents, natural justice and fairness demands that both parents are equally responsible for the consequences of their relationship'.

With the 1937 Act the child obtained the right to bear the father's name and to inherit from the father. The establishment of paternity was compulsory in cases where there was no voluntary recognition. In such a procedure the mother was under a criminal law obligation to state the father's name.[204] The Children Act of 1937 conferred rights on the child in relation to its father. It did not, however, confer any rights in relation to parental authority on the father. The mother continued to hold parental authority solely and the father could not have parental rights transferred to him against the mother's wishes. Not until the enactments of 1972 (access to obtain parental authority when the child had been given up for adoption)[205] and 1978 (the possibility to transfer parental authority to the father to the exclusion of the mother)[206] did the father gain an independent claim to parental authority.

---

203 Act No. 131 of 07.05.1937 (children born outside of marriage) and Act No. 132 of 07.05.1937 (legitimate children).

204 It was not always possible to establish biological proof of paternity. For this reason the 1937 Act maintained the possibility to establish a maintenance obligation for one or more possible fathers instead of establishing paternity. The 1960 Children Act removed this possibility. The 1960 Children Act included all provisions relating to the establishment of paternity in one Act, proclaimed the equal status of these children and provided the same maintenance obligation in respect of both, Act. No. 200 of 18.05.1960.

205 Act No. 280 of 07.06.1972.

206 Act No. 244 of 08.06.1978. The criteria for such a transfer were eased by Act No. 230 of 06.06.1985.

The 1986 reform made joint parental authority upon a joint request possible for unmarried legal parents. Once established, joint parental authority could always be terminated at the request of one parent when the parents did not live together or intended to end their relationship.

The 1996 reform strengthened the father's position in relation to parental authority. The 1994 Commission was positive towards giving unmarried parents who cohabited joint parental authority *ex lege*. The problem was the lack of registration concerning cohabitation. The Commission solved the issue by suggesting that the unmarried father who had cohabited with the mother, but had not shared parental authority, be given an equal right to obtain parental authority upon the dissolution of the relationship.[207]

II.3.4.1. The 2001 Children Act

The Children Act of 2001 abandoned the distinction between children born inside and outside marriage and introduced a paternity registration procedure for children born inside and outside of marriage.[208] The mother's obligation to state the possible father(s')'s name(s) when there is no designated father was strengthened insofar that the administrative case law, which provided that the mother could be freed of this obligation if she had attained a certain age and was considered to have sufficient means to support the child, was abandoned.

With the Children Act of 2001 the obligation for the mother to state the father's name and the establishment of paternity was seen as a means to ensure that a child has two parents, a father and a mother.[209] This obligation may only be dispensed with in special circumstances such as, for example, in cases of rape or incest. The Children Act of 2001 further strengthened the unmarried father's position in that he was granted a right to have his paternity established under certain conditions.

---

207 Art. 12 of the Act on Parental Authority and Contact.

208 Børneloven, Act No. 461 of 07.06.2001. The Commission preparing the draft act proposed this registration procedure should apply to married and co-habiting parents. Commission Report No. 1350/1998, *Betænkning om børns retsstilling*. The Justice Department changed the draft act so that it applied to all unmarried parents since there was no formal registration of cohabitation, see further C. Jeppesen, 'Moeder- en Vaderschap in Denemarken: de nieuwe Deense kinderwet gezien vanuit een Nederlands perspectief', *FJR* 2002, p. 174-181 and C. Jeppesen and A. Kronborg, 'Danish Regulation of the Parent-Child Relationship', in I. Schwenzer (Ed.), *Tensions Between Legal, Biological and Social Conceptions of Parentage*, Antwerp-Oxford: Intersentia, 2007, p. 141-157.

209 Commission Report No. 1350/1998.

The Children Act now provides that the unmarried father is registered at the time of the birth without any further procedures in the following situations:

a) The paternity is registered if the mother and a man state that they will *care for and be responsible* for the child together. It is not a condition that the man is the biological father of the child. A statement is not accepted if, during the last 10 months, the mother has been married to another man without being judicially separated.[210]
b) Paternity was already acknowledged before the birth of the child and the mother and the father stated that they *would care for and be responsible* for the child together, or paternity was acknowledged without such a statement, but with the mother's statement that the man is the only possible biological father.[211]

The most common paternity registration procedure for unmarried parents is the 'care and responsibility' statement. It is a simple procedure. A form must be completed, signed and submitted to the church registrar of the Danish State Church together with the birth certificate.[212] This procedure results in joint parental authority.

When the paternity is *not registered at the time of the birth* the administrative authorities will investigate the matter and ask the mother who the possible father(s) is/are. The mother is under a criminal law obligation to provide this information. A man who has had sexual intercourse with the mother at around the time of conception has the right, within 6 months after the birth of the child, to have his paternity established unless another man's paternity was already established involving joint parental authority (a registration based upon the mother's marriage or a statement of care and responsibility). This exception does not apply to the man who was married to the mother without being judicially separated, or cohabiting with the mother during the period of conception. A man who was married to the mother without being judicially separated within 10 months from the time of the birth is informed of the birth by the administration.[213]

210 Art. 2, Børneloven.

211 Art. 3, Børneloven.

212 The church registrar acts in a civilian function in this respect. Since 01.03.2007 registration is also possible on the internet.

213 C. Jeppesen and A. Kronborg, 2007, supra.

II.3.4.2. The 2007 Act on Parental responsibility

Pursuant to Article 7(2) of the Act on Parental Responsibility (2007) joint parental authority is established *ex lege* when the parents have cohabited during 10 months prior to the birth of a child irrespective of continued cohabitation and irrespective of the manner in which paternity has been established (voluntarily or enforced).

II.3.5. UNMARRIED PARENTS' RIGHT OF CONTACT

The administrative authorities were given a discretionary power to issue a contact order in respect of an unmarried legal father in 1969.[214] Article 27(2) of the 1922 Act provided that the administrative authorities could allow the father of a child born outside marriage a right to personally visit the child, if this was consistent with the welfare of the child, and that special circumstances, in particular the father's former connection with the child, were present.[215]

The 1996 Act on Parental Authority and Contact provided the same right to contact for all legal parents.[216] The consideration concerning the parent's former connection with the child was removed. The Ministry of Justice considered that the intention was to establish contact also in cases where the parents had not cohabited or had cohabited for only a brief period of time considering the child's age and maturity.[217] The Act on Parental Responsibility further strengthens this perspective in as much as it provides an increased possibility to establish more contact with very young children.[218]

II.4. MAIN COMPARATIVE FEATURES

The described development indicates a greater divide in the development of the law from the starting point at the beginning of the previous century up until the past few decades of the previous century as thereafter. During the first part of

---

214 Act No. 257 of 04.06.1969 amending the 1922 Act.

215 Act No. 244 of 08.06.1978 amending the 1922 Act established that the father who did not have parental authority had a *right* to contact (still depending on a former connection). Further, the 1986 reform provided a contact right for mothers and fathers alike (a former connection continued to be relevant).

216 See for the wording of the provision Section II.3.3. above.

217 Parliamentary discussions 1994/1995, *Folketings Tidende*, Section A, p. 2199.

218 L 133, p. 45.

the previous century Danish law was dominated by two major reforms which were aimed at creating equality between spouses in relation to their children (1922) and between children born inside and outside marriage in relation to, in particular, the judicial establishment of paternity (1937). The period which followed up until 1968 has been described as the 'happy times of Danish family law' because the various reforms removed the worst injustices in family law, without undermining the institution of marriage.[219]

In the Netherlands similar developments in law reform have generally been taken in smaller steps and have come later, for example full equality between the spouses in relation to the common children in 1984 and the judicial establishment of paternity in 1998.

Notwithstanding the above-mentioned differences, the developments in joint parental authority after divorce and for unmarried parents, although they are different in content and context and have developed differently, are strikingly concurrent. The possibility to exercise joint parental authority was enacted in Denmark in 1986 and developed in Dutch case law in 1984-1986 based upon parental agreement. In 1995 and 1996 the possibility to issue a contact order to a parent who shared parental authority was enacted in respectively the Netherlands and Denmark. Joint parental authority has since 1998 (the Netherlands) and 2002 (Denmark) continued automatically after divorce. The possibility of establishing joint parental authority (against the wishes of a parent) has developed in Dutch case law pursuant to the 1995 and 1998 reforms while this was enacted in Denmark in 2007.

The question which may be posed is whether, and to what degree, these developments represent the same or a different level of individualisation in the two countries. While there is plenty of evidence in this Chapter to support the thesis that Danish law developed in the direction of individualisation earlier than Dutch law, it would seem that joint parental authority developed into a strong legal norm in Dutch law before Danish law. Is this development indicative of a more rapid development towards individualisation in Dutch law than in current Danish law? A more rapid development in Dutch law would not correspond well with the more traditional family patterns in the Netherlands as depicted in Chapter I.4.2.

---

219 J. Graversen, 'Familieret som afspejling af familieideologien', in: J. Graversen (Ed.), *Familieretspolitik*, Copenhagen: CARNET, 1988, p. 197-216.

II.4.1. THE DEVELOPMENTS IN THE LAW

It is generally characteristic of the conceptual developments in the law concerning the parent-child relationship in the Netherlands during the past few decades that this development cannot be understood in the context of only law reform. The role of the judiciary in the creation of law is increasing.

In relation to the Danish law concerning the parent-child relationship, it is possible to describe all the major changes with regard to only law reform. This does not imply that the Danish judiciary does not influence the law, but rather that all the main conceptual changes have occurred as a result of law reform.

This discrepancy is the result of different factors. Perhaps the most direct factor is the influence of the ECHR upon Dutch family law during the past few decades,[220] but other factors also add to the puzzle, such as, for example, the enactment of Dutch legislation with an inherent complexity such as the 1998 reform in relation to the concept of 'good mutual understanding'. Furthermore, the Dutch parliamentary process, for example in relation to the regulation of contact, joint parental authority and parentage, has been very long compared with the Danish equivalent. The result has been that the Dutch judiciary, rather than the Dutch legislature, have been the primary instigators of the process of individualisation.

A main comparative feature which emerges is that developments which in Danish law are perceived as principal changes, have in Dutch law been left to develop in the case law. The consequence is that these changes have a more unsettled and unclear nature in Dutch law.

II.4.2. DISPUTE SETTLEMENT – A NATIONAL CHARACTERISTIC?

In the Netherlands and Denmark the discussions on the introduction of access to general dispute settlement procedures for married parents has been closely linked to the enactment of equality between spouses. In both countries there was resistance to a general dispute settlement mechanism at the beginning of the century. This resistance was based upon the notion that it would be inappropriate to intervene in family matters.

---

220 The influence of human rights is deliberated in detail in Chapter III.

In Denmark equality between the spouses in relation to the common children was enacted in 1922 without such access. In the Netherlands, the Dutch legislature reasoned that equality between the parents necessitated access to dispute settlement procedures in court and this was introduced in the Dutch Civil Code in 1984.

Leaving aside certain considerations of a more ideological nature, it is evident why access to dispute settlement may be perceived as necessary in Dutch law while there has been no pressing need for such access in Danish law. Dutch law historically linked joint parental authority with marriage and the termination thereof with divorce. The Danish Guardianship Act of 1922 made it possible to apply for joint parental authority to be terminated when the relationship between the parents had broken down.

It should be noted that joint parental authority after divorce and for unmarried parents in respect of access to general dispute settlement in the legislative reforms in both countries mirrored the situation in respect of married parents. In the Netherlands access to dispute settlement procedures came to apply also in these situations without much parliamentary debate before the 1995 reform. In Denmark it was a point of debate in the 1996 reform, but was then firmly rejected. The new Danish reform (2007) on parental responsibility does, however, suggest that the courts should have the possibility to settle a dispute concerning the residence of the child, but limits access to court to questions concerning the child's residence and contact.[221]

Notwithstanding the difference in access to dispute settlement procedures, it is a common feature that access to dispute settlement for parents who exercise joint parental authority has increased considerably.

---

221 The lack of access to the courts for general dispute settlement is a common Scandinavian feature (Sweden, Norway and Denmark) and has its origins in the enactment of harmonised Scandinavian Acts in the 1920s. While Sweden and Norway have increased access to the courts in respect of a residence order and Denmark has recently (2007) followed this line, it remains a general characteristic that there is no general access to dispute settlement, S. Danielsen, *Nordisk Børneret II, Forældreansvar*, Copenhagen: Nord, 2003, p. 112-116 (A comparative study of Danish, Finnish, Icelandic, Norwegian and Swedish law with discussions on the possibilities for harmonisation and the need for reform).

II.4.3. POST-DIVORCE REGULATION OF PARENTAL RIGHTS

In both the Netherlands and Denmark the belief that divorce constituted the end of shared legal parenting was dominant in the law at the beginning of the previous century. Law reform in Denmark (1922) did, however, somewhat reluctantly give the parent who was not allocated parental authority a right to have personal contact. Dutch law only gradually recognised such a right. Not until the reform of 1990 did the Dutch Civil Code actually explicitly provide contact as a right for the parent who had not been allocated parental authority.

On the other hand, Dutch law has generally given the non-resident parent an auxiliary or supervisory position in relation to parental authority which Danish law has not. Since the 1901 Children Act, Dutch law has contained the general rule that the parent who has not been allocated parental authority (then parental guardianship) could be allocated supervising guardianship thereby at least formally retaining most parents in a joint legal construction. The 1995 enactment which abandoned the position of the supervising guardian introduced a duty for the parent with sole parental authority to inform and consult the other parent without, however, providing a formal position for this parent. It is perhaps pertinent for the understanding of the Dutch reforms on parental authority in 1995 and 1998 where a consensus-based legislative system existed only shortly before the continuation of joint parental authority was enacted, that there seemed to be an underlying understanding of the value of retaining some formal position, even if it provided no more than the abandoned position of the supervising guardian. The lack of parental authority has been seen to constitute '*ontoudering*' (the lack of parentage).[222]

The recent Danish enactment (2007) and the pending Dutch proposal concerning 'Continued Parenting' further illustrate the difference in correlation between parental authority and contact. While both are deemed to provide more equal parenting, the Dutch proposal is rooted in the ongoing discussions concerning contact where the perceived problems are that many non-resident parents lose contact with their children, amongst other things because of poor means of enforcing contact. While the Danish enactment also strengthens contact rights in certain ways, it is placed in an ongoing debate where there is a perception that it has become too difficult to discharge a parent from contact rights.

---

[222] P. Vlaardingerbroek, 'Echtscheiding, ouderschap en voortgezet gezag', in: M. Antokolskaia, '*Herzienning van het echtscheidingsrecht*', 2006, supra, p. 156-175, S. Jansen, 'Gezamenlijk gezag na scheiding: over een dubieuze voorwaarde', *FJR*, 2002, p. 109-111.

In this perspective it is not evident that the earlier development of joint parental authority as a strong legal norm in the Netherlands is indicative of an earlier development towards individualisation as in Denmark.

II.4.4. THE DIVORCE PROCEDURE

In both the Netherlands and Denmark the allocation of parental authority has been an intrinsic element in the divorce procedure. In the former in terms of a positive requirement for the allocation of sole parental authority (or guardianship) to one parent upon divorce.[223] Pursuant to this, by providing the possibility for a joint request for joint parental authority subject to review. Presently, it could be said that the question of the allocation of parental authority has been removed from the divorce procedure in the sense that joint parental authority continues automatically. No court decision is necessary if the question of allocating sole parental authority is not raised by either of the parents.

The aforementioned is, however, not indicative of a similar approach. In Danish law the dividing line is now parental agreement/disagreement. If the parents agree they are free to allocate sole parental authority to one parent. The current Danish approach focuses upon attaining parental agreement through counselling or mediation only in cases where there is an actual dispute. In Dutch law only the court can terminate joint parental authority.

The pending Dutch proposal on 'Continued Parenting' implementing the 'parenting plan' as a precondition for a request for divorce widens the difference in approach. The condition is aimed at providing a duty for parents to substantiate their intentions concerning post-divorce parenting having regard to a set of minimum norms. The judicial review of these plans is an essential element.

A distinctly existing and furthermore emerging difference (if the pending Dutch proposal on 'Continued Parenting' is enacted) is the perception of the State's role in relation to the divorce procedure. The Danish approach is only directed at intervention when there is a dispute. The Dutch approach places substantive requirements for all parents and emphasises judicial review. The aforementioned indicates that the State has a more authoritative role in the Netherlands. The State defines the substantive legal norms and these norms are enforced also in situations where there is no dispute. Consequently Dutch law may be characterised as being less individualised than Danish law.

---

223 In the Netherlands since the 1901 Civil Children Act.

II.4.5. THE UNMARRIED FATHER'S RIGHTS

The law on the establishment of paternity in Denmark and the Netherlands has an inherently different starting point. In Denmark the law since the 1937 Children Act has developed and is based upon a principle of compulsory establishment. This principle is based, since the Children Act of 2001, solely upon the notion that a child should always have two parents, a mother and a father. Dutch law leaves the initiative for the establishment of paternity with the parties involved (the mother, father and child) and the establishment of paternity in cases where the parties do not agree upon recognition and consent pursuant to the 1998 reform depends upon a balancing of interests in a judicial procedure.

Turning to the beginning of the previous century paternity could not be established judicially in both countries, but a maintenance claim was possible (in the Netherlands from 1909). The voluntary recognition of paternity was possible in both countries, but only in the Netherlands did voluntary recognition actually establish legal ties. Once recognition had taken place the father exercised guardianship up until 1901. From 1901 he could, in principle, claim parental rights (parental guardianship) to the exclusion of the mother or be allocated supervising guardianship. Further, recognition by the father meant that the child would bear his name (until 1998). In Denmark the compulsory establishment of paternity (1937) initially mainly provided the child with certain rights, amongst others the right but not the duty to bear the father's name. The father's rights were only strengthened later in a series of enactments commencing with the right to personal contact in 1969 and the possibility to be allocated parental authority to the exclusion of the mother in 1978.

Parental rights in respect of children born outside marriage have consequently historically belonged more exclusively to the mother in Denmark in contrast to the Netherlands. It may, however, be tentatively suggested that the position of the father in Dutch law has perhaps been of a more formal nature considering that the main exception to this difference is that the contact right of the unmarried father was enacted much earlier in Danish law (1969) than in Dutch law (1995).

Presently, unmarried parents who thereby agree can establish paternity and exercise joint parental authority in both countries. Cohabitation is not required and once parentage and joint parental authority are established they have a similar legal position as that of married parents. However, for parents who do not agree Danish law provides more automatic rights in respect of both paternity and parental authority where Dutch law depends for both upon a balancing of interests in a judicial procedure.

The main difference may be seen as follows. It has been a matter of Danish family policy to always establish paternity when a child is born and to view the legal consequences in respect of parental authority and contact independently. Further, it has been a specific policy that paternity in respect of unmarried cohabiting parents should be established in the same manner as for married parents and have the same legal consequences in relation to parental authority. The Dutch approach has not been so directed; rather the approach has provided the possibility of an ad hoc ascertainment of rights in a judicial procedure. The difference is indicative of a stronger validation of the institution of marriage in the Netherlands than in Denmark and consequently of a less individualistic approach. It may also be noted that at the empirical level the number of children born outside marriage in the Netherlands has presently reached the Danish level of 1981.[224]

II.4.6. A RIGHT TO TWO PARENTS

It is a common recent feature that the parliamentary deliberations concerning joint parental authority and contact are debated in the context of a child's 'right to two parents' or a 'right to be cared for by two parents'. This notion was central in the legal and political discussions in Denmark in relation to the Children Act (2001) on the establishment of parentage and the regulation of parental rights following divorce or the breakup of a relationship with the latest reform on Parental Responsibility (2007). In the Netherlands this notion seems to have taken over from the non-interventionist approach or the 'right to family life' approach which was based upon Article 8 of the ECHR in the pending proposal concerning 'Continued Parenting'.

This notion is indicative of a gradual development where the law on parental authority is increasingly viewed as a means to secure an aim[225] rather than providing a legal concept, which clearly determines the rights and duties of the parent(s). The result is likely to generate, as stated in the Danish Commission Report from 1996, a more active role (of society) in determining the child's everyday life.

---

224 Chapter I, Section I.4.2. In the Netherlands 37% of children born in 2006 were born outside marriage. In Denmark 37% of children born in 1981 were born outside marriage. The Danish percentage has stabilised at approximately 45% during the past 20 years.

225 On the use of aims in a rights terminology, see Chapter I, Section I.2.2.

CHAPTER III
THE INFLUENCE OF HUMAN RIGHTS

III.1. INTRODUCTION

From Chapter II it may be deduced that the ECHR has played a vital role in the development of the parent–child relationship in Dutch family law. Indeed the consultation of any general Dutch family law book will provide such information.[1] The relevance of the ECHR for family law has also been the subject of several doctoral theses in the Netherlands.[2] This is not the case for Danish family law. General books on family law contain no reference or only a brief reference to the ECHR.[3] The purpose of this Chapter is to examine this discrepancy.[4] The main point to be made is how human rights influence national family law in the Netherlands and Denmark. The influence is ascertained in relation to the two most important conventions on the subject-matter of this study, namely the European Convention on Human Rights (ECHR) which came into force in 1953 and the UN Convention on the Rights of the Child (CRC) which entered into force in 1990.

1 C. Asser 2002, p. 7-18.

2 G.A. Kleijkamp, '*Family life and family interests*', Doctoral thesis (PhD), Utrecht, 1998. C.J. Forder, '*Legal Establishment of the Parent Child Relationship, Principles*', Doctoral thesis (PhD), Maastricht: University Press, 1995. M.L.C.C. de Bruijn-Lückers, '*EVRM, minderjarigheid en ouderlijk gezag, A whole code of juvenile law?*', Doctoral thesis (PhD), Deventer: Kluwer, 1994. C. van Wamelen, '*Ouderschap en ouderlijke gezag na scheiding: voorstellen tot wetgeving op basis van art. 8 EVRM, de Recommendation on parental responsibilties van de Raad van Europa (1984) en empirisch onderzoek naar opvattingen van kinderen over gezin en echtscheiding*', Doctoral thesis (PhD), Zwolle: W.E.J. Tjeenk Willink, 1987.

3 I. Lund Andersen, N. Munck, I. Nørgaard, *Familieret*, Copenhagen: Jurist- og Økonomforbundets Forlag, 2003 and L. Nielsen, J. Vorstrup Rasmussen, *Familieretten*, Copenhagen: GadJura, 2001.

4 This Chapter further serves as a referential framework for the comparison contained in Chapters V-VIII where the use of the simultaneous method of comparison does not support an extensive deliberation on the influence of human rights.

III.2. THE ECHR

The fact that the ECHR emerges as one of the most important conventions with respect to family law has to do with the fact that it has an enforcement body, the European Court of Human Rights (ECtHR), which interprets the Convention *in the light of present-day conditions,* rather than the actual content of the Convention provisions.

The decision of the ECtHR in the Marcx case raised the question whether the ECtHR's dynamic interpretation of the Convention provided 'a whole code of family law'.[5] Presently, the general opinion is that this is not the case. The case law of the ECtHR is not considered to have the effect of harmonising the national family laws of its member states, although it has in certain areas of law such as, for example, the equal treatment of children born within or outside marriage and perhaps will continue to influence the national laws of its member states bringing about a certain level of harmonisation.[6]

The dynamic interpretive style of the case law of the ECtHR is limited in particular by two notions, the common ground or consensus notion and the notion of the margin of appreciation and further as described by ANTOKOLSKAIA by a reluctance to intervene in sensitive policy areas.[7]

In this Chapter two Convention aspects are examined. The first concerns the question whether under the Convention there is a right to retain joint parental authority after divorce or a right to be allocated joint parental authority for unmarried parents. The second aspect concerns the right to contact for non-parents.[8]

Pursuant to this, the influence of the Convention is described and analysed in relation to the national law of the Netherlands and Denmark. Its influence on

---

5 Dissenting opinion of Judge Sir Gerald Fitzmaurice in Marxc v. Belgium, ECtHR, 13.06.1979.

6 M. Antokolskaia, *Harmonisation of Family Law in Europe: A Historical Perspective*, Antwerp-Oxford: Intersentia, 2006, p. 445-448, 493-500.

7 M. Antokolskaia, 'Human Rights as a basis for the Harmonisation of Family Law?' in P. Lødrup and E. Modvar (Eds.), *Family Law and Human Rights*, Oslo: Gyldendal Norsk Forlag A/S, 2004, p. 29-47.

8 The right to contact for parents is not examined. According to the established case law of the ECtHR, contact between parents and children is a fundamental Convention right, for example, ECtHR Hokkanen v. Finland 23.09.1994 19823/92 and is also now established as a right in Dutch and Danish law, Chapter II, Sections II.2.3, II. 2.2.5, II.3.3., II.3.5 and Chapter VIII, Section VIII.2.

Dutch law has, as initially mentioned, been extensive. Therefore the Chapter examines only the influence in relation to the allocation of joint parental authority after divorce and for unmarried parents. In relation to Danish law, where the influence is less prominent, it is necessary to adopt a wider approach in order to provide an insight into the influence of the ECHR upon national family law. For this purpose an analysis of the right to contact for near relatives is included in relation to Danish law.[9]

III.2.1. RELEVANT PROVISIONS OF THE ECHR

The relevant provisions of the ECHR in relation to family law are in particular Articles 6, 8 and 14.

Article 8 is the key provision. Article 8 provides a right to respect for one's personal and private family life. Article 8(1) of the ECHR is phrased so as to preclude the state from intervening in a person's family life. Such intervention may, however, be justified under Article 8(2) if the intervention is lawful, has a legitimate aim and is proportionate. Although the provision is phrased negatively – the state must not intervene – it is well established in the case law of the ECtHR that a State may also have a positive obligation to protect a person's family life. There is ample case law by the ECtHR which deliberates on the protection offered by Article 8 of the ECHR.

Article 6(1) provides certain procedural guarantees: access to the courts in relation to the establishment of civil rights and obligations. Article 6(1), however, only extends to disputes on civil rights and obligations, which can be said, at least on arguable grounds, to be recognised under domestic law. Consequently it does not in itself guarantee any particular content for the rights and obligations in the substantive law of the contracting states.[10]

Article 14 provides for the principle of non-discrimination. This principle is not a free-standing principle, however. It applies only in relation to rights protected by other Convention provisions as it prohibits discrimination only with regard to the 'enjoyment of the rights and freedoms' set forth in the ECHR. Protocol No. 12 of the ECHR, which was opened for signature on 4 November 2000, does, however, contain a general and free-standing non-discrimination principle. This

---

9 Dutch law provides a discretionary authority for the court to provide a contact order in respect of a person who has a close personal relationship with the child, Art. 377f, DCC.

10 See further; D.J. Harris, M. O'Boyle, C. Warbrick, *Law of the European Convention on Human Rights*, Londoon: Butterworths, 1995, p. 186.

Protocol has so far (June 2007) only been ratified by 11 member states.[11] Article 1 of the 12th Protocol provides that:

1. The enjoyment of any right set forth by law shall be secured without discrimination on any ground such as sex, race, colour, language, religion, political or other opinion, national or social origin, association with a national minority, property, birth or other status.
2. No one shall be discriminated against by any public authority on any ground such as those mentioned in paragraph 1.

Article 1 of the 12th Protocol contains a non-discrimination principle with regard to any right 'set forth by law' and concerns discrimination 'by any public authority'. It consequently provides a primarily negative obligation for the state. From the Explanatory report it may, however, be deduced that it may invoke certain positive obligations for the State to take measures to prevent discrimination even 'where discrimination occurs in relations between private persons, so-called indirect horizontal effects.'[12] The possibility that Article 1 of the 12th Protocol may include a positive obligation could arise, for example:

> 'If there is a clear lacuna in domestic law protection from discrimination. Regarding more specifically relations between private persons, a failure to provide protection from discrimination in such relations might be so clear-cut and grave that it might engage clearly the responsibility of the State and then Article 1 of the Protocol could come into play'.[13]

III.2.2. THE CASE LAW OF THE ECtHR ON JOINT PARENTAL AUTHORITY

There is little doubt that the exercise of parental authority is a core element of the right to respect for family life contained in Article 8 of the ECHR. The key question here is whether, based upon Article 8 of the ECHR, there is a right to retain and exercise joint parental authority after divorce and after the break-up of a relationship. Before turning to the case law of the ECtHR it should be noted that GRUNDERBEECK concluded in 2003 that 'no single binding instrument (...)

[11] It is mostly Eastern European countries which have ratified this Protocol. Further, Cyprus, Finland and the Netherlands have also ratified the Protocol, www.echr.coe.int.
[12] Explanatory Report to the 12th Protocol, No. 24.
[13] Supra, No. 26.

obliges the European States (...) to provide for the possibility of joint parental authority.'[14]

The right of an unmarried father to exercise joint parental authority has been addressed in a number of admissibility decisions by the European Commission of Human Rights.[15] In BN v. Denmark on 9 October 1989[16] an unmarried father complained about the fact that he could not obtain joint parental authority under Danish law except through an agreement with the mother. He alleged that Danish law on this point violated Articles 3, 6, 8 and 14 of the ECHR. The Commission found the complaints to be ill-founded and denied admissibility. The reasoning in relation to Articles 6(1) and 8 of the ECHR is relevant. In relation to Article 6(1) the Commission reasoned that this provision:

> '(...) Does not in itself guarantee any particular content for civil rights and obligations in the substantive law of the Contracting States and according to the established case-law of the ECtHR Article 6(1) extends only to disputes on civil rights and obligations which can be said at least on arguable grounds, to be recognized under domestic law'.

Since a right to joint parental authority did not exist in Danish law, the complaint under Article 6 failed. The father's complaint under Article 8 that the fact that he could not obtain joint parental authority was disrespectful of his right to family life also failed. The Commission reasoned as follows:

> 'Like in its previous case-law the Commission finds that the situation of children born out of wedlock necessitates a distinct legislative regulation which has to take into account the problems involved. The Danish legislator has opted for a regulation which is considered to be in the best interests of the child born out of wedlock. Such a premise is neither wrong nor arbitrary. Indeed the present case shows that when the parents do not live together and cannot agree on matters concerning the child it is indispensable in the interest of the child that it is kept away from situations which could be detrimental to its development owing to the existence of a loyalty conflict vis à vis one or both of the parents and the inevitable parental pressure causing feelings of insecurity and distress.'

---

14 D. Van Grunderbeeck, *Beginselen van personen- en familierecht, Een mensenrechtelijke benardering*, Doctoral thesis, Antwerp: Intersentia, 2003, p. 534.

15 Unpublished. Reference can be found in the case BN v. Denmark cited below.

16 European Commission of Human Rights, BN v. Denmark, 09.10.1989, 13557/88.

Two recent admissibility decisions by the ECtHR address the question of joint parental authority as a right under the ECHR. Both decisions concerned the situation in Austria (1996) where joint parental authority after divorce was only possible when the parents agreed upon the matter and continued to live in a common household.

In the case of Cernecki v. Austria[17] the parents jointly contested the prerequisite of continued cohabitation on the basis of Article 5 of Protocol No. 7 of the ECHR. Article 5 provides that:

> 'Spouses shall enjoy equality of rights and responsibilities of a private law character between them, and in their relations with their children, as to marriage, during marriage and in the event of its dissolution. This article shall not prevent states from taking such measures as are necessary in the interests of the children.'

The European Court did not find that Austrian legislation violated Article 5 of the 7th Protocol and rejected the application as being ill-founded. The ECtHR reasoned:

> 'The Court accepts that the need to provide a clear solution for custody immediately upon divorce is apparent in all cases where the former spouses are unwilling or unable to exercise joint custody.'

The ECtHR also considered that such clarity may be desirable in cases where the parents agree upon the exercise of joint parental authority because, amongst other reasons, a subsequent change of circumstances may hamper their good understanding considering that:

> 'If an award of joint custody were possible upon divorce, it may nevertheless prove necessary at a later stage to re-open custody proceedings in order to award sole custody to one parent, thereby subjecting the children concerned to another change in their situation. *In this case, the children are subjected to a period of uncertainty – which may take years – before a final decision on custody is taken.* On balance this seems to be a far heavier burden for the children to bear, than it is for the parents, who agree *de facto* on joint custody after divorce without official endorsement of their agreement.' (emphasis added)

---

17 ECtHR 22.11.2001, 31061/96.

In the case of R.W. and C.T.G.-W v. Austria[18] the claim for joint parental authority after divorce was also viewed in the light of Article 8 ECHR. The ECtHR considered that the necessity clause contained in Article 5 of Protocol No. 7 should be interpreted in the same way as the necessity clauses in other provisions of the ECHR (Article 8) and therefore saw no reason to distinguish this case from the Cernecki case. The ECtHR thereby concluded that:

> 'The exclusion of a possibility to award joint custody after divorce fell within the margin of appreciation left to the Contracting State when assessing what was 'necessary in the interests of the children'.

These admissibility decisions, in particular the Cernecki case, show that a wide margin of appreciation is left to the contracting member states with regard to the regulation of parental authority after divorce and for unmarried parents in relation to Article 8 of the ECHR. Even if there is no evidence of an immediate conflict of interest in cases where joint parental authority is based upon an agreement between the parents, the ECtHR finds that the allocation of sole parental authority can be justified with reference, in particular, to the clarity which an allocation of sole parental authority provides. Secondly, the ECtHR stresses the risk to children of continuous litigation where joint parental authority at a later stage must be replaced by sole parental authority. In respect of parental authority after divorce and for unmarried parents the necessary protection of children is deemed to carry greater weight than parental rights. In addition, it may be derived from the above-mentioned case of BN v. Denmark that a difference in the treatment of unmarried parents in the allocation of parental authority is not in itself arbitrary.

Further, it may be deduced that Art. 6(1) of the ECHR does not provide a right to joint parental authority, when such a right is not recognized 'at least on arguable grounds' under domestic law.[19]

III.2.3. THE ECtHR IN RELATION TO CONTACT FOR NEAR RELATIVES

Contact between parents and children is a fundamental aspect of the right to family life contained in Article 8 of the ECHR. In this respect it is a matter of

---

18 ECtHR 22.11.2001, 36222/97.

19 See further; ECtHR 12.02.2004, Perez v. France, 47287/99 and European Commission, 18.05.1999 Wolff Metternich v. the Netherlands, 45908/99.

well-established case law of the ECtHR that the State does not have merely a negative obligation not to intervene, but also a positive obligation to ensure that such contact is made possible.[20] The question whether Article 8 also provides near relatives with a more general right to contact based upon the right to family life, as provided for in Article 8, is subject to greater uncertainty. The case law of the ECtHR in this matter concerns the situation where the child has been placed in care.[21] In the case of Scozzari and Giunta concerning, inter alia, contact between a grandmother and her grandchildren, it was stated that family life within the meaning of Article 8 of the European Convention on Human Rights includes, at least, the ties between near relatives, for instance those between grandparents and grandchildren, since such relatives may play a considerable part in family life. 'Respect for a family life so understood implies an obligation for the State to act in a manner calculated to allow these ties to develop normally.'[22] It remains an open question how the ECtHR would decide the issue where contact was sought by a non-parent in a civil case, i.e. in a case where the holder(s) of parental authority oppose contact and the child has not been placed in care. It has been suggested that grandparents' rights in this situation 'carry less weight than those of parents'. Inherent in this issue is the notion that contact between a grandparent and a grandchild is normally at the discretion of the parents.[23]

III.3. INFLUENCE OF THE ECHR ON DUTCH LAW

The influence of the ECHR on Dutch family law is extensive. The analysis here will centre on two developments in the Dutch law on parental authority, where the Dutch courts have taken the lead and developed the law on parental authority based upon an interpretation of the ECHR. The first development concerned a right to exercise joint parental authority in post-divorce cases as well as for unmarried parents based upon parental agreement. This case law emerged in 1984-1986. The second development is more recent and concerns the right to exercise joint parental authority, when requested by one parent alone. This case law emerged in the period 2002-2006.

---

20 For example, ECtHR Hokkanen v. Finland 23.09.1994 19823/92.

21 For example, ECtHR Bronda v. Italy, 09.06.1998, 22430/93 and Boyle v. the UK, 28.02.1994, 16580/90.

22 Scozzari and Giunta v. Italy, ECtHR 13.07.2000, 39221/98 and 41963/98.

23 F. Kaganas and C. Piper, 'Grandparents and Contact: 'Rights v Welfare' revisited', *International Journal of Law, Policy and the Family*, 2001, p. 258-259, D. Van Grunderbeck, 2003, supra, p. 522-523.

III.3.1. CONSTITUTIONAL ASPECTS OF DUTCH LAW

The relationship between the legislature and the judiciary in the Netherlands is, at first sight, characterised by a firm rejection of a judicial review of legislation. The Dutch Constitution, which was revised in 1983, expressly prohibits the judiciary from reviewing parliamentary legislation. Article 120 of the Constitution provides that:

> 'The judge shall not review the constitutionality of statutes and treaties'.[24]

Further, Article 11 of the General Provisions Act of 1829 provides that: The judge should render justice in accordance with statutory law; under no circumstances may he review the inherent value or reasonability of that statutory law.[25] From this it can be observed that parliamentary legislation and treaties should not be reviewed in the light of the Constitution or unwritten principles of law.[26]

The Government's position in respect of the aforementioned Article 120 of the Constitution was argued as follows in the parliamentary process:

> 'The undersigned consider the political institutions to be the most qualified for the settlement of such conflicts. The view of the political institutions, such as it has been enacted in an Act, should not be liable to be deprived of legal force by one or more judicial institutions, whose members are not under Parliamentary control and possess life tenure. Furthermore, the undersigned take serious account of the possibility that the judiciary, if they would be empowered to review Parliamentary legislation in the light of the Constitution, could become *entangled in a political struggle*. This could affect their position of independence and impartiality and could result in a strong pressure by political parties on the appointment of judges'.[27] (Emphasis added)

---

24 Grondwet voor het Koninkrijk der Nederlanden of 24.08.1815, Stb. 1983, 70.

25 Wet algemene bepalingen, 15.05.1829, Stb. 1829, 28.

26 M.C.B. Burkens, 'The Complete Revision of the Dutch Constitution', *Netherlands International Law Review*, 1982, p. 323.

27 Parliamentary proceedings 1980/1981 (Kamerstukken), 16 162, No. 8, p. 21. Cited and translated by M.V. Polak & J.M. Polak in 'Faux pas ou pas de deux? Recent developments in the relationship between the legislature and the judiciary in the Netherlands', *Netherlands International Law Review*, 1986, p. 374.

The prohibition on a judicial review is, at least at first sight, fundamental to the separation of powers between the judiciary and the legislature in the Netherlands and represents the view, in the wording of the past Government, that the judiciary should not become 'entangled in a political struggle'.

The described separation of powers in the Netherlands does not reduce the role of the judiciary to that of merely a *bouche de la loi.* A development in the understanding of the sources of law suggests a move from a heteronymous towards a more autonomous perception of the sources of law, indicating, in broad terms, greater freedom for the judiciary in the application of legislation.[28] From a legal-philosophical perspective it indicates a move from a positivistic perception of law to a perception of law which encompasses the idea that law and morality are connected.[29]

The issue of reviewing legislation against a fundamental principle of law – that of judicial certainty, which is also enshrined in Article 43(1) of the Statute of the Kingdom of the Netherlands (ranking above the Constitution),[30] was considered by the Supreme Court in 1989. Legislation had been enacted to limit costs in respect of student grants. A maximum period in which a student could receive a grant had been fixed at six years. This maximum period also applied to students who had already transferred from a technical school to a university or vice versa and who were therefore likely to exceed the maximum period. The question was whether such retrospective effect was contrary to a general principle of judicial certainty. The 's-Hertogenbosch Court of Appeal decided in favour of the students. The Dutch Supreme Court overturned the decision stating that:

> 'Although it cannot be denied that the law has developed since the enactment of the Constitution in 1983, giving more weight to a restrictive interpretation of the prohibition on judicial review, nonetheless it must be stated that the judiciary would transgress the dictated boundaries by

---

28 P. Scholten, *Mr. C. Assers Handleiding tot de beoefening van het Nederlandse Burgerlijk Recht, Algemeen deel*, Zwolle: Tjeenk Willenk, 1974, p. 39-40, G.J. Wiarda, *3 typen van Rechtsvinding*, Zwolle: W.E.J. Tjeenk Willinck, 1988, Chapter 5.

29 C.E. Smith, *Regels van Rechtsvinding*, the Hague: Boom Juridische Uitgevers, 2005, p. 22-24. This does not imply a classic natural law perspective based upon meta-physical (universal) principles of morality, but a modest interactional, cultural, legal perspective, which can fulfil the same function as classic natural law, which is a critical review of positive law, H. Franken et al., *Inleiden tot de Rechtswetenschap*, Arnhem: Gouda Quint, 1995, p. 62.

30 Wet houdende aanvaarding van een statuut voor het Koninkrijk der Nederlanden, 28.10.1954, Stb. 1954, 503.

deciding that Article 120 of the Constitution did not (also) prohibit review of legislation against fundamental principles of law'.[31]

Seventeen years later the President of the Supreme Court at the time of the decision stated in his valedictory lecture that the notion contained in the decision *of the judiciary not transgressing the dictated boundaries*, related not so much to the primate of the legislature in shaping the law, but rather in the primate of politics.[32] The judiciary may accordingly create or shape law but should not take the role of the legislature in cases that have an expressly political nature.[33]

In contrast to the prohibition on a constitutional review, the judiciary has an active role to play in the matter of reviewing national law in the light of international law. In this respect it may be noted that the application of human rights principles and the expansion of such principles seem to be positively validated by the Dutch legislature. The Netherlands has ratified the 12th Protocol of the ECHR which provides for the free-standing principle of non-discrimination.[34]

The Dutch Constitution provides in Article 93 that:

> 'Provisions of treaties and decisions by international organisations which according to their content are directly applicable are of binding force after publication.'

Further, concerning the role of the judiciary Article 94 provides that:

> 'Legislative provisions in force in the Kingdom of the Netherlands are not applicable, if the application thereof is incompatible with directly applicable provisions in treaties and decisions of international organizations'.

The Dutch judiciary is thus allowed to review and set aside national law when national law infringes international law. This only applies, however, when such

31 Hoge Raad, 14,04.1989, *NJ* 1989, 469.

32 C.E. Smith, 2005, supra, p. 47 (emphasis added).

33 A critical analysis of the 'primate of politics' may be found in; C.E. Smith, 2005, supra, Chapter 3(1), *Rechtspraak in een min of meer rechtvaardige rechtsorde.*

34 See for an overview of the Dutch debate, J. Gerads, 'Protocol No. 12 – The Dutch Debate', in S. Lagoutte (Ed.), *Prohibition of Discrimination in the Nordic Countries: The Complicated fate of Protocol No. 12 to the European Convention on Human Rights*, The Danish Institute for Human Rights, 2005, p. 37-57.

international law is directly applicable or there has been a decision of an international organisation. The protection offered by Article 8 of the ECHR and the clear case law of the ECtHR is unquestionably directly applicable. The question, however, is whether the national judiciary is to apply only an international standard developed by the ECtHR or whether it may also interpret Article 8 in the light of national law.

This question was addressed by the Supreme Court in a decision from 2001.[35] The case concerned a child maintenance claim against a former same-sex partner of the mother. The two partners had cohabited and together cared for the child, which was born during their relationship. Article 394 of the Dutch Civil Code provides that only a male partner who, as a life-companion of the mother, has agreed to an act which could have resulted in the begetting of the child must provide for the cost of the care and upbringing of the child.[36] The mother argued that the limitation in Article 394 to a male life-companion was an infringement of Articles 8 and 14 of the ECHR in the light of recent national legislation which provided for the possibility of jointly exercising parental authority.[37] The Supreme Court ruled that international standards must be applied if national legislation is to be set aside according to Article 94 of the Dutch Constitution. The Supreme Court reasoned that:

> 'Article 53 of the ECHR leaves the national legislature with the freedom to create more extensive protection as provided for by the ECHR. The Dutch judiciary is nevertheless bound by Article 94 of the Constitution according to which acts that are binding in the Kingdom are not applicable if their application infringes a binding provision of a treaty. Such an infringement cannot be ascertained exclusively on the basis of an interpretation of the concept of family life by the national Dutch court in the light of recently enacted legislation, which provides more extensive protection than can be ascertained on the basis of the case law of the ECtHR concerning Article 8 of the ECHR.'

From this it can be deduced that, in principle, the judiciary must apply an international standard in order to set aside a legislative provision.

---

35 Hoge Raad 10.08.2001, *NJ* 2002, 278 annotated by J. De Boer.

36 It follows from this case that the legislature had expressly limited Art. 394 DCC to male life-companions.

37 These two partners had not exercised joint parental authority.

III.3.2. JOINT PARENTAL AUTHORITY 1984-1986

With its decision of 4 May 1984 the Dutch Supreme Court pulled the foundations from under the Dutch system which linked joint parental power solely with an existing marriage.[38] The parents had, in the course of the divorce proceedings, requested to be appointed joint guardians of their son rather than guardian and supervising guardian as provided for in Article 161(1) of the old Dutch Civil Code.[39] The parents argued that the child needed a father as well as a mother and that they continued to jointly care for and raise the child in good mutual understanding also after the divorce. The parents did not live far apart and the child would reside with both parents. The parents argued that the formal guardianship appointment should mirror this factual situation.

The Amsterdam Court of Appeal denied the request as joint guardianship was contrary to Article 161 of the old Dutch Civil Code. It did not find that this provision was an infringement of Article 8 ECHR. In its decision the Court of Appeal relied on the fact that the mother allowed the father to maintain substantial *de facto* family life with the child.

The Supreme Court set aside this decision. The Supreme Court found that the wording of the aforementioned provision was too stringent in as much as it prescribed an allocation of sole guardianship (and supervising guardianship) in all post-divorce cases. Such a general prescription could not be justified under Article 8(2) of the ECHR in the present case where the parents continued to raise the child jointly. The fact that the mother allowed the father to maintain substantial *de facto* family life could not mitigate the infringement as the obligation of the ECHR is directed primarily towards the contracting states. The *de facto* enjoyment of family life allowed by the mother should not present an excuse for not meeting these obligations.

With its decision the Dutch Supreme Court chose to set aside Article 161(1) and interpret 161(4) of the old Dutch Civil Code in a manner which was inconsistent with a historical interpretation of the provision and existing practice, on the basis of Article 8 of the ECHR and Article 94 of the Dutch Constitution.[40] This

---

38 Hoge Raad 04.05.1984, *NJ* 1985, 510, annotated by E.A.A. Luijten, E.A. Alkema.

39 This system has been described in Chapter II, Section II.2.2.2.

40 The old Art. 161(1) provided that guardianship (and supervising guardianship) was allocated upon divorce. The old Art. 161(4) provided that parental authority after divorce remained with those that had exercised parental power during the proceedings. The aim of Art. 161(4) was

result was favoured over creating joint guardianship, which was a legal institution not provided for in the Dutch Civil Code. The result was that the parents could continue to exercise joint parental power in the same manner as they had done during their marriage.

The decision of the Supreme Court to set aside a clear provision of the Dutch Civil Code was generally positively received.[41] Criticism emerged regarding two issues in particular. The first concerned the question whether the case law of the ECtHR and the Commission actually supported the notion that the denial of joint parental power was an infringement of Article 8. ALKEMA in his annotation to the case doubted this point.[42] The second issue was that the decision of the Supreme Court created legal uncertainty as to the scope of the right to joint parental power. For that reason LUIJTEN in his annotation to the case considered that a legislative action was warranted to counteract legal uncertainty.[43] ALKEMA considered that an important reason for this kind of review undoubtedly relied upon the notion of a fundamental right, the right to family life. In this respect it is primarily the parties involved who must provide the content of such a concept, while the legislature provides only the legal framework. In this separation of roles the State must exercise restraint in respect of citizens who take their responsibility seriously. ALKEMA thus explained the judicial activity on the basis of the tendency towards individualisation and the connected concept of self-determination.[44]

The decision of the Supreme Court led, as predicted, to great uncertainty as to the scope of the right to exercise joint parental power after divorce and also for unmarried parents. Four cases, resulting in the so-called spring decisions, reached the Supreme Court in 1986.[45]

---

to prevent that a custody void could arise before guardianship was allocated, G. Delfos & J.E. Doek, *Kinderrecht, Civielrechterlijk deel*, Zwolle, Tjeenk Willinck, 1974, p. 248.

41 However, N. Holtrust and I. de Hondt, 'Gezamenlijk ouderlijk gezag', *NEMESIS*, 1985, No. 5, p. 241-246 were critical considering that 'not only contact rights but now also parental authority has been bombarded into a human right' and they found that the decision went further than was warranted on the basis of the case law of the European Commission.

42 *NJ* 1985, 510.

43 *NJ* 1985, 510.

44 C.E. Smith, 2005, supra, p. 126.

45 Hoge Raad 21.03.1986, *NJ* 1986, 585, 586, 587, 588, annotated by E.A.A. Luijten and E.A. Alkema, *NJ* 1986, 588. In two of the cited cases (586, 588) an appeal was sought by the Advocate General in the interest of the act.

The first case concerned two unmarried cohabiting parents who had applied for the allocation of joint parental power. The District Court of Utrecht had rejected this request reasoning that the Supreme Court's decision of 4 May 1984 did not warrant the allocation of joint parental power to unmarried parents. The District Court considered this to be a matter for the legislature. The Supreme Court set this decision aside, reasoning that the right to family life contained in Article 8 of the ECHR applied equally to unmarried parents as well as married parents.[46]

The following case concerned two divorced parents who had already been allocated guardianship and supervising guardianship and subsequently applied for joint parental power. The 's-Hertogenbosch Court of Appeal denied this request on the ground that circumstances had not changed since the guardianship allocation. The Supreme Court also set aside this decision because it was an incorrect interpretation of the law.[47]

The third case concerned two divorced parents who had been allocated guardianship and supervising guardianship. The father subsequently appealed against the decision claiming that joint parental authority should have been continued. The 's-Hertogenbosch Court of Appeal denied this request and the Supreme Court upheld the decision because the parents did not agree on the matter of joint parental authority.[48]

The last case concerned two unmarried cohabiting parents who applied for joint parental authority. The Subdistrict Court of Amsterdam had allocated joint parental authority to the parents, subject to the condition that cohabitation continued. The Supreme Court set aside this decision because such a condition did not fit in with the legislative system.[49]

The reasoning of the Dutch Supreme Court in its first decision on post-divorce joint parental power and the following spring decisions was extensive. It centred on two themes. The first was the right to family life as contained in Article 8 of the ECHR. This theme was retained in rather vague terms in the sense that no reference was made to any particular case law of the ECtHR. In its first decision

---

46 Hoge Raad, 21.03.1986, *NJ* 1986, 585.

47 Hoge Raad, 21.03.1986, *NJ* 1986, 586. The Supreme Court thereby circumvented the interpretation of Article 161(4) of the old Dutch Civil Code in its decision of 4 May 1984, where it was deemed relevant for the interpretation of Article 161(1) that parental authority remained with those who had it *during the procedure*, see above in this Section and supra note 41.

48 Hoge Raad, 21.03.1986, *NJ* 1986, 587.

49 Hoge Raad, 21.03.1986, *NJ* 1986, 588, annotated by E.A.A. Luijten and E.A. Alkema.

of 4 May 1984, the Supreme Court made reference to the European Council Recommendation on Parental Responsibilities.[50] This recommendation does not, however, contain the principle that joint parental authority should be possible after divorce, but rather that it may be possible in cases of parental agreement.[51] The second theme was the perceived antiquated nature of the system of parental power, which linked joint exercise with an existing marriage.

A difference in approach between the 1984 and the 1986 decisions may be discerned. The 1984 decision tried, through interpretation, to stay within the limits of the wording of the relevant provision, albeit with an interpretation which derogated from a historic interpretation and the meaning given to it since its introduction in the Dutch Civil Code in 1901.

The result was that married parents who exercised joint parental power during their marriage could continue to do so after divorce under certain conditions. In its spring decisions this approach was extended. Joint parental power under certain conditions is also opened up to divorced parents, who have already been allocated guardianship and to unmarried parents who, according to the Dutch Civil Code, could only exercise guardianship. Perhaps more remarkable is that the Supreme Court in its decisions of 1986 laid down detailed conditions, which were to be fulfilled for the allocation of joint parental power as well as the procedural requirements. The last-mentioned gave rise to the use of the term *assistant-legislature.*

The spring decisions of the Supreme Court received a mixed response. Many welcomed the certainty which had been created in respect of the scope of joint parental power and the conditions according to which it could be allocated. Further, it was considered to be a positive step that an antiquated system had been abandoned.[52] Nonetheless, others were concerned with the constitutional implications of the separation of powers in the Netherlands.[53] In addition, the

50 Recommendation No. (84)4 of the Committee of Ministers to Member States on parental responsibilities.

51 Recommendation No. (84)4, Principle 6.

52 M. Rood-De-Boer, 'Duidelijkheid en Zekerheid', *NJB*, 1986, p. 601-603, A.W.M. Willems, 'Ouderlijke macht van ongehuwden', *NJB*, 1986, p. 604-607 with references to further articles and views.

53 L. de Vries, 'De Hoge Raad als pseudo-wetgever', *NJB*, 1986, p. 1117-1119.

described development has also received a great deal of attention from other disciplines of law.[54]

III.3.3. SOLE REQUEST FOR JOINT PARENTAL AUTHORITY

The development in the law on parental authority following the Supreme Court's decisions in 1984-1986 has been deliberated in Chapter II.[55] In short, law reform in 1995 provided a legislative basis for joint parental authority based upon parental agreement, but as soon as 1998 this starting point was changed in favour of a continuation of joint parental authority after divorce. Case law after 1998 soon established joint parental authority as a strong legal norm, leaving limited scope for the allocation of sole parental authority after divorce. The 1998 reform, however, had not generally discarded parental agreement as a basis for the allocation of joint parental authority.

Article 253o(1), 1st sentence of the Dutch Civil Code prescribes that in cases where the joint exercise of parental authority has been terminated and replaced with sole parental authority by a decision of the court, the court may, upon request, decide to reallocate parental authority if circumstances have thereafter changed or if the decision was based on incorrect or incomplete information. Such a decision concerns the reallocation of *sole parental authority*. Joint parental authority can only be reobtained upon joint request, Article 253o(1), 2nd sentence. This provision applies equally to divorced as well as to unmarried parents who have previously exercised joint parental authority.

For parents who have not previously exercised joint parental authority (typically unmarried parents) Article 253c(1) prescribes that sole parental authority can be allocated to the father if this is in the best interests of the child. Joint parental authority can only be obtained upon joint request, Article 252(1).

In 2002 Jansen suggested that the condition of a joint request for the reallocation of joint parental authority formed 'a dubious condition' from a 'human rights perspective'.[56] This analysis reviewed the development of joint parental authority in Dutch law set against the principles contained in Articles 6(1), 8 and 13 of the

---

54 G.J. Wiarda, *3 typen van Rechtsvinding*, 1988, supra, p. 71-78, C.E. Smith, 2005, supra, p. 124-127, C.W. Maris, F.C.L.M. Jacobs, *Rechtsvinding en de Grondslagen van het Recht*, Assen: Van Gorcum, 2001, p. 54-56, MV. Polak & J.M. Polak, 1986, supra, p. 374.

55 Sections II.2.2. and II.2.4.

56 S. Jansen, 'Gezamenlijk gezag na scheiding: over een dubieuze voorwaarde', *FJR*, 2002, p. 109-111.

ECHR without, however, substantiating the review with relevant case law of the ECtHR. The analysis dwelled on the fact that joint parental authority after divorce had become the norm or rather the standing interpretation of the best interest of the child. The condition of a joint request was argued to fit the system enacted in 1995, but not the system enacted in 1998 where joint parental authority became the norm after divorce. Considering that joint parental authority had become the norm after divorce, it was argued that parents who had 'lost' joint parental authority after 1998 or who had not been allocated joint parental authority prior to 1998 should have a right to access the court for the possibility of reallocating joint parental authority on the basis of Articles 8, 6(1) and 13 of the ECHR. In 2003 JANSEN changed the terminology from a 'dubious condition' to an 'unacceptable condition' and further argued for an extension of the right to access the court to make a sole request also in cases where the parents have never exercised joint parental authority.[57]

At present a pending act aims to scrap the condition of a joint request in both of the above-mentioned situations.[58] A number of cases have dealt with the issue of admissibility[59] for a request for joint parental authority by the parent who does not share joint parental authority.

Two situations may be discerned corresponding to the above-mentioned provisions of the Dutch Civil Code. In the first situation the parents have previously exercised joint parental authority.[60] These cases will be addressed below under: **(A Reallocation).**

In the second situation the parents have never exercised joint parental authority.[61] These cases will be addressed below under: **(B Allocation of joint parental authority).**[62]

---

57 S. Jansen, 'Gezamenlijk gezag moet, en omgang niet minder', in M.L.C.C. de Bruijn-Lückers, J.F.M. Giele, A. Heida, C.A. Kraan, L.H.M. Zonnenberg, M.J. Vos (ed.), *EB Klassiek*, Deventer: Kluwer, 2003, p.188-195.

58 Parliamentary proceedings, (*Kamerstukken*), 29 353 described in Chapter II, Section II.6.2.1.

59 All cases except one addressed only the question of admissibility. Whether joint parental authority was factually allocated was not addressed. This question was stayed upon advice from the Dutch Child Protection Board or, in the Supreme Court case, remitted to a lower court.

60 Art. 253o(1), DCC.

61 Arts 253c(2) and 252(1), DCC.

62 M. Vonk has made an analysis of a number of these cases in relation to the provision on parental authority based upon social parentage in her article: 'Enige overdenkingen bij de voorgestelde wijziging van art. 1:253o en de positie van de opvoeder niet-ouder', *FJR*, 2005, p. 34-39.

(A) Reallocation of joint parental authority

In 2002, a father contested the requirement of a joint request. The facts of the case were that the mother had obtained sole parental authority over the couples' four children after the divorce in 1997. In 2002 the father applied to the District Court to obtain joint parental authority once again. The District Court held that the claim was inadmissible because there was no joint request and the father appealed. The Leeuwarden Court of Appeal held that the claim was admissible and requested the Child Care and Protection Board to investigate whether joint parental authority was in the interest of the children.[63]

The Court of Appeal found that the claim was admissible by declaring that the wording of Article 253o was not applicable according to Article 94 of the Dutch Constitution because it was not in line with the ECHR. The reasoning of the Appellate Court may be summarized as follows: before 1998 parents should have made a joint request for joint parental authority if they wished to continue to exercise joint parental authority after divorce. Since 1998 the starting point is that joint parental authority continues automatically after divorce. This change to the Dutch Civil Code is the result of a change in the perception of the law on parental authority set against the case law of the ECHR where respect for family life, as contained in Article 8, has wide-reaching importance. Violation by the state of a person's right to respect for family life should be limited as far as possible. The law before 1998 was considered to be outdated.

Subsequently, the Arnhem Court of Appeal in its decision of 8 June 2004 also found that a request by a divorced father who did not exercise parental authority after divorce was admissible. In this case the mother had requested that she be allowed to share parental authority with her new husband, the child's stepfather. The claim was deemed to be admissible, thereby anticipating the above-mentioned proposed act and the arguments contained in its reasoning.[64]

(B) Allocation of joint parental authority

A number of cases before subdistrict, district and appeal courts have dealt with a request for joint parental authority by an unmarried father. These cases are discussed below. The Supreme Court settled the issue with its decision of 27 May 2005.[65] In this decision the Supreme Court set aside the decision of the Arnhem Appeal Court and declared an unmarried father's request for joint parental

63 Gerechtshof Leeuwarden, 05.02.2003, *NJ* 2003, 352.

64 Gerechtshof Arnhem, 08.06.2004, LJN: AQ5059.

65 Hoge Raad, *NJ* 2005, 485, annotated J. de Boer.

authority to be admissible. The Supreme Court reasoned that the rule contained in Article 252, whereby joint parental authority is conditional upon a joint request, is incompatible with the right to have access to the courts (Article 6(1) of the ECHR) for establishing the right to exercise parental rights contained in Article 8(1) of the ECHR. These rights also apply to unmarried parents with reference to the case law of the ECtHR.[66] The Supreme Court has confirmed its position in a recent case.[67] The decisions and the reasoning of lower courts prior to the decision of the Supreme Court were inherently different and therefore deserve to be mentioned.

Two decisions denied admissibility. The District Court of Haarlem did not find that the condition of a joint request contained in Article 252 infringed Article 8 of the ECHR.[68] Likewise, the Amsterdam Court of Appeal refused an argument based upon article 8 of the ECHR also in the light of the above-mentioned proposed Act, considering that this proposed Act was only relevant to parents who have shared parental authority previously.[69] The Court of Appeal further considered that the law on parental authority:

> '(...) Consists of a closed system with regard to the creation and termination of parental authority whereby a decision of this Court to allocate joint parental authority at the request of the father, contrary to this system, would exceed the law creating the powers of the Court'.[70]

In six cases, on the other hand, admissibility was allowed. The Subdistrict Court of Zwolle considered that Article 6 of the ECHR contained a right to have access to the court for the determination of civil rights and obligations. Further, the condition of a joint request contained in Article 253c was considered to be incompatible with Article 8 of the ECHR. Finally, it considered an argument based on asking 'less instead of more'; if the father could be awarded sole paren-

---

66 ECtHR: 08.07.1987 No. 10496/83 R v. UK, 28.11.1988, No. 10929/84 Nielsen v. Denmark and 27.10.1994, No. 18535/91 Kroon v. the Netherlands. All of the mentioned cases concern the position of the unmarried father, but none of them addressed the question of a 'right' to exercise joint parental authority or a 'right' to access the court for the establishment of such a right.

67 Hoge Raad 28.04.2006, *NJ* 2006, 284.

68 Rechtbank Haarlem, 02.12.2004, LJN: AR5017.

69 At this point the proposed act aimed only to scrap the condition of a joint request for parents who had previously exercised joint parental authority. Currently, the act aims to scrap the condition also for parents who have never exercised joint parental authority, Parliamentary proceedings (*Kamerstukken*), 29353, No. 8.

70 Gerechtshof Amsterdam, 17.02.2005, LJN AT2891.

tal authority to the exclusion of the mother, why not hear a request for less, i.e., a request for joint parental authority.[71] In its subsequent decision the Subdistrict Court of Zwolle relied more exclusively upon Article 8 of the ECHR.[72] The Court of Appeal of The Hague[73] and the District Courts of Utrecht[74] and Zutphen[75] relied upon the argument of asking 'less instead of more'. Finally, the decision of the Arnhem Court of Appeal[76] anticipated the above-mentioned proposed Act which now had been amended to scrap the condition of a joint request for unmarried parents.

III.3.4. THE INTERACTION BETWEEN THE JUDICIARY AND THE LEGISLATURE

There is no evidence of a conflict between the legislature and the judiciary. The legislature has not tried to turn back the clock in respect of the developments in the law on parental authority described above. In 1995 the legislature enacted a system which essentially was a codification of the law established by the Supreme Court in the period 1984-1986. Presently, a pending proposal intends to implement the development concerning a sole request for joint parental authority. Rather, it could be said that the legislature follows the judiciary or the law created by the judiciary. This interaction has been described as a successful *pas de deux*.[77]

In the following it will be ascertained which role the ECHR and the case law of the Dutch judiciary plays in the legislative process concerning the proposal to scrap the condition of a joint request for the reallocation of joint parental authority and the allocation of joint parental authority to a parent who has not previously shared parental authority.

71 Sector kanton Rechtbank Zwolle, 09.02.2004, LJN AO3270.
72 Sector kanton Rechtbank Zwolle, 24.02.2005, LJN AS7567.
73 Gerechtshof 's-Gravenhage, 12.05.2004, LJN AP0510.
74 Rechtbank Utrecht, 28.07.2004, LJN AQ9901.
75 Rechtbank Zutphen, 10.11.2004, LJN AR5611.
76 Gerechtshof Arnhem, 22.03.2005, LJN AT2560 with reference to the Parliamentary proceedings 2004/2005 (*Kamerstukken*), 29 353, No. 8.
77 M.V.Polak, J.M. Polak, 1986, supra, p. 374.

On 3 December 2003, the Dutch Minister of Justice proposed to scrap the condition of a joint request for the reallocation of joint parental authority.[78] In the preparatory notes the Minister wrote:

> 'Article 6 of the ECHR contains the right to have access to the court for the determination of civil rights and obligations. Although court access may be limited, there are no good reasons in such cases to limit such access to a joint request. (....). Article 8 of the ECHR is also of importance. Allocating sole parental authority to one parent can be viewed as an intervention in the right to family life. The court should accordingly be able to determine whether such intervention continues to be justified under Article 8(2) of the ECHR'.

In this context reference is also made to the decision of the District Court of Leuwaarden mentioned above.[79]

In the political debate on the proposed Act, one political party[80] raised the concern that:

> '(...) it may be more in the interest of the child that only two parents have the possibility of requesting that sole parental authority be changed to joint parental authority, than also allowing one parent to do so. A stable, peaceful parental authority may be more in the interest of children than the possibility of one parent being able to claim parental authority'.

The Minister of Justice recognised that:

> 'A procedure whereby the father or mother requests that sole parental authority be replaced with joint parental authority can lead to uncertainty for the person who has sole parental authority and the children. However, there is no reason to deny the father's or mother's access to the court. It should always be possible to determine whether joint parental authority is again possible. *If this is not the case, then only a provision which is incompatible with the ECHR will remain.*'[81] (emphasis added)

---

78 Parliamentary proceedings 2003/2004 (*Kamerstukken*) 29 353, No. 2, C, p. 2. *Wijziging van enige bepalingen van Boek 1 van het Burgerlijk Wetboek met betrekking tot het geregistreerde partnerschap, de geslachtsnaam en het verkrijgen van gezamenlijk gezag.*

79 Parliamentary proceedings 2003/2004 (*Kamerstukken*), 29 353, No. 3, p. 3.

80 D66, a social liberal party.

81 Parliamentary proceedings 2003/2004 (*Kamerstukken*), 29 353, No. 5, p. 3.

In an amendment to the proposed Act on 14 February 2005 the Minister of Justice proposed that the parent who has not previously shared parental authority (typically an unmarried father) is also granted the right to request joint parental authority.[82] The notes are short and refer to the change to Article 253o mentioned above and the reasoning in relation to Articles 6 and 8 of the ECHR. Further, the Minister referred to the decisions of the District Courts of Zwolle and Utrecht mentioned above.[83]

These proposals were made in 2003 and 2005. It is currently unclear if and when the proposal will be adopted. To date, the proceedings have focused on other aspects of the proposal. If these proposals are adopted it is clear that the legislature follows the law developed by the judiciary without much deliberation or regard for the concerns raised in the parliamentary proceedings. These concerns are disregarded because, according to the Dutch Minister of Justice, maintaining a provision where the allocation of joint parental authority is based upon parental agreement would infringe the ECHR.

III.3.5. ANALYSIS OF THE RIGHT TO JOINT PARENTAL AUTHORITY

The question is how are we to understand the development in parental authority after divorce and for unmarried parents, which has positioned joint parental authority as a human right in Dutch law based upon Articles 6(1), 8 and 14 of the ECHR in the light of the conclusion that this cannot be derived directly from these provisions or the case law of the ECtHR? There is a large gap between the ECtHR's understanding where the allocation of sole parental authority is justified, in particular, with regard to the best interests of the child, stressing the need for stability even when the parents agree, and the Dutch judiciary's interpretation based upon the ECHR that it should always be possible to asses whether joint parental authority is possible even when inherently the parents do not agree.[84]

In relation to the development of joint parental authority based upon parental agreement, in the development in the case law of the Supreme Court in the

82 Parliamentary proceedings 2004/2005 (*Kamerstukken*) 29 353, No. 8, Bb, p. 1-2 proposed change to Art. 253c, DCC.

83 Parliamentary proceedings 2004/2005 (*Kamerstukken*) 29 353, No. 8, under Article 253c, p. 3.

84 See also I. Sumner & C. Forder, 'The Dutch Family Law Chronicles: Constituted Parenthood notwithstanding divorce', in: A. Ed. A. Bainham, *The International Survey of Family Law*, Bristol: Jordan Publishing Limited, 2006, p. 268.

period 1984-1986 deliberated above,[85] ALKEMA in his annotation to the case considered that the State must exercise restraint in respect of citizens who take their responsibility seriously, which may be interpreted as applying the concept of self-determination. It is not possible, however, to understand the development in joint parental authority based upon a sole request (above III.3.3.) in this light. In this situation two parents have the right to 'personal and family life' and the child has a right to protection from parental conflicts. It involves a situation with an inherent conflict of interests where the development in the case law cannot be understood as involving only 'restraint'.[86] DE BOER has suggested in his annotation to the Supreme Court's case of 27.05.2005[87] concerning an unmarried parent's right to request joint parental authority that the Supreme Court 'overlooked' the relevant case law of the ECtHR.[88] The Supreme Court has repudiated this suggestion, however, and it reconfirmed its position in its decision of 28 April 2006.[89]

In the light of the aforementioned decision of the Supreme Court the developments in the case law concerning joint parental authority can perhaps be explained as the judiciary's adaptation of a more autonomous role in the creation and shaping of the law in this field. The decisions are reasoned in the light of the ECHR, but cannot be understood as a positive application of these provisions or the case law of the ECtHR. Rather, they depend upon a development in national law reviewed against an understanding of the general principles contained in the ECHR.[90] In this case the standard laid down by the Supreme Court in its decision of 10 August 2001 – which stated that in order to set aside national law on the basis of the ECHR, an international standard must be followed – is perhaps only relevant in relation to more recent legislation where the legislature has made an express choice.[91]

---

85 Section III.3.2.

86 It is quite clear that the judiciary considers the protection of the child. The cases concern admissibility. The development in the case law does, however, show that the judiciary has opted for a case by case evaluation of the 'right to joint parental authority'.

87 Above III.4.3.

88 J. de Boer in his annotation to the Supreme Court case of 27.05.2005, *NJ* 2005, 485.

89 Hoge Raad, *NJ* 2006, 284.

90 They may be viewed as an example of concealed reasoning (*verhullend argumenteren*) which according to Vranken is a characteristic of legal reasoning in civil law, J.B.M. Vranken, *Mr. C. Asser's Handleiding tot de beoefening van het Nederlands Burgelijk Recht, Algemeen deel, een vervolg*, Deventer: Kluwer, 2005, p. 28-41.

91 Supreme Court, 10.08.2001, *NJ* 2002, 278, annotated by J. de Boer.

If we turn to the pending legislative proposal to scrap the condition of a joint request for the allocation of joint parental authority, it is arguably not correct that national legislation which regulates parents' right to exercise joint parental authority or to access the court to establish this should necessarily infringe the ECHR. While the development in the case law necessitates legislative reform, such reform does not necessarily have to blindly follow the law developed by the judiciary when such a development is based upon a national standard. While the judiciary perhaps has no choice but to declare requests for joint parental authority admissible if it considers that the present law infringes fundamental principles of law, the legislature should have the freedom to consider alternative solutions.

III.4. INFLUENCE OF THE ECHR ON DANISH LAW

The influence of the ECHR on Danish family law is not very prominent. In the following this influence will be ascertained in relation to the Danish judiciary and the legislature in a broader parent–child relationship perspective and will also include the Danish position in relation to near relatives' right to contact.[92]

III.4.1. CONSTITUTIONAL ASPECTS OF DANISH LAW

The Danish Constitution does not address the issue of a constitutional review of national legislation.[93] Nevertheless, the judiciary has developed a claim to review the constitutionality of national legislation, but has at the same time long abstained from actually setting aside national law as being unconstitutional. This restrained review has been described as a sword which is rusting in its scabbard (…).[94] However, two decisions[95] by the Danish Supreme Court have

92 The influence of the ECHR is much more prominent in areas of law where Denmark has been found to infringe the ECHR, for example in relation to procedural law (Art. 6, ECHR) (unbiased judges) ECtHR, Hauschildt v. Denmark, No. 10486/83, (excessive length of civil proceedings), A and others v. Denmark, No. 60/95/566/652.

93 *Grundloven*, Act No. 169 of 05.06.1953. The act was partly revised in 1953.

94 H. Zahle, *Dansk Forfatningsret 4*, København: Christian Ejlers Forlag, 1987, p. 116.

95 Højesteret, *UFR* 1996.1300H (concerning a parliamentary Act aimed directly at terminating state aid for a particular School '*Tvind*' expressly providing that a judicial review was not possible; the Act was repealed by the Supreme Court as being unconstitutional) and *UFR* 1998.800H (the Supreme Court found that accession to the Maastricht Treaty was consistent with the Danish Constitution but also reserved the right for the Danish judiciary to review Community decisions for consistency with the Act on Denmark's accession to the EC Treaty), S. Harck, H. Palmer Olsen, 'Decision concerning the Maastricht Treaty', *The American Journal of International Law*, 1999, p. 209-214.

changed this perspective and placed constitutional review back on the legal agenda.[96]

The Danish Constitution is an old constitution and its catalogue of human rights contains classical freedom rights. But it does not contain, for example, a general principle of equality.[97] A constitutional review based upon the Danish Constitution has not played a role in the development of Danish substantive family law and cannot be expected to play such a role in the future given the contents of its human rights catalogue. The procedural requirements for changing the Danish Constitution are extensive. They involve, amongst other requirements, not only a majority vote in a referendum, but also that a high percentage of the voters participate in that referendum. Frequently calls have been made for the enactment of a new Constitution, but this has not yet resulted in an actual proposal.[98]

There is little doubt that the role of the Danish judiciary is more than that of merely 'bouche de la loi'. The law-shaping role of the judiciary is commonly accepted in areas of the law which are not or not regulated in detail, such as in private and commercial law contexts.[99] Traditionally, the source of law which permits the court to consider other factors as positive sources of law in a broad sense is described as *forholdets natur* (nature des choses). It may also be described as real considerations/reasons or general principles of law (*almene retsgrundsætninger*). *Forholdets natur* is not undisputedly an independent source of law in Danish law.[100]

Supreme Court judge TORBEN JENSEN reasons that when a court lacks a suitable basis for its decision (in emergency situations), it must support the decision on the basis of the 'antiquated concept' of *forholdets natur*. This concept covers a wide spectrum of general legal considerations including 'objective reasonability,

---

96 H. Zahle, *Dansk Forfatningsret 2*, Copenhagen: Christian Ejlers Forlag, 2001, p. 169 and O. Spiermann, 'Lovgivnings tilsidesættelse og det retlige grundlag herfor: Grundlov – menneskerettighedskonvention – traktat', *UFR*, Section B, 2006, p. 187.

97 A number of acts regulate the equality principle in relation to discrimination on the basis of sex, race, ethnicity, age, handicap, religion, ethnic or social origin and sexuality. The major part of these acts has only limited scope as they regulate equality solely in relation to the labour market.

98 For example, in the course of the Parliamentary conference on the necessity for a new Constitution, Report by J. Andersen, *Rapport fra Folketingets konference om behovet for en grundlovsrevision*, 1999 to be found on www.folketinget.dk.

99 J. Lookovsky in his contribution on precedents to the XVIIth Conference of the International Academy of Comparative Law, 'Precedent and the law in Denmark', p. 4-5, http://cisgw3.law.pace.edu/cisg/biblio/lookovsky15.html.

100 J. Evald,'Om forholdets natur', *Rettid*, 2002, p. 100-111.

equality principles and considerations concerning societal needs and developments'.[101]

The aforementioned should not be taken to mean that *forholdets natur* as understood today is based upon the legal-philosophical notion of natural law. Danish law is predominantly influenced by Scandinavian legal realism, most notably by the work of ALF ROSS. Scandinavian legal realism belongs to the positivistic side of the divide between natural law and positivism. ALF ROSS' fundamental idea was that law was a science seeking to ascertain the outcome of future judicial decisions (the prognosis theory). Further to strictly dividing legal reasoning, de lege lata, from political reasoning, de lege feranda implying a strong divide between law and morality. Perhaps the most notable practical influence on Danish legal reasoning has been the banning of, in particular, the concept of justice (*retfærdighed*).[102]

A constitutional review of legislation on the basis of general principles of law or *forholdets natur* which have no roots in the Danish Constitution such as, for example, a general principle of equality, has not been tried in Danish case law or deliberated in Danish jurisprudence. This is perhaps not remarkable considering the restrained application of a constitutional review. Furthermore, such a review would be more likely to be based upon international human rights instruments.

The Danish Constitution does not directly address the question of which status international law has in national Danish law. Traditionally, the Danish position in relation to international law has been described as dualistic. The dualistic theory considers international law and the national law of states as wholly separate legal entities, the former creating obligations only among sovereign nations and the latter allowing each state to determine the means and form by which it carries out its obligations. The monistic theory, on the other hand, views international and national law as part of a single legal system. It is probably misguiding to view the Danish position on international law in relation to monistic or dualistic theories. Classifying the Danish position as dualistic is not appreciative of the role that international law actually plays in Danish case law.

---

101 T. Jensen, 'Domstolenes retsskabende, retsudfyldende og responderende virksomhed', *UFR*, Section B, 1990, p. 442.

102 A. Ross, *Om ret og retfærdighed*, Copenhagen: Nyt Nordisk Forlag, 1953. The strict divide between law and morality is by no means undisputed and perhaps in decline, Bondesen (ed.) *Law and Morality*, Copenhagen: Forlaget Thomsen, 2006 and H. Zahle, *Omsorg for retfærdighed*, Copenhagen: Gyldendal, 2003.

On the other hand, the Danish position cannot be described as monistic. Therefore it has been suggested to use the term 'practical monism'.[103]

The position in Danish law is perhaps best explained with reference to how the judiciary factually uses international law.[104] Two generally accepted interpretative principles describe the relationship between international law and national law. The first is the interpretive rule (*fortolkningsreglen*) according to which 'national law which is ambiguous must be interpreted in a way which best brings it into line with international law'. Secondly, the application of the presumption rule (*formodningsreglen*) which states 'that it most often can (...) be assumed that it has not been the intention of the legislature to legislate contrary to the principles which the government recognises in its relations with other states'. ZAHLE adds the so-called instruction rule (*instruktionsreglen*) which contains a number of recommendations for the administration's use of international law, amongst others, that an administrative authority should use its discretionary powers to avoid a breach of international law.[105]

The ECHR was incorporated into Danish law by an Act of Parliament in 1992.[106] The Convention was incorporated to provide the courts with a clearer mandate to apply the ECHR. Simultaneously, however, it was stressed that the judiciary should apply the ECHR with restraint.[107] While the incorporation of the ECHR has provided the ECHR with a legislative basis in Danish law, which makes it indisputably an official source of law ranking above other instruments of international law, it remains a much debated issue how and to what extent the ECHR can be used to review and set aside national legislation. One point is clear, however; the ECHR does not have a constitutional status in Danish law. If the Danish legislature would explicitly choose to derogate from the protection offered by the ECHR, the judiciary would be bound to respect this position.

The question has been raised whether the Incorporation Act incorporated only the text of the ECHR or also the interpretation thereof in the case law of the ECtHR. In the latter case the question arises whether it concerns only the case law prior to the enactment of the Incorporation Act or also to 'new' case law of

---

103 O. Espersen, *Indgåelse og opfyldelse af traktater*, Copenhagen: Juristforbundets Forlag 1970, p. 163.

104 H. Zahle, *Menneskerettigheder*, Copenhagen: Christian Ejlers Forlag, 2003, p. 269.

105 H. Zahle, 2003, supra, p. 269-275.

106 Act No. 285 of 29.04.1992 replaced by Act No. 750 of 19.10.1998.

107 Commission Report No. 1220/1991, *Betænkning om inkorporering af EMRK* (Commission Report on incorporation of the ECHR), p. 149.

the ECtHR.[108] It may also be perceived as a question of an internal versus external standard, which court should interpret the ECHR, the national court or the ECtHR? This question has practical relevance since the principles of interpretation differ considerably. The ECtHR uses a dynamic style of interpretation in the light of present-day conditions 'whereas Danish courts tend to give the actual words and the legislative history of the different rules most weight in the interpretation'.[109]

The notion that the Incorporation Act incorporated only the text of the ECHR and the 'old' case law of the ECHR is not reflected in the parliamentary proceedings. Rather, the use of the case law of the ECtHR seems conditional upon a clarity requirement (*klarhedskravet*), that is, that it must be clear what the case law of the ECtHR requires in order to apply it.[110] Considering that the dynamic interpretive style of the ECtHR was well established at the time of incorporation, the notion that the case law of the ECtHR is relevant only within the application of the interpretive principles must be rejected.[111]

The Danish courts' use of the ECHR and the case law of the ECtHR to review national legislation is concurrently described as intense[112] and restrained.[113] The reason why such a difference of opinion may co-exist is due to the fact that there is no final decision by the Danish judiciary which clearly repeals national legislation based upon the ECHR, while there is ample case law which interprets national legislation and even the Danish Constitution in the light of the ECHR and the case law of the ECtHR. One decision by the Western High Court had the potential of shedding more light on this question. The High Court[114] had found

---

108 J. Garde, M. Hansen Jensen, 'Den Europæiske Menneskerettighedsdomstols praksis', *Juristen*, 2002, p. 76-82.

109 J. Albæk Jensen, 'Human Rights in Danish Law', *European Public Law*, 2001, Volume 7, Issue 1, p. 5.

110 Commission Report No. 1407/2001.

111 J. Albæk Jensen, 2001, supra, p. 6.

112 J. E. Rytter, *Den Europæiske Menneskerettighedskonvention – og dansk ret*, Copenhagen: Forlaget Thomson, Gad Jura, 2003, p. 67-69 and J. Christoffersen,'Højesteret og Den Europæiske Menneskerettighedskonvention', *UFR*, Section B, 2000, p. 593 modified and criticised in; J. Christoffersen, 'Højesterets prøvelse af folkeretlige diskriminationsforbud', *UFR*, Section B, 2002, p. 407 and J. Christoffersen, 'Den danske debat om den internationale menneskeret', *Nordisk Tidsskrift for Menneskerettigheder* (Nordic Journal of Human Rights), 2006, p. 97-114.

113 O. Spiermann, 'Tilbageholdenhed i anvendelsen af internationale menneskerettighedskonventioner', *UFR*, Section B, 2002, p. 412, and 'Lovgivnings tilsidesættelse og det retlige grundlag herfor: grundlov- menneskerettighedskonvention – traktat', *UFR*, Section B, 2006, p. 187.

114 Vestre Landsret, 17.05.2001.

that an Act, adopted after the incorporation of the ECHR in Danish law, which made the granting of new taxi licences conditional upon citizenship, infringed Article 14 of the ECHR. The Danish Supreme Court decided, however, that the Act did not infringe the ECHR based upon a different interpretation of the requirements of the ECHR.[115] The final decision by the Supreme Court means that it remains unclear whether the Danish courts would repeal clear national legislation on the basis of the ECHR.

The most predominant view is probably that the Danish judiciary is generally cautious in actually repealing national legislation on the basis of the ECHR. If repealing national legislation results in substantive changes to the law, the judiciary will mainly abstain from doing this because of the 'political' nature of the question.[116]

The cautious view in relation to the ECHR also has a political side. In 2005 MADS BRYDE ANDERSEN, a Professor of private law, launched an attack in the Danish press against 'the human rights thinking' directed in particular against the ECtHR's decisions in family law matters describing these as a 'politico-legal harmonisation project' and suggesting that the Danish Incorporation Act should be retracted.[117]

The article led to widespread debate and was also given an institutional element when the Danish Minister of Justice announced that she would not ratify the 12th Protocol to the ECHR because 'it was unreasonable that the ECtHR should decide when it was sufficiently justified to treat different groups in society differently.'[118] This debate has been analysed and relativated by CHRISTOFFERSEN where he, amongst others, points to the fact that Denmark along with the other Scandinavian countries and the UK formed a minority in the process of drafting the ECHR. These countries preferred drafting clear human rights provisions and not establishing a court to review and develop the human rights protection offered by the ECHR.[119]

---

115 Højesteret 21.05.2002, *UFR* 2002.1789H.

116 O. Spiermann, 2002, supra, p. 412, and 2006, supra, p. 187.

117 University of Copenhagen, 'Opgør med menneskerettighedstænkningen', *Berlingske Tidende* 13.03.2005.

118 In relation to the different treatment of foreigners in respect of provisions on child care and pension rights.

119 J. Christoffersen, 'Den danske debat om den internationale menneskeret', *Nordisk Tidsskrift for menneskerettigheder*, 2006, p. 97-114.

The status of Protocol 12 in relation to Danish law[120] was further debated in proceedings held in Copenhagen in 2004. The Danish representative put forward the Danish resistance towards the non-discrimination principle, amongst others, as follows:

> 'Danish ratification of Protocol No. 12 will presuppose going through each and every piece of legislation currently in force in Denmark and checking whether any sections thereof put emphasis on discriminatory criteria. That could be criteria such as age, sex, sexual orientation, social origin, language, physical or mental disability or other possibly discriminatory grounds bearing in mind that the list in Article 1 of the Protocol is not exhaustive. (...)
>
> The Danish Government is very concerned at the increasing transferral of legislative powers from the national parliaments to international non-legislative bodies which cannot be seen as democratically elected organs. Upon ratification, The European Court of Human Rights would be granted final jurisdiction in matters concerning whether Danish legislation is in compliance with Protocol No. 12.'[121]

As can be seen there seems to be a strong tendency in Danish politics to stress the role of the legislature and an inherent resistance against the transferral of powers to non-legislative bodies such as to the European Court of Human Rights.

Finally, one aspect of Danish administrative law which has constitutional implications must be mentioned. The competence to make decisions in various areas of private and public law are often placed with administrative authorities. Often this involves a two-tier system where the decision can be appealed to another administrative authority. Previously, legislation regulating this competence often contained a finality provision (*endelighedsbestemmelse*). It was recognised that the legislature could prevent a judicial review of administrative decisions with a finality provision. The constitutionality of such finality provisions must be seen in relation to Article 63(1) of the Danish Constitution, which

---

120 In fact in relation to a Nordic resistance (Denmark, Norway and Sweden); S. Lagoutte (Ed.), '*Prohibition of Discrimination in the Nordic Countries: The Complicated fate of Protocol No. 12 to the European Convention on Human Rights*', Proceedings from the Nordic Round Table on ECHR, held in Copenhagen on the 13th and 14th of December 2004, The Danish Institute for Human Rights.

121 Supra, p. 106-107.

provides that 'the judiciary is allowed to consider all questions relating to the boundaries of the administration'.

Today, it is generally assumed that a finality provision does not prevent the judiciary from reviewing the decision of the administration, but limits the review to legal questions. This implies that the discretion of the administration is reviewed only if the discretion can be legally qualified.

The Danish Act on Parental Responsibility places the competence to make contact orders primarily with the regional state administrations with the possibility of an appeal to another administrative authority. While the provision does not expressly contain a finality provision, the fact that the competence is placed with the administrative authorities means that a judicial review is limited to a review based upon Article 63(1) of the Constitution. The practical implication is that a case must be brought against the administrative appeal authority before the High Court. Few cases have been brought to court[122] and a review only recently resulted in setting aside the administrative decision.[123] From the case law it may be deduced that a review will only result in setting aside the administrative decision if this decision was contrary to a specific Act or infringed fundamental administrative principles.

III.4.2. THE INFLUENCE OF THE ECHR ON DANISH CASE LAW

The ECHR has been directly applicable in Danish law since 1992. Case law of the Danish judiciary and administrative authorities in family law cases concerning the parent-child relationship shows that the ECHR is directly applicable and is considered in decisions. Nonetheless, there are no examples, so far, of a clear legislative provision being set aside because of an infringement of the ECHR.

---

122 S. Danielsen, *Lov om forældremyndighed og samvær med kommentarer*, Copenhagen: Jurist og Økonomforbundets Forlag, 1997, p. 325-328. Published decisions Højesteret (Supreme Court), *UFR* 1989.398, Østre Landsret (Eastern High Court), 29.08.1996, *TFA* 1997.181, Østre Landsret (Eastern High Court) 24.02.2006, *UFR* 2006.1623Ø.

123 Østre Landsret (Eastern High Court), 01.11.2006, *UFR* 2007.673Ø. In this case a father (the paternity had been established judicially) had not had any contact with the child from its birth. When the child was 6 years old the father requested contact at the regional state administration. The mother opposed the request and the state administration denied contact on the basis of established legal practice, according to which contact is generally not established when there has been no contact for more than 5 years. The State Administration considered that the father had acted passively and relied solely upon the father's written request and the mother's written answer. The Court found that the case had not been sufficiently examined and annulled the decision.

In a case decided by the Western High Court on 15 December 1994 a clear legal practice was set aside on the basis of Article 8 ECHR.[124] The case concerned the establishment of paternity and adoption. The facts of the case were the following: A man and a woman had cohabited for two years until the birth of their child. The woman stated that the man was the only possible father of the child in the paternity proceedings. The man appeared in court and declared that he was willing to recognise the child subject to the condition that he could bring the child to Italy. The court could not accept such a conditional recognition and the case was adjourned for blood tests. Before the blood tests could be made the man moved to Italy. From Italy he requested that he should be allowed to recognise the child at the Danish Embassy in Italy.

Meanwhile, the Danish administrative authorities allowed the mother's new husband to adopt the child without hearing or involving the 'father' in the procedure. Pursuant to the adoption the Danish court then closed the paternity case in accordance with an established legal practice. The father appealed against the decision to close the case and requested that the case be reopened so that he could recognise the child. Before the High Court he no longer wished to contest the adoption or claim parental rights, he wished only to have his paternity established so that the child could later learn the identity of its biological father.[125] The Western High Court stated that the practice followed by the lower court and the administrative authorities was indeed in accordance with legal practice, but nonetheless reopened the case by reasoning as follows:

> 'The Appeal Court finds that it is doubtful whether the applied practice is in accordance with the principles in Article 8 of the ECHR in the present case where, according to the established facts, there was no reason to assume that another man was the child's father and where the result of the followed practice prevented the father from recognising the child and from making a statement in relation to Article 13 of the Adoption Act.'

The High Court further considered that reopening the case would not be substantially burdensome for the child. The reasoning of the Appeal Court did not contain an explicit analysis of the 'right to family life' as contained in Article 8 of the ECHR and did not make and reference to or an analysis of the case law of

124 Vestre Landsret, *UFR* 1995.249V.

125 Before the case had reached the High Court the father had contacted various authorities, amongst others, the administrative authorities seeking to establish a connection with the child and had unsuccessfully complained to the Danish *Ombudsmand.*

the ECtHR. The result in this case is probably best understood in its proper context, which was that at the time of the High Court's deliberations the conflicts of interests were considered to be minimal, given the fact that the biological father (no longer) claimed any parental rights or contested the adoption.[126]

Another example concerns the right of a near relative, for example a grandparent, step-parent or a sibling, to apply for contact with a child in a civil case. Danish law did not recognise such a right until recently.[127] In a case before the administrative authorities a stepfather had requested contact with the child of his ex-wife based upon Article 8 of the ECHR. The administration as well as the administrative appeal authority denied the request reasoning as follows:

> 'The administration is not entitled to make a decision, which is not founded on Danish law, referring to an international convention. This is not least when the decision will amount to a burden for a private person. It is of no relevance that the convention has been incorporated into Danish law by an Act, when this Act does not contain a provision empowering the administration to make a decision on contact.'[128]

The reasoning shows that the administrative authorities cannot rely directly upon the ECHR when there is no discretionary power.[129] There is no evidence that the decision or other (unpublished) administrative decisions on contact for a near relative have been brought before the Danish High Courts or the ECtHR.[130] It is also doubtful, however, if a review based upon Article 63(1) of the Danish Constitution would have changed the perspective given the fact that such

126 This case pertains to a situation similar to that raised in the ECtHR case Keegan v. Ireland, 26.05.1994, 16969/90. The difference was, however, that in the Danish case the father had had the opportunity to recognise the child and further the fact that paternity had not been established because the father had left the country before the blood tests had been made. For these reasons it is not entirely clear that the case would have constituted an infringement had it not been reopened.

127 If a child is placed in care, the local authorities have a discretionary power to determine whether contact between a non-parent and the child should take place, Art. 55(1), Lov om social service, Act No. 699 of 07.06.2006, Article 55(1).

128 *TFA*, 2001, p. 501.

129 Compare with the above-mentioned instruction rule, Section III.3.1. of this Chapter.

130 A case can only be brought before the ECtHR if all national remedies have been exhausted; this includes a review based upon Article 63(1) of the Constitution; J.F.Kjølbro, *Den Europæiske Menneskerettighedskonvention*, Copenhagen: Jurist- og Økonomforbundets Forlag, 2005, p. 103.

a review is limited to ascertaining whether the decision was 'contrary to the Act or infringed fundamental administrative principles'.[131]

III.4.3. THE LEGISLATURE

There is no tradition of extensive deliberation on the rights contained in the ECHR in relation to proposed legislation on family law in Danish parliamentary proceedings or parliamentary discussions. Typically it is concluded in the preparatory Commission Report that proposed legislation is in accordance with the ECHR.[132]

The possibility for a near relative to request a contact order has been laid down in the new Act on Parental Responsibility which entered into force on 1 October 2007. The preparatory Commission Report and the Explanatory Report did not, however, consider the rights of near relatives in relation to the ECHR, but only in relation to the possible ratification of the European Contact Convention[133] and the ratification of the Hague Child Protection Convention.[134]

Furthermore, the scope of the provision is clearly influenced by the same considerations, which in previous legislative reforms led to the conclusion that a right to request contact for near relatives should not be enacted. The consideration was that children should not be subjected to concurrent contact arrangements.[135] Consequently, Article 19(1) of the Act on Parental Responsibility provides the main rule that contact may be established with near relatives of the child with whom the child is closely connected where one parent or both parents are deceased.[136] Further, as an exception, in special cases where there is no contact or only very limited contact with the parent with whom the child

---

131 Above Section III.3.1.

132 The last Commission Report No. 1475/2006 contained a general overview in its annexes.

133 ETS No. 192 of 15.05.2003.

134 Convention on Jurisdiction, Applicable Law, Recognition, Enforcement and Cooperation in Respect of Parental Responsibility and Measures for the Protection of Children, 19.10.1996. Denmark signed this Convention on 01.04.2003 together with most other EC countries. The Convention has not yet been ratified, however. A Danish Act has been passed to implement the principles of the Convention into Danish law, Act No. 500 of 06.06.2007. The Act entered into force on 01.10.2007.

135 Commission Report Nos 1475/2006, p. 194-197, 1279/1994, p. 125-127, 985/1983, p. 45-46.

136 The scope of Art. 19(1) is not limited to the deceased parent's relatives, L. 133 , Comments to § 19.

does not reside, contact may be established with near relatives with whom the child is closely connected.[137]

III.4.4. ANALYSIS

There is no apparent evidence that the ECHR or the case law of the ECtHR has been considered in parliamentary proceedings in relation to a near relative's right to request contact with a child. In relation to children placed in public care the local authorities have discretionary powers to determine such contact. The discretionary power of the local authorities in respect of non-parents[138] was adopted in the recent reform on the placement of children in care.[139] Such discretionary power was, however, also acknowledged before the reform. The change in the wording of the relevant provision was not reasoned in the light of the ECHR, but lay in the general purpose of the reform, which was more to include the child's 'network' when a child was placed in public care.[140] It remains an open question why the ECHR and the case law of the ECtHR are not more explicitly considered or mentioned in the legislative processes.

III.5. COMPARISON – INFLUENCE OF THE ECHR

The influence of the ECHR on Dutch family law is undoubtedly stronger than on Danish family law. The principles contained in the ECHR have provided a kick-start for the Dutch development which has included a parent's right to joint parental authority in a human rights terminology. This has not been the case in Danish law where, so far, as deliberated in Chapter II, the conceptual development in joint parental authority has been based upon policy choices. In this respect it is worth repeating, however, that the general developments in joint parental authority have nonetheless been strikingly concurrent.[141]

There is little doubt that the Dutch judiciary has a clearer mandate to apply the ECHR and binding decisions of the ECtHR (a monistic approach) than the Danish judiciary where the mandate (neither monistic nor dualistic) is subject

---

137 Art. 19(2), Act on Parental Responsibility.

138 The term non-parents is used because its scope in this Act is wider than the term near relatives.

139 Lov om social service (Act on social services), Act No. 573 of 24.06.2005 which entered into force on 1 January 2007. This Act has now been replaced by Consolidated Act No. 58 of 18.02.2007 with later changes.

140 Information on this reform is available at www.anbringelsesreformen.servicestyrelsen.dk.

141 Chapter II, Section II.4.

to debate. In this respect it is also evident, however, that the influence cannot be understood only in a constitutional context because such a context does not explain why, on the one hand, the Dutch judiciary has adopted a more autonomous role in developing the law beyond what is required by the ECHR and the case law of the ECtHR and, on the other hand, why the ECHR does not more actively influence the development of the law by the Danish legislature.

Perhaps a more realistic explanation is that Danish family law concerning the parent-child relationship has been more in line with the requirements of the ECHR while Dutch law, in particular the law on parentage and contact, has been straggling behind resulting in a situation where, first, the Dutch judiciary and later also the legislature have become very attentive to the requirements of the ECHR. The Marcx decision, concerning the status of a child born outside marriage in relation to the mother and the mother's family, although directly involving Belgium, warranted action from the judiciary as well as the legislature to bring Dutch law into line with the ECHR.[142] The Marcx case had little relevance in Danish law where a child born outside marriage in relation to the mother and the mother's family enjoyed equal rights as a child born within marriage.[143] Furthermore, the Netherlands has been found to have infringed Article 8 of the ECHR on a number of occasions[144] while Denmark has not been censured in a family law case.[145] The influence of the ECHR is probably most dominant in a family law context in the Netherlands while in Denmark it has had more of an influence in areas of law where Denmark has been censured for a violation of the ECHR or where the Danish judiciary has based its decisions on an interpretation of the ECHR.[146] It is worth noting that the Danish judiciary in such cases has shown restraint in interpreting or going against national legislation where such an approach would have 'far-reaching consequences'. This indicates a different balance in the separation of powers between the judiciary and the legislature than the one struck in the Netherlands.[147]

---

142 Chapter II, Section II.2.4.

143 Chapter II.3.4.

144 ECtHR, Kroon v. the Netherlands, 27.10.1994, 18535/91 Lebbinck v. The Netherlands, 01.06.2004, 45582/99.

145 ECtHR, Rasmussen v. Denmark, 28.11.1984, 8777/79 Nielsen v. Denmark, 28.11.1988, 10929/84.

146 This line of reasoning may be substantiated with regard to the influence of the UN Convention on the Rights of the Child in Danish law where Denmark has received criticism from the Committee which has also resulted in legislative action, see below Section III.6.4.

147 Although such a balance in the Netherlands is presently not directly ascertainable in the constitutional framework.

Further, it is possible that the widespread use of administrative procedures in Danish law where legal representation is unnecessary and where court review may be limited means that 'a human rights violation' is argued less frequently.[148]

Finally, it is also quite clear that there seems to be a stronger resistance in Danish political and legal culture towards judicial activity which involves 'moral value judgments', which are considered to be political in nature, than is the case in the Netherlands. The developments depicted in this Chapter and the current Danish and Dutch stance in relation to the 12th Protocol to the ECHR illustrates this difference.

It is possible to view the difference as follows; while the enactment of equality has been a consistent matter of family policy in Danish legislation there is also resistance to a judicial review based upon general principles. Legislation provides the primary means for change. In the Netherlands the enactment of equality has to a lesser extent been the subject of family policy; however, there is a greater openness towards a judicial review based upon general principles. In this respect the extent to which human rights influence national law could be viewed as a reflection of the national legal culture.

Presently, it could be said that one of the primary differences in the concept of joint parental authority concerns an unmarried father's rights where Dutch law, inspired by the principles of the ECHR, relies upon an ad hoc ascertainment (balancing) of rights and Danish law provides more automatic rights. It should also be noted, however, that the present pending Dutch reform on 'Continued Parenting' does not rely upon the principles of the ECHR but rather upon 'the right to be cared for by two parents', a point which is very similar to the policy contained in recent Danish legislation.[149] It perhaps marks a shift in the terminology used in the conceptual development of joint parental authority in Dutch law, a shift which seems logical considering the present stance of the case law of the ECtHR. In this respect it is also possible to view the use of a human rights terminology by the legislature or the judiciary as a way to promote a develop-

---

148 S. Wortmann, 'Duidelijkheid en Zekerheid', *NJB*, 1996, p. 603 mentions the fact that the development in joint parental authority after divorce and for unmarried parents (Section III.4.2.) was triggered by young lawyers who inspired their clients to seek 'modern answers' to old legal questions and I. Foighel, 'Gælder menneskerettighederne', *UFR*, Section B, 1997, p .1, a former Danish judge at the ECtHR, who draws attention to the discrepancy in the amount of cases originating from different Member States and stresses the point that national lawyers must be conscious of the possibility of bringing cases before the ECtHR.

149 Chapter II, Sections II.2.6. and II.4.

ment which is considered desirable. It should also be noted that the Dutch lower courts in respect of the depicted developments in the case law concerning a sole request rely not only upon the principles contained in the ECHR, but also upon other considerations such as 'asking less instead of more' or by anticipating pending legislation.

III.6. THE CRC

The CRC provides the primary international source of human rights for children. The CRC, unlike the ECHR, does not have a court to interpret or enforce the rights contained in the Convention. It does, however, have a Committee on the Rights of the Child (the Committee) which examines the realisation of the obligations contained in the Convention.[150] This Committee considers the initial and the periodic reports submitted every five years by a State Party. The Committee may make suggestions and general recommendations. Further, the Committee may co-operate with non-governmental organisations, for example private children's rights organisations.[151]

III.6.1. RELEVANT PROVISIONS OF THE CRC

The provisions of the CRC which are most often cited in the context of parental authority and contact are: Article 3 containing the best interests principle, Articles 9 and 18 concerning a child's relationship with its parents and Articles 9(2) and 12 concerning the child's participation rights.

Article 18(1) provides that both parents have the primary responsibilities. The provision reads:

> 'States Parties shall use their best efforts to ensure recognition of the principle that both parents have common responsibilities for the upbringing and development of the child. Parents or, as the case may be, legal guardians, have the primary responsibility for the upbringing and development of the child. The best interests of the child will be their basic concern.'

---

150 Art. 43, CRC.
151 Art. 45, CRC.

Further, Article 9(1) of the CRC provides the circumstances under which a child may be separated from his or her parents. The provision reads:

> 'State parties shall ensure that a child shall not be separated from his or her parents against their will, except when competent authorities subject to judicial review determine, in accordance with applicable law and procedures, that such separation is necessary for the best interests of the child. Such determination may be necessary in a particular case such as one involving abuse or neglect of the child by the parents, or one where the parents are living separately and a decision must be made as to the child's place of residence.'

Finally, Article 9(3), first sentence provides that:

> 'States Parties shall respect the right of the child who is separated from one or both parents to maintain personal relations and direct contact with both parents on a regular basis, except if it is contrary to the child's best interests.'

Articles 9 and 18(1) of the CRC do not mention the concept of parental authority/responsibilities, although they are often cited as an authority for the principle that both parents should hold and further retain this concept upon divorce or the breakup of a relationship. The right of the child not to be separated from his/her parents is furthermore subject to the best interests principle and Article 9(1) states that the situation where the parents live separately is a special situation.[152]

III.6.2. THE CRC IN DUTCH LAW

The CRC entered into force in the Netherlands on 8 March 1995. The Dutch position with regard to binding treaty provisions has been deliberated above.[153] The position may be described as monistic. This entails that those provisions of the CRC which are sufficiently clear may have direct effect in Dutch law. At the time of incorporation the Dutch government considered that the CRC was not

---

152 The CEFL considers that the principle that both parents have common responsibilities for the upbringing and development of the child 'implies that both parents are holders of parental responsibilities'. Yet, with respect to the influence of the dissolution or weakening of a marriage the CRC 'does not mention this issue', Principles, principle 3:8, International instruments, p. 59 and principle 3:10, International instruments, p. 79.

153 Section II.2.1.

expected to have many consequences for the Netherlands. The Government considered that certain provisions could have direct effect. In relation to the above-mentioned provisions relevant for this study, it concerned Articles, 9(2) and (3), 12(1) and (2).[154]

III.6.2.1. The Dutch CRC Reports

The Netherlands submitted an initial report in 1997 and one periodic report thereafter and has received Concluding Observations of the Committee in respect of both.[155] The Concluding Observations did not contain any criticism particularly directed against the law concerning parental authority and contact.

III.6.2.2. The Dutch legislature

The CRC has not played as vital a role for the development of Dutch family law as the ECHR. The CRC is mentioned in the legislative processes concerning the subject-matter of this study, but does not seem to have been relied upon as directly as the ECHR. In the parliamentary proceedings concerning the pending proposal on 'Continued Parenting' the Dutch Minister of Justice rejected lowering the age where children have the right to be heard in the procedure (12+) considering that the courts already had the possibility of hearing younger children.[156]

III.6.2.3. Dutch case law on the CRC

A Dutch study has analysed 75 cases from the period 1995-2001 in relation to the application of relevant provisions of the CRC. The study found that several provisions of the CRC had been applied directly, including Article 3 which the Dutch Government had not initially presumed to have direct effect, and that the courts also applied the CRC *ex officio*.[157]

Two cases concerning contact deserve to be mentioned. In the first case the question was whether the court could request the Dutch Child Protection Board

---

154 G.C.A.M. Ruitenberg, *Het International Kinderrechtenverdrag in de Nederlandse rechtspraak*, Amsterdam: SWP, 2003, p. 17-18.

155 Initial report, April 1997 and periodic report, March 2002. Concluding Observations of 08.10.1999 and 30.01.2004.

156 Parliamentary proceedings 2006/2007 (*Kamerstukken*), 30 145, No. 6, p. 25.

157 G.C.A.M. Ruitenberg, 2003, supra, p. 217.

to provide supervised contact pursuant to a contact order.[158] The Leeuwarden Court of Appeal found that on the basis of Article 3(2) of the CRC the State has a positive obligation to attain the aim of family life based upon Article 8 of the ECHR and Article 16(1) of the CRC.[159] The Court of Appeal made a contact order and obliged the Board to supervise the contact. The Board appealed the matter to the Supreme Court. The Supreme Court quashed the decision of the Court of Appeal considering that 'the Board did not, according to the Act, have the function of supervising a contact order made by the Court and that the Act did not give the Court the authority to determine that function.' Further, the Supreme Court considered that such a function cannot be derived from Article 8 of the ECHR and Article 16 of the CRC.[160]

In proceedings before the Central Appeals Tribunal for social security matters, a father had requested that the local authorities should contribute to expenses concerning transportation and living costs relating to a contact arrangement with his child who resided with the mother. The local government and the District Court had dismissed the request. The Central Appeals Tribunal found that Article 9(3) of the CRC had direct effect but, however, also considered that:

> 'The protection offered by Article 9(3) of the CRC and Article 8 of the ECHR does not go as far as to provide an obligation for the social security authority to enable the father financially to exercise the contact right of the child with the parents and to enable the right to family life in respect of a child living in a different district.'[161]

III.6.3. THE CRC IN DANISH LAW

The CRC was ratified by Denmark on 19 July 1991. However, the Convention has not been incorporated into Danish law by an Act as is the case with the ECHR. This means that the Convention is only directly applicable by the courts within the scope of the interpretative principles deliberated above.[162]

---

158 Access to supervised contact is further deliberated in Chapter VIII, Section VIII.2.3.1.

159 Art. 16(1) provides that '*No child shall be subjected to arbitrary or unlawful intereference with his or her privacy, family, home or correspondance, nor to unlawful attacks on his or her honour or reputation*'.

160 Hoge Raad 29.06.2001, *NJ* 2001, 598.

161 Centrale Raad van Beroep 22.06.1999, RSV 1999, 235.

162 Section III.4.1.

The question whether the Convention should be incorporated was considered by a Commission in 2001. The Commission found that the CRC is 'central' to the protection of human rights, but did not recommend incorporation at the present time considering that the incorporation of other Conventions should be given priority. Further, it considered that the fact that there was no possibility to make an individual complaint under the CRC and that the Committee did not make general recommendations meant that there were insufficient interpretative contributions which could substantiate the content and extent of the provisions.[163]

III.6.3.1. The Danish CRC reports

Denmark submitted an initial report in 1993 and thereafter two periodic reports and has received Concluding Observations of the Committee thereon.[164]

The Concluding Observations have given rise to criticism of the Danish regulation of parental authority and contact. In the first Observations, the Committee expressed concern about the implementation of the CRC in respect of the child's right to be heard with respect to the minimum age of 12 years and the fact that children were often not heard when the parents agree.[165] In the second Observations the Committee stated the following:

> 'The Committee is concerned that the general principle of the best interests of the child is not fully applied and duly integrated into the implementation of the policies and programmes of the State party. In this regard the Committee notes that the rights of parents are often found more important than the best interests of the child.
>
> The Committee is aware of the various provisions in the law concerning the right of the child to be heard and that the legal minimum age, in this regard, is 12 years. However, the Committee remains concerned about the inadequate implementation of article 12 of the Convention and the fact that children below the age of 12 years do not have a right to be heard.'

---

163 Commission Report No. 1407/2001, *Betænkning om inkorporering af menneskerettigheder i dansk ret*, Chapter 12. The Commission considered the incorporation of various international conventions.

164 Initial Report, August 1993, periodic reports of September 1998 and August 2004. Concluding Observations of 15.02.1995, 08.06.2001 and 24.11.2005.

165 E. Caspersen, 'Børnekonventionen og dens efterlevelse i Danmark', *Juristen*, No. 6, 1995, p. 278-279.

In the third Observations the Committee noted that it 'welcomes the increased consideration given to the views of children in administrative decision-making processes, including children under the age of 12 years'.[166] However, the Committee noted that Denmark:

> 'Should ensure that all adults who work with children are trained to effectively assure that children capable to express their views are provided with adequate opportunities to do so and ensure that their views are taken into account.'

III.6.3.2. The Danish legislature

The criticism by the Committee led to a revision of the child's right to be heard. In 2002 the former Act on Parental Authority and Contact was revised and Article 29(2) came to provide that a conversation must also take place with a child under the age of 12 if the child's maturity and the circumstances make this reasonable.[167] It should be noted, however, that prior to this enactment children below the age of 12 often were heard in procedures and that the amended legislation was considered not to change the practices already in place.

Further, the Commission preparing the new Act on Parental Responsibility (2007) has extensively considered the requirements of the CRC and the criticism of the Committee. The new Act on Parental Responsibility accordingly intends to implement a 'child-centred perspective' which must ensure that the child's perspective is always present in a (disputed) case.[168] Article 5 of the Act on Parental Responsibility now provides that 'in all matters concerning the child regard must be had to the child's own views depending on age and maturity'. 'The child's perspective' is to be applied with regard to young children through the increased use of child experts.[169]

III.6.3.3. Danish case law on the CRC

The CRC has been mentioned in Danish case law, but there are no decisions relying directly on the CRC.

---

166 The legislation had been changed, see below Section III.6.4.2.

167 Act No. 461 of 07.06.2001 and L 3 04.11.2000, Comments to No. 6.

168 It continues to be the case that a child is not heard when the parents agree, see further Chapter VIII, Section VIII.4.2.

169 Further deliberated in Chapter VIII, Section VIII.4.2.

III.6.4. COMPARISON – INFLUENCE OF THE CRC

The influence of the CRC in Dutch law in relation to parental authority and contact has, as yet, been limited when viewed in the context of the influence which the ECHR has had. On the other hand, the influence on the Danish legislature has been more marked, which in relation to the conclusions contained above in respect of the ECHR could be viewed as a response to the Committee's criticism. It should be noted, however, that the Committee's criticism in respect of Danish law must also be viewed in the context of the internal criticism in Denmark and contributions by the Danish Child Rights organisations to the Committee.[170] The influence of the CRC could thus also be viewed as a response to internal criticism based upon the principles contained in the CRC.[171]

[170] The Organisation Børnerådet (The National Council for Children), for example, voiced its criticism to the Committee in respect of the third periodic report against the practises in some of the regional state administrations where children are heard by legal case workers rather than child experts, Report to the UN Committee on the Rights of the Child, Supplementary Report to Denmark's 3rd periodic report, January 2005, p. 15. This criticism was clearly adopted in the Observations, Above Section III.6.4.1. The National Council for Children is an independent national institution working to promote childrens rights administratively linked to the Ministry for Family and Consumer Affairs.

[171] The criticism of Danish law could also have been directed at Dutch law, for example, because children under the age of 12 do not have a 'right' to be heard in Dutch law, see further Chapter VIII, Section VIII.4.1.

CHAPTER IV
SOCIO-LEGAL DATA

IV.1. INTRODUCTION

The law regulating parental authority and contact after divorce and after the breakup of a relationship is dominated by changing perceptions of the child's welfare. Presently, the notion that a child has 'a right to two parents' implying that parents should continue to have joint parental authority and extensive contact after divorce and after the breakup of a relationship, even when the foundations for joint parenting are lacking, dominates the political and legal welfare ideology. It is, however, not a perception which is necessarily supported by research into children's well-being after divorce.

This Chapter aims to provide an insight into the research findings of primarily recent Dutch and Danish socio-legal studies concerning parental authority and contact. The term socio-legal is used to emphasise that the research should make a connection between social facts and the law.

Inspiration has been found, in respect of the Netherlands, in the recent study by SPRUIJT, which contains an overview of recent research into the consequences of divorce for children and young persons.[1] For Denmark, the recent contact studies from 2004, which were commissioned by the Minister of Justice, contain new research results, but also relate these to the findings of previous studies.[2]

---

1 E. Spruijt, *Scheidingskinderen*, Amsterdam: SWP, 2007.

2 M. Heide Ottosen, *Samvær til barnets bedste* (Contact in the best interests of the child) and *Samvær og børns trivsel* (Contact and the well-being of children), Copenhagen: Socialforskningsinstituttet (The Danish National Centre for Social Research), 2004. The latter was, as is the case with a great deal of other research, based upon the child survey data, a unique set of data pertaining to 6,000 randomly chosen children born in 1995 which therefore also yields information concerning the family before a divorce or the breakup of a relationship. The data were collected via interviews with the mothers in 1996, 1999 and 2003 and via questionnaires completed by the fathers in 1996 and 2003. At a later stage the children will also participate.

This Chapter aims to address two main themes. The first theme concerns parental authority and residence after divorce and the break up of a relationship. This theme includes a description of some main demographics concerning the allocation of parental authority and children's residence after divorce, the negative effects upon children associated with divorce and national perspectives concerning the development in the allocation of joint parental authority.

The second theme concerns national perspectives concerning contact after divorce and the breakup of a relationship.

IV.2. PARENTAL AUTHORITY AND RESIDENCE AFTER DIVORCE

IV.2.1. MAIN DEMOGRAPHICS

The vast majority of parents (approximately 90%) exercise joint parental authority after divorce in the Netherlands.[3] There is no dependable information on unmarried parents' exercise of parental authority. Children reside primarily with the mother, although the number of children having a shared residence is increasing steadily. Some 75% of children reside with the mother after divorce and the breakup of a relationship, 9% with the father and 16% are subject to a co-parenting (shared residence) agreement.[4]

In Denmark approximately 65% of the parents of children born in 1995 have joint parental authority. This estimation includes children born to both married and unmarried parents when the parents (no longer) live together. It is estimated that a larger number of children born after the enactment of the Children Act in 2001 will have parents holding joint parental authority.[5] Almost 90% of children who do not live with both parents, including children born to unmarried parents, have their registered address with the mother and 11% with the

3 See for more detailed statistics; Chapter V, Section V.4.5.5.

4 Co-parentage has been defined as encompassing children who spend more than 40% of their time with one parent. In 2001 the percentage of children subject to a co-parentage agreement was 4%; E. Spruijt, 2007, supra, p. 17-18. These data are based upon a group of children with divorced parents, including 17% of children whose parents had co-habited.

5 See further Chapter V, Section V.4.6.3.

father. Approximately 20% of all children spend more than one third of their time with one parent.[6]

These data show that the mother continues to be the primary carer after divorce in both the Netherlands and Denmark with, however, an increasing group of children who have shared residences. The data on children's residence with the mother or father are, however, not entirely comparable since the Danish statistics concern all children in Denmark including those born to single mothers while the Dutch data concern mostly children whose parents have divorced.

IV.2.2. NEGATIVE EFFECTS OF DIVORCE

It is internationally and nationally a well-established fact that parental divorce is associated with negative effects upon the well being of children. Rather surprisingly AMATO reported in his meta-analysis based upon internationally reported research results that the negative effects increased in the 1990s after showing a decrease in the 1980s (in comparison with the period 1950-1960). While the meta-analysis could not provide a direct explanation for these findings[7] the author notes that:

> '(...) Whatever the reason for the apparent decline in the relative well-being of children with divorced parents during the last decade, this shift occurred in spite of the growth of school-based interventions for children, parenting classes for divorcing parents, and divorce mediation. This conclusion does not mean that the spread of therapeutic and legal interventions has not benefited children – it only means that other social forces have operated even more strongly to disadvantage children from divorced families.'

---

6 M. Heide Ottosen (Contact and the well-being of children), 2004, supra, p. 14 based upon statistics from Statistics Denmark. The percentage of children living with the father has decreased from 12 to 11% over the past 10 years probably due to the increase in shared residences from 4% at the end of the 1980s to approximately 20% in 2004.

7 The author offers two possible reasons. The first has to do with a possible shift in the nature of marital discord, where more recent divorces increasingly include cases in which only moderately (rather than extremely dissatisfied) individuals leave their spouses. When low-discord marriages end in divorce it appears to be particularly stressful for children. The second reason refers to the increasing gap in economic well-being between children with single parents and children with married parents during the economic boom of the 1990s, P.R. Amato, 'Children of divorce in the 1990s: An Update of the Amato and Keith (1991) Meta-Analysis', Journal of Family Psychology, 2001, Volume 15, p. 365-366.

While the negative effects of divorce are considered to be significant enough to be a matter of concern, researchers also emphasize that the effects are not necessarily disastrous. The majority of children who have experienced divorce continue to do as well as their peers raised in intact families.[8]

The negative effects of divorce have been the subject of more research in the Netherlands than in Denmark.[9] The question whether other factors than divorce contribute to the negative effects is a commonly raised aspect.[10] Danish research consistently points to the fact that problems concerning joint parenting between parents who do not live together are strongly associated with social vulnerability and other problems such as substance abuse and physical and mental violence.[11]

VI.2.3. THE NETHERLANDS: JOINT PARENTAL AUTHORITY BEFORE AND AFTER 1998

The consequences of the shift towards continuing joint parental authority after the 1998 reform, leading to an abrupt increase in the allocation of joint parental authority after divorce, has not been extensively researched in the Netherlands and research results have only recently emerged. Moreover, little is known about the number of unmarried parents who exercise joint parental authority during their relationship and after a breakup.

Two studies provide some answers concerning the consequences of the automatic continuation of joint parental authority in comparison with the situation before 1998 where joint parental authority was consensus-based. In the first place SPRUIJT concludes that children have significantly more contact with the father when the divorce has taken place after 1998. The well-being of children

---

8 P.R. Amato, 2001, p. 366, M. Heide Ottosen (Contact and the well-being of children), 2004, supra, p. 30, E. Spruijt, 2007, supra, p. 48.

9 See for the Netherlands the overview in E. Spruijt, 2007, supra, p. 34-49 and for Denmark M. Heide Ottosen (Contact and the well-being of children), 2004, supra, p. 28. M. Heide Ottosen considers that this type of research is more prominent in countries such as the US where family policy discussions have a more moralistic character than in Scandinavia.

10 E. Spruijt, 2007, supra, p. 34.

11 Further, the negative influences of divorce upon children are relative in comparison with the negative effects upon children growing up in families where the parent(s) receive social benefits or has/have contact with the social authorities for other reasons. The negative effects upon children was 30% compared to 15% for children who had experienced divorce and 8% for children from non-divorced families, M. Heide Ottosen, Samvær og børns trivsel, 2004, p. 31. In Dutch research T. Fischer has pointed to the fact that parental conflict and financial difficulties before and after the divorce contribute to the negative effects; T. Fischer, 'Onderwijsachterstand door echtscheiding?', *Demos*, No. 8, 2004, p. 61-63.

has, however, decreased rather than increased. From 1998 onwards a constant and significantly higher conflict level is reported compared to before 1998.[12]

SPRUIJT makes a series of recommendations aimed at redressing the problem, for example compulsory counselling for the parents, the drafting of a 'parenting plan', compulsory conflict mediation, support groups for children, tax rewards when contact is successful and supervised contact. Furthermore, SPRUIJT considers that more attention should be directed towards threats to children's welfare such as violence, abuse and parental alienation and that the possibility of a temporary discontinuation of contact should be considered when this may be beneficial for the child.[13]

In the second place, however, a study from 2007 could not demonstrate that the 1998 Act had changed relationships between parents and children.[14]

IV.2.4. DENMARK: THE RELEVANCE OF LEGAL BONDS

A Danish sociological study from 2000 entitled 'Co-habitation, marriage and parental breakup' aimed to pin down the relevance of legal bonds (parental authority) for the *de facto* exercise of family life.[15]

This research concerned children born to married parents, unmarried co-habiting parents and single mothers.[16] The children included in the study were born

---

12 E. Spruijt, 2007, supra, p. 26-28. On a scale of 0-20 the reported conflict level was 8.4 in respect of divorces before 1998 and between 11.0-13.2 in respect of divorces after 1998. The analysis also shows that the conflict levels did not decrease with the passing of time after the divorce. The fact that the legal construction 'joint parental authority' may in itself bring about higher conflict levels was also reported by the Danish 2006 Commission in respect of Sweden, Commission report No. 1475/2006 and Chapter II, Section II.3.2.2.

13 E. Spruijt, 2007, supra, p. 72-74.

14 E.M. Mertz and H.J. Schultze, 'Relatie gescheiden ouders en hun kinderen', *Demos*, No. 5, 2007, p. 6-8. This study, however, was based upon the NKPS data which provided rather crude questions with respect to parental authority. The parents were asked if they had co-parentage arrangements rather than joint parental authority.

15 M. Heide Ottosen, *Samvær, Ægteskab og Forældrebrud*, Copenhagen: Socialforskningsinstituttet, 2000. The research was based upon the above child survey data concerning approximately 6,000 children born in the autumn of 1995, see above Section IV.1., supra note 2.

16 The research was based upon the respondents participating in 1996 and 1999 and amounted to 4,989 children in total. Of these 2,765 had married parents, 2,039 had co-habiting parents and 185 were born to single mothers during the first survey in 1996. The survey showed that 95 % of the parents who were married in 1996 continued to be married in 1999. 13% of the unmarried co-habiting parents had ended their relationship and 35% of the cohabiting parents had married by 1999. The majority of children born to single mothers continued to live in a

in 1996 before the enactment of the most common paternity registration procedure in 2001 (the care and responsibility statement) resulting in joint parental authority and before the automatic continuation of joint parental authority after divorce in 2002.[17] The research was thus in a context where joint parental authority after divorce and for unmarried parents could be viewed as a positive choice.[18]

The research had two main formulated problems; one concerned the legal bonds between the parents, that is, pinning down the differences between married and co-habiting parents. The other was pinning down the importance of legal bonds (parental authority) between younger children and their fathers focusing on the situation upon divorce and the breaking up of a relationship. The research further focused upon those children whose parents had serious *legal* conflicts concerning parental authority and contact.

Here the main results presented in Chapter 8 of the research: 'Parental authority, co-habitation and parental breakup' and Chapter nine of the research: 'When the child becomes a field of conflict' will be described.

'Parental authority, co-habitation and parental breakup'
This part of the research concerned the group of children whose parents had divorced or ceased co-habitation at the second measuring point in 1999. In total there were 419 children of whom two thirds were recruited from the group of parents co-habiting in 1996 and one third from the group of parents who were married in 1996.

The research provided an analysis at two levels. The first level focused upon the circumstances which may contribute to an understanding of the co-habiting parents' choice in respect of sole or joint parental authority at birth and the consequences thereof when a relationship comes to an end. The second level provided an analysis of the relevance of the absence or existence of legal bonds (parental authority) between the family members during the marriage/co-

single-parent family. However, in 23% of the cases the parents had become co-habitants and 6% had married. Half of these relationships had however terminated by the measuring point in 1999.

17 Chapter II, Section II.3.4.1. and II.3.2.1.

18 Presently (since 2007) co-habitating parents have joint parental authority *ex lege* and parental authority may only be terminated after divorce and the ending of a relationship if there are 'weighty grounds' or the parents agree to this, Chapter II, Sections II.3.2.2., II.3.4.2. and Chapter V, Sections V.3.2.2. and V.4.2.

habitation for the social shaping of post-divorce parenting. In this context the research aimed to examine whether children born to co-habiting parents in comparison with children born to married parents, at the time of divorce or the breakup of a relationship, are more or less likely to:

1. have the father as the primary carer;
2. have an extensive contact arrangement;
3. have loose contact with the non-resident parent, as well as to
4. have parents who co-operate extensively.

At both levels the analysis took account of background factors, which on the basis of other research was expected to have consequences for both legal and de facto social parenting. These background factors were: factors which as a consequence of life-phase differences between married and unmarried parents could be relevant for shaping the legal and social bond with the father,[19] socio-economic factors,[20] a number of variables illuminating the interpersonal interplay between the parents[21] and, finally, an indicator as to whether the child had been a 'common project'.[22]

The analysis showed that those families where the mother *had sole parental authority during the cohabitation* to a larger extent than families where the parents had joint parental authority could be characterised as being based upon a fragile foundation. The main variables were: that the mothers in this group were more frequently single at the time of birth,[23] that the child was more frequently unwanted because of a stormy relationship, that the families more frequently had a more traditional division of care for the child where the mother

19 The parents' age at the time of birth, the child's position (only child or siblings), the duration of the parents' relationship (cohabitation period) and the child's age at the time of the divorce or the ending of the relationship.

20 Concerning fathers' educational levels and occupations. The data relating to mothers were not included as preliminary analysis had shown that they were without importance when the data on fathers were included.

21 From the 1996 survey information was included relating to the child, that is, whether it was unwanted because of a stormy relationship. From the 1999 survey information was included about the breakup of a relationship and divorce, that is, whether it had occurred by mutual agreement, whether the parents had agreed to the allocation of parental authority, and whether the parents had initiated court proceedings. Finally, information was included on the reasons for the breakup or divorce, for example infidelity, substance abuse or violence.

22 Concerning the division of care during the first weeks after birth, that is whether the parents shared the caring activities (a symmetrical division) or whether the mother provided the primary care (a traditional division).

23 The co-habitation had thus commenced later than the first measuring point in 1996.

had provided the primary care, that the relationship was more frequently terminated because of violence and, finally, that the termination of the relationship took place early on.[24]

Further, the analysis showed that *cohabiting parents most often continue to hold joint or sole parental authority at the end of the relationship corresponding to the situation during cohabitation.* Only exceptionally (17%) was joint parental authority converted into sole parental authority or sole parental authority converted into joint parental authority (6%) at the time of the breakup.

For married parents the analysis showed that the most frequent variables which were *relevant for the choice between sole and joint parental authority at the time of divorce were identical with the variables which were relevant for co-habiting parents' choice of parental authority at birth.* These were: few socio-economic resources (father), that the father had not participated in the care after birth as well as violence in the relationship. The analysis thus indicates that the same motives determine the choice between sole and joint parental authority between co-habiting parents and married parents. The difference, however, is that this choice is made at two different points in time for married parents upon divorce and for unmarried parents at birth.[25]

The research further showed that 10% of children whose parents had held joint parental authority since birth (married and co-habiting parents) came to have the father as the primary carer after the divorce and the breakup of the relationship. This was only the case for 1% of children where the mother had held sole parental authority during co-habitation. In the analysis it is considered *that it cannot be excluded that the father's lack of parental authority at birth and during the co-habitation may have a discriminatory effect (on fathers) upon the breakup of the relationship.*[26]

When other factors were considered the analysis contributed to underpinning the notion *that the foundations for continued parenting after divorce and the*

---

24 The analysis showed that the mentioned variables together with the father's educational level (fathers with a higher education have a greater possibility of obtaining joint parental authority at birth) may contribute to an understanding of cohabitating parents' choice in respect of parental authority (joint/sole).

25 While married parents held joint parental authority *ex lege* only 60% of former cohabitants held joint parental authority during the cohabitation

26 However, the analysis in itself could not demonstrate this connection since other factors must be taken into account.

breakup of a relationship are founded through the social (de facto) *practices in the families at the time of birth.* The relevant factors for continued parenting were the duration of cohabitation with the child, the socio-economic conditions of the father, social vulnerability, an uneven distribution of care and violence.

'When the child becomes a field of conflict'

This part of the research focused upon the group of children who became the object of a legal conflict concerning parental authority or contact. First the research data concerning parental authority are presented.

Parental authority:

The table below shows how parental authority was distributed (including both agreements and decisions) in relation to the parents' level of agreement/disagreement.[27]

Table 4

	Parental authority at the time of the breakup		
Level of agreement	Joint p.a.	Sole p.a.	Total
Complete agreement	61	39	60
Predominat Agreement	44	56	9
Predominant Disagreement	35	63	3
Complete disagreement	25	75	11
The question was not raised	25	75	17

In the first place, it may be determined that the majority of parents (more than two thirds) agree upon the distribution of parental authority. While the majority chose joint parental authority there was also a considerable amount of parents who agreed to an allocation of sole parental authority (39%).

In the second place, it may be determined that 14% of the parents had disagreed on the allocation of parental authority. Amongst the parents who completely disagreed one fourth ended up with joint parental authority, which must be taken to indicate that joint parental authority is used as a means to settle a dispute rather than constitute a positive choice.

27 Concerning a total of 525 children.

Thirdly, it may be determined that in one in six cases the matter of distribution was not discussed at all. This primarily concerned cases where the result was an allocation of sole parental authority (75%). Several reasons were given for this, such as: the mother held sole parental authority during cohabitation, the family had been based upon a fragile foundation and a connection with other social problems, for example, the father's drug abuse.

The research further showed that the distribution of parental authority had been the subject of a legal dispute before the courts in approximately 7% of cases.[28] The analysis showed that four independent factors were relevant statistically. In the first place, legal disputes arose more frequently in families where the father received social security payments. In the second place, legal disputes emerged less frequently if the mother had held sole parental authority during cohabitation. Finally, the analysis showed that a legal dispute arose more frequently if the reason for the breakup had been the father's infidelity or the father had been guilty of mental violence towards the mother. The analysis thus points to the fact that legal disputes arise because of relational factors.

Summations and conclusions

The analysis shows that a majority of children (approximately three quarters) who have contact with the non-resident parent have parents who co-operate without substantial differences. However, approximately 10% of children have parents with seriously strained co-operation problems. In between those two groups are children whose parents have some difficulties and children without contact.

Further, the analysis showed that the type of conflict which led to a judicial decision was connected with the relational problems of the parents. In this connection the research also showed *a lack of any connection*. The analysis could not substantiate the hypothesis that conflicts are related to the modern perception of the 'father role' since conflicts occur with the same frequency whether or not the father had participated in the care of the young child.

The analysis also showed that the lack of parental authority between fathers and children from birth restrict the number of conflicts concerning parental authority possibly because these fathers tend to 'give up' in advance. However, the legal construction of joint or sole parental authority was not decisive for the emergen-

28 In principle 9%, but in some cases the legal dispute did not concern the allocation of parental authority. It generally related to other aspects of the divorce.

ce of a conflict as to contact at a later stage. The determining factor was whether the parents had agreed upon the construction.

The analysis did not point to the fact that conflicts are rooted in increased 'rights consciousness amongst modern and caring yet rightless fathers'. Rather, the analysis points to the fact that the number of absent fathers and the amount of legal cases concerning parental authority and contact have been constant since the 1980s and that the reported increases in the total number of legal cases has to do with the fact that the minority group of parents who have legal disputes repeatedly initiate proceedings.

The impression that 'rights consciousness' amongst fathers has increased may therefore have other explanations such as the angle provided by the media coverage of 'the child as a victim', 'the dispute concerning the child' or 'the individual's fight against the family law system.' Furthermore:

> 'The family political aims concerning childrens' rights for both parents become extremely easily confused with the parents' right to the children. A confusion which, to a large degree, is created by interest organisations. This confusion, however, is also caused by the fact that there is a lack of any substantial discussion on and an agenda for what the child's right actually is and should be'.

IV.3. CONTACT

The legal, political and sociological discussions on contact in the Netherlands and Denmark as well as internationally can be seen as reflecting the same basic question: whether contact is always in the best interests of children also in cases where parental conflict or other detrimental aspects hamper such contact.

Yet the discussions also reflect some differences, which perhaps may overall be explained by the fact that family forms at the empirical level have been more individualised for a longer period and the fact that contact has been a right of the parent for a longer period of time in Danish law strongly influenced by the notion of 'the right to two parents.'

IV.3.1. MAIN DEMOGRAPHICS

While legal parents currently have a right to contact in both countries, there seems to have been some differences in the percentages of children who actually have factual contact with the non-resident parent after divorce. In the Netherlands the percentage of children who have no contact with the non-resident parent has decreased from approximately 25% in 1998[29] to approximately 17% in 2006.[30]

In Denmark there are no recent research results relating only to the post-divorce situation. Research includes children in single-parent families and children whose parents have divorced (after co-habitation or marriage). This research indicates that approximately 13% of children have no contact with the non-resident parent. This percentage has remained steady over the past 20-25 years and the main reason for the lack of contact is considered to be that the non-resident parent does not actually exercise his right to contact.[31]

IV.3.2. DUTCH PERSPECTIVES ON CONTACT

Dutch discussions on contact may be viewed to reflect three aspects: until recently a relatively large percentage of children (25%) did not have any contact with the non-resident parent; the perception that the enforcement of contact orders often does not take place; and the fact that there is a perceived lack of support possibilities, for example with respect to supervised contact.[32]

SPRUIJT concluded in 2002 that contact frequency between a non-resident parent and a child is not generally connected to children's well-being. When there are high levels of conflict, contact has a negative effect upon children.[33]

Consequently SPRUIJT recommends that a range of measures be employed in order to support contact, such as mediation, research and supervised contact.[34]

---

29 Spruijt, 2007, supra, p. 18 with reference to A. de Graaf, 'Onder moeders paraplu. Ervaringen van kinderen met relaties na echtscheiding', *Demos*, No. 17, 2001, p. 33-37.

30 Spruijt, 2007, supra, p. 19 with reference to the Conamore studies, Utrecht University 2006, Kinder- en Jeugdstudies.

31 M. Heide Ottosen (Contact and the well-being of children), 2004, supra, p. 7.

32 The pending proposal on 'Continued Parenting' has developed in the course of parliamentary proceedings concerning contact, Chapter II.2.6.2.

33 E. Spruijt, *Het verdeelde kind*, Utrecht, 2002, p. 51.

34 E. Spruijt, 2002, supra, p. 86-89.

IV.3.3. DANISH PERSPECTIVES ON CONTACT

The political debate on contact diversified in Denmark after the 1996 legislation. While the perception of the difficult position of the non-resident parent is also present in Denmark, an increasing critical focus has been directed towards Danish contact practices. Since the end of the 1990s private and public organisations aiming to promote the interests of children have become increasingly concerned with the Danish regulation of contact[35] and a private interest organisation concerned only with the interests of the child in relation to contact has emerged.[36]

This concern was voiced by a politician who had previously strongly supported Danish contact practices in the parliamentary debate:

> 'How can we improve it and to a greater extent secure the child's welfare? That is what we wanted last time, in particular with the major changes in 1996, and I actually thought we all felt that we had completed our task. We had taken the right steps and we thought they were good. But I must admit that something has developed differently. Something is wrong; we hear about situations that should not happen.'[37]

As a consequence of this criticism the Danish Minister of Justice initiated two sociological studies aimed at inventorying the Danish regulation of contact in 2001. In 2004 two reports emerged. One report was based upon the child survey data[38] and aimed to provide perspectives on contact generally.[39] The second report contained an analysis of legal constructions of 'the child's best interests' concerning 75 contact cases involving a major conflict.[40] This report raised serious concerns. The new Danish Act on Parental Responsibility aims, amongst

---

35 For example, *Børns Vilkår* and *Børnerådet;* the last mentioned had a representative in the 2006 Commission. This representative, together with the sociologist M. Heide Ottosen, formed a minority opinion against the proposal that joint parental authority could be established against the wishes of one parent.

36 *Landsforeningen Børn og Samvær.*

37 Lissa Mathiesen (Social democrat) taken from; B. Boserup and H. R. Hansen, *Samværsklemmen*, Copenhagen: Gyldendal, 2003, p. 61.

38 Above Section IV.1. supra note 2 and Section IV.2.2.

39 M. Heide Ottosen (Contact and the well-being of children), 2004, supra.

40 M. Heide Ottosen (Contact in the best interests of the child), 2004, supra.

other things, to redress this criticism by adopting a more 'child-centred perspective'.[41]

The first report concluded overall that contact is relatively uncomplicated for two-thirds of children, including children with normal contact (every other week), extended contact and share arrangements (shared residences).[42] One-third of children had experienced problems with contact and one-quarter of children had been the subject of a contact case at the regional state administration.

HEIDE OTTOSEN concluded that the number of children who do not suffer negative consequences and who are content with the contact is highest when both parents agree that contact works well, when the contact parent participates in the daily care, when the child can influence the contact arrangement and when there have never been any serious disputes over contact.

On the other hand, the study concerning 75 major conflict cases raised concerns.[43] The data showed that a complicated dispute over contact generally concerned children below the age of eight, took about two years to pass through the administrative system and involved an average of 5 decisions. Some cases, however, contained more than 20 decisions and extended almost throughout most of the minor's childhood. The parents' seldom held joint parental authority and upon the conclusion of the case one-third of the children no longer had any contact with the non-resident parent.

The data suggested that in approximately 60% of the cases there were signs of social marginalisation indicating that families involved in family legal disputes deviate markedly from the average population and this is consistent with other Scandinavian research.

The cases could overall be divided into the following main categories: disputes concerning the extent and details of contact; the unstabile contact parent, violent behaviour towards the resident parent; violence against the child; incest; the

41 The new Act has nonetheless been substantially criticised by the named organisations because the good intentions concerning a 'child-centred perspective' which were initially proposed by the 2006 Commission have given way to a strong equality principle between parents in the amended Act; see the considerations to be found on www.boernsvilkaar.dk.

42 Slightly more negative factors were registered with respect to share arrangements than for children with normal and extended contact. Share arrangements are generally practised by the socio-economically strongest part of the population, M. Heide Ottosen (Contact and the well-being of children), 2004, supra, p. 21.

43 M. Heide Ottosen (Contact in the best interests of the child), 2004, supra, p. 210-221.

unknown father and contact frustration. The research could not confirm the notion that there are many cases of contact frustration. Only 1 out of the 75 cases concerned a situation where the resident parent could be considered to frustrate contact without any apparent reason.

Children were involved differently in the various types of cases. The research showed that the age of 12 seemed to have a distinct function. In these cases the proceedings were concluded quickly because the authorities accepted the child's wish not to have contact. However, younger children from the age of 5 or 6 were heard on a number of occasions before a decision was made.

PART II
THE COMPARISON OF DUTCH AND DANISH LAW AND THE CEFL PRINCIPLES

CHAPTER V
THE ALLOCATION OF PARENTAL AUTHORITY

V.1. INTRODUCTION

This Chapter provides a description and comparison of Dutch and Danish law and the CEFL principles concerning the allocation of parental authority and further takes account of relevant features of the pending Dutch reforms.[1] The Chapter covers the initial allocation, the allocation upon divorce and the break-up of the relationship and subsequent changes (reallocation). Further, it addresses two specific matters concerning the allocation of parental authority. The first is the possibility for a parent who holds sole parental authority to obtain joint parental authority together with a non-parent, for example, with the parent's new partner. The second concerns the allocation of parental authority after a parent's death.

The division between the subject-matter of this Chapter and that of Chapter VI, which concerns the establishment of residence and relocation, and Chapter VII, which concerns the content and subsequent exercise of parental authority, is predominantly a practical division, which to some extent is reflected in the national laws of the Netherlands and Denmark and in the CEFL principles.[2]

This Chapter is further divided into the following main Sections:

1. Section V.2. describes and compares some systemic features of the law concerning the distinction between holding and exercising, the persons who may hold or exercise parental authority as well as the connection between parental authority and child protection measures.

---

[1] The primary features of these reforms have been deliberated in Chapter II, Section II.2.6. There are no pending Danish reforms. Danish law has been substantially revised with the Act on Parental Responsibility entering into force on 01.10.2007, Chapter II, Section II.3.

[2] The distinction between holding and exercising is addressed below, Section V.2.1.

2. Section V.3. describes and compares the initial allocation of parental authority to parents who are married or have been married and the allocation of parental authority to unmarried parents.
3. Section V.4. describes and compares the law which regulates the allocation of joint parental authority in connection with divorce or the breakup of a relationship (the choice between joint parental authority and sole parental authority).
4. Section V.5. describes and compares the law which regulates a subsequent change in the allocation of joint parental authority in Dutch and Danish law (the choice between joint parental authority and sole parental authority).
5. Section V.6. describes and compares the allocation of sole parental authority to one parent and the reallocation of sole parental authority at a later stage in Dutch and Danish law (the choice of a parent).
6. Section V.7. describes and compares the possibility of one parent to obtain joint parental authority together with a non-parent.
7. Section V.8. describes and compares the allocation of parental authority following the resident parent's death.
8. Section V.9. *portrays* and compares the relevance of a private agreement in the national law of the Netherlands and Denmark.

V.2. MAIN SYSTEMIC FEATURES

Certain general features of the law on parental authority may be deemed to be systemic in the sense that they have a bearing upon the concept of parental authority and/or the system in which decisions on parental authority are made. In the first subsection the difference between the terminology of holding and exercising is addressed. The subsequent Section addresses the persons who may hold parental authority, thereby covering the question of which persons may do so, the number of persons who can do this and their capacity. Finally, the connection between parental authority and child protection measures is addressed.

V.2.1. TO HOLD AND TO EXERCISE

V.2.1.1. The Netherlands: To exercise

Dutch law contains an implicit distinction between the holding and the exercising of parental authority.[3] The term *exercise* is generally used to describe the situation where a parent holds or is allocated parental authority. Two married parents consequently *exercise* joint parental authority during marriage and after divorce.[4] The unmarried mother exercises parental authority *ex lege* or the unmarried parents, pursuant to the registration of a joint request in the Custody Register, *jointly exercise* parental authority.[5] Further, in relation to child protection measures a parent who exercises joint parental authority together with the other parent may be discharged from *exercising* this parental authority.[6]

This terminology indicates, although not expressed directly in the relevant provisions, that joint parental authority is vested in married parents and in unmarried parents who have registered a joint request in the Custody Register. If a parent who jointly exercises parental authority is discharged from doing so, the discharged parent retains parental authority without being able to exercise it.[7] However, in the situation where a parent is allocated sole parental authority, for example, upon divorce or upon the breakup of a relationship, the other parent no longer retains parental authority since not only the exercise of that authority but the parental authority as a whole is vested in this one parent.[8]

The origins of the distinction between holding and exercising parental authority in the legislative framework may be traced back to the 1901 Civil Children Act and before this to the Dutch Civil Code of 1838 where the distinction was relevant because married parents held joint parental authority, but only the father exercised parental authority.[9]

---

3 E.A.A. Luijten, *Het Nederlandse personen- en familierecht*, part 1, Deventer: W.E.J. Tjeenk Willink, 1997, p. 112.

4 Art. 251, DCC.

5 Art. 253b(1) and 252(1), DCC.

6 Art. 274(1), DCC.

7 J. de Boer, *Asser's Handleiding tot de beoefening van het Nederlands Burgerlijk Recht, Personen en Familierecht*, Deventer: Kluwer, 2006, p. 758 (hereafter referred to as ASSER-DE BOER, 2006).

8 Art. 252(2) and 253n(1), DCC.

9 Chapter II, Sections II.2.1. and II.2.2.

Furthermore, the general dispute settlement provision contained in Article 253a provides for access to the courts in relation to all disputes between the holders of parental authority in respect of the *exercise* of parental authority. Consequently, Dutch law considers the holding of parental authority to be something different from the exercising of parental authority. Even though the distinction is only implicit and not always consistent, the distinction is still made.

V.2.1.2. Denmark: To hold

Danish law does not make a distinction between holding and exercising parental authority.[10] Danish law provides three main types of decisions in respect of parents who do not live together: (1) the allocation of parental authority, (2) the establishment of residence, and (3) a decision on contact.

V.2.1.3. The CEFL principles: Holding and exercising

The CEFL principles concerning parental responsibilities draw a very distinct line between the holding of parental responsibilities and the exercising thereof. Paramount to the understanding of this distinction are three notions.

The first general notion is that once parental responsibilities belong to a person, this person 'cannot divest him or herself of the whole package of rights and duties'.[11] Secondly, that it is possible to have parental responsibilities without exercising them.[12] Thirdly, that the termination of joint parental responsibilities is not viewed as a means to solve disputes between the holders. Rather, the principles provide the possibility for the discharge (wholly or partly) of parental responsibilities to apply only in exceptional cases. These cases may pertain to situations involving fault or behaviour which adversely affects the child.[13] Disputes between the holders may be alternatively solved by dividing the exercise of parental responsibilities or deciding the dispute.[14]

---

10 Since the 1922 Act. Before this Act parents held joint parental authority, but according to the so-called law of the principal, the father was supreme and could decide where the wife and children should live during the marriage; the father could thus be viewed as exercising parental authority, Chapter II, Section II.3.1.

11 Principles, Introduction, p. 14.

12 Principles, principle 3:15, p. 100. Principle 3:13, p. 91, 3:14, p. 95.

13 Principles, principle 3:33, Comment 1, p. 216.

14 Principles, principle 3:14, p. 95.

The distinction between holding and exercising in the CEFL principles is viewed as a means to provide a modern and comprehensive conceptual framework, which, amongst other things, allows for the attribution of parental responsibilities to third persons[15] and which also allows for a concrete division of the exercise of parental authority between the parents.

V.2.1.4. Comparison: Holding and exercising

The distinction (in the Netherlands and the CEFL principles) or the lack of a distinction (in Denmark) between the holding and the exercising of parental authority may be viewed as providing technically different solutions in respect of a conceptual development of parental authority, which Chapter II has already revealed to have become fragmented. A few points can, however, be made. While the distinction in the CEFL principles is regarded as providing a comprehensive and modern conceptual framework, the origins of such a distinction in Dutch and Danish law seem to be related to the subservient position of the mother who previously yielded the exercise of parental authority to the father. Furthermore, the CEFL principles provide the distinction to allow for attribution to third parties. This distinction is neither relevant to Dutch nor Danish law in relation to allocation to third persons because Dutch law generally provides for the *exercise*[16] of parental authority also in respect of third persons and Danish law relies upon the *transfer*[17] of parental authority.[18]

Finally, it should be noted that the notion that a person 'cannot divest him or herself of the whole package of rights and duties' does not apply in Danish law where parents who do not live together are free to allocate sole parental authority to one parent whereby the whole 'package of rights and duties' inherent in the concept of parental authority is lost.[19]

15 Principles, principles 3:9, 3:17. International instruments p. 66-67, Comment 1, p. 114.

16 For example, Art. 253t, DCC.

17 Art. 13(2), Act on Parental Responsibility.

18 It should be noted that the CEFL principles do not rely upon a common core in relation to the conceptual framework, Principles, International Instruments p. 66 and Comments p. 76-78.

19 Below, Sections V.3.–V.5. Rights and duties inherent to parentage, for example, the duty to pay maintenance and the right to contact continue to exist in both Dutch and Danish law, Chapter VII, Section VII.4.1. and Chapter VIII, Section VIII.2.1.

V.2.2. PERSONS

V.2.2.1. The Netherlands

In Dutch law parental authority can only be exercised by two persons at most. The exercise of parental authority is generally reserved for legal parents.[20] There is, however, a possibility for parental authority to be jointly exercised by one legal parent and a non-parent and this is deliberated below.[21] Non-parents and legal institutions may be allocated guardianship.

The exercise of parental authority *ex lege* or pursuant to a court order in Dutch law depends upon the capacity to exercise parental authority. This implies that a minor parent, a parent whose mental capacity is diminished (more than just temporarily)[22] or a parent who has been discharged or suspended of parental authority cannot exercise parental authority.[23]

V.2.2.2. Denmark

In Danish law parental authority can only be exercised by two persons at most. The concept of parental authority is not reserved for legal parents. Parental authority may also be transferred to a legal parent and the parent's spouse and to a non-parent or two married non-parents.[24]

Danish law has no formal conditions for the allocation of parental authority. The age of majority is not a condition for the allocation of parental authority.[25] If the holder or both holders of parental authority are temporarily prevented from making decisions concerning the child's person, the Regional State Administra-

---

20 An exception is that joint parental authority may apply when a child is born during a registered partnership or marriage between two partners of the same (two female partners) or opposite sexes where one of the partners is not the legal parent and where the child has no legal ties with another parent, Art. 253sa, DCC.

21 Section V.7.1.

22 Art. 246, DCC. A minor woman may be declared to be of full age if she has reached the age of 16, Art. 253ha, DCC.

23 Title 14, Section 5, DCC and Articles 253q and 253r, DCC.

24 Art. 13(2), Act on Parental Responsibility.

25 A minor will, however, be subject to parental authority unless he/she has entered into a marriage, Art. 1(1), Guardianship Act, Værgemålsloven, Act. No. 388 of 14.06.1995 with later amendments.

tion may appoint a new holder of parental authority for the duration of the period during which the holder(s) is/are prevented from doing so.[26]

V.2.2.3. The CEFL principles

From the comments to the CEFL principles it may be derived that parental responsibilities may be held by more than two persons depending, however, upon national law.[27] Parental responsibilities are not reserved for legal parents. Non-parents may be attributed with parental responsibilities instead of or in addition to the parents.[28]

The CEFL principles do not contain formal capacity requirements. A discharge of parental responsibilities is, however, also possible in situations not involving fault and a third person may be attributed with parental responsibilities.[29]

V.2.2.4. Comparison: persons

Dutch and Danish law provide that a maximum of two persons may hold or exercise joint parental authority while the CEFL principles provide for the possibility of parental responsibilities to be attributed to more than two persons depending, however, upon national law.

Only Dutch law has specific capacity requirements for the exercise of parental authority. Neither Danish law nor the CEFL principles have such requirements.

V.2.3. CHILD PROTECTION MEASURES

V.2.3.1. The Netherlands

The law on child protection measures is regulated in Title 14 of the Dutch Civil Code and may be viewed as belonging to private law.[30] A child protection measure in Dutch law may discharge a parent of parental authority voluntarily or this may be enforced through a court decision.[31] The most common child

---

26 Art. 25, Act on Parental Responsibility.
27 Principles, principle 3:2, Comment 1, p. 33.
28 Principles, principle 3:9, p. 66.
29 Principles, principle 3:9, p. 66 and 3:32, p. 212.
30 Although the function of the Dutch Child Protection Board in such cases may be viewed as pertaining to administrative (public) law, ASSER-DE BOER, 2006, supra, p. 639.
31 Book 1, Title 14, Section 5, DCC.

protection measure, the supervision order, does not, however, discharge parent(s) of parental authority.[32] The District courts have the competence to make decisions in cases concerning child protection measures as well as in cases pertaining to the allocation of parental authority. The fact that the District courts have jurisdiction in both types of cases means that the distinction between the two is not always distinct.[33]

V.2.3.2. Denmark

Child protection measures in Danish law, whether voluntary or enforced, do not formally discharge the holder(s) of parental authority although they are directed collectively at the holder(s) and the child.[34] The limitations in the factual exercise of parental authority, which a care order may invoke, for example, the right to determine the child's residence, depends upon the content of the care order.[35] In Danish law child protection measures are regulated in the field of social (public) law and parental authority in the field of family (private) law.[36] The competence to make decisions in these two separate fields of law is also distinctly different. Child protection decisions are made by a standing committee under the auspices of the local government while the competence to take decisions in the field of parental authority is split between the regional state administrations and the ordinary courts. There is consequently a sharp distinction between civil and social cases.[37]

---

32 Book 1, Title 14, Section 4, DCC.

33 In a case where the Dutch Child Protection Board had sought to discharge the father of parental authority in connection with the risk of abduction, the District Court of Haarlem awarded sole parental authority to the mother instead of discharging the father, Rechtbank Haarlem (District Court) 26.07.2005, LJN AU0323. Further, the courts may use the supervision order (the most common child protection measure) in contact cases, Chapter VIII, Section VIII.2.4.2.

34 J. Graversen and I. Koch Nielsen, *Fælles forældremyndighed ved separation og skilsmisse*, Copenhagen, Socialforskningsinstituttet, 1984, p. 21.

35 I. Lund Andersen, N. Munck, I. Nørgaard, *Familieret*, Copenhagen: Jurist- og Økonomforbundets Forlag, 2003, p. 111-120.

36 Before the Welfare Act of 1976 (*Bistandsloven*), now replaced by the Act on Social Services, the private law measure of *transferring* parental authority was applied in child protection cases.

37 A judge who has been a member of the Committee and has participated in decisions pertaining to child protection measures may not (depending on the extent of the measure) be able to hear a civil case concerning parental authority, Vestre Landsret (Western Appeal Court) 01.12.1995, *UFR* 1996.428V and 15.11.1991, *UFR* 1992.186V. The subject of an increase in co-operation and the exchange of information between the regional state administration and the social authorities concerning contact cases has been addressed in a research project resulting in the report: *Forsøgsprojekt om øget samarbejde mellem Kommune og Statsamt i sociale og familieretlige sager*, February 2004. See Chapter VIII, Section VIII.3.2.3. on the new approach

V.2.3.3. The CEFL principles

The CEFL principles contain the possibility for the competent authority to discharge, wholly or partly, a holder of parental responsibilities. Discharging is possible when there is behaviour involving fault, such as violent behaviour towards the child or the other parent, and when there is behaviour not involving fault, for example a long-term physical or mental illness which adversely affects the child. While the principles generally cover only private law excluding '*public welfare, intervention by the state (...), health law and the law regarding foster care*', they do nonetheless provide for the possibility to discharge.[38]

V.2.3.4. Comparison: child protection measures

In Dutch law and the CEFL principles the possibility to discharge a parent of parental authority/responsibilities is regulated within the ambit of the law concerning parental authority/responsibilities. Moreover, child protection measures in Dutch law are generally regulated in the field of private law albeit also with a public law function.[39] In contrast, child protection measures in Danish law are regulated separately in social (public) law.[40] The result is that the distinction between the regulation of parental authority and child protection measures is less sharp in Dutch law and in the CEFL principles than in Danish law.

V.3. THE INITIAL ALLOCATION OF PARENTAL AUTHORITY

The initial allocation of parental authority forms the cornerstone of this Section. For married parents this concerns, in particular, children born before the parents' marriage or after the parents' judicial separation or divorce in respect of the father's right to parental authority. For unmarried parents it concerns, in

concerning co-operation between social authorities and the regional state administration in contact cases.

38 Principles, introduction, p. 21-22 and principle 3:32 and Comment 2, p. 216.

39 The CEFL principles only regulate child protection measures to a limited extent.

40 The private law approach is shared by many continental civil code countries, K. Schweppe, 'Child protection in Europe: Different systems – Common challenges', *German Law Journal*, Vol. 3, No. 10, 2002. This system does not generally fit the 'Scandinavian model' (Denmark, Norway, Sweden) separating civil and social law. There has, however, been a development in Swedish law where the social authorities have been given an increasing role in civil cases, S. Danielsen, 2003, supra, p. 322 see also in respect of contact cases in Denmark, supra note 37.

particular, the unmarried father's right to parental authority. Chapter II has already revealed substantive differences between Dutch and Danish law. It was concluded that Danish law provides the unmarried father who has cohabited with the mother with more automatic rights in respect of parental authority[41] and that Dutch law relies upon an ascertainment of rights[42] in a judicial procedure when the parents have not agreed to an allocation of joint parental authority. The difference was seen to be indicative of a stronger validation of the institution of marriage in the Netherlands than in Denmark and consequently of a less individualistic approach.[43]

V.3.1. MARRIED PARENTS

V.3.1.1. The Netherlands

Married parents exercise joint parental authority during their marriage.[44] If the parents are judicially separated at the time of the birth of the child, they also exercise joint parental authority.[45] If the parents remarry and parental authority was exercised by one parent alone, joint parental authority is restored.[46]

The question whether the (legal) parents, according to Article 251(1), exercise joint parental authority or the mother exercises sole parental authority[47] in respect of a child that was born before the parents' marriage or after the parents' divorce has raised uncertainty in Dutch law pursuant to the changes in the law on parentage and the law on parental authority in 1998.[48] The wording of Article 251(1) is the following: 'During their marriage, the parents exercise joint parental authority'. It makes no reference to when (before or after the marriage) the child is born.[49] In the following, the legal situation of children born before the parents' marriage and after divorce will be described.

41 Danish law also provides the unmarried father with more automatic rights in respect of the establishment of paternity.

42 Dutch law also relies upon such an ascertainment of rights in a judicial procedure concerning the establishment of paternity.

43 Chapter II, Section II.4.5.

44 Art. 251(1), DCC.

45 Art. 251(1) in connection with Art. 251(2), DCC.

46 Art. 253(1), DCC.

47 Pursuant to Art. 253b(1), DCC.

48 Chapter II, Section II.2.4.

49 Before 1998 Art. 246 of the old DCC provided that (legal) parents exercised joint parental authority over their children thus including children born before the parents' marriage. Children born within 307 days after the marriage were legitimate and the parents thus had joint parental authority, Art. 197 old, DCC.

Children born before the parents' marriage

Initially, the District courts dealt differently with the situation of children born before the parents' marriage. The Leeuwarden and Alkmaar District Courts found that the (legal) parents exercised joint parental authority by virtue of the marriage.[50] The Rotterdam District Court came to the opposite conclusion. The reasoning of the Rotterdam District Court was as follows:

> 'The intention of the legislature in 1998 was to abolish the difference between legitimate and illegitimate children. The result is that unmarried parents must record an agreement on joint parental authority in the Custody Register to acquire joint parental authority, regardless of a subsequent marriage.'[51]

VONK[52] has convincingly argued that it follows from the explanatory notes to the Act that parents exercise joint parental authority over children born before the parents' marriage by virtue of the marriage, when the child has been recognised by the father. In its decision of 23 August 2006 The Hague Court of Appeal reversed the above-mentioned decision of the Rotterdam District Court so that the parents exercised joint parental authority by virtue of the marriage. In its decision the Court did not rely specifically on the point that the father had recognised the child as opposed to the judicial establishment of paternity.

It remains unclear whether joint parental authority is established by virtue of the marriage when paternity is established judicially as opposed to the situation where the father has recognised the child. The combination of judicial establishment and a subsequent marriage is not an entirely impossible combination considering that judicial establishment may be sought by the mother or the child for reasons other than the father's resistance to the establishment of paternity, for example because judicial establishment has retroactive effect while recognition does not.[53]

---

50 Rechtbank Leeuwarden 15.02.2006, LJN AV5268, Rechtbank Alkmaar 16.02.2006, LJN AV2146.

51 Rechtbank Rotterdam 11.10.2005, LJN AU4409.

52 M. Vonk, 'Voorkinderen en gezamenlijk gezag door huwelijk', *WPNR*, 2006, No. 6671, p. 457-459. Coppens, however, is uncertain on this point, H.P. Coppens, 'Is door huwelijk gezamenlijk gezag ontstaan?', *EB*, 2002, No. 7-8, p. 103-105.

53 Art. 207(5) and 203(2), DCC.

Children born after divorce

If the parents are divorced at the time of birth it is also unclear whether the parents exercise joint parental authority. The 's-Hertogenbosch Court of Appeal decided on 13 January 2005[54] that parents exercised joint parental authority in respect of a child born in 1994 within 307 days after the parents' divorce because of its status as a legitimate child pursuant to Article 197 of the old Dutch Civil Code. According to the present regulation there is no presumption of paternity when parents are divorced and the paternity must be established through recognition or judicially.[55] If paternity is established it is unclear whether the parents exercise joint parental authority. On the one hand, Article 251(1) prescribes that the parents exercise joint parental authority '*during their marriage*'. On the other hand, Article 253b of the Dutch Civil Code, which regulates parental authority in respect of a child where only maternity is established or the parents are not married, applies only when the parents are not married '*and have not been married*'.

The possibility to obtain joint parental authority

If Article 251(1) of the Dutch Civil Code is to be understood as providing that children born before the parents' marriage where paternity has been established judicially and children born after divorce are not subject to joint parental authority then the situation formally arises that the parents cannot obtain joint parental authority (in the case of children born before the marriage only after the marriage has been celebrated).[56] This situation seems to be an unintended result of ill-coordinated legislation rather than an explicit choice by the legislature. Further, it does not very well correspond with the developments in case law allowing one parent to request joint parental authority based upon Article 8 of the ECHR and upon the notion that it should always be possible to reassess whether joint parental authority is possible.[57]

---

54 Gerechtshof 's-Hertogenbosch, LJN AS2624.

55 Art. 199(1) e.c., DCC.

56 Art. 252(1), DCC concerns the recording of a joint request in the Custody register. This provision applies only to parents who are unmarried and have never been married. Art. 253o, DCC provides that in cases of changed circumstances the parents may apply to the court to reobtain joint parental authority. This provision only applies to parents who have previously exercised joint parental authority.

57 Chapter III, Section III.3.3. and M. Vonk, 2006, supra, p. 457-459. The Gerechtshof 's-Hertogenbosch (Court of Appeal) 04.06.2002, LJN AE4053 disregarded the formal requirement in Art. 253o(1) of a joint request in a case where the mother had informally agreed to the reallocation of joint parental authority on the basis of Art. 8, ECHR.

Pending legislation to rectify this situation
A pending legislative proposal aims to create the possibility to record a joint request in the Custody Register for parents who have previously been married and have not exercised joint parental authority.[58]

V.3.1.2. Denmark

If the parents are married at the time of birth or marry later, they have joint parental authority.[59] This provision applies to legal parents and irrespective of the manner in which paternity is established. If the parents are judicially separated at the time of the birth, the mother has sole parental authority unless the husband is the legal father (irrespective of the manner in which paternity is established), the parents have made a statement to the effect that they will care for and be responsible for the child (the care and responsibility statement)[60] or have entered into an agreement on joint parental authority.[61] In case the parents remarry and sole parental authority is held by one parent, joint parental authority is restored.

Children born after the parents divorce
If the (now divorced) legal parents were married in the period prior to ten months before the birth of the child they have joint parental authority irrespective of the manner in which the paternity is established.[62] Danish law consequently currently places emphasis not only upon the marital status at birth, but also upon the previous marital status for the duration of the conception period.

V.3.1.3. The CEFL principles

The CEFL principles provide that parents whose legal parentage has been established hold joint parental responsibilities. This principle has been chosen, based among other things, on the notion that a common core exists on the point that parental responsibilities are '*a consequence of affiliation*'.[63]

58 Parliamentary proceedings 2004/2005 (*Kamerstukken*), 29 353, No. 8, p. 2.
59 Art. 6(1), Act on Parental responsibility.
60 A care and responsibility statement is a paternity registration procedure, Chapter II, Section II.3.4.1.
61 Art. 6(2) of the Act on Parental Responsibility. According to the law prior to the 2007 Act, the mother held sole parental authority for children born after a judicial separation.
62 Art. 6(3) of the Act on Parental Responsibility. According to the law prior to the 2007 Act, the mother held sole parental authority for children born after the divorce.
63 Principles, principle 3:8, p. 59, Comment 4, p. 65.

V.3.1.4. Comparison: married parents

The CEFL principles provide that parental responsibilities are a consequence of established parentage and the parents' marital status is consequently irrelevant for the allocation of parental authority. Neither Dutch nor Danish law provides that parental authority is solely a consequence of parentage.

The main rule in Dutch and Danish law is that married parents hold or exercise joint parental authority. This also applies if the parents are judicially separated at the time of birth. Further, it applies to children born before the legal parents' marriage although it is uncertain in Dutch law if it applies to a child born before the parents' marriage where paternity has been judicially established.[64]

If the child is born after the parents' divorce, the legal parents hold joint parental authority in Danish law if they were married ten months prior to the birth of the child,[65] while it is unclear whether the parents exercise joint parental authority or the mother exercises sole parental authority in this situation in Dutch law.

While neither Dutch nor Danish law provides for joint parental authority to be a consequence of established parentage, Danish law has changed in this respect and has expanded the scope of joint parental authority with the 2007 Act. The general rule is now that legal parents hold joint parental authority also when the child is born after the parents have obtained a judicial separation or divorce as opposed to the law prior to the 2007 Act. This corresponds with the tendency towards joint parental authority as a general legal norm.[66]

In contrast, Dutch law pursuant to the 1995 Act concerning parental authority and the 1998 Act concerning parentage could be understood, due to the wording '*during their marriage*' in the relevant provision, to have limited the scope of joint parental authority, which would be inconsistent with the development where joint parental authority has increasingly become the legal norm. The initial uncertainty has, however, been redressed by case law providing for joint parental authority in respect of children born before the parents' marriage. For children born before the parents' marriage where paternity has been established judicially and for children born after divorce the situation remains uncertain.

---

64 A pending proposal intends to make it possible to record a joint request for joint parental authority in this situation.

65 Or agree to the allocation of joint parental authority.

66 Chapter II, Section II.4.3.

V.3.2. UNMARRIED PARENTS

V.3.2.1. The Netherlands

Legal parents who have never been married to each other or exercised joint parental authority[67] over their minor children will exercise joint parental authority if they have recorded a joint request to do so in the Custody Register administered by the District courts.[68] Such a request will be denied if either or both of the parents lack the necessary capacity to exercise joint parental authority, have been discharged of parental authority, custody has been entrusted to a guardian, a specific provision pertaining to the custody of the child has ceased to exist[69] or the parent who has parental authority exercises it jointly with a person other than a parent.[70] If no agreement has been registered the mother exercises sole parental authority *ex lege.*[71]

The joint exercise of parental authority by unmarried parents is thus consensus-based.[72] A recent development, however, is that the courts have declared a sole request for joint parental authority by a legal parent to be admissible based upon Article 8 of the ECHR. These requests have all originated from unmarried fathers who did not or no longer cohabited with the mother.[73] In this case the Supreme Court has ruled that the relevant criterion for the allocation of joint parental authority depends on a balancing of interests based upon Article 8 of the ECHR.[74]

The pending legislative proposal enacting the possibility to make a sole request for joint parental authority[75] mentions only the present criterion of the relevant

---

67 If the parents have previously exercised joint parental authority it is possible to submit a joint request to the courts, Art. 253(1), DCC.

68 Art. 252(1), DCC.

69 For example, if the guardian has died or the mother is a minor.

70 Art. 252(2), DCC.

71 Art. 253b(1), DCC.

72 S.F.M. Wortmann advocated joint exercise *ex lege* in her inaugural speech '*Als een eigen kind*', 1998, p. 10. This was considered by the legislature, however, and it was found to go too far, Parliamentary Proceedings (*Kamerstukken*) 2000/2001, 27 047, No. 12, p. 1.

73 Chapter III, Section III.3.3.

74 Hoge Raad 27.05.2005, LJN AS7054. In an earlier decision by the Subdistrict Court of Zwolle the father was allocated joint parental authority based upon the best interests of the child, Sector Kanton Rechtbank Zwolle 24.02.2005, LJN AS7567.

75 Chapter II, Section II.2.6.1.

provision in Article 253c which is '*that the application must be desirable in the best interests of the child*'.[76]

V.3.2.2. Denmark

Unmarried (legal) parents have joint parental authority *ex lege* if they have cohabited during a period of 10 months prior to the birth of the child and paternity has been established (irrespective of the manner in which paternity is established).[77] This also applies to parents who, before the birth of the child, have broken off their relationship and ceased to cohabit. Furthermore, unmarried parents hold joint parental authority if paternity has been established in the most common paternity registration procedure (the care and responsibility statement) or they have entered into an agreement on joint parental authority.[78]

In other situations the mother holds sole parental authority *ex lege*. However, the legal father may at any time request the court to allocate joint parental authority.[79] This possibility was laid down in the 2007 reform in connection with changes pertaining to the possibility of allocating joint parental authority against the wishes of one parent.[80] The criterion of this provision is the general best interests criterion contained in Article 4 of the Act. In the notes to the Act it is mentioned that it is relevant why the parent does not hold parental authority, the relationship between the parent and the child is also relevant and further reference is made to the criterion for the termination of joint parental authority: the '*weighty grounds*' criterion.[81]

---

76 Chapter II.2.6.1. and Parliamentary proceedings (*Kamerstukken*) 2004/2005, 29353, No. 8, p. 2-3. However, in an amendment to the above-mentioned proposal, raised by private members of parliament, it is proposed to apply the 'torn or lost' criterion also in this situation, Parliamentary proceedings (*Kamerstukken*) 2004/2005, 29 353, No. 10.

77 Based upon information derived from the Central Personal Register (*Folkeregisteret*). There are no minimum requirements concerning the duration of the cohabitation, L 133, Comments to § 7.

78 Art. 7, Act on Parental Responsibility.

79 Art. 14(1), Act on Parental Responsibility.

80 It has been reported that a 'boom' in cases may be expected after 01.10.2007 when the Act on Parental Responsibility enters into force as parents (primarily fathers) who do not hold parental authority or have previously 'lost' parental authority will request a new decision. There is serious concern that the courts will become overloaded with 'old' cases, *Politiken*, 25.09.2007.

81 L 133, comment to § 14. The 'weighty grounds' criterion is deliberated below, Section V.4.6.

V.3.2.3. The CEFL principles

As deliberated above the CEFL principles provide that parental responsibilities are a consequence of established parentage.[82] Consequently, the Principles place no emphasis on marital status and unmarried legal parents hold joint parental authority *ex lege*.

V.3.2.4. Comparison: unmarried parents

Neither Dutch nor Danish law provides that parental authority is a consequence of established parentage such as the CEFL principles. Danish law has, however, expanded the scope for joint parental authority with the 2007 Act providing that the vast majority of unmarried (legal) parents will hold joint parental authority *ex lege* based primarily upon cohabitation.[83] Further, the most common paternity registration procedure results in joint parental authority. Dutch law, on the other hand, does not provide for the establishment of joint parental authority *ex lege*. The establishment of joint parental authority for unmarried parents remains consensus-based. The possibility of an ad hoc decision by the court in cases where the parents do not agree has, however, been developed in case law and is presently contained in a pending legislative proposal.

The differences may be viewed in relation to the conclusion in Chapter II.[84] It has been a matter of family policy in Denmark to treat unmarried cohabitating parents in the same way as married parents in relation to the establishment of parentage and the allocation of parental authority. The Act on parental responsibility from 2007 has cemented this development by providing for joint parental authority *ex lege* for cohabiting parents. Further, for unmarried parents, just as for married parents who divorce, it is the previous status (marriage/cohabitation) rather than the status at birth which is relevant. Dutch law in respect of the establishment of parentage as well as the establishment of joint parental authority relies upon an ad hoc decision by the court unless the parents agree upon such an establishment. This approach is indicative of a stronger validation of the formal relationship status in the Netherlands as in Denmark and consequently of a less individualistic approach.[85] Joint parental authority is consequently *the predefined substantive legal norm* for cohabiting parents in Danish law but not in Dutch law.

---

82 Above Section V.3.1.3.

83 Only approximately 4% of children are born to single mothers in Denmark, Chapter I.4.2.

84 Section II.4.5.

85 Chapter II, Section II.4.5.

V.4. AFTER DIVORCE AND THE BREAKUP OF A RELATIONSHIP

The historical background in Dutch and Danish law of the development in the allocation of parental authority after divorce and after the breakup of a relationship has been deliberated in Chapter II and the influence of human rights upon this development, in particular for Dutch law, has been discussed in Chapter III. The main rule in the Netherlands and Denmark is that joint parental authority continues after divorce or after the breakup of a relationship when the parents held or exercised joint parental authority prior thereto. This means that the allocation of parental authority only becomes an *intrinsic* element in the divorce procedure when a request for sole parental authority is made.[86]

The main theme of this Section is to describe the allocation of parental authority upon divorce or after the breakup of a relationship in the context of the choice between sole and joint parental authority. It is also intended to describe, compare and analyse the criteria determining the choice between joint and sole parental authority.[87]

V.4.1. THE NETHERLANDS

V.4.1.1. After divorce

The regulation is contained in Article 251(2) of the Dutch Civil Code. This provision provides that upon divorce parents 'continue to exercise joint parental authority unless the parents, or either one of them, request that parental authority over a child or children shall vest in only one of them in the best interests of the child.' From this provision it may be deduced that the allocation of sole parental authority to one parent requires a request from one or both parents and that such a request must be based upon the best interests of the child. Further, it has been established in case law that the courts are not bound by a request for sole parental authority.[88] This applies when the request is made by one parent,

86 However, in the Netherlands the courts may hear the child also when joint parental authority continues and further may issue an order *ex officio* when it appears that a minor aged twelve or older would appreciate this, Art. 251a, DCC, see further Chapter VIII, Section VIII.4.1. concerning the child's procedural rights.

87 The CEFL principles do not contain such a criterion as deliberated below in Sections V.4.1.3. and V.4.2.3.

88 Hoge Raad (Supreme Court) 15.12.2000, *NJ* 2001, 710 annotated by S.F.M. Wortmann.

both parents request sole parental authority (for themselves) and when both parents request that sole parental authority is allocated to one parent.[89]

The main criterion to determine an allocation of sole or joint parental authority is the 'torn and lost' criterion as already described in Chapter II.[90] This criterion is further examined below.[91]

V.4.1.2. After the breakup of a relationship

The Dutch Civil Code does not contain a provision specifically dealing with the situation for unmarried parents after the breakup of a relationship as it does in respect of parents who divorce. Article 253n of the Dutch Civil Code provides a general provision for the subsequent termination of joint parental authority in respect of parents who are not married to each other (after divorce and for unmarried parents). Termination is possible when circumstances have changed (after the initial allocation or continuation of joint parental authority) or the initial decision was based upon incorrect or incomplete information.[92]

The Supreme Court has ruled, however, that the termination of joint parental authority in respect of unmarried parents is subject to the same criterion as that which applies to married parents upon divorce: the 'torn or lost' criterion.[93]

In cases where the parents did not exercise parental authority prior to the breakup the possibility to make a sole request for joint parental authority has been deliberated above.[94]

---

89 Gerechtshof's-Hertogenbosch (Court of Appeal), 15.04.2004, LJN AO7714. This case is further deliberated below in Section V.9.1.

90 Section II.2.2.2.

91 Section V.4.5.

92 The pending proposal concerning 'Continued Parenting' incorporates the 'torn and lost' criterion and a secondary criterion in Art. 253n, Parliamentary Proceedings (*Kamerstukken*) 2004/2005, 30 145, No. 2, p. 3-4 pending as 30 145, No. A. It does not however provide a provision formally dealing with the situation of unmarried parents after the breakup of their relationship. There is little doubt, however, that the intention is that unmarried parents who break up and who exercised joint parental authority are treated in the same way as married parents upon divorce.

93 Hoge Raad 28.03.2003, *NJ* 2003, 359 annotated by S.F.M. Wortmann.

94 Section V.3.2.1.

V.4.2. DENMARK

Article 8 of the Act on Parental Responsibility provides that joint parental authority continues after the breakup of a relationship and divorce. No distinction is therefore made based on the marital status of the parents. Further, Article 10 of the Act provides that parents who do not live together may agree upon the allocation of parental authority to one parent. Such an agreement becomes valid upon notification to the Regional State Administration.

The background to the present regulation of the termination of joint parental authority has been described in Chapter II.[95] As may be derived from this Chapter it is only since the entry into force of the Act on Parental Responsibility on 1 October 2007 that Danish law has abandoned the principle that a parent may always request sole parental authority in situations where the parents no longer live together. Consequently the current Danish case law regarding the allocation of parental authority always concerns the allocation of sole parental authority to one parent. Article 11 of the Act on Parental Responsibility now provides that:

> 'If parents who have joint parental authority, and who do not live together, cannot agree upon (the allocation) of parental authority, the court will determine whether joint parental authority must continue, or if one of the parents must be (allocated) sole parental authority. The court may only terminate joint parental authority when there are weighty grounds'.

The 'weighty grounds' criterion thus supplements the general best interests criterion contained in Article 4 of the Act on Parental Responsibility. The possibility for the court to determine that joint parental authority must continue requires that at least one of the parents wishes to maintain joint parental authority.[96] The 'weighty grounds' criterion is examined below.[97]

V.4.3. THE CEFL PRINCIPLES

The CEFL principles contain the principle that neither a divorce nor factual separation affects parental responsibilities.[98] Consequently the CEFL principles place no emphasis upon the relationship status of the parents. The termination

---

95 Section II.3.2.1.
96 L 133, Comments to § 11.
97 Section V.4.6.
98 Principles, Principle 3:10, p. 79.

of joint parental responsibilities is only possible in the context of discharge which, as discussed above,[99] is reserved for exceptional circumstances and requires a decision by a competent authority. The principles also do not provide for the possibility of a parental agreement concerning the holding of parental responsibilities. Any adjustment is only possible in respect of exercising parental responsibilities.[100]

V.4.4. COMPARISON

The general rule is that joint parental authority continues after divorce and after the breakup of a relationship in Dutch and Danish law and in the CEFL principles. The main difference between Dutch law, on the one hand, and Danish law and the CEFL principles, on the other, is that the continuation of joint parental authority or an allocation of sole parental authority in Dutch law is formally regulated in the context of the divorce procedure,[101] while in Danish law and the CEFL principles this is not the case. In Danish law the matter is regulated in the same way for married and unmarried parents with no emphasis on the divorce procedure. Consequently a request for sole parental authority may be made before, in connection with or after the request for divorce or the breakup of a relationship. Contrary to the Danish approach, however, the CEFL principles do not provide for this possibility since parental responsibilities are *unaffected* by divorce and factual separation.

While the continuation of joint parental authority in both Dutch and Danish law is the main rule, the laws of both countries contain the possibility of allocating sole parental authority upon divorce or a breakup. As such it cannot be said that joint parental authority *is unaffected by divorce or factual separation* as provided for in the CEFL principles.

A request for sole parental authority in Dutch law is subject to a review as to whether the parents agree or not. The CEFL principles only provide for the discharge of parental responsibilities in exceptional cases to be decided by the competent authority. In contrast, in Danish law the parents are free to make an agreement on the allocation of sole parental authority. The approach taken in Danish law, as concluded in Chapter II, is to focus upon *parental conflict* while

99 Section V.2.3.3.

100 Principles, to be derived from Comment 4 to principle 3:8, p. 65. See further Chapters VI and VII in relation to the exercise of parental authority.

101 For unmarried parents the matter depends upon a request for sole parental authority to the District court.

Dutch law distinguishes between *joint and sole* parental authority.[102] Joint parental authority is consequently the *predefined substantive legal norm* in Dutch law and the CEFL principles, but not in Danish law.

The difference between Dutch and Danish law concerns the perception of the role of the State, the authority it exercises and the value which is attributed to the institution of marriage and the joint exercise of parental authority by unmarried parents. In the Netherlands the State continues to assume a protective and authoritative role. Parents are not free to agree upon the allocation of parental authority. Joint parental authority is the given substantive legal norm and the courts have the authority to enforce this norm. Marriage, the family and the family members are, as expressed by the former Dutch Minister of Justice, '*a concern of the state*'.[103]

In Denmark the development has been marked by a high level of individualisation based upon a notion of equality and self-determination. The State no longer has a role to play in the divorce procedure or upon the breakup of a relationship when parents agree and the institution of marriage has little relevance for the allocation of parental authority. There are no given substantive legal norms in respect of parents who agree. Reviewing a parental agreement on the allocation of parental authority has been abandoned because it is viewed as paternalistic and outdated.[104] In Danish law the conflict has become the determinant.[105]

V.4.5. THE DUTCH 'TORN OR LOST' CRITERION

V.4.5.1. General

The origins of the 'torn or lost' criterion, which has developed in case law, have been deliberated in Chapter II.[106] The criterion has been adopted by the legislature and is phrased as follows in the pending proposal concerning 'Continued Parenting':

102 Section II.4.4.

103 Parliamentary proceedings 2006/2007 (*Kamerstukken*), 30145, No. 6, p. 29. This concern, however, is evidently not shared by all members of Parliament, see Chapter II, Section II.6.2. and, for example, the recent Parliamentary discussions 2006/2007 (*Kamerstukken*), 51-2997-3020.

104 Chapter II, Section II.3.2.1.

105 Chapter II, Section II.4.4.

106 Section II.2.2.2. The phrasing of this criterion by the Supreme Court in its decision of 10.09.1999, *NJ* 2000, 167 was also included in this Section.

'The court can (...) at the request of the parents or one of them decide that parental authority should belong to one parent if there is an unacceptable risk of the child becoming torn or lost between the parents and it is not expected that a sufficient improvement can be expected within a reasonable time.'[107]

When consideration is given to the criterion formulated by the Supreme Court, it consists of three elements: the serious nature of the communication problems, the unacceptable risk that the child is torn or lost and the assessment whether a sufficient improvement may be expected within a reasonable time.

In its second decision on this criterion the Dutch Supreme Court upheld the Amsterdam Court of Appeal's decision to allocate joint parental authority.[108] The facts and the procedure in the case were the following. The mother had requested sole parental authority over the son aged four in the course of the divorce proceedings before the District Court of Haarlem in 1999. The father also requested sole parental authority for himself or, failing this, an allocation of joint parental authority. The son was temporarily entrusted to the mother in June 1999. Two expert reports were delivered in August 1999 and February 2000. The last-mentioned concluded the following:

'Joint parental authority is (...) at this moment not feasible because the parents are not capable of communicating, have no faith in each other and the father has no confidence in the mother. Joint parental authority would mean that (the child) would experience more fear and anxiety, because the parents repeatedly fight about questions pertaining to the raising of the child, which is not in the interest of (the child).'[109]

The Haarlem District Court allocated joint parental authority considering that:

'It is necessary for the exercise of joint parental authority that the parents can consult each other over matters concerning the raising and care of the child. The sole condition that communication does not run smoothly is nevertheless not a reason for terminating joint parental authority. It may be expected of both parents that they will make every effort, in the interest of the child, to bring about and maintain mutual communication.'

---

107 Parliamentary proceedings (*Kamerstukken*) 2004/2005, 30145, No. 2, p. 3.

108 Hoge Raad 19.04.2002, *NJ* 2002, 458.

109 (Added).

The District Court of Haarlem further relied upon the parties' stated willingness to attempt to reach a settlement through the use of mediation. The mother appealed against the decision to allocate joint parental authority to the Amsterdam Court of Appeal requesting sole parental authority. The father also requested sole parental authority in these proceedings and a temporary decision entrusting the child to him. During these proceedings the parties attempted to reach an agreement through mediation. This attempt was unsuccessful. The father submitted a statement from the mediator. This statement contained the following passage:

> '(...) I have reached the conclusion that in this case it is impossible to set points of view, positions and feelings in motion: the fundamental lack of trust in each other is such that the gap is deeper and wider than I have ever experienced.'

The mediator further mentioned the fact that the parents had such deviating notions as to how to raise the child that joint parental authority was a practically 'impossible task'. On 12 April 2001 the Amsterdam Court of Appeal upheld the decision of the District Court of Haarlem to allocate joint parental authority and establish the child's main residence with the mother considering, amongst other things, that:

> '(...) joint parental authority must be continued now that it does not appear that the parties differ in their opinion on the decisions which must be made concerning (the child), the parties in so far as is necessary communicate via e-mail or by post and they appear to be able to overcome their personal problems so that a contact arrangement between (the child) and the father, which perhaps does not run smoothly but after all is factually not in conflict, has been established and that the parties, with sufficient effort, are considered to be able to deal with joint parental authority in a manner which will not be detrimental to (the child).'[110]

The mother appealed against this decision to the Supreme Court claiming that the Court of Appeal had misinterpreted the 'torn or lost' criterion or misapplied this criterion to the facts of the case. The appeal further contained the information that the contact arrangement was not without conflict, rather it had been necessary to request enforcement measures to have the child returned from a

110 (Added).

contact visit. The appeal was dismissed because the Court of Appeal's decision contained a correct application of the law to the facts of the case.

The application of the 'torn or lost' criterion by the District and Appeal courts has been extensively analysed in the legal literature. Several points may be deduced therefrom. In the first place that the application of this criterion seems to have provided diverging decisions. PUNSELIE[111] mentions a decision by the Amsterdam Court of Appeal where the Court allocated sole parental authority to the mother considering that 'joint parental authority requires a minimum ability to communicate positively between the parents'.[112] Secondly, that the general impression seems to be that something more than communication problems is required. HEIDA describes this as a requirement of misbehaviour by the non-resident parent, for example when this parent stubbornly refuses to communicate with the other parent or continuously questions the children's main residence with this parent.[113] Finally, that the courts rely upon a stated intention of the non-resident parent not to intervene in daily matters or upon the perception that this will not occur or even upon the notion that decisions will be taken by the resident parent alone.[114] VAN LEUVEN has described the role of the caring (resident) parent as 'the captain of the ship' indicating that the non-resident parent would only lose parental authority when he/she does not respect this position.[115]

A case which determined the limits of the 'torn or lost' criterion reached the Supreme Court in 2004.[116] In this case the mother (a Dutch national) had requested and been allocated sole parental authority over a son born in 2002 by the District Court of Leeuwarden on 23 April 2003. The father (an Egyptian national) appealed to the Leeuwarden Court of Appeal, which on 7 January 2004 reversed the decision of the District Court and allocated joint parental authority. The Court of Appeal considered that the father's mental condition (according to

111 E.C.C. Punselie, 'Gezamenlijk gezag', *FJR* 2001, p. 313.

112 Gerechtshof Amsterdam 20.09.2001, *FJR* 2001, p. 342/343 annotated by P. Dorhout.

113 A. Heida, 'Gezamenlijk ouderlijk gezag na scheiding', *EB*, 2000, No. 7/8.

114 P. Van Teffelen, 'Gezamenlijk gezag na echtscheiding: tijdbom, lege huls of groeimodel?', *FJR*, 2000, p. 27 with reference to Gerechtshof Amsterdam (Amsterdam Court of Appeal) 07.01.1999, *FJR* 1999, No. 12, p. 259. Further, Gerechtshof 's-Gravenhage (The Hague Court of Appeal) 22.03.2006, LJN AX7311, Gerechtshof 's-Hertogenbosch 07.07.1999, Rechtspraak Nemesis, No. 1271, Hoge Raad (Supreme Court) 07.02.2003, LJN AF0892 (which, however, concerned a subsequent request for the termination of joint parental authority).

115 C.A.R.M. van Leuven, 'Het gezamenlijk gezag van ouders na scheiding, een praktijkmodel', *EB*, 1998, No. 10, p. 4.

116 Hoge Raad 18.03.2005, LJN AS8525.

the mother the father used drugs, received psychiatric treatment and medication which, however, he did not take, was homeless and had been violent and aggressive towards the mother):

> '(...) did not provide – even if the mother's statements were true – an obstacle to the exercise of joint parental authority, when (the son) lives with the mother and she is the designated parent to care for and raise (the son) and in that respect makes the daily decisions.'[117]

The Supreme Court found that the decision of the Court of Appeal was incomprehensible and it annulled the decision remitting the case to another Court of Appeal. The Supreme Court considered that on the basis of the stated information, which the Appeal Court accepted as true and the fact that the father was homeless which made communication practically impossible, that there 'was an unacceptable risk that (the son) would become torn or lost between the parents if they were to exercise joint parental authority and that it was not to be expected that a sufficient improvement could be expected within a reasonable time'.[118] The Supreme Court thus applied the 'torn or lost' criterion to this case.

V.4.5.2. A secondary criterion

WORTMANN had considered that next to the 'torn or lost' criterion there could be other reasons to allocate sole parental authority in the interests of the child considering, for example, situations involving drugs or alcohol abuse, a (plausible) incestuous relationship or abuse.[119]

The Court of Appeal of 's-Hertogenbosch applied such a secondary criterion in a decision in 2004.[120] In this case the Appeal Court allocated sole parental authority to the mother of a daughter born in 1993 and a son born in 1995 considering that (the father had been convicted of sexually abusing the daughter and a niece):

> 'The mother, in view of the criminal conviction of the father for sexual abuse, no longer has faith in the norms and values and qualities for raising

117 The Dutch Child Care and Protection Board in its advice to the Court had found that there were no reasons not to allocate joint parental authority.

118 The Procurator General had considered that the appeal should be dismissed.

119 S.F.M. Wortmann in her annotation to *NJ* 2000, 167.

120 Gerechtshof 's-Hertogenbosch 15.12.2004, LJN AS2646. The District Court of 's-Hertogenbosch had allocated sole parental authority to the mother based upon the 'torn or lost' criterion.

a child of the father, (and) on this basis it cannot reasonably be required that she should continue, together with the father, to decide on matters concerning the children, so it is therefore in the interests of the children that parental authority is allocated to the mother. The Court of Appeal assumes that the mother will inform and consult (the father) in important matters concerning the children.' (Added)

The pending Dutch reform on 'Continued Parenting' lays down the 'torn or lost' criterion as well as a secondary criterion 'where a change in the parental authority is otherwise necessary in the best interests of the child'.[121] In the Explanatory Report an example is given pertaining to the situation where 'a parent continuously questions the main residence established by the court by which tensions between the parents may arise which have repercussions for the child.'[122] The described situation would seem to fit the 'torn or lost' criterion directly.

At a later stage in the parliamentary proceedings the relevance of the secondary criterion was argued by the Minister of Justice in relation to the possibility to allocate sole parental authority to one parent where one parent frustrates the other parent's right to contact. Simultaneously, the Minister rejected a suggestion from Members of Parliament who considered this criterion 'difficult to operate' and proposed to enact a 'best interests' criterion instead. The Minister considered that the 'torn or lost' criterion was well established in case law and that no operational difficulties had emerged.[123] From the above-mentioned it must be concluded that the distinction between the two criteria does not become any clearer if these are enacted in their present form.

V.4.5.3. Parental authority: factual care and contact

It is well established in case law that the allocation of joint parental authority does not depend on factual care provided by the non-resident parent.[124] While the exercise of joint parental authority implies the right to contact since the

121 Chapter II, Section II.6.2.1 and Parliamentary proceedings (*Kamerstukken*) 2004/2005, 30 145, No. 2, p. 3.

122 Parliamentary proceedings (*Kamerstukken*) 2004/2005, 30 145, No. 3, p. 14.

123 Parliamentary proceedings (*Kamerstukken*) 2006/2007, 30 145, No. 6, p. 30.

124 For example, Rechtbank 's-Gravenhage (The Hague District Court) 21.11.2005, LJN AU8801 where the mother had left the father and the three children indicating that she wished to have no contact with any of them. The father requested sole parental authority in the course of the divorce proceedings and presented a written note from the mother agreeing to such an allocation. The District Court allocated joint parental authority considering that the 'torn or lost' criterion did not warrant an allocation of sole parental authority.

reasons for discharging contact rights contained in Article 377a(3) of the Dutch Civil Code do not apply to the parent who exercises joint parental authority, it has been established by the Supreme Court that contact may be *temporarily* discontinued, but not discharged, in cases where the parents exercise joint parental authority.[125] The origins of the distinction between the parent who exercises parental authority and the parent without parental authority in relation to contact stems from the 1995 revision where the exercise of joint parental authority was consensus-based. It has been debated to what extent the lack of a possibility to discharge in the light of the developments in the allocation of parental authority after divorce and after the breakup of a relationship should continue to apply.[126] The Supreme Court has, however, maintained the general principle that contact cannot be discharged.[127]

A number of cases have concerned the situation where the non-resident parent lives abroad, is moving abroad or spends long periods abroad and therefore provides limited care. In these situations the cases also concern the communication and decision-making possibilities of the parents. The general trend is that this does not prevent the continuation of joint parental authority based upon the 'torn or lost' criterion. The District Court of Roermond consequently allocated joint parental authority in a situation where the non-resident parent lived in Ecuador and was expected to come to the Netherlands once a year.[128] Similarly the 's-Hertogenbosch Court of Appeal changed the decision of the District Court to allocate sole parental authority to the mother of two children aged one and four and allocated joint parental authority in a case where the father was going to immigrate to the US. The father would come to the Netherlands every two months.[129]

---

125 Hoge Raad 18.11.2005, *NJ* 2005, 574 annotated by S.F.M. Wortmann, Hoge Raad 31.03.2006, *NJ* 2006, 392 and Hoge Raad 23.03.2007 LJN: AZ5443 see further Chapter VIII, Section VIII.2.1.1.

126 S.F.M. Wortmann, 'Bij gezamenlijk gezag kan rechter toch omgang met kind ontzeggen', *Perspectief*, 2002, No. 4, p. 26. E. Nicolai, 'Bij gezamenlijk gezag geen ontzegging van omgang', *Perspectief*, 2002, No. 5, p. 17.

127 The pending legislative proposal concerning 'Continued Parenting' lays down the possibility to temporarily discontinue contact, Parliamentary proceedings (*Kamerstukken*) 2004/2005, 30 145, No. 2, p. 3 and 30 145, A.

128 Rechtbank Roermond 11.02.1999, Rechtspraak Nemesis, No. 1038, p. 17.

129 Gerechtshof 's-Hertogenbosch 07.07.1999, Rechtspraak Nemesis, No. 1271.

V.4.5.4. Analysis of the criteria

The criterion 'torn or lost' seemingly refers to the welfare of the child, that is to an ascertainment of the risks involved when parents cannot communicate or co-operate. The way this criterion is applied by the courts is nonetheless complicated because in a number of situations where the criterion is applied it would seem to relate to other factors such as the risks to the child. In the Supreme Court decision concerning the father who was mentally ill, on drugs, abusive and homeless, the risks to the child who was one year old would seem to be more associated with contact (which was also established). Further, it could be viewed as unreasonable, dangerous and impractical that the mother should be obliged to seek approval for decisions in respect of matters pertaining to joint decision making. Finally, the implications of joint parental authority, for example the allocation of parental authority to the father *ex lege* if the mother should die, could be viewed as an argument against joint parental authority.[130] The Supreme Court did, however, consider the case under the 'torn or lost' criterion.

The cases pertaining to the non-resident parent's stay in another country seem to depend upon a practical ascertainment of the possibility of the resident parent to get in touch with this parent. These cases are nonetheless also considered in relation to the 'torn or lost' criterion.

For cases pertaining to the core of the principle: communication problems, it would seem that something more than communication problems and the inherent risks involved for the child are necessary. Rather, these cases seem to depend upon some qualified misbehaviour (fault) on the part of the non-resident parent.

A secondary criterion has not been applied, as far as it can be ascertained, in other published cases such as the one mentioned above[131] pertaining to a situation where the parent could be considered to be unsuitable to exercise joint parental authority (incest). At present, however, there is not much clarity to be derived from the parliamentary proceedings pertaining to the enactment of the secondary criterion.

The criteria for the termination of joint parental authority may be considered to point in the direction of a decision based upon the welfare of the child. The

---

130 Below, Section V.8.1.

131 Section V.4.3.1.

application of these criteria seem, however, to rely more upon some qualified fault on the part of the non-resident parent than upon an ascertainment of the risks for the child. It would thus seem that the welfare of the child is associated with the level of fault attributed to the parent.

V.4.5.5. Statistics on parental authority

The schedule below containing the Dutch Statistical Authority's[132] registration of parental authority allocations in divorce procedures from 1993-2005 clearly shows the move towards joint parental authority as the legal norm. The shift to the continuance of parental authority, which took place in 1998, and the pursuant shift in the courts' perception of the relevance of a request for sole parental authority is clearly visible. The declining percentage in respect of the allocation of joint parental authority from 2001-2005 from 93% to 86% seems to be related to an increase in the number of undecided cases (indicative of stayed proceedings) and the relatively high number of divided allocations of sole parental authority to both parents. There are no statistics pertaining to the allocation of joint parental authority to unmarried parents.

Table 5: Statistics on the allocation of parental authority

Allocation of parental authority %						
Periods	Total divorces/ minor children	Joint p.a. %	Mother p.a. %	Father p.a. %	Both[133] p.a. %	Undecided
1993	17,952	16	76	5	3	0
1994	19,642	16	76	5	3	0
1995	18,952	17	71	5	7	0
1996	19,065	27	66	4	4	0
1997	18,128	34	59	3	4	0
1999	19,364	74	16	1	9	0
2001	21,630	93	5	0	2	0
2003	19,546	92	3	0	0	4
2005	20,020	86	4	1	5	4

132 CBS on www.statline.nl.

133 The term 'both' covers the situation where the children are divided between the parents and each of them are allocated sole parental authority over one or more of the children.

V.4.6. THE DANISH CRITERION OF 'WEIGHTY GROUNDS'

V.4.6.1. General

The content of the Danish criterion is based upon the deliberations in the notes to the Act on Parental Responsibility since this Act only entered into force on 1 October 2007.

The notes to the Act mention two main reasons for the allocation of sole parental authority. The first is the parental conflict level and the second is the unsuitability to exercise parental authority.

The relevance of the parental conflict level is formulated so as to mean that, on the one hand, complete agreement is not required, but, on the other, that the co-operation problems between the parents in relation to the child must not be so serious and irreconcilable that the child suffers. The central point according to the notes is that 'the parents can deal with the problems in a way which is not detrimental to the child'.[134] A dispute over the child's residence is not sufficient for the allocation of sole parental authority. The court may determine, pursuant to Article 17, the child's residence. It is generally assumed that most conflicts regarding parental authority actually concern the establishment of the child's residence.

If the conflict level relates to the fact that one parent has been violent or has committed a sexual offence against the other parent, the child or other members of the family, the notes to the Act consider that joint parental authority will not be in the best interest of the child.[135]

If the conflicts concern contact and one parent is considered to be obstructing the other parent's right to contact, the notes to the Act state that the court must consider the child's future best interest. This could involve the establishment of the child's residence and/or the allocation of sole parental authority to the parent who has the best co-operation potential and who in the long run can secure the child's contact with the other parent. Countering any obstruction to contact runs like a thread through the notes to the Act. Although the obstruction of contact is no longer mentioned in the Act concerning the transfer of parental autho-

[134] L 133, Comments to § 11.
[135] L 133, Comments to § 11.

rity,[136] it nonetheless seems to be given increasing importance. KRONBORG[137] has described the relevance of obstructing contact within the term 'co-operation norm' (*samarbejdsnormen*). This norm was well established also before the 1996 Act. The norm will be further deliberated below in relation to the allocation (transfer) of sole parental authority and the reallocation of parental authority.[138]

Unsuitability to exercise (joint) parental authority is present in cases where one parent has an *overwhelming* abuse problem (drugs, alcohol), a serious mental illness or other conditions which make the parent unsuitable to participate in decisions concerning the child.[139]

While the Danish Explanatory notes explicitly provide for the possibility to terminate parental authority based upon a welfare assessment in relation to the child, the situations involving the reprehensible behaviour of a parent are described in more detail as those exceeding the tolerable conflict level. It remains to be seen how Danish case law will develop in relation to the criterion 'weighty grounds'.

V.4.6.2. Parental authority: factual care and contact

There is no direct link in Danish law between the holding of parental authority and the right to contact. The right to contact is formulated in the same way for all (legal) parents. The notes to the Act on Parental Responsibility considered that it is not in the best interest of the child to establish joint parental authority against the wishes of the resident parent when the other parent is not interested in caring for the child and has demonstrated no intention of participating in the child's life. This may be the case where, for example, the parent has not had stabile contact or has been absent for many years and the parent would not be granted contact when the lack of contact may be ascribed to conditions pertaining to this parent as opposed to the situation where the other parent has obstructed contact.[140]

---

136 This consideration was laid down in the 1996 reform, ChapterII, Section II.3.2.

137 A. Kronborg, *Forældremyndighed og menneskelig integritet*, Copenhagen: Jurist- og Økonomforbundest Forlag 2007, p. 158.

138 Sections V.5.2.1. and V.5.2.2.

139 L 133, Comments to § 11.

140 L 133, Comments to § 11.

V.4.6.3. Statistics on parental authority

There is no registration of the allocation of sole/joint parental authority in Denmark. This means that the statistics which are available are based upon the estimations and results of sociological research.[141] When the continuation of joint parental authority was laid down in 2001 it was estimated that parents agreed upon the continuation of joint parental authority in approximately 90% of divorce cases.[142]

The contact study[143] from 2004 showed that in 1990 approximately 40% and in 2003 approximately 65% of parents held joint parental authority. The study includes children born to single, cohabiting and married parents who (no longer) live with both parents. The last mentioned percentage (65%) relates to children born in 1995. The percentage must be expected to be higher in respect of children born after the changes to the Children Act in 2001 where the paternity registration procedure (the care and responsibility statement) results in joint parental authority and in respect of children born to married parents after the automatic continuation of joint parental authority after divorce enacted in 2001 in connection with the Children Act.[144]

V.4.7. COMPARISON BETWEEN THE DUTCH AND DANISH CRITERIA

The Dutch criterion of 'torn or lost' and the secondary criterion have evolved in the case law pursuant to the 1998 revision which has provided the criteria with a changing and unclear nature and which, as yet, have not been clarified in the legislative procedures enacting these criteria. The Danish criterion of 'weighty grounds', on the other hand, has not yet been applied by the courts and the manner in which it will be applied is consequently still unknown.

Nonetheless, the Dutch criteria and the phrasing of the Danish criterion of 'weighty grounds' for the allocation of sole parental authority have many common features. In the first case they concern an assessment for the future relying upon the notion that conflicts in divorce are likely to diminish with time. Secondly, they rely upon a duty on the part of the parents to co-operate,

---

[141] See for an overview of the relevant statistics, Commission Report No. 1475/2006 p. 245-261.

[142] Explanatory notes to L 198, Forslag til ændring af retsplejeloven og forskellige andre love, 2000, p. 11.

[143] See Chapter IV, Section IV.2.1.

[144] Chapter II, Section II.3.2.1.

described in relation to Danish law as the *co-operation norm*. Thirdly, Dutch law relies informally upon the non-resident parent's subsidiary position. This is, however, also true in respect of Danish law where the establishment of residence gives the resident parent inherent rights such as the right to relocate within the country.[145] Finally, the criteria, while seemingly pointing in the direction of the child's welfare, seem to rely more upon something which may be described as involving reprehensible behaviour on the part of the parent(s), thereby making them unsuitable, unavailable or unreachable.

In this respect it is worth drawing a parallel with the development in Dutch law concerning the requirement that the court should asses whether joint parental authority would be 'properly exercised' pursuant to the 1995 reform where it soon appeared that the courts relied upon a joint request.[146] It raises the question whether the courts are actually capable of or willing to make such welfare assessments concerning the future.

It would seem that Dutch and Danish law, while in principle allowing for the possibility of allocating sole parental authority upon divorce or the breakup of a relationship, comes close to the solution contained in the CEFL principles where a parent may only be discharged of parental responsibilities in exceptional cases.

V.5. SUBSEQUENT CHANGES: JOINT PARENTAL AUTHORITY

The question of a subsequent termination of joint parental authority[147] or a subsequent reallocation of joint parental authority is addressed in this Section. The allocation and reallocation of sole parental authority in the context of the *choice of a parent* is addressed in the following Section.

---

145 Chapter VI, Section VI.4.2.2.

146 Chapter II, Section II.2.2.2.

147 After the divorce when joint parental authority is continued. In relation to unmarried parents 'a subsequent termination' must be viewed in relation to the initial allocation of joint parental authority or a case concerning the termination of joint parental authority where the request for sole parental authority has been rejected.

V.5.1. SUBSEQUENT TERMINATION

V.5.1.1. Subsequent termination: Dutch law

Article 253n(1)1st sentence of the Dutch Civil Code provides that

> 'On the application of parents who are not married to one another or of either one of them the district court may terminate the joint parental authority (...), if the circumstances have changed thereafter or if its decision was based, when taken, on incorrect or incomplete information. In this case the district court shall lay down which of the parents shall thereafter have parental authority over each of the minor children in the best interests of the child'.

Article 253n applies both to married parents where joint parental authority has continued after divorce and to unmarried parents who exercise joint parental authority. It is important for understanding this provision in relation to the development in joint parental authority after divorce and after the breakup of a relationship as well as the development in the leading 'torn or lost' criterion that the wording of this provision has not been changed since the 1995 Act where joint parental authority was based upon agreement.[148] The 'torn or lost' criterion concerns an assessment for the future. Inherent in the criterion is the assessment that 'it is not expected that a sufficient improvement can be expected within a reasonable time'. The question may be raised how the criteria 'changed circumstances' or 'incorrect or incomplete information' fit the situation where the court has rejected a request for sole parental authority in the divorce procedure or in a procedure concerning the termination of joint parental authority where subsequently after some time a new request for sole parental authority is made pursuant to Article 253n(1). Are changed circumstances required or is it sufficient that the conflict level continues? WORTMANN has suggested that termination must be considered if the conflicts continue although in this situation consideration must continuously be given to the effects on the child.[149]

---

148 Chapter II, Section II.2.2.2. Save for the adding of the best interests principle in Art. 253n(1)2nd sentence in connection with the 1998 reform.

149 In her annotation to *NJ* 1999, 167.

Case law does not provide much clarity although the tendency is clearly to maintain joint parental authority.[150] The pending proposal concerning 'Continued Parenting' provides in Article 253n(1) a reference to 'torn or lost' and the secondary criterion contained in the proposed Article 251a.[151] The Act will thus confirm the courts' dependence upon the 'torn or lost' criterion but contains no further enlightment as to the correlation between 'changed circumstances' and the other criteria.[152] It is probable that despite the requirement of 'changed circumstances' the same criteria will apply as in divorce situations.[153]

V.5.1.2. Subsequent termination: Danish law

In Danish law the parents are free to agree upon the termination of joint parental authority when they do not live together.[154] The agreement becomes valid upon notification to the Regional State Administration. Further, a parent may request sole parental authority either before, in connection with or after the request for divorce or in connection with the breakup of a relationship. Termination is possible when the parents do not live together.[155] The criterion 'weighty grounds' thus applies in all situations also when the court at an earlier stage has rejected a request for sole parental authority. It is currently estimated that a request for sole parental authority is only rarely made in the divorce procedure and that most requests are consequently made after the divorce procedure.[156]

V.5.1.3. Subsequent termination: The CEFL principles

The CEFL principles only provide for the possibility to terminate joint parental authority in the context of a discharge of such authority which, as discussed above,[157] is reserved for exceptional circumstances and requires a decision by a

---

150 In the majority of cases the request for sole parental authority is rejected based upon the 'torn or lost' criterion often supplemented by the notion that joint parental authority does not concretely hinder the exercise of parental authority, Hoge Raad (Supreme Court) 31.03.2006, LJN AV2863, the decisions of the Gerechtshof 's-Hertogenbosch (Court of Appeal) 09.09.2004, LJN AR5959, 26.02.2007 LJN BA1915 and Gerechtshof Amsterdam (Court of Appeal) 07.01.2004, LJN AO5637. In some cases the courts seem to rely upon a requirement of changed circumstances, for example, Gerechtshof 's-Hertogenbosch (Court of Appeal) 09.07.2007, LJN BB1541 and 11.06.2007, LJN BB1534.

151 The present Art. 251, DCC concerning allocation upon divorce.

152 Parliamentary proceedings (*Kamerstukken*), 2004/2005 30 145, No. 3, p. 15.

153 ASSER-DE BOER, 2006, supra, p. 674.

154 Art. 10, Act on Parental Responsibility.

155 Art. 11, Act on Parental Responsibility.

156 S. Danielsen, 'Foreløbig forældremyndighed', *TFA*, 2007, p. 5.

157 Section V.2.3.3.

competent authority. The Principles consequently do not distinguish between the moments in time where termination is requested.

V.5.1.4. Comparison: Subsequent termination

The main difference in the subsequent termination of joint parental authority is that Danish law and the CEFL principles do not distinguish between the moments in time where termination is requested, which Dutch law formally does. It must be assumed, however, that the same criteria apply to a subsequent termination in Dutch law as provided for in Danish law and in the CEFL principles. Further, only Danish law allows for a parental agreement on termination.

V.5.2. REALLOCATION OF JOINT PARENTAL AUTHORITY

V.5.2.1. Reallocation: Dutch law

The present regulation of the possibility to reobtain joint parental authority is contained in Article 253o(1) 2nd sentence of the Dutch Civil Code. This provision has not been changed since the 1995 reform. Consequently the provision must be understood in the light of the developments in the continuation of joint parental authority since the 1998 reform.

Article 253o(1) 2nd sentence provides that:

> 'An application to still be charged with joint parental authority over their minor children may only originate from both parents.'

In the legislative framework reallocation is thus consensus-based and is subject to review. However, as deliberated in Chapter III[158] developments in case law have provided the parent who has 'lost' parental authority with the possibility to make a sole request for joint parental authority in this situation. The mentioned cases, except for one, concerned only the question of admissibility. It is unclear to what extent the parent will actually reobtain joint parental authority.[159]

---

158 Section III.3.3., A (Reallocation).

159 In the one case where the actual reallocation was addressed the father was not allocated joint parental authority, Gerechtshof Arnhem (Court of Appeal) 08.06.2004, LJN AQ 5059. The criterion was the 'best interests' principle. See also M. Vonk, 'Enige overdenkingen bij de voorgestelde wijziging van art. 1:253o en de positie van de opvoeder niet-ouder', *FJR*, 2005, p. 34-39.

A pending proposal foresees a legislative basis for a sole request for parents who have previously exercised joint parental authority.[160]

V.5.2.2. Reallocation: Danish law

Parents may agree to reobtain joint parental authority.[161] The agreement becomes valid upon notification to the Regional State Administration.

Further, a parent may at any time since the 2007 Act request the court to reallocate joint parental authority.[162] In this case the court must take account of the reason why this parent 'lost' parental authority and further consider the main criterion of 'weighty grounds'.[163]

V.5.2.3. Reallocation: The CEFL principles

The CEFL principles provide that the restoration of parerntal responsibilities is possible if the circumstances that led to the discharge no longer exist and the restoration is in the best interests of the child.[164] Further, it is stressed in the comments that based upon the case law of the ECtHR 'all measures should always be consistent with the ultimate aim of possibly reuniting the family'.[165]

V.5.2.4. Comparison: Reallocation

The main difference is that Danish law and the CEFL principles provide for the possibility of reallocation in the legislative framework. In Dutch law, however, case law has provided this possibility and a proposal aiming to enact this possibi-

---

160 Chapter II.2.6.1. and Parliamentary proceedings (*Kamerstukken*) 2004/2005, 29 353, No. 1-2, p. 2. The criterion seems to be the present criteria contained in Art. 253o(1) in respect of the reallocation (transfer) of sole parental authority: 'changed circumstances' or 'incorrect or incomplete information'. The proposed criterion for the allocation of joint parental authority to a parent who has not previously exercised joint parental authority is the 'best interests' principle or, pursuant to an amendment, the 'torn or lost' criterion, see above Section V.3.2.1. and supra note 76.

161 Art. 9, Act on Parental Responsibility.

162 Art. 14, Act on Parental Responsibility.

163 L 133, Comments to § 14. As mentioned above a 'boom' in old cases is expected after 01.10.2007 when the Act on Parental Responsibility enters into force whereby parents (primarily fathers) who do not hold parental authority or have previously 'lost' parental authority will request a new decision. There is serious concern that the courts will become overloaded with 'old' cases, supra note 80.

164 Principles, principle 3:34, p. 221.

165 Principles, Comment 1, p. 223.

lity is pending. The criteria for the reallocation are, as yet, not as clear in Dutch law compared with Danish law and the CEFL principles. Further, only Danish law allows for a parental agreement on reallocation.

V.6. SOLE PARENTAL AUTHORITY

The purpose of this Section is to examine the law relating to *the choice of a parent.*[166] That is, the law regulating the allocation of sole parental authority to one parent upon the termination of joint parental authority and a subsequent reallocation (change or transfer) of such an allocation. The difference between allocation and reallocation is typically that in the first situation the parents are, at least formally, equal and the deciding principle is the best interests principle. Reallocation typically requires something more such as *changed circumstances*.

An allocation of sole parental authority upon divorce or the breakup of a relationship[167] has become the exception in Dutch law. This must also be expected in Danish law following the 2007 Act.[168] In view of what has been considered above in respect of the criteria determining the choice between sole and joint parental authority where fault, unsuitability and unavailability play a central role, it is to be expected that only a few cases will concern the situation where a choice must be made between equally able parents immediately after divorce or the breakup of a relationship. A subsequent allocation of sole parental authority (sometime after the divorce or the breakup of the relationship) will mostly only concern two equal parents when the child has had a shared residence or an extensive contact arrangement.

Notwithstanding the exceptional status of an allocation of sole parental authority, it is relevant to examine the law pertaining to *the choice of a parent* in respect of an allocation of sole parental authority as well as the possibility to change or transfer such an allocation to the other parent. Two general principles

---

166 In Danish law the parents are free to agree upon an allocation or reallocation; the law is thus only relevant for parents who have a dispute. In the Netherlands only the court may decide upon an allocation or reallocation of parental authority.

167 In cases where the parents held/exercised joint parental authority.

168 It has probably already become the exception that an allocation of sole parental authority is made in the course of the divorce proceedings, see above Section V.5.1.2. and supra note 156.

– the principle of continuity[169] and the principle of non-discrimination[170] – play a role in the allocation and reallocation of sole parental authority. Further, the relevance of the co-operation norm has been described in relation to Danish law by KRONBORG.[171]

V.6.1. SOLE PARENTAL AUTHORITY: THE NETHERLANDS

V.6.1.1. Allocation of sole parental authority

If both parents request sole parental authority for themselves and the court does not allocate joint parental authority, the court must decide which decision (allocating sole parental authority to one parent) *is most in the best interests of the children.*[172] A parent who does not have the capacity to exercise parental authority will not be allocated parental authority. The court must, however, allocate parental authority to a parent even if both parents lack capacity.[173] It is not possible to allocate guardianship to a third person in a procedure concerning the termination of joint parental authority.

The court must 'in the light of what the interests of the child require, weigh the possibilities which either of the parents offers or may offer and on this basis assess which of the parents will be allocated with parental authority.'[174] The aforementioned indicates that the parents are *entitled* to a decision which weighs the possibilities that each parent may offer. This decision may pertain to the qualities of each parent, the factual possibility to care for and raise the child (relating to living, work and family circumstances), the relationship which the child has with each parent, the changes which the requests will invoke upon the child's life,[175] the opinion of the child and – in cases where each parent requests

[169] Also referred to as the status quo, changes to the child's life, and changes in the child's environment.

[170] The ECtHR has decided that a parent may not be discriminated against on the ground of homosexuality, ECtHR Salgueiro da Silva Mouta v. Portugal 21.12.1999, 33290/96, or in respect of religion ECtHR Hoffmann v Austria 23.06.1993, 12875/87.

[171] A. Kronborg, 2007, supra.

[172] P. Vlaardingerbroek et al., *Het hedendaagse personen- en familierecht*, Deventer: W.E.J. Tjeenk Willinck, 2002, p. 145, ASSER-DE BOER, 2006, supra, p. 676.

[173] Save in the situation where both parents have been discharged of parental authority. In such a situation a guardian will be appointed.

[174] Hoge Raad (Supreme Court) 25.05.1990, *NJ* 1991, 267 annotated by E.A.A. Luijten.

[175] The principle of continuity.

parental authority only in respect of some of the children – the interests of the child in not being separated from his/her siblings.[176]

As far as can be ascertained, however, there are no recent decisions allocating sole parental authority to one parent in situations where both parents are considered equally able and where the principle of continuity does not favour one parent, for example because the child has already resided with this parent for a considerable period of time.[177] A decision on sole parental authority, except in graver situations involving fault, as deliberated above, is not likely to be made at an early stage after divorce or after the breakup of a relationship. The courts are likely to stay the proceedings pending advice from the Dutch Child Care and Protection Board,[178] mediation attempts[179] or, as illustrated by the case of The Hague Court of Appeal, upon a one-year trial period of joint parental authority.[180]

In most cases where there is a dispute, a decision concerning the child's main residence will replace the decision on the allocation of sole parental authority. It is however not evident that the role of the court pertaining to such a decision is the same in respect of *the choice of a parent* as a decision concerning sole parental authority.[181]

In respect of non-discrimination or equality between the parents, it may be deduced from Chapter II[182] that the courts were free to allocate parental authority (guardianship) to either parent pursuant to the 1901 Civil Children Act in the interests of the child. In case law an experience-based rule favouring maternal care in respect of younger children was established and confirmed by the

176 Vlaardingerbroek et al., 2002, supra, p. 145.

177 Factually or pursuant to an interim decision entrusting the child to one parent.

178 Which will often cause serious delay.

179 For example, Gerechtshof 's-Gravenhagen (Appeal Court) 03.07.2002, LJN AE8529 where the Appeal Court subjected the parents to an obligation to participate in mediation. The divorce procedure seemed to have been commenced in 1999-2000.

180 The decision concerned a divorce procedure initiated in November 1999 and the proceedings were stayed by the Appeal Court until January 2003, Gerechtshof 's-Gravenhage 13.02.2002, LJN AE2305. The increase in stayed proceedings is also illustrated by the statistics contained above in Section V.4.5.5.

181 Chapter VI, Section VI.2.1.

182 Section II.2.2.

Supreme Court in 1997.[183] While the rule has not been directly repealed, more recent case law does not seem to rely explicitly on this rule.[184]

It is generally acknowledged in the legal literature that the non-discrimination principle applies.[185] In a recent appeal to the Supreme Court, however, a father complained, amongst other things, against a certain consideration contained in the Amsterdam Court of Appeal's decision. The Court of Appeal had considered that '*it shared the concern of the mother over the father's behaviour as a transvestite now there is a hypothetical risk that the children will become confused, which could damage their development.*' The appeal was rejected; in relation to this point the Supreme Court considered that the decision of the Court of Appeal was not based upon this consideration.[186]

V.6.1.2. Reallocation of sole parental authority

Article 253o(1) of the Dutch Civil Code provides that:

> 'Decisions, whereby one parent is vested with parental authority (...) may, on the application of the parents or of either one of them, be varied by the district court on the ground that there has been a change of circumstances thereafter or that when the decision was taken, it was based on incorrect or incomplete information.'[187]

---

183 Hoge Raad 21.11.1997, *NJ* 1998, 164 and ASSER-DE BOER, 2006, supra, p. 677.

184 For example, Gerechtshof Amsterdam (Court of Appeal) 06.07.2006, LJN AY3929 concerning, however, the main residence of the child as further deliberated in Chapter VI, Section VI.2.1.

185 ASSER-DE BOER 2006, supra. p. 606.

186 Hoge Raad 10.11.2006, LJN AY8753.

187 The text of this provision originates from the 1995 Act, Chapter II, Section II.2.2.2. According to the Explanatory report 'changed circumstances' are present 'when there is a change in the situation whereby it is no longer in the interest of the child to uphold the existing exercise of parental authority. It is evident that the simple fact that the parent who, for example, has not been allocated with parental authority after divorce, has remarried, is in itself not enough to change the exercise in his or her favour.' This may be deduced from the Parliamentary proceedings 1992/1993 (*Kamerstukken*), 23 012, No. 3, p. 44. An analysis of 50 cases may be found in a report by L. Combrink-Kuiters, 'Gelet op de feiten; een analyse van 50 rechtbankdossiers inzake voogdijwijziging', *EB*, 1997, p. 6-9. From this analysis it appears, amongst other things, that the father will request a change in parental authority in the majority of cases (92%), that the father is allocated parental authority in 52% of cases and that only a small percentage (14%) involved a factual change of the child's residence. In none of the cases did the court rely upon the continuity principle or the willingness of the parents to co-operate with a contact arrangement as a main argument.

This provision applies when a parent pursuant to divorce or after the breakup of a relationship or subsequently in accordance with Article 253n of the Dutch Civil Code has been allocated (vested) with sole parental authority pursuant to a court decision.[188]

The requirement of a transfer is thus based upon the requirement of changed circumstances or an initial decision based upon incorrect or incomplete information.[189] As mentioned in Chapter II, the Supreme Court had already considered in 1939 that a parent's complete rejection of contact between the child and the parent not holding parental authority (then guardianship) without good reason, could provide a reason for the reallocation of parental authority (guardianship) to the other parent.[190] There are, however, no clear indications in published case law that such reallocations have actually taken place based only upon the frustration of contact.[191]

A new development in the case law is, however, that the reallocation of parental authority is temporarily used as a last resort in cases where the resident parent frustrates contact. In these cases the courts have temporarily reallocated parental authority to the father with the purpose of establishing a contact arrangement, but relying upon the presumption that the children's factual residence with the mother will not change. The father will thus hold parental authority and formally have the competence to make decisions on the child's residence and have the possibility to request enforcement measures while the child continues to be cared for by the mother.[192]

---

188 The unmarried legal father who has never exercised joint parental authority may request the allocation of sole parental authority in accordance with Art. 253c, DCC and ASSER- DE BOER, 2006, supra, with references to the relevant case law, p. 687-688.

189 The legal literature does not generally contain extensive deliberations on the substantive requirements, see, for example, ASSER-DE BOER, 2006, supra, p. 607. The Hague Court of Appeal reallocated sole parental authority to the father in a decision in 2003 where the child had factually changed residence to that of the father considering that 'from a practical point of view it is preferable that the parent with whom the child resides has parental authority', Gerechtshof 's-Gravenhage 03.09.2003, LJN AL8181.

190 Chapter II, Section II.2.3, Hoge Raad 28.08.1939, *NJ* 1939, 948 annotated by P. Scholten.

191 See the analysis by L. Combrink-Kuiters, 1997, supra and the decisions of the Supreme Court, Hoge Raad 05.04.2002, LJN AD9142 and 19.11.1999, *NJ* 2001, 214 annotated by Th.M. de Bolkenstein Boer. In the last-mentioned case the mother had frustrated contact for many years, amongst other things, by relocating to Germany. The Amsterdam Court of Appeal had found that a reallocation of parental authority was not in the interests of the child considering that the child had had no contact with the father for many years and firmly rejected any contact with the father.

192 Gerechtshof Amsterdam (Court of Appeal) 27.01.2005, LJN AS6020 and Gerechtshof 's-Gravenhage (Court of Appeal) 31.08.2005, LJN AS6020.

V.6.2. SOLE PARENTAL AUTHORITY: DENMARK

V.6.2.1. Allocation of sole parental authority

The possibility to establish joint parental authority against the wishes of one parent has only existed since the 2007 Act. From this it follows that all disputes before the courts concerning the allocation of parental authority up until 1 October 2007 have resulted in an allocation of sole parental authority to one parent.[193] This means that there is ample case law illustrating the criteria for the 'choice of a parent'. Moreover, it has been a tradition in Danish family law literature to arrange and qualify the case law, in particular of the Courts of Appeal and the Supreme Court, in accordance with a number of criteria[194] derived from the Commission report from 1994[195] and further to register changes according to these criteria.[196]

The criteria contained in the 1994 report concerned: (1) parental ability; (2) the child's connection with each parent; (3) the risk of a change to the child's environment;[197] (4) the opinion of the child of a certain age; (5) considerations concerning the best possible contact with both parents; (6) sibling relations; (7) the parents' new family situations; (8) the child's sex and age; and finally (9) each parent's possibility to be together with and care for the child.

Since the 1996 Act which provided the obstruction of contact as the only mentioned consideration in relation to the transfer of parental authority,[198] the criterion of 'best possible contact with both parents' has carried great weight. Further, the continuity principle, the child's connection with each parent and the child's own opinion have been especially emphasised.[199]

---

193 Except if the case was settled. Cases which have not been decided before 01.10.2007 must be decided according to the new Act, L 133, Comments to § 42.

194 Rather than criteria, they may be referred to as legal standards or themes of evidence, S. Danielsen, *Lov om forældremyndighed og samvær*, Copenhagen: Jurist- og Økonomforbundets Forlag, 1997, p. 171.

195 Commission report No. 1279/1994, p. 103.

196 For example, Danielsen, 1997, supra, p. 171-187, I. Lund-Andersen et al., *Familieret*, Copenhagen: Jurist og Økonomforbundets Forlag, 2003, p. 59-66 and before then in relation to the criteria contained in Commission report No. 369/1964.

197 Also referred to as status quo points of view (the continuity principle) referring to both continuity in relation to the primary caring parent and the environment.

198 Chapter II, Section II.3.2.1.

199 Danielsen, 1997, supra, p. 171.

The principle of non-discrimination in relation to the parents' different religions was addressed by the Supreme Court in its decision of 25 September 2001.[200] In this case the parents had divorced in 1998 and agreed upon joint parental authority. The parents had further made the agreement that the child, a daughter who at the time of the divorce was aged 4, would reside alternately 8 days with the mother and 6 days with the father. In 1999 the father requested the termination of joint parental authority and an allocation of sole parental authority to him as the child had experienced some problems which the father associated with the mother's membership of Jehovah's Witnesses and which also actively involved the child. The father's primary reason for requesting sole parental authority was his wish to prevent his daughter from having involvement with Jehovah's Witnesses.[201] The mother also requested sole parental authority for herself because she was the primary carer further claiming that her membership of Jehovah's Witnesses should not be taken into consideration.

The District Court allocated sole parental authority to the mother, mainly taking into consideration that she was the primary carer and that the daughter, if she remained with the mother, would be raised together with her brother (born within the mother's new marriage).[202] The Eastern High Court changed this decision on 15 January 2001 and allocated sole parental authority to the father considering all the elements of the case[203] and especially that:

> 'The conflicts which may be feared will arise as a result of the parents' difference in attitudes must be assumed to be resolvable in the best possible manner if the father is allocated parental authority, and that consequently the father will be able to ensure the best possible contact with both parents'.

The Supreme Court delivered an extensively deliberated decision on 25 September 2001 in which the majority (three judges) voted for the allocation of parental authority to the mother while two dissenting judges found that parental authori-

---

200 Højesteret, *UFR* 2001.2518H.

201 The mother had returned to this religion after the divorce. The father was a member of the Danish (Protestant) State Church.

202 Further, the Court relied upon the stated intention of the mother to continue the extended contact arrangement, decision of the District Court 21.06.2000.

203 The fact that both parents were able and that although the mother had been the primary carer, the father as a result of an extensive contact arrangement had cared almost as much for the child and the fact that they lived close to each other which meant that the child could remain in her usual environment and have extensive contact with the other parent.

ty should be allocated to the father. The majority reasoned in respect of the religious aspect that:

> 'We find that no importance should be attached to one parent's membership of Jehovah's Witnesses and the doctrines and attitudes which Jehovah's Witnesses generally preach and represent, but to how that parent in relation to the child practises these doctrines and attitudes, and how (the parent) deals with the problems which may arise as a consequence of the fact that the parents' have different religions. The mother has expressed a clear acceptance of the fact that the daughter will encounter a different religious understanding and culture with her father, and has factually acted in agreement therewith, thereby accepting that (the daughter) celebrates Christmas and birthdays (with her father). (...). The father does not object to, for example, the daughter saying grace with the mother, but does not want her to participate in meetings so that she is kept from being influenced by Jehovah's Witnesses. On these grounds we find that the mother must be expected to be able to deal with the problems which are a consequence of a difference in religion and to ensure the best possible contact with both parents.'[204] (Added)

The Supreme Court thus found that the relevant factor was how the parent practised religion with respect to the child and further emphasised that allocation to the mother who respected the different religious understanding of the father would ensure the best possible contact with both parents, thus emphasising the *co-operation norm.*[205]

KRONBORG has described the evolvement of the co-operation norm in Danish law. The evolving of the norm is placed in the context of increased individualisa-

---

204 There is no mention of the ECtHR case of Hoffmann v. Austria, 23.06.1993, 12875/87, which also concerned the allocation of parental authority to the father where the mother had become a member of Jehovah's Witnesses. Austria was found to have infringed Art. 8 in conjunction with Art. 14 of the ECHR by relying decisively upon the point that the mother's religious upbringing of the children contravened a certain Austrian Act on religious upbringing, which would seem to require that children are raised in the religion of the parents' first choice (Roman Catholic).

205 The dissenting judges also relied upon the co-operation norm considering, amongst other things, that 'it would be better for (the daughter) if both parents in their contact with her would exercise restraint in influencing her with respect to religion (...) so that her everyday life with each of them would not be very different'. The dissenting judges consequently relied upon a duty to exercise restraint in the upbringing of a child when the parents had diverging opinions thereon.

tion, which took place after 1968[206] when the institution of marriage and its inherent norms (fault and tradition) lost their relevance compared to the principle of 'best interests'. This principle requires the courts to assess the parents individually and the courts increasingly tend to depend more upon expert evidence for this assessment.[207] With these assessments general societal norms (including the co-operation norm) became a decisive factor in cases where the welfare of the child does not warrant an allocation of parental authority to one particular parent.

Illustrative is a case decided by the Supreme Court in October 2004.[208] In this case the parents divorced in 2003 and parental authority over their children (two daughters born in November 1997 and October 2002) was allocated to the mother. The mother was a Danish national and the father an American national. The parents had met and married in the US and relocated to Denmark before the birth of the youngest daughter. The parents had agreed that the youngest daughter should remain with the mother, but parental authority in respect of the eldest daughter was disputed.

The District Court found that the parents were equally able to care for the daughter and allocated parental authority over the eldest daughter to the mother considering that she had been the parent who had spent the most amount of time with the daughter and the fact that the children would then be raised together. The father appealed against this decision to the Eastern High Court which upheld the decision of the lower court in its decision of 23 June 2003. The father then sought and was awarded leave to appeal the case to the Supreme Court.

During the procedures before the lower courts the extent of and the conditions for the contact arrangement between the eldest daughter and the father had been disputed and the Regional State Administration had been requested to decide on these issues. Initially the parents had agreed that the children should reside with the mother and that the eldest daughter would spend the weekends with the father. Consequently, the Regional State Administration decided on a 9:5 contact arrangement (in the summer of 2003) and later upon an 8:6 contact

---

206 The period before 1968 has been described as the happy times of Danish family law because the worst injustices (against illegitimate children) had been removed without undermining the institution of marriage, Chapter II, Section II.4.

207 A. Kronborg, 2007, supra, p. 135.

208 Højesteret 28.10.2004, *UFR* 2005.363H.

arrangement (August 2004).[209] The question of the father taking the eldest daughter on holiday to the US had also been disputed. The mother was initially in favour (after having been allocated sole parental authority by the High Court), but changed her opinion after the father had sought and been granted leave to appeal to the Supreme Court, because she was afraid that the father would remain in the US with their daughter.

The Supreme Court changed the decision of the lower court and allocated parental authority to the father. From the extensive quotations from the expert evidence it may be deduced that the decisive factor was that the mother was considered fragile in relation to the co-operation norm. The expert considered, amongst other things, that:

> 'The mother has a great wish to co-operate with the father in respect of (the daughter), but her co-operation potential is assessed as being fragile, because in stressful situations she has reacted with fear and has acted inappropriately in respect of positive co-operation with the father. This was the case, for example, in the beginning when she requested sole parental authority instead of trying to make joint parental authority work and she has also subsequently rejected the father's suggestion to settle the case (joint parental authority). She does not recognise that she has a share in the involvement of (the daughter) in the conflict, amongst other things, by not allowing (the daughter) to travel to the US with the father. The mother acts as if (the daughter) is primarily her child and she is considered to have difficulties in sharing (the daughter) with the father.'

KRONBORG has criticised this decision in relation to, in particular, the decisiveness attached to the co-operation norm within the perspective that the parents are not equal in relation to this norm. The father had nothing to lose by stating an intention to co-operate. The mother, on the other hand, was afraid that he may have taken the child to the US.[210]

The *co-operation norm* is given increasing importance in the Explanatory notes to the 2007 Act. It must be expected that this norm will increasingly determine an allocation of sole parental authority or perhaps rather an establishment of the

---

209 This means that the child would reside with the mother and spend 5, respectively 6 days with the father.

210 A. Kronborg, 2007, supra, p. 143-144. The expert had stated that the father did not seem to intend to relocate to the US without, however, substantiating on which basis this assessment had been made.

child's residence in cases where the contact rights of the other parent are disputed.[211]

The question of *factual equality* between the parents or the non-discrimination of fathers has been addressed in relation to legislation and in the legal literature. The 1994 Commission investigated how often a father won the case when there was a dispute and came to the conclusion that in 25% of cases the father was allocated sole parental authority.[212] In a case study from 2002 the conclusion was that fathers were allocated parental authority in 40% of cases before the district courts and in 36% of cases before the appeal courts. The study considered that 'the percentage is expectantly so high that it may dismiss the myth that fathers only obtain parental authority if the mother is unsuitable'.[213]

V.6.2.2. Reallocation of sole parental authority

The Danish regulation on the reallocation (transfer) of parental authority from one parent to the other has been changed on a number of occasions. These changes have toned down the importance of the continuity principle.[214] In the 1986 reform of parental authority[215] the criterion became that a transfer was possible 'if it was necessary considering what was best for the child, especially due to changed circumstances.'[216] In the 1996 reform the criterion became that a transfer was possible when 'special reasons indicate this (...) if it is best for the child, especially due to changed circumstances.' Further, the 1996 reform provided the only mentioned consideration that 'the decision should attach

211 L 133, Comments to § 11. Further, the Act on Parental Responsibility contains a new provision in Article 18 concerning contact, providing that 'Both parents have responsibility for the child's contact (with the other parent)'.

212 Commission report No. 1279/1994, p. 43 and p. 100 pertaining to all cases decided in October-December 1993.

213 M. Højgaard Pedersen, 'Når den fælles forældremyndighed skal ophøre', *TFA*, 2002, p. 81-83. This article has been criticised for making this conclusion considering that the information is (probably) based upon cases which reach the two high courts. Such cases are probably cases where the father has a good possibility of succeeding. As such they are not representative, O. Bjerg, 'Er kønsmæssig diskrimination i forældremyndighedssager en myte – eller ej?', *TFA*, 2005, p. 277-279.

214 Amongst other things, because a change is considered to be less dramatic because the amount of contact has increased, L. Frost, 'Ændring af forældremyndighedsdomme og –aftaler efter forældremyndighedsloven §13', *TFA*, 2003, p. 352.

215 See generally on these reforms, Chapter II, Section II.3.2.1.

216 The insertion of the word 'especially' indicated that in special circumstances a transfer was possible also when circumstances had not changed.

importance to the fact that the holder of parental authority hinders contact (with the other parent) without any reason'.[217]

The present regulation (the 2007 Act) has further toned down the continuity principle. The provision is contained in Article 14 of the Act on Parental Responsibility. According to this provision the court may transfer parental authority to the other parent. This provision applies to all situations where one parent holds sole parental authority. The guiding criterion is the general 'best interests' principle.[218] Further, the consideration concerning the obstruction of contact has been omitted. The 2006 Commission considered that the obstruction of contact could only rarely justify a transfer of parental authority considering the best interests principle.[219] The obstruction of contact nonetheless continues to occupy an (increasingly) central position in relation to the provision on the transfer of parental authority.[220]

As is the case with the allocation of parental authority, it has been a tradition in Danish family law literature to arrange and qualify case law in relation to reallocation and to register changes in the categories of cases.[221]

V.6.3. SOLE PARENTAL AUTHORITY: THE CEFL PRINCIPLES

The CEFL principles only allow for the discharge of parental responsibilities in exceptional situations and further contain no *choice of parent criteria* save for the principle of non-discrimination deliberated below. The principles depart

217 L. Frost, 2003, supra, p. 352.

218 Art. 4, Act on Parental Responsibility.

219 Commission report 1475/2006, p. 86. The leading case is Højesteret (Supreme Court) 03.11.2003, *UFR* 2004.296H where the mother had obstructed contact for many years and where the father had previously unsuccessfully requested the transfer of parental authority. In this case the District and the High Court had allocated sole parental authority to the father, but the Supreme Court overturned this decision. Nonetheless, a large number of cases from the district and high courts have obstruction as a central reason for the transfer, see L. Frost, 2003, supra, p. 361-363. Further, the Supreme Court transferred parental authority to the father in a case where the child was born after the parents had ended their beief relationship, paternity had been judicially established when the child was 2 years old and the father had had no contact during the first two and a half years and thereafter only limited contact, Højesteret 30.10.2000, *UFR* 2001.153H.

220 L 133 p. Comments to § 14 and Commission report 1475/2006, p. 86.

221 L. Frost, 2003, supra, p. 352-363 with reference to an earlier article. Apart from the categorisation of cases, it may be deduced that the number of cases concerning a transfer is increasing, that approximately 50% of cases result in a transfer and that the age of the children encompassed by a request for a transfer has decreased. A. Kronborg, 2007, supra, p. 146-170 handles a different categorisation.

from the notion of an equal exercise '*whenever possible*' but do allow for the sole exercise of parental authority pursuant to an agreement or a decision by a competent authority.[222]

The principles contain a general principle of non-discrimination against the child on grounds such as sex, race, colour, language, religion, political or other opinion, national, ethnic, or social origin, sexual orientation, disability, property, birth or other status, irrespective of whether these grounds refer to the child or to the holders of parental responsibilities.[223]

V.6.4. COMPARISON: SOLE PARENTAL AUTHORITY

A comparison between Danish and Dutch law and the CEFL principles in respect of an allocation of sole parental authority (the choice between parents) may be considered to be fruitless, at the present moment in time, as Danish law is in a transitory phase, whereas Dutch law has developed a strong legal norm favouring joint parental authority and the CEFL principles provide for the allocation of sole parental authority only in the context of a discharge of parental responsibilities.

However, a few pointers may be derived from the descriptions. In the first place, it should be noted that the question of equality in respect of 'the choice of the parent' and the qualification of the criteria for the allocation and reallocation of parental authority has had a far more prominent place in Danish law than in Dutch law.[224] While mothers continue to be the primary resident parents in most cases in both countries,[225] it is probable that there are more disputed cases in Denmark where the parents are considered to be equally able and where the court allocates parental authority to the father.[226] The family patterns in relation to the division of work and care are also more traditional in the Netherlands than in Denmark. In respect of Denmark, DANIELSEN has pointed to the fact[227] that the increasing labour participation of women means '*that the choice more*

---

[222] Principles, principle 3:11, p. 82, Comment 2, p. 85. See further Chapter VI and VII.

[223] Principles, Principle 3:5, p. 44.

[224] Also taking account of the law prior to the 1998 Act.

[225] Chapter IV, Section IV.2.1.

[226] Above Section V.6.2.1. concerning allocation to fathers in Denmark. There are no statistics on the allocation to fathers in the Netherlands concerning specifically the situation where the allocation is disputed, see Section V.4.5.5. above concerning allocations in divorce proceedings.

[227] S. Danielsen, 2003, supra, p. 175. See Chapter I.4.2. concerning female work participation in the Netherlands and Denmark.

often now concerns two full-time working parents' where the children spend their day in creches, day-care facilities or schools.

In the second place, it should be noted that in both the Netherlands and Denmark parents are expected to co-operate. In the Netherlands this applies to parents who exercise joint parental authority but, in principle, also to parents who exercise sole parental authority because there is a duty to consult the other parent in important matters. In Denmark this duty formally only applies to parents who hold joint parental authority. The development of the co-operation norm in Denmark does, however, provide parents with a strong incentive to co-operate because not doing so factually places a parent in a position where he/she may lose parental authority. In this respect the paradox appears that the employment of the co-operation norm in Denmark even under the law prior to 2007, which provided that a parent may always request the termination of joint parental authority, probably provided a stronger means to enforce co-operation than an allocation of joint parental authority in the Netherlands where these are maintained even when contact cannot be established and where the allocation of joint parental authority has been described as a rag to wipe off the blood.[228]

It remains to be seen whether the reallocation of parental authority in the Netherlands, where the child is not meant to change its residence as in Danish cases, will work as a means to enforce co-operation. The reallocation is meant primarily as a means for the parent (the father) to use enforcement measures (the physical fetching of the child) if necessary.[229]

V.7. ALLOCATION OF PARENTAL AUTHORITY TO A NON-PARENT

This Section addresses the possibility of a parent holding or exercising parental authority to acquire joint parental authority together with a non-parent. In Dutch and Danish law there can only be two holder(s) of parental authority while the CEFL principles contain the possibility of more holder(s) depending, however, upon national law.[230]

228 Chapter II.2.2.2.

229 In Denmark such enforcement measures are possible in respect of a contact order, see further Chapter VIII, Section VIII.5.2.

230 Above, Section V.2.2.

V.7.1. NON-PARENT: THE NETHERLANDS

The possibility for a parent to exercise joint (parental) authority together with a non-parent was introduced in Article 253t of the Dutch Civil Code in 1998. It was part of an enactment regulating, in particular, the possibility to exercise joint guardianship (non-parents), which had not been previously possible. In the course of the parliamentary proceedings an amendment to the Act provided for the automatic continuation of joint parental authority after divorce.[231]

According to Article 253t the parent who exercises sole parental authority and his/her partner or, in principle, another person who has a close personal relationship with the child, for example the parent's sibling, a grandparent or a close friend may apply to the court for an allocation of joint parental authority. If legal ties exist between the child and another parent, the court will only allocate joint authority if, prior to the application, the parent and the other person have continuously cared for the child for at least one year and the parent has exercised sole parental authority for at least 3 years. The application will be denied if there is a well-founded fear that the best interest of the child would be neglected if the application was granted.[232]

The starting point is thus that joint (parental) authority will be allocated to a parent and a non-parent if they meet the requirements of this provision and such allocation is not contrary to the best interests of the child. The interests of the other legal parent play a role, but are, in principle, not decisive.[233] The other legal parent does not have a right of veto. While the position of the other legal parent played an important role in the parliamentary discussions, intrinsically no clear guidance may be derived from the parliamentary proceedings as to the relevance of an objection from the other legal parent.[234]

The matter has been further complicated by the possibility for one parent to make a sole request for the reallocation or first-time allocation of joint parental authority as developed in case law and as is presently contained in a pending

231 Chapter II, Section II.2.2.2.

232 The Supreme Court denied a request for joint parental authority in a situation where the mother and the mother's same-sex partner had discontinued cohabitation before the request was made, Hoge Raad 13.07.2004, LJN ZC3639. The Maastricht District Court allocated joint parental authority to the male partner of the mother where the cohabitation had been discontinued. In this case the child lived with the ex-partner, Rechtbank Maastricht 18.11.2003, LJN AN8695.

233 Hoge Raad (Supreme Court) 13.07.2004, LJN ZC3639.

234 Parliamentary proceedings 1995/1996 (*Kamerstukken*) 23 714, No. 6, p. 9.

legislative proposal.[235] This means that the court will often hear competing claims from the non-parent and the legal parent for joint parental authority. In this case there is no clear line to be derived from case law as to the preference to be given to two competing requests.[236]

When a non-parent is allocated joint authority together with a parent they hold parental authority on equal terms. This means that they have the same rights and duties deriving from Article 247 of the Dutch Civil Code pertaining to the care for the child and they have, in principle, an equal right to retain joint parental authority in cases where the relationship or marriage breaks down and a right to contact.[237] Furthermore, the non-parent has a duty to provide for the child financially also after the termination of joint authority.[238]

V.7.2. NON-PARENT: DENMARK

It is possible for the holder of sole parental authority to be allocated joint parental authority together with his/her spouse. Such an agreement is subject to approval by the Regional State Administration that must ascertain that the allocation is in the best interest of the child.[239] If the other legal parent objects to this allocation, administrative case law shows that permission will not be granted.[240]

The possibility for a parent to hold parental authority together with his/her spouse was introduced by the 1986 Act on Parental Authority and Contact.[241] The scope of the provision, for example in relation to a co-habitating or a registered partner, was not considered in the 1996 or 2007 revision.

---

235 Chapter III, Section III.3.3.

236 In some cases both requests are denied, for example Gerechtshof Arnhem (Court of Appeal) 08.06.2004, LJN AQ5059. In some cases the new partner is allocated joint parental authority, for example Rechtbank Haarlem (District Court) 06.02.2007, LJN AZ9643, Gerechtshof The Hague (Appeal Court) 27.08.2003, LJN AI1828 and M. Vonk, 2005, supra, p. 34-39. There seems to be no published cases where the legal parent has been reallocated joint parental authority.

237 See Chapter VIII, Section VIII.2.1. and VIII.2.2.

238 For a period corresponding to the period that he/she has held parental authority, Art. 253w, DCC.

239 Art. 13(2), Act on Parental Responsibility.

240 S. Danielsen, 1997, supra, p. 205-206.

241 Chapter II, Section II.3.2.1.

When the married partner obtains joint parental authority together with the parent they hold parental authority on equal terms. This means that the rights and duties (concerning the raising of the child) contained in Article 2 of the Act on Parental Responsibility apply equally to both. In the case of divorce the married partner has an equal right, in principle, to retain joint parental authority or to be allocated sole parental authority as the legal parent.[242] Further, the married partner has a right to contact after divorce.[243] The married partner who has obtained joint parental authority is under a duty to care for, but not to support the child financially. This duty rests upon the child's legal parents. He/she also cannot be obliged to pay maintenance upon divorce.[244]

V.7.3. NON-PARENT: THE CEFL PRINCIPLES

The CEFL principles provide the possibility for the attribution of parental responsibilities to a non-parent (a third person) instead of or in addition to a parent, but leaving the further regulation of how, to whom and subject to which conditions to national law.[245] The CEFL has made a choice for a broad concept of parental responsibilities, but simultaneously considering that parents are the most important persons in a child's life and primarily in charge of the exercise of parental responsibilities.[246]

V.7.4. COMPARISON: NON-PARENTS

The scope of the Dutch provision in terms of the persons who may be allocated joint parental authority together with a parent is considerably broader than the Danish provision, which provides this possibility solely in respect of the parent's spouse. The Dutch provision, on the other hand, has more specific time requirements in relation to the period during which the non-parent has cared for the child and the time when the parent has held sole parental authority than the Danish provision. The main difference, viewed in the context of the subject-

242 By analogy to Art. 11 of the Act on Parental Responsibility (this Article uses the term 'parent'), S. Danielsen, 1997, supra, p. 213.

243 By analogy to Art. 18 of the Act on Parental Responsibility (this Article uses the term 'parent'), Commission Report No. 985/1983, p. 81 in relation to the previous provision and L. Frost, 'Samspillet mellem forældremyndighedslovens og bistandslovens regler om samvær og anden kontakt', *Skarrildhus*, 27.10.1997. S. Danielsen is doubtful hereof considering that the term used is 'parent', S. Danielsen, 1997, supra, p. 303.

244 Only legal parents have a duty to pay maintenance, Lov om børns forsørgelse, Consolidated Act No. 352 of 15.05.2003 with later amendments.

245 Principles, principle 3:2, p. 32, principle 3:9 and Comment 4, p. 66, p. 77.

246 Principles, principle 3:2, Comment 1, p. 33.

matter of this study, is that Danish law provides the other parent with a right of veto, which Dutch law does not.

The CEFL principles provide ample possibility for attribution to a non-parent, but leaving further regulation to national law. Consequently, the CEFL principles do not contain more specified requirements.

Presently it is probably true for the development in both Dutch and Danish law that the position of a social parent in relation to the allocation of parental authority in cases where there are two legal parents, a father and a mother, will be pushed to the background considering the emergence of joint parental authority as a strong legal norm.[247]

V.8. PARENTAL AUTHORITY AFTER ONE PARENT'S DEATH

This Section addresses the allocation of parental authority *ex lege* or pursuant to a decision of the competent authority after the death of a parent who held parental authority.

V.8.1. AFTER DEATH: THE NETHERLANDS

If the parents hold joint parental authority and the resident parent dies, the surviving parent retains parental authority *ex lege*, Article 253f of the Dutch Civil Code.

If the deceased parent had sole parental authority then the court determines whether the surviving parent or a third person will obtain custody (parental authority or guardianship) over the child.[248] A request from the surviving parent is only denied if there is reason to believe that the interest of the child would be harmed if this request was granted.[249]

247 This is less true for the CEFL principles which allow for an attribution in addition to the parents.

248 Art. 253g(1), DCC.

249 Art. 253g(3), DCC.

V.8.2. AFTER DEATH: DENMARK

The Danish provision regulating the allocation of parental authority upon the resident parent's death makes two distinctions. One concerns the surviving parent's holding of parental authority and the other whether the child resided with the surviving parent.

If the parents hold joint parental authority and one parent dies, the other parent retains parental authority. If, however, the child did not reside with the surviving parent then another person may apply for parental authority. The application from a third party will only be granted if it is considered to be inconsistent with what is best for the child to allow parental authority to remain with the surviving parent.[250]

If the deceased parent had sole parental authority, then parental authority must be placed with the remaining parent, a third person or a married couple. If the surviving parent applies for parental authority he or she is given priority.[251]

Further, Danish law contains special provisions concerning the situation where the surviving parent has caused the other parent's death. If the child resided with the surviving parent, the parents held joint parental authority, and the surviving parent has caused the other parent's death, then another person may apply for parental authority. The application is only granted if it is decisively important for the child that parental authority does not remain with the surviving parent.[252] The same applies when the surviving parent held sole parental authority.[253]

V.8.3. AFTER DEATH: THE CEFL PRINCIPLES

The CEFL principles provide that the surviving parent retains parental responsibilities *ex lege* when the parents held joint parental authority. If only one parent held joint parental responsibilities the competent authority must attribute parental responsibilities to the surviving parent or a third person upon a decision of the competent authority.[254] The Principles do not contain a rule favouring the surviving parent. It is considered that the common core approach is that the law

250 Art. 15(1), Act on Parental Responsibility.
251 Art. 15(2), Act on Parental Responsibility.
252 Art. 15(1), Act on Parental Responsibility.
253 Art. 15(3), Act on Parental Responsibility.
254 Principles, principles 3:31(1) and (2), p. 203.

does not distinguish between attribution to the surviving parent depending upon this parent holding parental responsibilities and further that a 'better law approach seems to require' such a distinction.[255]

V.8.4. COMPARISON: PARENTAL AUTHORITY AFTER DEATH

The main difference is that Danish law, as opposed to Dutch law and the CEFL principles, contains two distinctions: the holding of parental authority and the residence of the child. Further, Danish law contains a more specific regulation in the situation where one parent has caused the other parent's death. Paramount for understanding the more detailed Danish regulation is that Danish law does not contain the possibility to *discharge* parental authority.[256] In Dutch law and pursuant to the CEFL principles an unsuitable parent could be discharged of parental authority.[257]

Dutch and Danish law as well as the CEFL principles clearly favour parental authority to be held by the legal parent after the other parent's death.[258]

V.9. THE RELEVANCE OF A PRIVATE AGREEMENT

The purpose of this Section is to portray and compare the relevance of a private agreement in respect of the allocation of *parental authority* in Dutch and Danish law. The CEFL principles do not provide for the possibility for parents to make agreements on the allocation of parental responsibilities since only a discharge determined by a competent authority is possible.[259]

---

255 Principles, principle 3:31, Comment 2, p. 210. Considering that the CEFL principles provide for a discharge of parental authority only in exceptional cases, the distinction is logical.

256 If there was no detailed regulation, the only possibility in cases where the parents held joint parental authority and the surviving parent was not suitable would be to place the child in care.

257 For example, in Dutch law a father who had caused the mother's death was discharged of parental authority, Gerechtshof 's-Gravenhage (Court of Appeal) 06.06.2007, LJN BA9040. Principles, Principle 3:31, Comment 2, p. 210.

258 The CEFL principles do not favour an attribution of parental authority to the legal parent when this parent did not hold parental authority. The CEFL principles also only provide, however, for the possibility of sole parental authority to apply in exceptional cases (discharge).

259 Principles, principle 3:32, p. 212. The possibility to make agreements in respect of the exercise of parental authority is, however, endorsed and further deliberated in Chapters VI and VII.

The approach in respect of the possibility to make agreements on the allocation of parental authority is considerably different in Dutch and Danish law. In Chapter II and in this Chapter it has been concluded that Dutch law distinguishes between joint and sole parental authority while in Denmark the dispute has become the determinant factor. The difference has been associated with the role and the authority of the State where Dutch law adopts a more protective role and exercises authority also in respect of parents who agree. The Danish position is more individualised and the State does not generally intervene when parents agree.[260]

V.9.1. A PRIVATE AGREEMENT IN DUTCH LAW

Dutch law does not contain the possibility for parents to make agreements on the allocation of parental authority.[261] The only exception is the possibility for unmarried parents, who have not previously jointly exercised parental authority, to register a joint request in the Custody register. This possibility was introduced with the 1995 reform of parental authority. The purpose was not to introduce contractual freedom, but rather to equate unmarried parents with married parents in the sense that the initial allocation of joint parental authority would not be subject to a substantive review.[262] All other changes to the allocation of parental authority, whether they concern an allocation of joint or sole parental authority, must be decided by the court.[263] The aforementioned does not mean that parental agreement on allocation is not relevant to the court's decision.[264] The majority of divorces in the Netherlands are so-called covenant divorces[265] where the parties submit a covenant containing the parties' agreements concerning the consequences of divorce.

---

260 Chapter II, Section II.4. and above, Section V.4.7.

261 This principle was contained in Art. 195 of the old DCC, which was abandoned in 1956 considering that the prerogative character could be derived from the provisions concerning parental authority, ASSER-DE BOER, 2006, supra, p. 342.

262 Chapter II, Section II.2.4.

263 A less restrictive view concerning a joint request for joint parental authority is demonstrated through a recent enactment which provides that legal representation is unnecessary in such cases, Wet van 22 november 2006 tot wijziging van Boek 1 van het Burgerlijk Wetboek in verband met herschikking van de bevoegdheidsverdeling tussen rechtbank en kantonrechter, alsmede van artikel 12 van dat boek en van artikel 268 van het Wetboek van Burgerlijke Rechtsvordering, Stb. 2006, 589.

264 For example, concerning an allocation of sole parental authority, Gerechtshof 's-Hertogenbosch (Court of Appeal) 30.03.2006, LJN AX9618 where the father was often unreachable and had agreed to an allocation of sole parental authority. The court allocated sole parental authority to the mother.

265 52% (2003), CBS (Statistics Netherlands).

Illustrative is a case decided by the 's-Hertogenbosch Court of Appeal. In this case both parents had requested in the divorce procedure an allocation of sole parental authority to the mother. One of the children had brain damage and the parents disagreed on the manner in which the child should be raised. The parents wanted the mother to exercise sole parental authority to prevent conflicts and problems in the future. The Court of Appeal rejected the request considering that it was in the interest of the child that decisions were made jointly also in a case where the parents had diverging opinions on how to raise the child.[266]

The court may, however, consider an agreement to be relevant to its decision. In a divorce procedure before the District Court of Breda (the divorce decree had been issued in 2001) where the parents had submitted a covenant in respect of the consequences of the divorce providing for the continuation of the joint exercise of parental authority in 2006, the Court rejected the father's subsequent request for sole parental authority (the children resided with the father). The 's-Hertogenbosch Court of Appeal considered, amongst other things, that it was '*incompatible*' with the signing of the covenant to request an allocation of sole parental authority.[267]

When a common request from the parents forms the basis of the court's decision, this decision may be changed if the court had not properly reviewed the agreement and a proper review would have provided a different result.[268] This may be derived from the 's-Hertogenbosch Court of Appeal's decision of 31 August 2006. In this case the father had been allocated sole parental authority over the children in the divorce procedure in 2004. In this procedure the parents had submitted a joint request for sole parental authority to the father. The parents had also agreed upon a co-parentage (shared residence) arrangement in the covenant. The mother subsequently (in 2006) requested a reallocation of joint parental authority from the (same) District Court of 's-Hertogenbosch, which rejected the request considering that circumstances had not changed since the allocation (the parents continued the shared residence arrangement) and that the

266 Gerechtshof 's-Hertogenbosch 09.09.2004, LJN AR5959.

267 Gerechtshof 's-Hertogenbosch 11.10.2006, LJN AZ3900.

268 The question of how intense the review which the courts factually provide in respect of joint requests, for example concerning 'covenant divorces', has been a recurrent theme in the Luchtenveld proposal and the pending proposal on 'Continued Parenting', Chapter II., Section II.2.6. It is probable that a review has not been as intense as presumed, M. Antokolskaia, 'Administratieve echtscheiding vanuit national en international perspectief' in: M. Antokolskaia (Ed.), *Herzienning van het echtscheidingsrecht*, Amsterdam: SWP, 2006, p. 51.

decision had not been based upon incorrect or incomplete information.[269] The 's-Hertogenbosch Court of Appeal changed this decision and allocated joint parental authority considering, primarily, that the District Court in the divorce procedure had neglected to investigate if the allocation of sole parental authority was in the interests of the children and further that such an investigation would have resulted in an allocation of joint parental authority. Finally, the Court of Appeal considered that there was no risk of the children becoming 'torn or lost' between the parents.[270]

It may be derived from these decisions that an agreement may be relevant to the court's decision. The agreement is not decisive, however.

V.9.2. A PRIVATE AGREEMENT IN DANISH LAW

Parents are not free to make agreements on parental authority in Danish law. The possibility to make agreements is restricted to the possibilities contained in the Act on Parental Responsibility.[271] These concern the possibility for parents who do not live together to agree upon the allocation of sole and joint parental authority. Such an agreement must be notified to the State Regional Administration to become valid or in the situation where a case on the allocation of parental authority is pending before the courts, to the court itself.[272] Such agreements are no longer subject to a substantive review.[273]

An agreement which has been notified has, in principle, the same validity as a decision by the court. The court may, at the request of one parent, amend an agreement subject to the same conditions for amending a decision.[274] The agreement may thus be viewed as having limited validity.[275]

An agreement may be declared invalid based upon general contractual rules,[276] in principle based upon the failure of basic assumptions (*bristende forundsæt-*

---

269 Art. 253o, DCC, which in the legislative framework only allows for a reallocation of joint parental authority based upon a joint request, above Section V.4.5.1.

270 Gerechtshof 's-Hertogenbosch 31.08.2006, LJN AZ2571.

271 The parents cannot, for example, make a conditional agreement, Østre Landsret (Eastern High Court) 28.01.2002, *TFA* 2002.938Ø.

272 Further regulated in a Ministerial decree, Bekendtgørelse om forældremyndighed, barnets bopæl og samvær m.v., No. 1071 of 06.09.2007.

273 Chapter II, Section II.3.2.

274 Art. 14(2), Act on Parental Responsibility and above, Section V.2.2. on reallocation.

275 A. Kronborg, 2007, supra, p. 82.

276 Contained in the Aftalelov, Consolidated Act. No. 781 of 26.08.1996.

ninger).[277] The starting point, however, is clearly that an agreement is binding. Illustrative is the Eastern High Court's decision from 2006.[278] In this case the parents had submitted a divorce petition to the Regional State Administration requesting that sole parental authority over their three children be allocated to the father.[279] The State Administration confirmed the allocation of parental authority. The mother complained about this allocation to the State Administration claiming that she had not agreed to this allocation. According to the mother the papers had been signed during a hectic moment and the father had put pressure on her to sign; further, she did not think that the section on the allocation of parental authority had been completed when she signed. The father claimed that they had discussed the papers over a few days, that he had helped the mother to understand the forms and that they had agreed upon the allocation of parental authority.[280] The State Administration advised the mother to seek legal aid and the mother then initiated court proceedings claiming that the agreement was void or, alternatively, that parental authority be transferred to her.[281] The District and the Eastern Appeal Court found that the agreement was valid and rejected a transferal of parental authority to the mother considering that the children were doing well with the father.[282]

---

277 In a case where the parents had held joint parental authority since the birth of the child they agreed to allocate sole parental authority to the mother in May 2000. In October 2000 they agreed to reobtain joint parental authority. Both agreements were notified and approved (under the previous law). In August 2001 the father requested the court to allocate sole parental authority to him in a case concerning the termination of joint parental authority (under the previous law). The mother claimed that it had been a basic assumption that the father would not request sole parental authority and that therefore she still had sole parental authority, which should result in the dismissal of the case (the father would then need to request a transfer of parental authority). The court considered that even if she had assumed that the father would not request sole parental authority, this assumption could not result in a dismissal of the case, Østre Landsret (Eastern Appeal Court) 28.01.2002, *UFR* 2002.938Ø.

278 Østre Landsret 27.03.2006, *UFR* 2006.1959Ø.

279 The mother had entered into a new relationship and left the marital home.

280 Pursuant to the simplification reform, a divorce may be obtained through the completion and submission to the State Administration of a form when the parents agree. A meeting (*vilkårsforhandling*) at the State Administration is not required, and neither is legal representation, see on this reform C.G. Jeppesen de Boer, 'Administratieve Ectscheiding in Denemarken, *FJR*, 2005, p. 231-235 and further Chapter VIII, Section VIII.3.2.1.

281 Pursuant to Art. 14(1) of the new Act on Parental Responsibility, it would also have been possible to request joint parental authority.

282 A similar case decided by the Eastern High Court also concerned the validity of an agreement and the possibility of a subsequent transfer. In this case the mother had signed a form allocating sole parental authority to the father in the course of an 'unofficial divorce proceeding', in which an Iman had assisted the parents. The agreement had been notified to the State Administration. The mother claimed that she thought that they had agreed upon joint parental authority (which they already held). The High Court transferred parental authority to the

There has been a divergence in the case law of the two high courts as to the character of a settlement (agreement) entered into in court.[283] The Eastern High Court found in its decision of 28 June 2006 that the fact that the parents in the course of the divorce procedure before the district court had agreed upon the allocation of sole parental authority to the mother, did not preclude the father from claiming parental authority in the appeal. The High Court considered that the primary purpose of the provision concerning disputes on parental authority was to establish what was best for the child.[284]

The Western High Court, on the other hand, found in its decision of 28 September 2006 that the court only has a function in cases where there is a dispute. The fact that the parties before the District Court had agreed upon the allocation of parental authority over two of the parents' three children to the father (the court allocated parental authority over the third child to the father) precluded the mother from appealing in respect of the two children.[285] This case was brought before the Supreme Court (with leave from the Appeals Permission Board). The Supreme Court found that the court settlement was to be regarded as a valid agreement. Nonetheless, the Supreme Court found that the High Court should have allowed the mother to claim parental authority over one of the children encompassed by the agreement.[286] It would thus seem that the Supreme Court shares the approach of the Eastern High Court that notwithstanding a valid agreement entered into in court, a parent may still claim parental authority on appeal.[287]

On the basis of these decisions, it may be concluded that an agreement on the allocation of parental authority in Danish law has limited validity when a dis-

---

mother considering that she had been the primary carer and that the child had primarily resided with the mother, since the parents had ceased cohabitation without mentioning the agreement, Østre Landsret 21.02.2006, *TFA* 2006.250Ø.

283 Pursuant to the enactment of the rule simplification, Chapter II.3.2.1.

284 Østre Landsret 28.06.2006, *UFR* 2006.2816Ø.

285 Vestre Landsret 28.09.2006, *UFR* 2007.92V. Before the High Court the mother requested parental authority only in respect of one of the two children encompassed by the agreement and further requested an amendment of the Distric Court's decision in respect of the third child.

286 Based upon the general provisions of the Civil Procedural Act, Retsplejeloven Art. 383 and 384 concerning the possibility to extend a claim on appeal.

287 Højesteret (Supreme Court), 24.08.2007, case No. 82/2007, still unpublished (October 2007), and based upon a brief summary of the decision. One judge delivered a dissenting opinion corresponding to the approach of the Eastern High Court. The Supreme Court allocated parental authority over both children to the father and he consequently came to hold parental authority over all three children.

pute subsequently arises. Although the agreement is valid and forms the starting point, all cases have eventually resulted in a decision considering the best interests principle. The possibility to enter into an agreement in Danish law is consequently primarily relevant for parents who continue to agree.

V.9.3. COMPARISON: A PRIVATE AGREEMENT

While only Danish law allows for private agreements concerning the allocation of parental authority, a private agreement may nonetheless be relevant in both Dutch and Danish law. A private agreement in Dutch law is, however, subject to review and the relevance therefore depends upon the circumstances of the individual case and the general legal norm pointing in the direction of joint parental authority. In Danish law a private agreement is primarily relevant for parents who continue to agree since that an emerging dispute will be decided according to the best interests principle.

CHAPTER VI
RESIDENCE

VI.1. INTRODUCTION

This Chapter addresses the concept of the child's residence with one or both parents who hold or exercise joint parental authority. Further, the Chapter addresses one of the main sources of parental disputes: the relocation of a resident parent.

VI.2. CONCEPT OF RESIDENCE

In both Dutch and Danish law, in the latter since 2007, the establishment of a (main) residence may be viewed historically as a substitute for an allocation of sole parental authority when parents who hold or exercise joint parental authority cannot agree upon the child's residence.

VI.2.1. MAIN RESIDENCE: THE NETHERLANDS

The 1998 Act did not provide for the possibility of establishing the main residence. As deliberated in Chapter II it could not be derived from the parliamentary proceedings that joint parental authority should become the legal norm also in cases where the parents had fundamental disagreements such as a dispute over the child's residence.[1] The authority of the Dutch courts to establish a main residence (*hoofdverblijf*) when the parents exercise joint parental authority was, however, confirmed by the Supreme Court's decision of 15 December 2000.[2] The authority is derived from the general dispute settlement provision contained in Article 253a of the Dutch Civil Code.[3]

---

1 Section II.2.2.2.

2 Hoge Raad, *NJ* 2001, 123 annotated by S.F.M. Wortmann.

3 Art. 253a provides that 'In the case of the exercise of joint parental authority, disputes between the partners in respect thereof may, on the application of both or either of them be submitted to the district court. The district court shall first attempt to reach an agreement between the

In this case the Supreme Court upheld the decision of the Arnhem Court of Appeal to determine the child's main residence instead of, as requested by both parents, an allocation of sole parental authority to one of them. From the Supreme Court's decision it may, however, be deduced that the court may only establish a main residence when this has been requested by the parents and not *ex officio* as the Court of Appeal had done. Further, it may be deduced from the case that the establishment of a main residence belongs to the ancillary provisions which may be decided in the course of the divorce procedure.[4] While it is not required, most divorce decrees will contain a decision, if requested, or mention the agreement which the parents have reached concerning the child's residence.[5]

The general rule in respect of the registered residence (address) of a child as far as the council administration is concerned is that the child is registered with the parent who exercises sole parental authority or in the case of a joint exercise with the parent with whom he/she factually resides or has stayed most recently, Article 12(1) of the Dutch Civil Code.[6] If a main residence has been established and the child resides with this parent, the child will be registered at the address of this parent. The registration of the child with the council administration is, however, to be viewed as an independent matter as the court can decide upon the child's registered address without establishing a main residence.[7] It is consequently possible for the court to alternatively decide upon the child's main residence and the registered address.

---

parents prior to taking a decision. The court shall give such an order as it shall consider desirable in the best interests of the child.'

4 Critical of this approach is S.F.M. Wortmann in her annotation to the case, *NJ* 2001, 123.

5 The question of which effect the mentioning of the child's residence in the *dictum* has is not clear; M.J.C. Koens, C.G.M. van Wamelen, *Kind en scheiding*, the Hague: Koninklijke Vermande, 2001, p. 58-59.

6 The child has a dependent residence (dependent upon the parent who holds parental authority). Registration of a change in the child's residence with the council administration (*Gemeentelijke Basis Administratie Persongegevens*) requires the consent of the holder(s) or a decision of the court.

7 Gerechtshof's-Gravenhage (Court of Appeal) 18.10.2006, LJN AZ2072. In this case the parents had agreed to a shared residence (co-parentage). The child was registered at the father's address. The mother requested the court to establish the child's main residence with her so that she would qualify for subsidised housing and other benefits. The Court of Appeal rejected the mother's requested main residence and decided that the child's registered address was to be with the father.

It has been suggested that the concept of a main residence is a more flexible instrument than the concept of parental authority.[8] It is indeed also based upon a provision which provides the courts with extensive power with the best interest principle being the only guiding criterion. The court is not bound by the request(s) of the parent(s) but may give an order which it considers desirable in the interests of the child. As such it may be used, according to VAN LEUVEN, for example to resolve contact cases where the resident parent frustrates contact in the sense that the court may change the main residence to the contact parent. An illustrative example of the use of the main residence as a flexible concept is provided by the decision of the District Court of Roermond where the court established a *conditional* main residence.[9]

While there is little doubt that the establishment of the main residence in most divorce procedures will replace an allocation of sole parental authority, it is not evident that the court's role in this procedure is the same as in a procedure concerning the termination of joint parental authority and the allocation of sole parental authority. In a divorce procedure before the Hague Court of Appeal it would seem that the court adopted the approach that it was not its role and not the role of the Dutch Child Protection Board to assess which of the parents was the most suitable to provide the child's main residence. Rather, it adopted the more limited approach of ascertaining whether a change of the factually established residence (with the mother) was indicated.[10] If this approach is correct

---

8 C. van Leuven, 'De verblijfplaats van het kind na echtscheiding', *EB*, 1998, p. 1-5, p. 3.

9 Both the interim and the final decision were conditioned upon the mother's co-operation in respect of contact. Such a decision, according to the court, fitted the extensive powers which the court had according to Art. 253a, DCC, Rechtbank Roermond 10.11.2004, LJN AR5891. In this respect, however, it should be noted that this development is also visible in respect of parental authority, see, for example, the decision referred to in Chapter V, Section V.5.1.1.; Gerechtshof 's-Gravenhage (Court of Appeal) 13.02.2002, LJN AE2305 where the court had established a trial period of joint parental authority and the cases on temporary reallocation of parental authority (without factual residence) in relation to the frustration of contact mentioned in Section V.5.1.2. It is not clear whether such conditional, trial periods and temporary reallocations represent a correct application of the law. It is worth considering the decision mentioned in Chapter III, Section III.3.2. where the Supreme Court set aside the Subdistrict Court's decision to allocate joint parental authority (then parental power) conditional upon continued cohabitation because it did not fit within the legislative system, Hoge Raad, 21.03.1986, *NJ* 1986, 588 annotated by E.A.A Luijten and E.A. Alkema and Gerechtshof 's-Hertogenbosch (Court of Appeal) 28.06.1973, *NJ* 1974, 6. An interim decision cannot, as a main rule, be appealed.

10 Gerechtshof 's-Gravenhage 21.09.2005, LJN AU3030. In this case the Court of Appeal made a rather unclear distinction between the best interests principle in a case concerning the allocation of sole parental authority and in a case concerning the establishment of the main

then it means that the presumption that each parent is *entitled* to a decision which weighs the possibilities that each parent may offer, which is presumed to apply in a case concerning the allocation of sole parental authority, does not apply in the situation where the dispute concerns the child's residence.[11]

In a more recent case, however, it would seem that the Amsterdam Court of Appeal did adopt the approach that each parent was entitled to such a decision weighing the possibilities that each parent could offer.[12] The proceedings in this case were the following:

The parents' separated (factually) in June 2003 and their marriage was converted into a registered partnership in December 2003 and judicial proceedings pertaining to the dissolution of this registered partnership were initiated. Pursuant to the factual separation in June 2003 the (Swedish) mother moved to Sweden bringing the child, a daughter aged one, with her. The parents subsequently made an agreement that the child should reside alternately with the mother in Sweden and the father, who had Dutch nationality, in the Netherlands. The child thereafter stayed with the father in the Netherlands from approximately September to October 2003 and from mid October to the end of October with the mother in Sweden. From the end of October the sharing arrangement was discontinued and the parents' ceased to agree upon the residence arrangement for the child.

The child was temporarily entrusted to the father with the decision of the District Court of Amsterdam of 14 May 2004. On 19 January 2005 the District Court determined the child's main residence to be with the father. The mother appealed against this decision to the Amsterdam Court of Appeal. The Court of Appeal requested an expert opinion from the Dutch Child Protection Board concerning the question with whom the child's residence should be. Pending the proceedings, the Court of Appeal determined on 7 July 2005 that the child should reside alternatively with both parents.[13] This residence arrangement was possible because the mother had established a secondary residence in the Netherlands for the duration of the proceedings.

---

residence, indicating that in a decision concerning the main residence, the interests of the parent could also be taken into account.

11 Chapter V, Section V.6.1.1.

12 Gerechtshof Amsterdam, 06.07.2006, LJN AY3929.

13 Gerechtshof Amsterdam, 07.07.2005, LJN AY3928.

The Dutch Child Protection Board considered both parents to be equally able to care for the child, but recommended that the child's main residence was to be with the father, based upon the continuity principle. The Board considered that the child had factually resided in the Netherlands and had primarily been cared for by the father since October 2003, that the child went to a day-care centre in the Netherlands and was due to start school here in the near future. On these grounds the Board considered that it would not be in the best interests of the child to change the child's residence to that of the mother, a change which would mean the child moving to Sweden.

The Amsterdam Court of Appeal did not follow the advice of the Board but determined the child's main residence to be with the mother in Sweden in its decision delivered on 14 July 2006 (a year after the interim decision establishing a temporary shared residence arrangement). In doing so the Court of Appeal relied upon, amongst other things, the fact that school starts later in Sweden than in the Netherlands, which meant that a more extensive contact arrangement was possible if the child stayed in Sweden (for the duration of approximately two years), and it further relied upon the fact that the mother was able to care for the child at home (for a certain period given the more extensive parental leave possibilities in Sweden and the fact that the mother was again pregnant) whereas the father made use of day-care facilities.

In this decision the Amsterdam Court of Appeal established a shared residence in order to be able to weigh the possibilities which each parent could offer and as such provided a very different view of its role in a case concerning the main residence than the one portrayed above by the Hague Court of Appeal. In the case before the Amsterdam Court of Appeal, the parents had, however, also initially agreed upon a shared residence. It is perhaps possible to reconcile the two decisions with the understanding that the court relied upon a continuation of the existing arrangement.[14]

Based upon these two decisions, it must be viewed as being uncertain whether and to what extent the court's role in a case concerning the main residence differs from its role in a case concerning the allocation of sole parental authority. Perhaps the uncertainty must be understood in the context of the extensive powers the court has pursuant to Article 253a.[15]

---

14 In the decision of the Amsterdam Court of Appeal for the *duration* of the proceedings only.

15 As cited above in Section VI.2.1., supra note 3.

The pending Act on 'Continued Parenting' lays down the possibility to establish a main residence without, however, further clarifying this concept or the court's role in the procedure. From the Explanatory report to the 1998 Act it followed that the parents were free to divide the care and responsibilities when they exercised joint parental authority. If the pending proposal concerning 'Continued Parenting' is adopted the division of care and responsibilities, including the child's residence, should follow from the obligatory 'parenting plan', which must be submitted with the divorce petition. It must be expected that the establishment of residence, also when the parents agree, to a greater extent than is now the case, becomes part of the obligation to make '*verifiable agreements*'.[16]

VI.2.2. RESIDENCE: DENMARK

The authority of the courts to establish the child's residence (*bopæl*) has been introduced with the 2007 Act. Article 17(1) of the Act on Parental Responsibility provides that the court will decide with whom the child should reside in cases where the parents hold joint parental authority and disagree on the child's residence. The court will not be bound by the parents' request for sole parental authority, but may *ex officio* provide a decision on residence. A decision on residence follows procedurally the same lines as a decision on the allocation of sole parental authority.[17] In most cases the parents will agree upon the residence of the child and such an agreement need not be notified and is not subject to a substantive review.[18]

Further, it follows from Article 17(2) that the court can change an agreement or a decision on residence. The provision or the Explanatory notes do not mention any specific criteria for the establishment or subsequent change of residence.[19] The notes specify that such a decision should be duly reasoned, so that the grounds for the decision are well established. The grounds may be relevant for a later change to the child's residence, for example, if the resident parent has

---

16 Chapter II, Section II.2.6.2.

17 L 133, Comments to § 17.

18 The registration in the persons administration (*Folkeregisteret*) is based upon *factual residence* and is thus not dependent upon the residence of the holder(s) of parental authority, Art. 8(1), Lov om det Centrale Personregister, Compilated Act No. 1134 of 20.11.2006 with later amendments.

19 The guiding principle of 'best interests' is now contained in a general provision rather than in the individual provision, Art. 4, Act on Parental Responsibility. Further it is specified that cases on the residence must be dealt with in the same manner as cases concerning parental authority, L 133, Comments to § 17.

agreed to or accepted an extensive contact arrangement and then later opposes this arrangement or decides to relocate with the child.[20]

VI.2.3 RESIDENCE: THE CEFL PRINCIPLES

Principle 3:20 provides that the holders of parental responsibilities who are living apart should agree upon the child's residence. If the parents cannot agree, the matter will be deferred to the competent authority that will proceed according to Principle 3:14.[21] This Principle provides the general principle regulating parental disputes of a more important nature. The principle provides two alternative solutions to settle a dispute. The competent authority may divide the exercise of parental responsibilities or decide the dispute. The principles consequently leave the choice between two different solutions to national law considering that there is no common core. It may, however, be derived from the comments that the solution of establishing a residence with one parent is (probably) the preferred solution,[22] when it is also taken into account that a relocation is separately regulated in Principle 3:21.

The question whether a competent authority should review the parents' agreements on the exercise of parental responsibilities including the matter of residence is regulated differently depending on the context. In general, the Principles leave the question of a review to national law.[23] In two specific situations, however, the Principles provide more substantive requirements. In the case of a divorce by mutual consent, an agreement must be in writing and is subject to a review by the competent authority.[24] Further, as deliberated below, an agreement concerning an alternate residence is subject to review.

VI.2.4. COMPARISON: RESIDENCE

A decision on (main) residence in Dutch law and in the CEFL principles is a decision concerning the *exercise* of parental authority/responsibilities. As such

[20] L 133, Comments to § 17.

[21] Principles, principle 3:20(1), p. 130 and Principle 3:14, p. 95.

[22] Principles, principle 3:14, p. 99, Comment 3. The principles states that: 'Authorising one of the parents to act alone will be preferable where it can be established that a specific, separable issue has to be resolved and one of the holders of parental responsibilities has a sufficient degree of competence or knowledge to pursue the best interests of the child concerning this question'. This statement would not seem to relate to a dispute concerning the residence.

[23] Principles, principle 3:13(2), p. 91, 'The competent authority may scrutinize the agreement' and principle 3:15, p. 100, Comment No. 2, p. 104.

[24] Principles, Comment No. 4, p. 94 to principle 3:13.

it is the general dispute settlement provision which regulates the determination of (main) residence and a change thereof when there is a dispute.[25] In Danish law it is a new separate type of decision.

While the establishment of the (main) residence may be viewed historically as a substitute for an allocation of sole parental authority in Dutch and Danish law, it is not evident that it has the same character in Dutch law. In the first place, the court may assume its role to be different in respect of *the choice of a parent*. In the second place the court may alternatively determine the main residence or determine with whom the child should have its registered address. In Danish law the establishment of the main residence follows the same procedural lines as the allocation of parental authority.

In respect of the *registration* of the child's residence (address) both the Nether lands and Denmark rely upon the child's factual residence when the parents hold or exercise joint parental authority. In the Netherlands the parents must, however, agree to a change in the registration or request a decision by the court while in Denmark the factual residence must be registered. The child's registered residence has relevance in both countries in relation to social benefits.

In both the Netherlands and Denmark parents are free to enter into an agreement on the child's (main) residence although in the Netherlands there is some uncertainty as to the status of an agreement compared to a court decision. In the Netherlands, however, the proposal on 'Continued Parenting' makes the determination of the child's residence part of the obligation to make 'verifiable agreements'. Also the CEFL principles provide that the agreement should be subject to review in case of a divorce by mutual consent.

VI.3. SHARED RESIDENCE

While joint parental authority after divorce and the breakup of a relationship has developed as a strong legal norm in both Danish and Dutch law and the CEFL principles provide only for the discharge of parental responsibilities in exceptional cases, the notion that the factual care of the child should be divided equally between both parents implying that the child should have a shared residence with both parents is a more disputed *de facto* implementation of joint parental authority.

---

25 The CEFL principles alternatively provide for the possibility of dividing the exercise.

VI.3.1. SHARED RESIDENCE IN DUTCH LAW

The parents are free to agree on shared residence according to Dutch law. The term generally used is co-parentage (*co-oudershap*) or bilocation (*bilocatie*).[26] The question whether the court can establish a shared residence against the wishes of one parent is not clear in Dutch law.[27] In a decision by the District Court of Zutphen of 5 February 2003 the court had established an alternate residence, against the wishes of the mother, which meant that the children would have an alternate residence with each parent for a period of two years and then change residence.[28] This decision was changed by the Arnhem Court of Appeal in its decision of 13 May 2003, according to which the children's main residence should be with the mother in order to meet their need for safety, stability and continuity.[29]

It may, however, be inferred from the case law of the lower courts that it is possible to uphold a shared residence which has been agreed upon by the parents.[30] In a decision by the Amsterdam Court of Appeal from 2005 which has

---

26 C. van Wamelen, 'De eerbiediging van een zorgrelatie', *NEMESIS*, 1996, 79 advocates the use of the term *bilocatie* (bilocation) considering that this term implies shared residence. The term *co-ouderschap* is, however, the term wich is most used. Shared residence does not have a legislative foundation, J. Gerritse, 'Blijft co-ouderschap na echtscheiding een uitzondering?', in K. Boele-Woelki (Ed.), *Actuele ontwikkelingen in het familierecht*, Oprichtingssymposium UCERF, Nijmegen: Ars Aequi Libri, 2007, p. 17.

27 J. Gerritse, 2007, supra, p. 25-26 describes the conditions that should be met in order to establish a shared residence (good communication between the parents and a flexible approach as well as a short distance between the two homes) and further advocates a preference for the establishment of a main residence and an extensive contact arrangement with the other parent above the establishment of a shared residence.

28 Pending the proceedings the children, who were born in 1991 and 1993, had been entrusted to the mother. The Dutch Child Protection Board had recommended that the children should have their main residence with the mother.

29 The father's appeal to the Supreme Court was dismissed, Hoge Raad, 29.10.2004, LJN AR1213. See also Rechtbank Haarlem (District Court) 06.02.2007, LJN AZ9635 where the father's request for co-parentage against the mother's wishes was rejected.

30 Rechtbank Utrecht (District Court) 12.04.2006, LJN AZ1191. In this case the parents had agreed to a co-parentage arrangement but also provided for the children's main residence to be with the mother. The Court rejected the mother's request to relocate, which would mean that the co-parentage arrangement would factually come to an end. The Court considered that such an agreement required the parents to agree on important decisions concerning the children including the residence of the children. When the mother thereby initiated the move, the Utrecht District Court changed the children's main residence to that of the father in its decision of 18.08.2006, LJN AZ1192. Further, the Hague Court of Appeal rejected a mother's request for the establishment of the main residence with her (a co-parentage agreement) in order to change the council registration in its decision of 18.10.2006, LJN AZ2072. Finally, the

been deliberated above in detail,[31] the Appeal Court established a temporary shared residence pending the procedures (in this case the parents also initially had agreed upon an alternate residence changing every 8 weeks which, however, had been discontinued). In the only case which seems to have reached the Supreme Court, it upheld the decision of the lower court to establish the child's main residence with the mother in a situation where the parents initially had agreed upon shared residence.[32]

From Chapter IV it may be derived that an increasing amount of children in the Netherlands grow up in a share arrangement.[33] It could, however, also be derived that there is uncertainty concerning the definition of a shared residence. From the case law it emerges that parental agreements on shared residence also often concern a situation where a main residence has been established. It is not possible to derive from this case law whether such an establishment only had a practical purpose or represented a choice of a 'primary parent'.[34] A dispute concerning the registration of the child with the council administration may be decided separately without the establishment of a main residence.[35]

The pending legislative proposal concerning 'Continued Parenting' codifies the court's authority to establish the main residence and it may be derived from the parliamentary proceedings that it is assumed that a court already has the authority to establish a shared residence.[36] It is not entirely clear, however, from the parliamentary proceedings whether an equal division of care and responsibilities decided by the court concern only the time allocation or an actual shared residence (without the establishment of the main residence).

Rechtbank Haarlem (District Court) rejected a request for the termination of the co-parenting agreement, which the parents had committed themselves to after they had decided to end their relationship and to establish the main residence with the mother, decision of 20.03.2007, LJN BA1738.

31 Gerechtshof Amsterdam, 07.07.2005, LJN AY3928, see above Section V.2.1.

32 Hoge Raad 10.11.2006, LJN AY8773.

33 Section IV.2.1.

34 In the decision of the District Court of Utrecht, supra note 30, the mother had requested a change in the *contact arrangement* and further provided more de facto care during the week.

35 Gerechtshof 's-Gravenhage (Court of Appeal) 18.10.2006, LJN AZ2072, above Section VI.2.1., supra note 7.

36 Chapter II, Section II.2.6.2. To be derived from the Explanatory report: 'The court can divide the care and responsibilities (the care arrangement) according to the best interests of the child. The care (...) may be divided equally between the parents (both parents half) but a division of 12 days with one parent and two days with the other parent is also possible', Parliamentary proceedings 2004/2005 (*Kamerstukken*), 30 145, No. 3, p. 14. The Explanatory report assumes that this is in accordance with the present Art. 377h, DCC concerning contact.

By an amendment to the proposed act, the child retains the right to be cared for and brought up equally[37] by both parents after divorce and after the breakup of a relationship when the parents exercise joint parental authority. This norm, according to the proposed amendment, is directed towards the parents and forms the basis upon which the parents may come to an agreement concerning the continuation of parenting. In the discussions in the Second Chamber, however, the norm was also presented as being relevant for the court's decision when the 'care and responsibility' must be divided. While it is clear that the norm represents a move towards more equal parenting, it is nonetheless unclear if this norm will extend the scope for the establishment of shared residence. In the Parliamentary discussions the Member of Parliament who introduced this amendment also expressed concern in respect of the establishment of shared residence by the court.[38]

VI.3.2. SHARED RESIDENCE IN DANISH LAW

The notion of a shared residence is not a legal concept in Danish law. The term generally used in Danish law to describe the parents' agreement on a shared residence is a 'divided arrangement' (*deleordning*). Generally, the term describes an equal share arrangement agreed upon by the parents, for example, alternating 7 days with each parent.[39]

The courts cannot establish a shared residence against the wishes of one parent, but it is possible for the courts or regional state administrations to establish a contact arrangement, which in the sense of time allocation amounts to a shared residence. The Explanatory report considers the following in relation to shared residence:

37 The term used is '*gelijkwaardig ouderschap*' which may be understood to imply equal parenting or equal value parenting, Parliamentary proceedings 2006/20007 (*Kamerstukken*) 30 145, No. 26 pertaining to Art. 247(4), DCC. The question of an equal share norm has been the subject of debate in the Parliamentary proceedings also in the Luchtenveld proposal, Chapter II, Section II.2.6.2. See for a critical analysis in respect of the unclear equal share norm and the fact that it applies only after divorce in relation to the Luchtenveld proposal, J. Kok, 'Gelijkwardig ouderschap, een nieuwe norm in het scheidingsrecht', in: M.V. Antokolskaia (Ed.), *Herzienning van het ectscheidingsrecht*, Amsterdam: SWP, 2006, p. 176-190.

38 Parliamentary discussions 2006/2007 (*Kamerstukken*) 30 145, No. 51-3002. The norm and its scope has further led to debate in the Dutch Parliament's First Chamber, Parliamentary proceedings 2007/2008 (*Kamerstukken I*), 30145, No. B.

39 According to the previous law the State Administration could not make a contact arrangement amounting to equal sharing but an arrangement amounting to 8/6 (6 days with the contact parent) was possible, Østre Landsret (Eastern High Court) 24.02.2006, *UFR* 2006.1623Ø.

> 'The Ministry finds that consideration for the child indicates that in cases where the parents disagree, only a decision concerning one residence may be given. Shared residence requires a high degree of potential co-operation between the parents concerning daily matters which are difficult to put into practice, if the parents do not agree. The risk is that the child's everyday life would be affected by problems concerning basic matters with the effect that the child is restrained in its development and well-being. It is important that the child in such cases has a fixed base.'

The Ministry further refers to the 2006 Commission report. The Commission had also considered the legal effects of a shared residence in relation to matters such as the public registration of residence and the effect upon social benefits.[40] Further, the Commission had considered that a contact arrangement is a more flexible instrument which can be adjusted to the child's age and situation.[41]

Pursuant to article 17 of the Act on Parental Responsibility, the Court must establish a residence with one parent if the parents' hold joint parental authority and disagree upon the question with whom the child should reside. This rule applies in all situations where the residence is disputed and thus also in cases where the parents have initially made an agreement on a shared residence.

VI.3.3. SHARED RESIDENCE: THE CEFL PRINCIPLES

The CEFL principles provide that it should be possible for the parents to agree upon an alternate (shared) residence and contemplates the possibility that a competent authority may establish an alternate residence.[42] An agreement on alternate residence must be approved by the competent authority, which must take into account factors such as: the age and opinion of the child, the ability and willingness of the holders of parental responsibilities to cooperate with each

---

40 When the child resides equally with both parents who hold joint parental authority and the parents cannot agree upon the child's registration, the child must be registered in the persons administration with the parent with whom a residence has been established. If no residence has been established, the child remains registered at the last address if this address is one of the parent's addresses, Article 8(3), Lov om det Centrale Personregister, Compilated Act No. 1134 of 20.11.2006 and Act No. 500 of 06.06.2007 (Changes pursuant to the Act on Parental Responsibility).

41 L 133, p. 24-25.

42 Principles, principle 3:20(2), p. 130, Comments No. 7, p. 135. The principles leave the question whether alternate residence is the main rule or the exception to national law and further leave the question whether it requires a request by one parent to the national law, Comments No. 6 and No. 8, p. 135.

other in matters concerning the child, as well as their personal situation and the distance between the residences of the holders of parental responsibilities and the distance from the child's school.

While the Principles allow for an alternate residence, concern is simultaneously expressed in the comments because an alternate residence may 'deprive the child of a stable environment and thus be harmful to the child.'

VI.3.4. COMPARISON: SHARED RESIDENCE

It is only Danish law which unequivocally provides that a shared residence is possible based only upon parental agreement. But shared residence in the sense of time allocation is possible.[43]

In Dutch law the question is somewhat unsettled. There are no final decisions establishing a shared residence against the wishes of one parent, but decisions of the lower courts uphold a shared residence agreement after the parents have ceased to agree. It is furthermore uncertain if and to what extent the proposal concerning 'Continued Parenting', if adopted, will change the law in this respect. The equality norm contained in the proposal is unclear. Further, it emerges that the court may decide alternatively upon the child's main residence or decide with whom the child should be registered in the council administration.

The CEFL principles provide that it should be possible to establish a shared residence based upon parental agreement and contemplate the possibility of establishing such by decision of the court, however relying upon the ability and willingness of the parents to co-operate and generally expressing concern in respect of such arrangements. Unlike Dutch and Danish law the CEFL principles explicitly provide a guideline concerning the circumstances that should be taken into account before a shared residence can be established.

---

[43] The distinction between shared residence and a contact arrangement must be viewed in the context of inherent rights, for example, the right to relocate within Denmark, that the parent has when residence is established and the clarity it brings in respect of the child's registration with the council administration.

VI.4. RELOCATION

Dutch and Danish case law provide ample evidence of the fact that the resident parent's relocation within or outside the jurisdiction is a main cause of disputes between parents who hold or exercise joint parental authority. The CEFL principles also contain a specific regulation in relation to relocation considering the need to respond to 'an ever increasing mobility in European Society' and further considering the importance in the context of the free movement of persons and the likeliness of a growing number of such disputes.[44]

Neither Dutch law, Danish law, nor the CEFL principles regulate the relocation of the non-resident parent.[45]

VI.4.1. RELOCATION: THE NETHERLANDS

VI.4.1.1. General

A dispute between the parents exercising joint parental authority concerning the resident parent's relocation within or outside the jurisdiction concerns the exercise of parental authority and may be decided by the Dutch courts according to the general dispute settlement provision in Article 253a of the Dutch Civil Code. A decision pursuant to this provision may or may not allow the resident parent to relocate or change the child's main residence if this has been requested. From the case law it may be deduced that a decision pursuant to Article 253a primarily distinguishes between two relocation determinants. In the first place, it is relevant whether the resident parent is relocating within or outside the jurisdiction. Secondly, it is relevant if a main or shared residence has been established.

VI.4.1.2. Relocation within the jurisdiction

There is, as far as can be ascertained, no published case law which has not allowed the resident parent to relocate with the child within the jurisdiction (the European part of the Netherlands, as opposed to Aruba and the Netherlands Antilles) when the child has its main residence with this parent. In principle, however, any relocation probably requires the other parent's consent or the

---

44 Principles, principle 3:21, Comment 2, p. 141.

45 Save for the duty to notify in Danish law, see below Section VI.4.2.2. of this Chapter.

replaced consent of the court irrespective of the distance and whether a main residence has been established.[46]

In cases where the parents have agreed to a shared residence (co-parentage) arrangement, the main rule inferred from the case law of the lower courts seems to be that a parent cannot relocate with the child when the other parent objects to the relocation. This seems to apply also in cases where, notwithstanding the co-parentage agreement, one parent (typically the mother) emerges as the primary carer or when next to the co-parentage agreement a main residence has been established with this parent.[47] Illustrative is the case in which the District Court of Utrecht provided two decisions.[48] In this case the parents had in the course of the divorce proceedings in 2004 agreed upon co-parentage and the establishment of the children's (two children born in 1993 and 1996) main residence with the mother. The children were to stay with the mother from Monday to Wednesday and with the father on Thursday-Friday and every second weekend with each parent. The father was to have ten extra holiday days with the children. The mother wished to relocate together with the children and a new partner to a location which was too far away for a well functioning shared residence arrangement. The District Court of Utrecht upheld the shared residence agreement and rejected the mother's request to change the 'contact arrangement' with the father. When the mother relocated anyway, the Court changed the children's main residence to that of the father.

However, in the only published case which reached the Supreme Court and where the decision of the Court of Appeal was upheld, the Court had allowed the mother to relocate by establishing the child's main residence with the mother.[49]

---

46 See, for example, Vorzieningenrechter Rechtbank Haarlem (District Court) 14.08.2007, LJN BB1817 concerning an intended relocation (probably to a neighbouring council). It is, however, not evident from case law that relocation always requires consent; notable is the decision of Gerechtshof Leeuwarden 01.08.2007, LJN BB1198 where the Court of Appeal seemed to rely upon a right of the parent with whom the child had its main residence to determine the place of residence. Consent is also required for the registration of the child's new address in the Municipal Personal Records Database (*Basisadministratie Gemeentelijke Persoongegevens*).

47 Above Section VI.3.1. and supra note 30.

48 Rechtbank Utrecht 12.04.2006, LJN AZ1191 and 18.08.2006, LJN AZ1192.

49 Hoge Raad 10.11.2006, LJN AY8773. In this case the parents had changed the co-parenting agreement and the mother was the primary carer. The mother wished to relocate together with a new partner who was under a duty to relocate in connection with his work.

VI.4.1.3. Relocation outside the jurisdiction

The general trend concerning the resident parent's relocation outside the jurisdiction seems to be that this is only rarely allowed.

A typical case, also often seen in the context of the law pertaining to child abduction, is the case where the resident parent wishes to relocate to his/her country of origin. In 2001, the District Court of Haarlem delivered a decision in a case which involved the relocation of the mother to Spain (although it was not explicitly stated, it would seem that the mother was a Spanish national). The parents had been married in the period between 1992 and 2001 and had three children born in 1992, 1994 and 1998. They had lived in Spain prior to 1993 and from then onwards in the Netherlands. The divorce decree contained the provision that the parents continued to exercise joint parental authority after the divorce without mentioning the childrens' residence. The children, however, had had their main residence with the mother since the divorce and had contact on a regular and frequent basis with the father. Pursuant to the mother's announced intention to relocate to Spain by the end of the school year, the father started proceedings claiming that he should be allocated sole parental authority supplemented at a later stage with a claim for main residence. The mother claimed sole parental authority or a decision allowing her to change the children's main residence to Spain where she considered that she had better work opportunities.

The District Court of Haarlem rejected both parents' claim for sole parental authority as well as the father's claim for a change in the main residence of the children dependent on, however, the mother's continued residence in the Netherlands. The mother was thus not allowed to relocate (with the children) to Spain. In case she decided to relocate the Court would change the childrens' main residence so that they could be with the father.

On the other hand, the Leeuwarden Court of Appeal[50] decided in its decision of 1 August 2007 that the mother could relocate to her country of origin, Brazil, with a daughter over whom the parents exercised joint parental authority and where the daughter's main residence with the mother had been established by the District Court in the course of the divorce procedure in 2004. In this case the father sought sole parental authority over the daughter and refused to consent to the mother's relocation and the issuance of a passport for the daughter. It was

50 Gerechtshof Leeuwarden 01.08.2007, LJN BB1198.

not possible for the mother to remain in the Netherlands because she no longer had a right to stay. The interesting aspect of this case is that the Court of Appeal seemed to rely upon a right of the parent with whom the child had its main residence to determine the place of residence.

Another type of case concerns the situation where the resident parent wishes to relocate to pursue a job abroad. In this situation relocation is typically denied. In the first case decided by the District Court of Utrecht in 2005, the father of a child born in 2000 was denied the right to relocate to Dubai in the course of the divorce proceedings. The parents agreed upon the child's main residence with the father but the mother did not consent to the relocation (the mother was being cared for in an institution).[51]

Further, in a decision by the District Court of Alkmaar, the court denied the mother the right to relocate to Crete with a younger son who had his main residence with the mother since the parents' divorce. The mother wished to relocate to Crete with the son, two children from a previous relationship and her new partner in order to take over a restaurant. The mother had stated that she would go irrespective of the decision of the court. The court changed the main residence of the son so that he could be with the father. The court, amongst other things, relied upon the fact that the parents had not shared the care of the son in a traditional manner (during the mother's part-time work, the father had cared some extra days during the week) and that although the relocation was well prepared, also in respect of the children (schooling), the well-being of the son had not been the primary concern of the mother in her choice to relocate.[52]

Finally, the situation where the resident parent wishes to relocate in order to establish a new family in another country should be mentioned. In a case before the Hague Court of Appeal in 2003, the question was whether the Court would substitute the father's consent to permit the mother to relocate to Australia.[53] The facts of the case were the following:

The parents had two children born in 1989 and 1991. The parents divorced in 2001 and continued to exercise joint parental authority. The children's main residence was with the mother. In 2002 the mother requested permission from the District Court of the Hague to relocate to Australia. The mother wished to

51 Rechtbank Utrecht 26.01.2005, LJN AS 6703.

52 Rechtbank Alkmaar 05.04.2006, LJN 8683, see also Rechtbank Haarlem (District Court) 27.02.2007, LJN BA1742 where the mother was not allowed to relocate to Spain.

53 Gerechtshof 's-Gravenhage 05.03.2003, LJN AG1643.

relocate to Australia in order to settle there with her new partner who could not obtain permission to reside in the Netherlands. The father would not consent to such a relocation and claimed that the children's main residence should be changed so that they could be with him. The District Court denied both parents' requests and the mother appealed the decision to the Hague Court of Appeal. The Court of Appeal changed the decision of the District Court and permitted the mother to relocate to Australia. The Court of Appeal first considered that it was in the children's best interest to remain living with the mother given the fact that the parents had agreed to choose a traditional family pattern where the mother had been the primary carer both during the marriage and after the divorce. In this light the Court considered that 'it is in keeping with this carer role that she should have sufficient room to fulfil that role, in principle also if she chooses to continue her life and the life of the children in another place'. The Court then considered whether the relocation was in the interests of the children, which it found to be the case taking into account that the mother had planned the relocation carefully and that the mother's new relationship was a stable one.

However, in two similar cases the mother was denied permission to relocate.[54] In a decision by the Arnhem Court of Appeal from 2006,[55] the Court changed the District Court of Almelo's decision to allow the mother to relocate to the US with three children who had resided with her since the divorce in 2004 and had contact with the father every second weekend, although this depended on the father's work abroad.[56] The mother wished to relocate to the US in order to be with her new husband who had settled there in 2005. The Arnhem Court of Appeal found that a main residence did not entail a right to relocate in a situation where the relocation would hinder frequent contact and where the other parent did not consent. The Court of Appeal further considered that the mother had not provided adequate contact possibilities after the relocation. The decision of the Court of Appeal provided that the children should continue to reside with

---

54 Similar because they concerned the establishment of a new family abroad and the main residence was with the mother who was the primary carer, Rechtbank Rotterdam (District Court) 23.07.2007, LJN BB0581 denied permission to the mother to relocate to Bonaire where she wished to marry and see also Gerechtshof Arnhem (Court of Appeal) 29.08.2006, LJN AZ5530.

55 Gerechtshof Arnhem (Court of Appeal) 29.08.2006, LJN AZ5530.

56 The case before the District Court had been initiated by the father before the mother's factual relocation to the US. The father had requested that the children's main residence should be with him. Before the Court of Appeal the father stated that he did not wish to change the children's main residence with the mother considering that she had been the primary carer, also during the marriage, but he would not consent to the relocation.

the mother but have contact with the father every other weekend which would mean that the mother could not reside in the US.[57]

These decisions show that each case is decided on its own merits and that there is no clear line to be derived. Most of the recent cases seem to depart from the starting point that the parent with whom the children have their main residence should be granted permission to relocate; however, often rejecting permission based upon an ascertainment of the contact possibilities of the other parent and child. If viewed in the context of the results of the decisions, a relocation was only allowed in two cases where the resident parent could be viewed as having a limited choice in respect of relocation. In one case because the parent (the mother) no longer had the right to remain in the Netherlands[58] and in the other because the mother's new partner could not obtain a permit to stay in the Netherlands.[59] Further, it appears that the co-operation potential of the resident parent in respect of consulting the other parent and the contact possibilities are important.[60]

VI.4.2. RELOCATION: DENMARK

VI.4.2.1. General

The possibility of obtaining a decision on residence or relocation has only been possible in Danish law since the 2007 Act. Prior to this Act parents who held joint parental authority should have agreed on the child's residence or relocation.[61] If the parents could not agree, there existed only the possibility to request the termination of joint parental authority. A number of cases concerning the

---

57 Gerechtshof Arnhem 29.08.2006, LJN AZ5530. The court further added that 'needless to say' the mother had not requested permission to relocate pursuant to Art. 253a, DCC before the Court of Appeal. A somewhat odd addition considering that the District Court had allowed the mother to relocate. It is not clear whether or not the Court of Appeal considered this to be of importance.

58 Gerechtshof Leeuwarden 01.08.2007, LJN BB1198

59 Gerechtshof 's-Gravenhage (Court of Appeal) 05.03.2003, LJN AG1643.

60 Gerechtshof Arnhem (Court of Appeal) 29.08.2006, LJN AZ5530. In this case the mother had taken the decision to relocate without consulting the father and had not provided adequate contact possibilities. The Court of Appeal denied the mother the right to relocate to the US and the Court did not seem to depart from the starting point that permission should be granted.

61 Factually, the parent could relocate, the registration of the child in the persons administration (*Folkeregisteret*) is based upon the child's factual residence irrespective of who holds parental authority, Art. 8(1), Lov om det Centrale Personregister, Act No. 1134 of 20.11.2006. Relocation outside of Denmark, however, may be a criminal offence, see Chapter VII, Section VII.4.5.2. and Chapter VIII, Section VIII.5.2.

termination of parental authority and an allocation of sole parental authority to one parent have, however, indirectly concerned the intended or factual relocation of the resident parent.[62] In these cases the courts have been obliged to allocate sole parental authority to one parent. This means that it has not been possible to prevent a resident parent's relocation. It has only been possible to allocate sole parental authority to the other parent requiring that this parent is able and willing to hold sole parental authority.

Decisions on the allocation of sole parental authority containing relocation as an element are concrete decisions in which, naturally, not only the relocation plays a role. From the published case law it seems that the relocation or the intention to relocate does not in itself provide a reason to allocate parental authority to the other parent. This applies in respect of relocations within the jurisdiction[63] and presumably also in respect of relocation outside the jurisdiction.[64] Individual circumstances such as parental ability, contact obstruction and the child's own opinion may, however, provide a reason to allocate parental authority to the other parent.[65]

The present regulation enacted in 2007 makes a sharp distinction between relocations within the jurisdiction and relocations outside the jurisdiction. Further, the Act introduces a duty to notify the other parent in the case of any relocation.

---

62 Also a number of cases concerning the transfer of sole parental authority from one parent to the other have concerned the relocation of the parent holding sole parental authority, L. Frost, 'Ændring af forældremyndighedsdomme og – aftaler efter forældremyndighedslovens §13', *TFA*, 2003, p. 360-361.

63 For example, Østre Landsret (Eastern High Court) 15.09.2005, *TFA* 2006.450Ø where the child had previously had a shared residence with the parents. The mother was allocated parental authority (over a daughter aged 6) and intended to relocate to Funen which made no difference. See also Vestre Landsret (Western High Court) 24.08.2004, *TFA* 2004.535V where the father was allocated parental authority over two daughters aged 5 and 8 despite the fact that he would have to relocate within a few years.

64 For example, the decision of the Østre Landsret (Eastern High Court) 16.02.2006, *TFA* 2006.238Ø and 14.02.2006, *TFA* 2006.227Ø. In these two cases, parental authority was allocated to the mothers who relocated to, respectively, Japan and Bulgaria with a young child. See also Vestre Landsret (Western High Court) 04.06.2003, *TFA* 2003.395V where the father was not allocated parental authority despite his fear that the mother would relocate to Venezuela and, finally, Østre Landsret (Eastern High Court) 28.05.2003, *TFA* 2003.392Ø where parental authority was allocated to the father who resided with the child in the Comoros.

65 Vestre Landsret (Western High Court) 28.11.2003, *TFA* 2004.139V and 14.12.2001, *TFA* 2002.144V where the mother was allocated sole parental authority by the district court and relocated to the Netherlands. The Western High Court allocated parental authority to the father on appeal considering, amongst other things, problems relating to contact.

VI.4.2.2. Notification in the case of relocation

If a legal parent, irrespective of whether he/she holds parental authority (sole/joint), wishes to relocate (within and outside the jurisdiction) he/she is placed under an obligation to notify the other parent six weeks in advance.[66] The obligation to notify is thus placed upon all parents, not just upon the resident parent. The reason for this is that, according to the Explanatory notes, the relocation of also the non-resident parent may provide a reason to reconsider a contact arrangement. There is no direct sanction in cases where the parent has not notified the other parent prior to or in accordance with the requirements of the provision, for example if the notification is sent later than six weeks before the relocation. The lack of notification or a notification which has not met the requirements may, however, be deemed to be relevant in a subsequent case on the child's residence or contact.[67]

VI.4.2.3. Relocation within the jurisdiction

A resident parent has the right to relocate within the jurisdiction which in this case is the territory of Denmark, thus excluding any relocation to Greenland and the Faeroe Islands.

While the resident parent has a right to relocate irrespective of whether the child's main residence has been established by the court or the parents have agreed to this residence, the relocation may nonetheless provide a reason for the court to change the child's residence depending upon the individual circumstances of the case. In this respect the Explanatory notes mention the situation when a contact arrangement does not run smoothly.[68]

VI.4.2.4. Relocation outside the jurisdiction

When the parents hold joint parental authority, they must agree upon the relocation of the child outside of the territory of Denmark (including Greenland and the Faeroe Islands). If they cannot agree the court may decide that the child can have its residence outside the jurisdiction.[69] Such a decision must relate to a specific residence abroad. It does not, in principle, allow the resident parent subsequently to relocate to another country. The Explanatory notes consider that

---

66 Art. 3a, Act on Parental Responsibility.

67 L 133, Comments to § 3a.

68 L 133, Comments to § 17.

69 Art. 17(1)2nd sentence, Act on Parental Responsibility.

a decision on relocation may be granted where the court finds that the child is best served with residence with this parent.[70] It must be expected that the present case law concerning the termination of joint parental authority and the allocation of sole parental authority to one parent will serve as guidance.

VI.4.3. RELOCATION: THE CEFL PRINCIPLES

VI.4.3.1. Relocation

The CEFL principles contain the general rule that parents must agree on any relocation and if they cannot agree that the competent authority must decide the matter: principle 3:21. This principle does not distinguish between relocation within and outside the jurisdiction. The principles do not provide a main rule in respect of relocations, but provide six guiding (non-exhaustive)[71] factors which are:

(a) the age and opinion of the child;
(b) the right of the child to maintain personal relationships with the other holders of parental responsibilities;
(c) the ability and willingness of the holders of parental responsibilities to cooperate with each other;
(d) the personal situation of the holders of personal responsibilities;
(e) geographical distance and accessibility;
(f) the free movement of persons.

The principles do not provide relocation as the starting point or the right of the resident parent, rather they provide for a balancing of interests between the right of the child to maintain personal relationships with the non-resident parent and other relatives and the right of the resident parent to move in pursuit of a 'valid purpose', for example in order to improve his or her professional situation or to accompany a new partner (free movement rights).[72]

VI.4.3.2. Notification in the case of relocation

The principles provide an obligation on the part of the resident parent (the parent wishing to change the child's residence) to inform the other parent.[73]

---

70 L 133, Comments to § 17.
71 Principles, principle 3:21, Comment 7, p. 141.
72 Principles, principle 3:21, Comment 7, p. 141-142.
73 Principles, principle 3:21(2).

VI.4.4. COMPARISON: RELOCATION

A decision on relocation in Dutch law is a decision concerning the *exercise* of parental authority/responsibilities. As such it is the general dispute settlement provisions which regulate the allowed or non-allowed relocation or alternatively in cases where this has been requested, the possibility of changing the child's main residence. The CEFL principles provide that in case of a dispute the competent authority must decide if the parent may relocate (with the child). In Danish law the court may only decide upon relocation outside the jurisdiction.

In Dutch case law and formally in Danish law, the most important distinction in relation to relocation is the distinction between relocation within and outside the jurisdiction. The CEFL principles do not provide such a distinction, which is logical given the fact that the principles aim to serve as guiding principles for the harmonisation of family law in Europe viewed in the context of an increase in and the desirability of free movement rights in Europe.[74]

In Danish law the resident parent has the right to relocate within the jurisdiction. The CEFL principles do not provide a right of relocation, but do provide for a balancing of interests without determining a starting point. In Dutch law the resident parent does not have the right to relocate within the jurisdiction but will probably be granted this right by the court, if a request is made, save perhaps in situations where notwithstanding the established main residence an agreement on shared residence has been established.

Danish law and the CEFL principles formally provide a duty for the resident parent to notify the other parent before relocating and Danish law provides this duty also in respect of the other legal parent. Dutch law does not formally contain such a duty. It may, however, be derived from the case law that the resident parent has a duty to consult the other parent.

With respect to relocations outside the jurisdiction Dutch case law seems to point in the direction that this is only possible when the resident parent may be viewed to have little choice. As such the case law suggests a duty on the part of the resident parent to remain within the jurisdiction when the parents exercise joint parental authority and cannot agree upon the child's relocation. Danish

---

74 Further this is logical considering that in some countries the distance within the jurisdiction may be great.

case law, so far, does not point in this direction. Rather, a factual or intended relocation does not in itself seem relevant without additional circumstances.

CHAPTER VII
THE CONTENT AND EXERCISE OF PARENTAL AUTHORITY

VII.I. INTRODUCTION

This main focus of this Chapter is to describe and compare the competence of parents holding or exercising joint parental authority, the possibility of regulating this competence through a decision or an agreement and the access to dispute settlement procedures. These elements may also be described as pertaining to the *exercise* of joint parental authority.[1] Furthermore, this Chapter deals with a number of different types of disputes covered by Dutch and Danish law.[2]

First, however, a summary description and comparison of the general content of parental authority; on the one hand, the rights and duties of parents and, on the other, the child's position in relation thereto.

VII.2. THE CONTENT OF PARENTAL AUTHORITY

The focus of this Section is the general content of parental authority, that is the rights and duties of parents and the child's general position in relation to parental authority. The child's position in a procedure concerning parental authority and contact is discussed separately in Chapter VIII.[3]

---

1 Danish law does not use the terminology of exercising, Chapter V, Section V.2.1.2.

2 Section VII.4. is based upon a problem approach in relation to types of disputes. The perspective is broad as it aims to assess not only the access to dispute settlement, but more generally to ascertain how the law deals with such disputes. Disputes concerning residence and relocation have already been dealt with separately in Chapter VI and contact is dealt with separately in Chapter VIII.

3 Section VIII.4.

VII.2.1. CONTENT: RIGHTS AND DUTIES OF PARENTS

VII.2.1.1. Dutch law

The Dutch Civil Code provides that a minor is subject to custody.[4] The concept of custody covers parental authority and guardianship. Parental authority is exercised primarily by legal parents and guardianship by person(s) other than a parent.[5] The term custody and consequently parental authority relates to the child's person, the administration of his or her property and legal representation judicially and extra-judicially.[6]

Article 247 of the Dutch Civil Code provides that parental authority 'comprises the duty and the right of the parent to care for and raise his or her minor child' and that 'care and upbringing include the care and responsibility for the mental and corporal well-being of the child and the fostering of the development of its personality.' Finally, parents 'in caring for and raising the child must not use mental or physical violence or any other degrading treatment.'[7]

The exact content of the rights and duties of parents as contained in the concept of parental authority in respect of the child's person is not listed but it is generally assumed that they encompass the provision of and the competence to decide on matters concerning clothing, food, accommodation, medical treatment and education.[8] Furthermore, it is assumed that parents should acknowledge the increasing maturity and needs of the child to develop according to his or her own vision.[9]

---

4 Art. 245(1), DCC. A minor is a person who has not reached the age of 18, is not or has not been married or in a registered partnership and it has not been determined that the minor in question should have full capacity and be treated as an adult, Art. 233, DCC. Since the 1995 revision a minor has conditional capacity; see E.A.A. Luijten, *Het Nederlandse personen- en familierecht, deel 1*, Deventer: Kluwer, 1997, p. 97-99.

5 Art. 245(2), DCC and Chapter V, Section V.2.2.1.

6 Art. 245(4), DCC.

7 This provision aiming to prohibit the use of lawful chastisement was adopted on 08.03.2007, Stb. 2007, 145.

8 J.H. Nieuwenhuis, C.J.J.M. Stolker, W.L. Valk, M.J.C. Koens, A.P.M.J. Vonken, *Personen- en Familierecht, Tekst en Commentaar*, Deventer: Kluwer, 2004, p. 295. Parents have a duty to ensure that their children attend school from the age of five onwards, Leerplichtwet 1969 with later amendments.

9 J.H. Nieuwenhuis a.o., 2004, supra, p. 295. In the course of the 1995 revision it had been proposed to adopt this duty explicitly. The provision was not explicitly adopted, however, but is nonetheless considered to be inherent in the content of parental authority.

Administration of the child's capital and representation of the child in civil law proceedings is inherent in the concept of custody and parental authority and is regulated separately in § 3 of Title 14 of the Dutch Civil Code. While separately discharging these rights is not possible, administration and legal representation may be carried out by the parent who does not exercise parental authority upon the application of the parents or either one of them and if the other parent does not oppose this.[10] A discharge or suspension of the exercise of parental authority also includes the administration of property and legal representation. Parents who exercise parental authority have a right of usufruct.[11]

VII.2.1.2. Danish law

Children or young persons under the age of 18 are subject to parental authority unless they have entered into a marriage or registered partnership.[12] The holder(s) of parental authority 'must care for the child and may make decisions concerning the child's person from the perspective of the child's interest and needs'. Further, 'the child has the right to care and safety. It must be treated with respect and must not be subjected to physical punishment or other degrading treatment.'[13]

The exact content of the rights and duties of parents is not listed in the provision. It is generally assumed, however, that the parents have a duty to provide clothing, food, accommodation, medical treatment and education.[14]

The parent(s) who hold joint parental authority are also the legal representatives and administer the minor's property *ex lege*. The administration of this property and legal representation in respect thereof pertains to the parent's/parents' exercise of guardianship as regulated in the Guardianship Act.[15] The distinction between parental authority and guardianship in Danish law is important,

10 Art. 253i(4)b, DCC.

11 Art. 253l(1), DCC.

12 Art. 2, Act on Parental Responsibility and Art. 2(1), Lov om registreret partnerskab (Act on Registered Partnership), Act No. 938 of 10.10.2005 with later amendments.

13 Art. 2, Act on Parental Responsibility. The prohibition on the use of lawful chastisement was adopted with Act No. 416 of 10.06.1997.

14 S. Danielsen, *Lov om forældremyndighed og samvær*, Copenhagen: Dansk Jurist- og Økonomforbund, 1997, p. 58.

15 Children and young persons under the age of 18 who have not entered into a marriage or registered partnership are minors and are subject to guardianship, Art. 1, Værgemålsloven (Guardianship Act), Act. No. 388 of 14.06.1995 with later changes. Legal representation in relation to the child's person concerns parental authority.

because the regulation is considerably different. Guardianship is regulated in more detail and it is the regional state administration which has sole competence in these matters.[16] Furthermore, a parent may be released or discharged from guardianship when he/she is not capable of carrying out this task, while the discharge of parental authority is not possible.[17]

In Danish law the parents may reasonably use the child's income to support the child.[18] Parents do not have a right of usufruct, which must be viewed in the context that a child does not have an obligation to support its parents financially.[19]

VII.2.1.3. The CEFL principles

The CEFL principles define parental responsibilities as 'a collection of rights and duties aimed at promoting and safeguarding the welfare of the child,' encompassing in particular: (a) care, protection and education; (b) maintenance of personal relationships; (c) determination of residence; (d) administration of property; and (e) legal representation.[20]

Furthermore, Principle 3:19 describes the content of parental responsibilities as encompassing: care, protection and education in accordance with the child's distinctive character and developmental needs and it prohibits corporal punishment and any other humiliating treatment. Inherent in the concept of care are decisions concerning medical treatment and within the concept of care and education, the child's religious upbringing is included.[21]

---

16 Subject to a limited review based upon the Constitution, see Chapter III, Section III.4.1. for this type of review.

17 Art. 2, Guardianship Act. A parent is only released or discharged from guardianship in exceptional circumstances if this is necessary with respect to the administration of the child's property. A child protection measure, such as the placement of the child in care, does not lead to an automatic discharge of guardianship. Near relatives as well as the public authorities may request a discharge, Art. 12 and 15, Guardianship Act. See in relation to parental authority Chapter V, Section V.2.2.2.

18 Art. 2(3), Act on Parental Responsibility.

19 The child's income may, however, also benefit the parents; for example, if the child's income in special cases covers some of the living expenses such as rent, S. Danielsen, 1997, supra, p. 98.

20 Principles, principle 3:1, p. 25. The administration of property and legal representation are regulated separately in principles, 3:22, p. 143, 3:23, p. 152 and 3:24, p. 159.

21 Principles, principle 3:19, p. 119, Comments 3 and 4, p. 128-129.

The content of parental responsibilities, as defined by the CEFL, must be viewed in connection with the child's rights to autonomy, protection and participation as contained in Chapter II of the principles.[22]

VII.2.1.4. Comparison: Rights and duties of parents

In Dutch and Danish law the provisions defining the content of parental authority are formulated broadly to encompass care. The CEFL principles, on the other hand, provide that the concept encompasses, in particular, care, protection and education; maintenance of personal relationships; determination of residence; administration of property; and legal representation. These elements, however, are also considered to be inherent in the Dutch and Danish concepts.[23] It is a common feature that, although formulated differently, it is the child's perspective, welfare or well-being which is central to the concept of parental authority/responsibilities. Furthermore, it emerges as a common feature that there is a general prohibition on the use of violence and other degrading treatment.

In both Dutch and Danish law and in the CEFL principles the parent(s) who hold or exercise joint parental authority are also the legal representatives and administer the child's property *ex lege*. In Danish law, however, the administration of property and legal representation in respect thereof pertains to the parent's/parents' exercise of guardianship as regulated in the Guardianship Act. This distinction in Danish law is important because the regulation contained in the Guardianship Act differs considerably from that in the Act on Parental Responsibility as it provides a more detailed regulation, provides the possibility for a discharge and competence rests solely with the regional state administration.

However, the administration of property and legal representation is also regulated in separate and more detailed provisions in Dutch law and in the CEFL principles. Additionally, in Dutch law it is the sub-district court, rather than the district court, that is competent and the possibility exists that the parent who does not hold parental authority will be responsible for administration and legal representation.[24] There is not a great difference between Dutch law and the

[22] Below, Section VII.2.2.3.

[23] A difference concerns the 'maintenance of personal relationships'. It may be derived from Chapter V, Section V.4.3.2. that a parent exercising parental authority in Dutch law cannot formally be discharged from the right to contact, only a temporary discontinuation is possible. In Danish law it cannot be deduced that a parent holding parental authority cannot be discharged from the right to contact, see further Chapter VIII, Section VIII.2.

[24] The CEFL principles also provide the possibility to divide this task, see below Section VII.2.2.

CEFL principles compared to Danish law considering that the main rule is that parents administer the property and are the legal representatives *ex lege*. Nonetheless, the distinction has particular relevance for Danish law.

Dutch law and the CEFL principles provide the parent(s) who exercise parental authority with a right of usufruct. In Danish law, the parents may reasonably use the child's income to support the child. The parents do not, however, have a right of usufruct, which must be viewed in the context that a child does not have an obligation to support needy parents as is provided for in Dutch law.[25]

VII.2.2. CONTENT: THE CHILD'S POSITION

VII.2.2.1. Dutch law

In Dutch law a minor has conditional legal capacity.[26] He/she is, however, subject to custody (parental authority) and it is the parents who are the legal representatives and have decision-making competence in respect of his or her person, administering that child's property and legally representing him/her.

Dutch law lays down a duty for the child to 'take into account the powers vested in the parent or guardian within the framework of the exercise of custody and the interests of the other members of the family of which he or she forms a part.'[27] This provision was adopted in order to counteract the duty of the parents to acknowledge the increasing maturity of the child.[28]

A child or young person is not granted an increasingly autonomous position *generally* in relation to parental authority, although the matter has been extensively discussed and deliberated in Dutch literature and Parliamentary proceedings over the past forty years.[29] Rather, the law has provided various regulations relating to the child's autonomy and participation rights with regard to specific matters. An example of an autonomous position is that a child of 16 has auton-

25 Art. 392(1), DCC. The CEFL principles do not address the law relating to maintenance.

26 Since the 1995 revision, see E.A.A. Luijten, 1997, supra, p. 97-99.

27 Art. 249, DCC. A child or young person who earns an income from work has a duty to contribute to household costs, Art. 253l(1), DCC.

28 Although this provision was not formally adopted, see above Section VII.2.1.1., supra note 9.

29 See hereon: M.L.C.C. de Bruijn-Lückers, *EVRM, minderjarigheid en ouderlijk gezag, A whole code of juvenile law?*, Doctoral thesis (PhD), 1996, p. 84-89.

omy in respect of medical treatment.[30] In relation to child protection measures, Dutch law does not provide explicitly for an autonomous position of the child, for example, to appeal against decisions on being taken into care. Rather, Dutch law relies upon the general provision providing that a child aged twelve should be heard in the procedure and that a child below this age may be heard in the procedure.[31] However, the child does have the possibility to make certain requests[32] and there are examples from case law where the child has been granted a more autonomous position, for example, to appeal against a certain decision.[33]

A special guardian (*bijzondere curator*) may be appointed when there is a conflict of interests between the holder(s) of parental authority and the child. Article 250 of the Dutch Civil Code stipulates that:

> 'When in matters regarding the care and upbringing or in respect of the capital of the minor there is a conflict between the interests of the minor and the parents entrusted with parental authority or of either of them or of the guardian or both guardians, the sub-district court shall appoint a special guardian to represent the minor in respect thereof, both judicially and extra-judicially at the request of an interested person or ex officio, if it considers this necessary in the best interests of the minor, having regard to the nature of the conflicts of interests.'

This provision was given a broader scope in the 1995 reform.[34] The provision applies to both conflicts of interests regarding the child's person and the administration of property and legal representation. A special guardian can only be appointed if it is necessary and it involves a conflict of an important nature. The child may request such an appointment.[35] The task of the special guardian is to represent the child as stipulated by the court. The special guardian's tasks may be to seek a settlement with the parents or to initiate legal proceedings on behalf of the child and represent the minor during these legal proceedings. The

---

30 Book 7, Title 7, Art. 447, DCC. A child between the age of 12 and 16 must consent together with the parents; see further M.L.C.C. de Bruijn Lückers, E.C.C. Punselie, 'Medisch handelen en kinderbescherming', *Tijdschrift voor gezondheidsrecht*, 2004, No. 28, p. 578-579.

31 Art. 809(1), Dutch Code of Civil Procedure.

32 Title 14, Section 4, Art. 256, 260, 263, DCC.

33 K. Lünnemann, M. Steketee, Annuska, M., Overgaag, M., *Minderjarigen als procespartij*, Utrecht: Verwey-Jonker Instituut, 2003, p. 27.

34 Parliamentary proceedings 1992/1993 (*Kamerstukken*), 23 012, No. 3, p. 11-12. Before 1995 the scope of the provision related, in particular, to conflicts of interests concerning financial matters.

35 Parliamentary proceedings 1992/1993 (*Kamerstukken*), 23 012, No. 3, p. 12.

special guardian does not substitute the authority of the parents and does not have the authority to make decisions instead of the parents.[36]

In 2003, the institution of the special guardian was assessed. The assessment also more generally concerned minors' access to the courts. It appeared that the appointment of a special guardian was used only rarely and primarily in cases concerning financial matters.[37] Several reasons were given. In the first place it was noted that the provision to appoint a special guardian is not well known. In the second place, the special guardian is appointed only after legal proceedings have commenced, and, finally, that only the sub-district court may appoint a special guardian.[38]

VII.2.2.2. Danish law

Danish law does not *generally* provide for the increasingly autonomous position of the child or young person in relation to parental authority, although it is assumed that the powers inherent in the concept of parental authority decreases as the young person approaches the age of eighteen.[39] The general starting point, however, is that parents 'in the interests of the child' have the competence to take decisions on behalf of that child and to represent him/her.[40]

A minor cannot undertake obligations of an economic nature unless such a right is established by law since the parents act on behalf of the minor in economic matters.[41] However, the parents must consult the minor in important matters if

---

36 Parliamentary proceedings 1992/1993 (*Kamerstukken*), 23 012, No. 5, p. 8.

37 Primarily concerning inheritance.

38 K. Lünnemann, M. Steketee, M. Annuska, M. Overgaag, *Minderjarigen als procespartij*, Utrecht: Verwey-Jonker Instituut, 2003, p. 17 and p. 116 (English summary). The possibility that the district court may appoint a special guardian is contained in the pending proposal on 'Continued Parenting', Parliamentary proceedings 2006/2007 (*Kamerstukken*) 30 145, No. A.

39 It has been suggested in legal litterature to lower the minority age to 15, see hereover; S. Danielsen, Nordisk Børneret II, Copenhagen: Nord, p. 261.

40 S. Danielsen considers the legal position of children in relation to their parents to be a neglected area in Danish law, S. Danielsen, 'Børns rolle under forældremyndighedstvister', *TFA*, 2004, p. 280. I. Lund-Andersen considers that it may be an advantage to regulate the child's autonomous position in specific matters so that the age requirement may be adapted to the specific nature of the matter, although acknowledging that the present regulation has a coincidental character, I. Lund-Andersen, N. Munck, I. Nørgaard, *Familieret*, Copenhagen: Jurist- og Økonomforbundets Forlag, 2003, p. 103.

41 Art. 1, Guardianship Act.

he/she is aged fifteen or over. A minor aged fifteen or over is entitled, for example, to dispose of his/her own income earned through labour.[42]

The law further provides various regulations relating to the child's autonomy and participation rights with regard to specific matters, for example, in respect of medical treatment the child has an autonomous position from the age of fifteen.[43] Danish law provides greater autonomy for the child in respect of procedures concerning child protection measures. In such procedures the child's 'views should always be considered and given proper weight corresponding to the child's age and maturity' and a child aged fifteen (and for some decisions a child aged twelve) is granted independent legal standing, for example, to appeal against decisions on child protection measures.[44]

In Danish law the Regional State Administration may appoint a special guardian when there is a conflict of interests between the holder(s) of guardianship and the child regarding matters pertaining to guardianship.[45] There is no corresponding provision in relation to parental authority concerning the child's person.[46] It is not entirely excluded, however, that the possibility exists to appoint a temporary holder of parental authority when a conflict of interests regarding the child's person arises.[47] The reason why there is no general 'conflict of interests" provision is twofold. In the first place, to avoid parental abuse of such a rule in cases where the parents in reality seek a decision concerning their dispute.[48] In the second place, it has not been considered desirable that in such cases the Regional State Administration could eliminate the rights of the holder(s) of parental authority in favour of the child's independent rights.[49]

---

42 Art. 26(1) and 42, Guardianship Act.

43 Sundhedsloven (Health Act), Act No. 546 of 24.06.2005. See further on other consent requirements, for example, with respect to religious decisions, I. Lund-Andersen a.o., 2003, supra, p. 102-103.

44 Art. 32(3), 48 and 167, Serviceloven (Act on social services), Compilated Act. No. 58 of 18.01.2007 with later amendments.

45 Art. 47, Guardianship Act.

46 It may however be deduced from a decision of the Family Agency that the limitation to matters pertaining to guardianship is not strict when there is a conflict of interests, *TFA* 2006.356CS and S. Danielsen, 1997, supra, p. 449.

47 Pursuant to Art. 25 of the Act on Parental Responsibility concerning the impediment of the holder(s) and S. Danielsen, 1997, supra, p. 449.

48 There is no such general access in Danish law, see below Section VII.3.2.

49 S. Danielsen, 1997, supra, p. 449.

VII.2.2.3. The CEFL principles

The content of parental responsibilities as defined by the CEFL must be viewed in connection with the child's rights contained in Chapter II of the Principles. The Principles stipulate that the child's autonomy should be respected 'in accordance with the developing ability and need of the child to act independently.'[50] The CEFL principles provide general and broad autonomy, participation and protection rights which are not limited to applying to situations where a legal dispute has arisen, as they are directed at both parents and the competent authorities. Additionally, they state no specific age requirements.[51] The inspiration for the child's position is based upon international conventions, in particular the Convention on the Rights of the Child recognising the child as an autonomous individual.[52]

While the Principles provide for the child's self-representation in legal proceedings in accordance with the 'developing ability and need of the child to act independently,' the Principles do not clarify whether the right to self-representation includes a more independent legal standing, for example, the right *to initiate court proceedings* against the parents or third persons.[53]

The Principles state that the interests of the child 'should be protected whenever they may be in conflict with the interests of the holder(s) of parental responsibilities.'[54] The holder(s) of parental responsibilities should consequently not represent the child when there is a conflict of interests.[55] In such cases, the competent authority should appoint a special representative for the child whose task it is to represent the child in the current proceedings.[56]

VII.2.2.4. Comparison: The child's position

The Dutch Civil Code and the Danish Act on Parental Responsibility do not provide explicitly for the increasingly autonomous position of the child as do the

---

50 Principles, principle 3:4, p. 39.

51 Principles, principle 3:3, p. 34 (best interests), 3:4, p. 39 (autonomy), 3:6, p. 49 (right to be heard, 3:7, p. 56 (conflict of interests).

52 Principles, principle 3:4, International Instruments, p. 39.

53 Principles, principle 3:4, Comment 2, p. 42 and principle 3:38, Comment 3, p. 258.

54 Principles, principle 3:7, p. 56.

55 Principles, principle 3:24(2), p. 159.

56 Principles, principle 3:38, p. 253 and Comment 3, p. 258.

Principles of the CEFL.[57] The CEFL principles do not, however, clarify the scope of the autonomy, for example, whether the child has an independent legal standing that would enable it to initiate court proceedings. The approach taken in Dutch and Danish law provides various regulations relating to the child's autonomy and participation rights with regard to specific matters, but with the common starting point that a child or young person is not competent to make his or her own decisions or to represent him or herself.

A common example of an autonomous position in Dutch and Danish law is the young person's independent position from a certain age in respect of medical treatment. Furthermore, the child or young person has autonomy and participation rights in a procedure concerning child protection measures. This is particularly so in Danish law, where the child or young person of a certain age has an explicit independent legal standing, for example, to appeal against decisions on child protection measures.

The protection of the child in a situation where there is or may be a conflict of interests with the parents is a complex issue because the regulation thereon may fall within the scope of child protection measures or be regulated separately in relation to particular matters. If viewed in a private law context the CEFL principles stipulate, both explicitly and broadly, that the child should be protected, whereas the institution of the special guardian in Dutch law seems to have the broadest scope as it applies to conflicts of interests both judicially and extra-judicially. The scope of the Danish provision providing for a special guardian is considerably narrower as it applies primarily to a conflict of interests concerning guardianship.[58]

The Dutch institution of the special guardian and the Principles' provision on a special representative are, however, not comparable to the possibilities to appoint a special guardian in Danish law because the special guardian in Danish law *replaces* the parent(s) within the scope of the appointment and is thus bestowed with the decision-making competence of the parent(s) while the special guardian in Dutch law and the special representative provided for by the CEFL principles *represent* the child.

---

57 Although a minor aged 15 in Danish law has a more explicated position in relation to guardianship.

58 Although it is not entirely excluded that the provision may be given a broader scope or that *exceptionally* there is a temporary allocation of parental authority.

The role of the special guardian in Dutch law exists to some extent in Danish law, particularly concerning the appointment of a legal representative for the child in a legal procedure, something which, however, is also possible in Dutch law. On the other hand, the possibility of 'replacing' the parent in Dutch law would be regulated in the context of the suspension of parental authority, which is possible only when the parent lacks the capacity to exercise parental authority or in the context of child protection measures.

VII.3. THE EXERCISE OF PARENTAL AUTHORITY

The exercise of parental authority is reviewed in the context of the internal and external competence of the holders of joint parental authority, the possibility to regulate the exercise through a decision or an agreement and access to dispute settlement. This Section is supplemented by the next Section, which aims to review Dutch and Danish law in relation to the law regulating a number of *concrete disputes*.

VII.3.1. INTERNAL AND EXTERNAL COMPETENCE

VII.3.1.1. Dutch law

The competence of two parents who exercise joint parental authority in respect of decisions concerning the child's person is not specifically regulated in the Dutch Civil Code. With respect to the administration of property and legal representation, Article 253i of the Dutch Civil Code provides that parents exercise parental authority jointly, although one parent also has the capacity to do so alone provided that there are no objections by the other parent.

It is generally assumed that the resident parent can make day-to-day decisions concerning the child's person while more important decisions such as, for example, educational choices and important medical decisions, such as surgery or the treatment of life-threatening illnesses, require agreement between the parents. However, it is not specifically regulated when third persons, for example, teachers and medical practitioners, dentists and so forth have an independent duty to ensure that both parents exercising joint parental authority are in agreement. It must be generally assumed that third persons have a duty to investigate the custody position and ensure that both parents consent to more important matters such as a change of school or surgery or medical treatment for a serious illness.[59]

There has been increasing focus on the position of third persons, particularly medical practitioners, in relation to the parents' exercise of parental authority. PUNSELIE recently warned doctors to be alert concerning the requirement that both parents exercising joint parental authority consent to the medical treatment of the child on the basis of a decision where a psychiatrist has received a warning from the Central Disciplinary Tribunal.[60]

Two recent decisions by disciplinary tribunals relating to health care also issued warnings to doctors who had failed to seek the consent of the parent who exercised parental authority. Both cases related to situations where the parents had ongoing disputes over parental authority or contact.

The first case concerned a doctor who, at the request of the father who did not exercise parental authority but had unlawfully placed the children in a place which was unknown to the mother, carried out an examination of two children because the father suspected that the mother had used physical violence against them. The doctor claimed, amongst other things, that it had been an emergency situation. The Central Disciplinary Tribunal issued a warning stating that the doctor should not have carried out the examination without informing the mother and seeking her consent. Furthermore, the Tribunal considered that it had not been an emergency situation and that the doctor could have followed standard procedures by contacting the relevant authorities.[61]

In the second case a psychiatrist had written a report, at the request of the mother, concerning contact between the father and the son to be used in pending contact proceedings. The psychiatrist had not contacted the father or sought his consent. The parents exercised joint parental authority. The psychologist received a warning.[62]

---

59 A custody register exists and is administered by the district courts, Art. 244, DCC. This register may be consulted by everyone. The register only contains decisions, for example an allocation of sole parental authority or an allocation of joint parental authority to unmarried parents and is consequently not complete.

60 E.C.C. Punselie, 'Artsen let op!', *FJR*, 2007, No. 57, p. 133.

61 Centraal Tuchtcollege voor de Gezondheidszorg 23.11.2006, *Tijdschrift voor Gezondheidsrecht*, 2007, No. 31, p. 161-165.

62 Regionaal Tuchtcollege voor de Gezondheidszorg te Eindhoven 01.02.2007, *Tijdschrift voor Gezondheidsrecht*, 2007, No. 31, p. 321-324.

VII.3.1.2. Danish law

Important decisions concerning the child's person and matters pertaining to guardianship require agreement between the parents who hold joint parental authority.[63] The parent with whom the child resides may make overall decisions concerning the child's daily life.

The notes to the Act consider that, in practice, both parents can make decisions on a daily basis concerning matters such as food, clothing, bedtime and the entertaining of friends. Both parents may also decide on leisure activities separately and individually when they take place within the period of time that the child spends with one parent.[64]

The notes to the 2007 Act on Parental Responsibility illustrate the competence of parents in relation to the possible decisions:[65]

Table 6

Holders jointly	The resident parent	The contact parent
Guardianship Important medical treatment and important surgery Choice of school Relocation outside the jurisdiction incl. Greenland and the Faeroe Islands Choice of names Religious matters Marriage Passport	Direct daily care Day care After-school care Leisure activities Relocation within the jurisdiction	Decisions related to contact – direct care, Leisure activities

The division of competence in relation to possible types of decisions concerning the child's person deals primarily with the internal competence of the holders of parental authority. There is no general regulation of external competence.[66]

63 A guardian may provide the other guardian with a power of attorney, Art. 3(1) and (2), Guardianship Act.

64 L 133, Comments to § 3.

65 L 133, Comments to § 3. The list is non-exhaustive.

66 S. Danielsen, 1997, p. 64.

It is generally assumed that doctors must ensure that in more important matters both parents holding joint parental authority agree to the treatment of a child under the age of 15.[67]

In 2004 the Ministry of Family and Consumer Affairs informed all hospitals, doctors and dentists of procedures that must be followed in respect of the obligation to inform parents without parental authority.[68] The information was highly detailed and concerned not only the right to information but also regulated, for example, the right to visit a child in hospital. The information placed an extensive obligation upon doctors to investigate the parent's legal position in relation to his or her right to receive the information requested.[69] A doctor commented upon this in a medical journal under the title 'New rules are silly'. It read as follows:

> 'No matter whether we receive the information or not, it actually means that we have to suspect every consultation concerning children (...). Considering that few children, especially very young children, rarely call the doctor for an appointment themselves, it concerns many consultations – and consequently creates a considerable amount of extra work for doctors.
>
> Would it not be fair to assume that when a child is placed in the care of other adults, whether it is a parent with parental authority, grandparents or others, we may examine and treat (the child) and send the bill to the public medical insurance scheme without asking?'[70]

KRONBORG places this reaction in the context of an individualisation which has gone too far and raises the question whether conflicts between parents should

67 Although the Act concerning the legal position of patients formally operates with the presumption that the consent of one holder is sufficient, Art. 17(1), Health Act; see also Commission report 1475/2006, p. 303-304. The Ministry of the Interior and Health has issued a Guideline concerning specifically the circumcision of boys. If the boy in question is under the age of 15 and the parents hold joint parental authority, both parents must consent to the operation. Boys above the age of 15 may give consent themselves, Vejledning No. 9267 of 23.05.2005. The circumcision of girls is a criminal offence whether it takes place within or outside Denmark, Art. 245 Straffeloven (The Penal Code).

68 The right to information is further deliberated in Chapter VIII, Section VIII.2.3.2.

69 There is no register with information on a parent's status in relation to parental authority in Denmark. Consequently, third persons must request relevant information from the parent.

70 S. Meyer, 'Nye regler er hul i hovedet', *Dagens medicin*, 19.11.2004.

not be dealt with elsewhere rather than in the context of the documentation required in connection with a medical consultation.[71]

VII.3.1.3. The CEFL principles

When parentage has been established in respect of both parents, the parents hold parental responsibilities and have an equal *right and duty* to exercise these responsibilities. Parental responsibilities should, whenever possible, be exercised jointly.[72]

The Principles distinguish between daily matters and important and urgent decisions. In daily matters each parent has the right to act alone. Important decisions concerning matters such as education, medical treatment, the child's residence and the administration of the child's property should be taken jointly. In urgent cases a parent has the right to act alone, but should inform the other parent without undue delay.[73] The Principles do not contemplate the position of third persons if a parent has acted alone in a situation where the parent was not competent.

The principles further contain a provision allowing the partner of the parent, who lives with the child, to take part in decisions regarding daily matters such as, for example, deciding on the child's bedtime or how much time the child may watch television. This applies implicitly with the resident parent's consent, unless the other parent having parental responsibilities objects.[74]

The source of this principle which allows the parent's partner to have a quasi-legal position[75] may be found in the law of some countries, for example, in Germany where it only applies when the resident parent exercises sole parental responsibilities.[76] Viewed in the context of a joint exercise by two parents as generally provided for by the CEFL principles, it could become an issue of contention. Not because of the limited competences granted to the partner

---

71 A. Kronborg, 2007, p. 14.

72 Principles, principle 3:11, p. 82.

73 Principles, principle 3:12, p. 86.

74 Principles, principle 3:18, p. 116, Comments 1 and 2, p. 117. The principles also contain the possibility that the parent's partner is formally attributed with the exercise of parental responsibilities in addition to or instead of the other parent, principle 3:17, p. 110 or is attributed with parental responsibilities, principle 3:9, p. 66.

75 The principle has a quasi-legal character since it does not rest upon a formal attribution and the exercise is further unregulated.

76 Principles, principle 3:18, Comparative overview p. 116.

considering that such could be viewed as inherent in caring for a child (whether by a babysitter, grandparents, day-care facilities or the parent's partner). Rather, because of the implications of the other parent's objection. The fact that the principle does not apply when the other parent objects, seems to provide the other parent with an extraordinary means of interference in the private life of the resident parent.[77]

VII.3.1.4. Comparison: Internal and external competence

Danish and Dutch law, as well as the CEFL principles, provide a distinction between important and less important matters; with the general rule that important matters require agreement while each parent has competence in less important matters. The right to act alone can only be found explicitly in the CEFL principles.

With respect to the administration of property, Dutch law provides that a parent may act alone with implied consent while Danish law provides for the possibility of providing one parent with a power of attorney. The CEFL principles do not regulate this matter specifically.

The developments in joint parental authority mean that the question of the external competence of parents holding or exercising joint parental authority is clearly becoming increasingly important in both Dutch and Danish law. In the future we can expect that third persons, such as teachers and medical practitioners, will increasingly have to investigate the competence of parents in order to avoid liability on their part.

VII.3.2. DECISIONS AND AGREEMENTS ON THE EXERCISE

VII.3.2.1. Dutch law

The distinction between holding and exercising parental authority in Dutch law is not made to allow for a division at the level of exercising such authority.[78] Dutch law does not *currently* contain specific regulations concerning the division of exercising parental authority whether pursuant to an agreement or court

---

77 Although the principle applies only to the resident parent's partner who lives with the child, it would seem a natural corollary that also the resident parent could object to care decisions provided by the 'contact' parent's partner.

78 Chapter V, Section V.2.1.1.

decision, other than the possibilities described in Chapter VI in relation to the establishment of a main or shared residence.

If parents draw up more specific agreements, it is not clear whether such agreements can be included in the divorce decree, or the decision on parental authority and the legal validity of such agreements is uncertain.[79] It is clear, however, that some decisions which allocate joint parental authority depart from a limited perception of the subsequent exercise. As illustrated in Chapter V, some decisions rely upon the subsidiary position of the non-resident parent or even upon the perception that the resident parent has decision-making competence.[80] Yet, such decisions do not set out a division formally providing the resident parent with more competence and is consequently probably only relevant in a subsequent procedure.

The pending proposal on 'Continued Parenting' obliges parents to make a parenting plan, which is used to substantiate the division of care and responsibilities, and this must be submitted with the divorce petition.[81] If the parents do not reach an agreement, the court may decide upon the division.[82] The parenting plan, or alternatively the court's decision, could be viewed as providing a division at the level of exercising such responsibilities. However, it is not clear from the parliamentary proceedings to what extent the parenting plan may be viewed as providing a division at the formal level or to what extent the parenting plan may be regarded as legally binding. The proposal foresees the enforcement of the parenting plan only if the court so decides.[83]

VII.3.2.2. Danish law

The Danish Act on Parental Responsibility does not provide for any other decisions than the three main types; the allocation of parental authority, the establishment of residence and contact.[84]

---

79 Art. 819, Civil Procedural Code.

80 Section V.4.5.1.

81 Unmarried parents also have a duty to draw up such a plan, see Chapter II, Section II.2.6.2.

82 Chapter II, Section II.6.2.2. and parliamentary proceedings 2006/2007 (*Kamerstukken*), 30 145, No. A pertaining to Art. 253a.

83 Parliamentary proceedings 2006/2007 (*Kamerstukken*), 30 145, No. A pertaining to Art. 812 of the Civil Procedural Code.

84 A new provision provides that the Regional State Administration may allow a parent to travel when the parents have a dispute concerning parental authority and residence, Art. 25, Act on Parental Responsibility, see further below Section VII.4.5.2.

Furthermore, the Act on Parental Responsibility does not regulate agreements between the holder(s) of parental authority other than those that concern the allocation of parental authority, the establishment of residence or contact. While it is possible, and probably quite common, to enter into agreements concerning other matters, for example, more specific agreements concerning the raising of the child or educational choices, such agreements are not legal in nature and remain unenforceable.[85]

VII.3.2.3. The CEFL principles

The CEFL principles draw a distinct line between the holding and exercising of parental responsibilities. While the termination of parental responsibilities is only possible through a discharge reserved for exceptional situations,[86] the Principles provide the possibility of dividing the exercise as a means of solving differences between the holder(s), for example, in cases of divorce or factual separation.

The principles provide that one holder may exercise parental responsibilities alone with the agreement of the parents or a decision taken by the competent authority, subject to the best interests of the child.[87] Depending upon national law, an agreement may be subject to scrutiny by the competent authority. However, in the case of divorce by mutual consent the agreement should be in writing and subject to scrutiny.[88]

A decision on the sole exercise of parental responsibilities may cover situations where the parents do not share the same views or cases where a parent is unable to exercise parental responsibilities, for example, due to mental illness, absence or because a parent is not interested in taking care of the child.[89] The guiding criterion for sole exercise is the *best interests of the child*.

---

85 See generally on enforcement, Chapter VIII, Section VIII.5.2.

86 Chapter V, Section V.2.1.3. and V.4.3.

87 Principles, principle 3:15, p. 100.

88 Principles, principle 3:13, p. 91, Comment 4, p. 94. The somewhat inconsistent approach concerning scrutiny, where this is only required in the case of divorce by mutual consent, must be viewed in connection with the requirements of the CEFL divorce principles: K. Boele-Woelki, F. Ferrand, C. González Beilfuss, M. Jäntera-Jareborg, N. Lowe, D. Martiny, W. Pintens, *Principles of European Family Law Regarding Divorce and Maintenance Between Former Spouses*, Antwerp-Oxford: Intersentia, 2004, principle 1:6(1)(a), p. 37.

89 Principles, principle 3:15, Comment 3, p. 104-105.

Furthermore, the parents may make more detailed agreements concerning aspects such as care, protection and education.[90]

VII.3.2.4. Comparison: Decisions and agreements

The CEFL principles provide explicitly for the possibility of agreements and decisions on the exercise at the formal level. Such a division may also include sole exercise and is possible as a means of solving differences between the holders, for example, after divorce or factual separation. The division at the level of exercising such responsibilities may be seen to serve a function comparable to the possibility of allocating sole parental authority in Dutch and Danish law upon divorce or the breakup of a relationship.[91] The CEFL's guiding criterion of ' best interests' is clearly a more open criterion than the Dutch 'torn or lost' or the Danish 'weighty grounds', although the CEFL criterion provides little guidance.

Dutch law does not provide specifically for a formal division at the level of exercising parental responsibilities comparable to the CEFL principles, yet the pending proposal on 'Continued Parenting' could be viewed as pointing in the direction of an informal division of 'care and responsibilities.[92] Danish law does not provide for this possibility at all.

VII.3.3. DISPUTE SETTLEMENT

VII.3.3.1. Dutch law

Dutch law provides general access to the settlement of any disputes which may arise between parents who exercise joint parental authority, whether the dispute concerns the child's person, the administration of the child's property or his/her legal representation.[93] Art. 253a of the Dutch Civil Code provides that:

---

90 Principles, principle 3:13, Comment 5. Subject to scrutiny in the same manner as applies to agreements on the sole exercise of parental responsibilities, above in this Section.

91 Chapter V, Sections V.4.5. and V.4.6.

92 This division in Dutch law must be considered informal or of a quasi-legal nature since it does not expressly provide the parents with a formal division of competence or a division which is necessarily enforceable. The enforceability of the parenting plan has been a discussed and disputed issue in the legislative proceedings. See further Chapter VIII, Section VIII.3.1.1.

93 When the matter concerns the administration of property or legal representation, the sub-district court is competent rather than the district court, Art. 253i(2), DCC.

> 'In the case of the exercise of joint parental authority, disputes between the parents in respect thereof may, on the application of both or either of them be submitted to the district court. The district court shall first attempt to reach an agreement between the parents prior to taking a decision. The court shall give such an order as it shall consider desirable in the best interests of the child'.[94]

As can be deduced from this provision, the court is not bound by the requests of the parents but may give a decision which it considers desirable in the interests of the child. The parents are, however, free to subsequently agree on a different result.[95]

VII.3.3.2. Danish law

Disputes between the holders of guardianship, normally the parents holding joint parental authority, concerning matters relating to guardianship, may be brought before the regional state administration, which will decide the disputed matter.[96]

In Danish law there is no general access to the settlement of disputes concerning the child's person. Danish law relies upon the three main types of decisions; an allocation of parental authority, the establishment of residence and a decision on contact.[97] The parents may, however, request counselling or mediation at the regional state administration.[98]

VII.3.3.3. The CEFL principles

The CEFL principles provide two alternative solutions for settling an important disagreement on the *exercise* of parental responsibilities, if the competent authority cannot conciliate the parents. The competent authority may divide the exercise of parental responsibilities or decide the dispute. The Principles consequently leave the choice between two different solutions to national law, consid-

---

94 See Chapter II, Section II.2.2.2. for the historical background to this provision.

95 ASSER-DE BOER, 2006, supra, p. 671. Certain types of disputes are separately regulated such as, for example, a dispute over child maintenance and the name of the child, see below Section VII.4.

96 An administrative appeal to the Family Agency is possible as well as limited court review based upon the Constitution, see Chapter III, Section III.4.1. for this type of review.

97 Further, the Regional State Administration may allow a parent to travel, see below Section VII.

98 Chapter VIII, Section VIII.3.2.3.

ering that there is no common core and that 'the practical result will often be the same because deciding on the most competent parent will be difficult without taking into account the disputed issue itself'.[99] However, the CEFL probably favours the division of the exercise to a decision on the disagreement.[100]

The principle concerns only *important matters* but there is no restriction upon the types of disputes that the parents may bring before the competent authority as the CEFL considers that 'the competence should not be limited to certain issues'.[101]

VII.3.3.4. Comparison: Dispute settlement

Dutch law and the CEFL principles provide for general access to the settlement of disputes, which Danish law does not. The CEFL principles provide an alternative: the division of the exercise or deciding the dispute depending on national law, while Dutch law provides for a decision on the dispute.

VII.4. CONCRETE DISPUTES: DUTCH AND DANISH LAW

The purpose of this Section is to review how Dutch and Danish law deal with the following types of disputes: child maintenance, the child's name, medical issues, educational choices and the child's passport and travel.

The access to dispute settlement is reviewed broadly in the context of the relevant national law and in relation to parents who hold or exercise joint parental authority and, where relevant, also in respect of parents who hold or exercise sole parental authority. The child's position is also summarily mentioned.

99 Principles, principle 3:14, p. 95, Comment 3, p. 99.

100 Principles, principle 3:14, Comment 3, p. 99 stating; 'Authorising one of the parents to act alone will be preferable where it can be established that a specific, separable issue has to be resolved and one of the holders of parental responsibilities has a sufficient degree of competence or knowledge to pursue the best interests of the child concerning this question'.

101 Principles, principle 3:14, p. 98.

VII.4.1. CHILD MAINTENANCE

VII.4.1.1. Dutch law

Dutch maintenance law relating to children is of a complex nature; on the one hand, because the obligation towards a child may be based upon different and competing foundations, such as: legal parentage, begetter status,[102] or step-parentage;[103] on the other hand, because Dutch law departs from the notion of an individual assessment depending upon the needs of the child and the financial capacity of the parents.[104] The obligation to pay maintenance ends when the child or young person reaches the age of 18. A young person may, however, also instigate a claim for maintenance from the age of 18 until the age of 21.[105]

The parents may agree upon the payment of child maintenance or request the court to decide the matter. An agreement exempting a parent from this obligation is void.[106] The request can be made in the course of the divorce procedure as an auxiliary provision.[107] Young persons from the age of 16 have a right to be heard in a procedure concerning child maintenance.[108]

Changes to an agreement or court decision are possible when it no longer meets the legal standards on account of a change of circumstances.[109]

Three public institutions are involved in the collection of child maintenance in the Netherlands:

---

102 The biological father who, together with the mother, has conceived the child in a natural way where paternity has not been established, see further ChapterII, Section II.2.4.1. and II.2.4.2. The begetter may be liable for the payment of the child's living expenses until the age of 18; if the child is handicapped the liability may continue after the age of majority, Art. 405, DCC.

103 The obligation is a mutual obligation of parents, children, children-in-law and step-parents, Art. 392, DCC.

104 Legal parents and step-parents have a duty to provide for their children irrespective of their needs, Art. 392(2), DCC. The need of the child is nonetheless a relevant yardstick, M.J.C. Koens, C.G.M. van Wamelen, *Kind en Scheiding*, The Hague: Koninklijke Vermande, 2001, p. 198-199. While there are non-binding guidelines for the calculation of child maintenance, the actual calculation is based upon an individual assessment, p. 209-212.

105 Art. 395a(1), DCC.

106 Art. 400(2), DCC.

107 Art. 827(1)c, Civil Procedural Code. The division of costs (maintenance) becomes part of the obligation to make verifiable agreements in the 'parenting plan' if the proposal on 'Continued Parenting' is adopted, see Chapter II, Section II.2.6.2.

108 Art. 809(1), Civil Procedural Code.

109 Art. 401(1), DCC.

1. The court which decides on the amount to be paid when the parents do not reach an agreement;
2. The social services of the local council enforce the collection when the parent who has a right to receive child maintenance requests public aid; and
3. The National Maintenance Collection Agency (Landelijk Bureau Inning Onderhoudsbijdragen, L.I.B.O.) collects and pays out maintenance under certain conditions.[110]

The law concerning child maintenance has been under review because, amongst other things, more than half of single mothers do not receive child maintenance payments due to the fact that it has not been determined (by the court) and because of problems with enforcement.[111] The proposed amendments have nonetheless been retracted.

VII.4.1.2. Danish law

Legal parents are obliged to provide for their children. In cases where a parent does not live with the child, the other parent may apply to the regional state administration for a decision on child support.[112]

The Act on Child Support points in the direction of an individual assessment dependent upon the needs of the child and the financial circumstances of the parents. Nonetheless, the amount of maintenance to be paid is generally calculated as a percentage of the income of the parent who has to pay and the amount of children this parent has to support or pay maintenance to.[113] The obligation to pay child support ends when the child reaches the age of eighteen.[114]

Child support procedures are administrative procedures decided on a written basis. There are no costs involved. Only the parents are party to the procedure

---

110 Het Kind Centraal: verantwoordelijkheid blijft, Eindrapport van de werkgroep alimentatiebeleid, p. 3, Parliamentary proceedings 2002/2003 (*Kamerstukken*), 28 795, No. 1.

111 Supra, p. 2.

112 Art. 13, Lov om børns forsørgelse (Act on child support), Compilated Act No. 352 of 15.05.2003. Step-parents do not have such an obligation. This also applies to a step-parent who holds or has held parental authority; see Chapter V, Section V.7.2.

113 I. Lund-Andersen a.o., 2003, supra, p. 134.

114 Art. 14(2) of the Act on Child Support. The parent may be obliged to pay an educational contribution until the age of 24. This contribution is paid to the other parent when this parent provides for the young person. The young person cannot request maintenance him or herself. Mostly such a contribution is not due because the child receives publicly funded student grants or has other income, I. Lund Andersen et al., *Familieret*, 2003, p. 135.

and a child or younger person is never heard in such a procedure.[115] The decision taken by the regional state administration may be appealed to the Ministry of Family and Consumer Affairs.

It is always possible to request a review of the decision, if the request is reasoned, for example, on the basis of changes in income. If the parents have reached an agreement, the regional state administration may amend this agreement if it is considered to be unreasonable, circumstances have changed or the decision is inconsistent with the best interests of the child.[116]

In cases where the parent does not comply with the maintenance obligation, the other parent may request the local council to collect the maintenance which is due[117] and may, additionally, request an advance payment of the fixed basic amount.[118]

VII.4.2. THE LAW ON NAMES

VII.4.2.1. Dutch law

The Dutch law on names was revised in 1998 to allow for a more liberal system.[119] A child bears the first name laid down on the birth certificate, given by the person who comes to register the child. The registration of the birth must take place at the Registry within three working days after the birth.[120] Where no name is chosen or the chosen name is rejected, the Registrar gives the child one or more first names *ex officio*.[121]

---

115 This also applies to the educational contribution in respect of a young person aged between 18-24. It is also not possible for the young person to claim maintenance him or herself.

116 Art. 17, Act on Child Support; see further on agreements; L. Tøgersen and C. Fogt-Nielsen, 'Aftaler om børnebidrag og ægtefællebidrag – en gennemgang af regler og praksis' *TFA*, 2007, p. 35-40.

117 Bekendtgørelse af lov om indrivelse af underholdsbidrag (Compilated Act on collection of maintenance obligations), Act No. 946 of 10.10.2005.

118 Bekendtgørelse af lov om børnetilskud og forskudsvis betaling af børnebidrag, Act. No. 909 of 03.09.2004, Chapter 3.

119 The process of changing the law began in 1984. The old law provided that children born within marriage or recognised by the father always carried the father's surname, ASSER-DE BOER, 2006, supra, p. 44-46.

120 Both parents are authorised to register the child and the father has an obligation to do this, Art. 4(1) and 19e, DCC.

121 Art. 4(3), DCC.

The parents can make a choice in respect of the child's surname. The parents must choose one of their surnames. It is not possible to give the child another surname or a combination of the parents' surnames. If no choice is made at the time of registering the birth, a child born within marriage acquires the surname of the father and a child born outside of marriage the surname of the mother.[122] The choice of surname is only possible after the birth of the first child since the choice is binding in respect of children born to the parents subsequently.[123]

A child's first name(s) may only be changed by the district court at the request of the child's representatives, that is, the parents who exercise parental authority, if there are sufficiently important reasons to justify the change.[124] A child aged twelve or over must be heard and a child under the age of twelve may be heard, in accordance with the general provision concerning the hearing of children.

A surname may be changed by Royal Decree (*Koninklijk Besluit*) upon the recommendation of the Minister of Justice.[125] Changing the surname of a minor must be requested by both legal representatives, that is, by both parents when they exercise joint parental authority.[126] The wishes of children over the age of twelve are important and should be taken into account.[127] Furthermore, it is possible to request a change of the child's surname in a procedure concerning the allocation of joint authority between a parent and a non-parent.[128]

When a parent exercises sole parental authority over a child born outside marriage the surname of the child may be changed. For children who were born within marriage, the possibility of changing the child's surname depends upon the number of years the parent has solely cared for the child.[129]

---

122 Art. 5, DCC.

123 Art. 5(8), DCC.

124 Art. 4(4), DCC and J.H. Nieuwenhuis et al., 2004, supra, p. 6, for example, in cases of transexuality and adoption.

125 The starting point is not that such a right exists. 'The authority is inclined to take a negative decision with respect to so-called vanity petitions; P. Vlaardingerbroek, in: J. Chorus, P. Gerver and E. Hondius, *Introduction to Dutch law*, Alphen aan den Rijn: Kluwer Law International, 2006, p. 77.

126 Art. 7(1), DCC.

127 ASSER-DE BOER, 2006, supra, p. 55.

128 Art. 253(5). See for this type of allocation Chapter V, Section V.7.1.

129 5 years if the child is younger than 12 and 3 years if the child is older than 12; Koninklijk Besluit Geslachtsnaamswijziging of 06.10.1997 with later amendments.

VII.4.2.2. Danish law

The Danish law on names was revised in 2005. The new Act on Names has provided considerable freedom of choice to choose, add to or change first names, middle names and surnames.[130]

When a child is born, the parent(s) holding parental authority is/are obliged by law to choose a first name within six months.[131] There is no possibility to bring a dispute thereon before a competent authority. When a child is not given a first name the Regional State Administration may fine the holder(s) of parental authority.

The child must also be given a surname within six months and may be given a middle name.[132] The child may be given the family name, the surname of the mother or the father, a combination of both or another name. If a choice is not made or the parents cannot agree on a surname, the child acquires the mother's surname.[133] This also applies to married parents. Each child of the family may be given a different surname.

If the parents hold joint parental authority they must both agree to any changes to the child's first name, middle name or surname. A child who has reached the age of twelve or older must consent to a change. A child younger than twelve must be heard depending on the child's maturity and the circumstances of the case; the views of the child must be considered.[134]

Where one parent holds sole parental authority, this parent can request a change to the child's first, middle or surname, subject to consent by the child aged twelve or older. Furthermore, a child younger than 12 must be heard during the case. If, however, the child bears the other parent's middle name or surname, this parent must also be heard. The regional state administration may deny the request if it considers that this result is indicated.

Giving a name or changing name(s) are administrative procedures and the competence to register names and changes rests with the regional state administration and the Ministers of the Danish State Church in their civil function as

130 Navnelov (Act on Names), Act No. 524 of 24.06.2005.
131 Art. 12(2), Act on Names.
132 Art. 1(1), Act on Names.
133 Art. 1(2), Act on Names.
134 Art. 22, Act on Names.

administrators of the Registers of Births and Deaths. Registration is also possible on the internet.

VII.4.3. MEDICAL CARE

VII.4.3.1. Dutch law

A dispute concerning the medical care of the child may be brought before the district court pursuant to Art. 253a of the Dutch Civil Code when the parents exercise joint parental authority.[135] The court will try to reconcile the parents and, if this is not successful, it will decide the dispute. There are not many cases concerning medical decisions. Published case law has provided decisions in respect of vaccination and circumcision. In the first case the non-resident father wanted the children to be vaccinated and the resident mother resisted because she was of the opinion that previous vaccinations had had serious side-effects. The Arnhem Court of Appeal upheld the decision of the District Court, deciding that the children should be vaccinated, following the advice of the Dutch Child Protection Board, considering that the mother had not proven that the side-effects were a result of the vaccinations.[136]

The second case concerned the resident mother's request to allow the circumcision of the son to be performed at the age of five, in accordance with her religious beliefs. The father did not consent to the circumcision. The 's-Hertogenbosch Court of Appeal overturned the decision of the District Court, which had allowed the circumcision, on the ground that it was an irreversable and medically unnecessary operation.[137]

VII.4.3.2. Danish law

If parents holding joint parental authority cannot reach agreement concerning an important decision on a young child's medical treatment, for example, after having participated in counselling or mediation at the regional state administration, either parent may request the termination of joint parental authority.

135 Concerning children younger than 16. Children aged 12 or above should also consent to the treatment, above Section VII.2.2.1.

136 Gerechtshof Arnhem 16.11.2004, LJN AR8769. Similarly, Rechtbank Haarlem (District Court) 15.04.2005, LJN AT4422.

137 Gerechtshof 's-Hertogenbosch 26.11.2002, LJN AF2955.

Termination is possible if there are 'weighty grounds'. A normal vaccination will probably not constitute an important decision requiring agreement.[138]

The notes to the Act consider that joint parental authority may be terminated, if disagreements on important matters result in a situation where the child does not receive necessary medical or psychological treatment. The notes also point towards the possibility *of a temporary allocation of sole parental authority* pending the proceedings allowing one parent to determine the matter.[139]

VII.4.4. EDUCATIONAL CHOICES

VII.4.4.1. Dutch law

A dispute concerning educational matters may be brought before the district court pursuant to Art. 253a of the Dutch Civil Code, when the parents exercise joint parental authority and cannot agree upon important educational choices, such as the choice of a particular school.

In a decision by the District Court of Zwolle from 2004, the court was asked to rule on a situation where the parents could not reach an agreement on the choice of a school. The resident mother wished to change the childrens' school because the child of the father's new partner went to the same school and relations between the mother and the new partner were not amicable. The father could agree to a change of school, but did not approve of the mother's choice of a Montessori school. The court rejected the mother's request, considering that the parents should make every effort to agree on a new school. The court consequently did not decide on the dispute.[140]

VII.4.4.2. Danish law

The legal position with regard to educational choices[141] is the same as that concerning important medical decisions: a solution to a dispute over an educational choice would thus have to be reached through counselling or mediation, the termination of joint parental authority or through a temporary allocation of sole parental authority. It should be noted that it is somewhat inconsistent that

---

138 Circumcision is only possible if the parents agree, supra note 68.

139 L 133, p. 25.

140 Rechtbank Zwolle 19.08.2004, LJN ATAQ7125.

141 Day care or after-school care may be decided by the resident parent, see above Section VII.3.1.2.

a resident parent has the right to relocate within the jurisdiction but not necessarily the authority to register the child at a new school.[142]

VII.4.5. PASSPORT AND TRAVEL

VII.4.5.1. Dutch law

When parents exercise joint parental authority both must consent to the issuing of a passport. If a parent refuses consent, the other parent may request the consent of the court.[143]

A passport cannot be issued directly to the minor him or herself but in a case of a conflict of interests the sub-district court may appoint a special guardian to represent the minor in a legal procedure.[144]

It does not seem to be specifically regulated in Dutch law to what extent parents exercising joint parental authority are allowed to travel outside the jurisdiction or whether this requires the consent of the other parent.[145]

VII.4.5.2. Danish law

In Denmark the local authorities are authorised to issue passports. Decisions concerning the issuing of a passport or the denial thereof may be appealed to the Danish Justice Department.

Usually the issuing of a passport to a child or young person requires the consent of the holder(s) of parental authority. However, the authorities have discretionary powers in exceptional cases to issue a passport at the request of only one parent or at the request of the child. Furthermore, they may also issue a passport to a parent who does not hold parental authority in situations where this parent has the right to have contact abroad.[146]

---

142 On relocation see; Chapter VI, Section VI.4.2.3.

143 Art. 34(2), Paspoortwet 26.09.1991 with later amendments.

144 Based upon the example provided in, M.J. Steketee, A.M. Overgaag and K.D. Lünnemann, 2003, supra, p. 19.

145 Save for situations where the law relating to child abduction becomes relevant or the parent illegally retains the child, see further on this Chapter VIII, Section VIII.5.2.4. The fact that the issuing of a passport requires consent indicates that consent is also necessary for travelling.

146 Art. 19, Bekendtgørelse om pas m.v., Ministerial Decree No. 1003 of 06.10.2006.

Parents who hold parental authority and a parent who has the right to have contact abroad are generally allowed to travel with the child outside Denmark.[147] The Danish Act on Parental Responsibility contains a special rule applying to situations where there is a dispute concerning parental authority. Article 3(2) of the Act provides that when 'parents have joint parental authority and disagree about the allocation of parental authority, both must consent to the child leaving the country, or upon the prolongation of the child's stay abroad beyond what has been agreed, presumed or set out.' This provision must be understood in the context of the Penal Act where, accordingly, it is a criminal offence to take the child outside Denmark.[148] This provision was enacted in support of the law concerning child abduction, but also applies in situations outside the scope of child abduction, for example, in respect of a planned holiday abroad. The provision applies when there is a dispute as to parental authority. It is not necessary that judicial proceedings have been initiated, a stated intention to do so or other evidence of a disagreement is sufficient.[149]

A particular case raised concern and provided a reason to amend the first proposed 2007 Act on Parental Responsibility. The amendment provided the possibility to request permission to travel in situations where the other parent holding parental authority will not consent to the journey. In this case, the resident mother, holding joint parental authority together with the father, had initiated court proceedings for the termination of joint parental authority. The father had limited contact with the child. The mother was then given a free holiday for a week in Turkey and wished to bring the child. The father would not consent to the journey[150] and the mother was contacted by the police in connection with the issuing of the passport. The police advised that she was not allowed to travel but further also made a remark[151] which the mother took as an indication that she should go. When the mother and child returned as planned a week later, she was arrested and later criminally convicted.[152]

---

147 The contact parent only in accordance with the contact order.

148 Art. 215(2) in connection with Art. 251(1), Straffeloven (Penal Act), see further Chapter VIII, Section VIII.5.2. on the enforcement of parental authority.

149 L 133, Comments to § 3.

150 Amongst other things, because the mother had previously rejected consent for the father to take the child on holiday abroad.

151 'Have a nice trip to Bornholm', Bornholm is a Danish Island.

152 Østre Landsret (Eastern High Court) 19.12.2006, *TFA* 2007.267Ø. The District Court had acquitted the mother considering that it was only a week's holiday and that the primary purpose of the provision was to punish real child abductions. The High Court was divided, three judges voted for conviction (resulting in a fine) where the fine would be repealed due to the circumstances of the case and three judges found that the mother should pay the fine.

Article 25 of the Act on Parental Responsibility now provides that the Regional State Administration can decide that a parent is allowed to travel with the child abroad or to Greenland or the Faeroe Islands, for a short period, when there are disagreements on the allocation of parental authority.

VII.4.6. COMPARISON: CONCRETE DISPUTES

Danish law does not provide for general access to dispute settlement in relation to matters concerning the child's person, as is provided for by Dutch law. Nonetheless, it may be argued that on a practical level in relation to the type of disputes dealt with in this Section, and in the light of the access to residence and relocation decisions dealt with in Chapter VI, the lack of general access does not provide a substantive difference in respect of the possibility to obtain a ruling on a concrete dispute.[153]

It is clear that Danish law provides a more simplistic, yet also more effective regulation of child maintenance and disputes thereon than Dutch law where one of the main problems is that child maintenance is often not paid. The substantive content of Danish maintenance law is simpler as it provides purely an obligation for the parent(s) internally, whereas Dutch maintenance law is based upon a mutual parent-child obligation and further provides more and competing foundations for a manintenance obligation. Furthermore, the Danish procedures are written administrative procedures, without costs for the parties concerned, whereas the Dutch procedures are (primarily) judicial procedures involving costs.

The discretionary powers in Danish law with respect to the possibility of issuing passports, in situations where one or both parents do not consent, also provide a more simplistic solution compared with the judicial procedure required in Dutch law. The requirement that both parents must consent to the child travelling outside the jurisdiction, when there is disagreement on the allocation of parental authority, provides a more specific regulation of the competence of the holders of joint parental authority than in Dutch law.

The regulation of names in Dutch and Danish law operates with the common starting point that a dispute over the child's name, between parents who hold or exercise joint parental authority, does not provide the parents with the possibil-

---

153 As far as can be ascertained, no other types of decisions with respect to the child's person have been decided pursuant to Art. 253a, DCC under Dutch law.

ity to have the dispute judicially decided. Dutch law rather provides that the child receives a first name *ex officio* and, for the child born to married parents, the surname of the father, while the child born to an unmarried mother receives the mother's surname. Danish law provides an obligation for the parents to agree on a first name, enforceable through fines, and for children to receive the mother's surname when the parents cannot agree. Subsequent changes require agreement between parents who hold or exercise parental authority in both countries.

With respect to disputes such as educational choices and medical treatment, it is characteristic of Danish law that the lack of any possibility to obtain an official decision on the dispute is connected with the notion that this would involve 'public parenting'.[154] While access to dispute settlement has undoubtedly increased with the 1996 reform and, in particular, with the 2007 reform, Danish law nonetheless maintains this position, which primarily affects immaterial disputes concerning matters such as educational choices and medical treatment.

The CEFL has considered that the practical result between a decision and a division of the exercise of responsibilities will often be the same, because deciding on the most competent parent will be difficult without taking into account the disputed issue itself.[155] The solution which could become relevant with respect to a dispute over a medical issue in Danish law is the temporary allocation of sole parental authority during the procedure. This solution could be seen as a decision on the exercise of parental authority, since it provides one parent with the competence to decide. It is not evident, however, that the practical result would be the same. The Dutch case on vaccination mentioned above may illustrate this point. The Dutch court ruled that the children residing with the mother should be vaccinated, as requested by the father. It would not seem likely that a Danish court would allocate sole parental authority to the father *temporarily* in such a situation *with the only purpose* of providing for the vaccination considering that vaccinations are recommended but not obligatory in Denmark.

The matter may also be viewed in the context of relocation. It was concluded in Chapter VI that the Dutch case law on relocation outside the jurisdiction points in the direction that relocation is only possible when the resident parent could be viewed to have limited choice. Current Danish case law, based upon the law

154 Chapter II, Section II.3.2.1.

155 Above, Section VII.3.2.3.

before the 2007 reform, does not point in this direction. Rather, a factual or intended relocation does not seem relevant in itself without additional circumstances.

It is consequently not evident that a decision or a division of exercise provides the same actual results. It should also be noted, however, that it seems inherent in Dutch law generally to rely upon general substantive legal norms, for example, with respect to the allocation of joint parental authority and with respect to names, thereby providing for the unity of family names. Consequently, it is a complex matter to ascertain whether it is the legal construction (decision/division) in itself which is the determining factor.

CHAPTER VIII
CONTACT, PROCEDURES AND ENFORCEMENT

VIII.1. INTRODUCTION

The purpose of this Chapter is to include the 'related perspectives' which play a central role in the main subject-matter of this study. In the first place, this concerns contact rights after divorce and after the breakup of a relationship. In the second place, an inventory is made of the main features of the procedural systems in which decisions on parental authority and contact are taken. Thirdly, the child's procedural rights in such procedures are taken into account. Finally, this Chapter addresses the possibility of enforcing decisions on parental authority and contact.

VIII.2. CONTACT

This Section addresses contact; that is, the right to contact between the parent and child, the content of such contact including the right to information and the possibility of placing restrictions or conditions upon the exercise of contact rights. Before turning to the description and comparison, a few general features of the law should be noted.

Contact law and procedures differ considerably in the Netherlands and Denmark. Contact is regulated in extraordinary detail in Danish law. The Danish Act on Parental Responsibility is supplemented by hundreds of pages of Ministerial decrees and guidelines. This is far less so in Dutch law. Further, contact procedures are (primarily) administrative procedures in Denmark embedded in an increasing 'welfare' ideology. The Danish regional state administrations offer a wide range of 'services', mostly free of charge, such as: child expert counselling, mediation, partner counselling, children's 'talk' groups, various types of supervised contact, in-house child experts, substance and alcohol abuse treatment for parents and an interdisciplinary approach involving the social services. These types of 'services' are only available to a limited degree in Dutch judicial procedures, but the necessity of such services, especially supervised contact and mediation, is frequently argued in the Dutch legal and sociological literature. The approach taken in Danish law could be seen to promote the process of individualisation in family law.

Further, it may be noted that the relevant provisions of the Dutch Civil Code regulate contact between parents and children generally, thus including situations where the child has been placed in care within the context of child protection measures. The CEFL principles on contact also apply in situations where parental responsibilities have been discharged. In Danish law the contact rights of and in respect of children placed in care are regulated by the Act on Social Services.[1]

VIII.2.1. THE RIGHT TO CONTACT: PARENT-CHILD

VIII.2.1.1. The Netherlands

Parental authority in Dutch law presupposes the existence of contact between the parent and the child. Contact between the parent who exercises parental authority and the child is thus viewed as *a consequence of parental authority.*[2] The court may, however, substantiate this right by deciding on contact in respect of a parent who exercises parental authority and who does not reside with the child. The relevant provision, Article 377h of the Dutch Civil Code, does not contain the possibility of discharging a parent from contact, as provided for in respect of a legal parent who does not exercise parental authority.[3] The terminology of these provisions originate from the 1995 reform of parental authority and contact, which provided a joint request procedure for the establishment of joint parental authority.

In the light of the developments in joint parental authority, where the allocation of sole parental authority has become the exception, also in the situation where the parents have serious disagreements, the contact parent is unstable or has had little contact with the child, a number of decisions from the lower courts have

1 Art. 22a, Act on Parental Responsibility. The content of these provisions is not further deliberated in accordance with the general limitation to private law, Chapter I, Section I.2.3. The difference in the scope of these provisions compared to the provisions contained in private law have, however, been mentioned in Chapter III, Sections III.4.3. and III.4.4.

2 ASSER-DE BOER, 2006, supra, p. 818.

3 Art. 377a, DCC.

discharged or rejected contact for the parent who exercised joint parental authority. A number of these cases have reached the Supreme Court. The Supreme Court has decided that a discharge is not possible and contact may only be temporarily discontinued for a specified period of time pursuant to the general dispute settlement provision contained in Article 253a of the Dutch Civil Code. The Supreme Court has consequently remitted all cases to other Courts of Appeal for renewed consideration.[4] The question whether it should be possible to discharge a parent who exercises joint parental authority from contact has been discussed in the legal literature. WORTMANN has considered that this should be possible based upon Article 8 of the ECHR and Article 253a of the Dutch Civil Code while others have argued that it should not be possible.[5] A recent decision by the District Court of Roermond provided a new approach towards temporary discontinuation when the Court decided that contact with the father had to be discontinued for the *duration of the children's minority*, thereby indicating that contact would only be possible upon the initiative of the children who were twelve and fourteen years old.[6] It must be expected that the matter of a discharge versus temporary discontinuation will continue to play a role in Dutch law.

The right to contact between the legal parent who does not hold parental authority and the child is stated as a mutual right, which must be viewed in the context of Article 8 of the ECHR.[7] The parents may apply to the district court for a decision on contact.[8] The Court shall then establish a contact arrangement, which may be limited in time or discharge the right to contact, which may also be limited in time, based upon four limitative reasons, Article 377a(2)(3) of the Dutch Civil Code.

---

4 Hoge Raad 18.11.2005, *NJ* 2005, 574 and 31.03.2006, *NJ* 2006, 392 annotated by S.F.M. Wortmann, 23.03.2007, LJN AZ5443 and 14.09.2007, LJN BA5198.

5 S. Wortmann, 'Bij gezamenlijke gezag kan rechter toch omgang met kind ontzeggen', *Perspectief*, 2002, No. 4, p. 26, E. Nicolai, 'Bij gezamenlijke gezag geen ontzegging van omgang', *Perspectief*, 2005, No. 5, p. 17 and R.M.H.H. Tuinstra, 'Ontzegging omgang aan gezagouder via achterdeur van art. 1:253a BW', *EB*, 2006, p. 64-66.

6 Rechtbank Roermond 12.09.2007, LJN BB3532.

7 ASSER-DE BOER, 2006, supra, p. 820-821. Dutch law on contact has developed in the light of the ECHR as deliberated in Chapter II, Sections II.2.3. and II.2.5. Art. 377a, DCC concerns the legal parent, see for this concept Chapter II.2.4. Although the scope of the provision would seem to apply to all legal parents, the Explanatory report stated that the intention of this provision related to, in particular; 'the non-marital relationship where the father has recognised the child , Chapter II, Section II.2.5.

8 Further, the court may *ex officio* issue a decision, if it appears to the court that a minor aged twelve or older or a younger child who is considered able to reasonably appraise his or her interest in the matter would appreciate this, Article 377g of the Dutch Civil Code. This possibility is further deliberated below, Section VIII.3.1.1.

Discharge of the right to contact is possible if:
(a) contact would result in serious detriment to the mental or physical development of the child, or
(b) the parent is manifestly unfit or clearly must be considered not to be in a position to have contact, or
(c) a child aged twelve or older while being heard has demonstrated that he/she seriously objects to contact with the parent, or
(d) contact is otherwise contrary to the paramount interests of the child.

The reasons for discharging the right to contact are formulated in a manner which emphasises the serious nature of a discharge. The important issue is not whether contact is viewed to be in the interests of the child or whether the child wishes to have contact with the parent. A discharge is only possible where contact may be viewed to be detrimental to the child or the child has *serious objections*.[9]

Illustrative of the notion of a 'serious objection' is a case decided by the District Court of The Hague from 2007 in which a father had applied for contact in respect of two children whom he had not seen for six years, although there had been various procedures since the parents' divorce. One of the children had reached the age (12+) where he was heard in the procedure and had rejected contact with the father. The father was ill and possibly had only a limited time to live. The court decided that a supervised contact arrangement should be established. In an annotation to the case, it is considered that the obligation to hear children above the age of twelve does not mean that the child's opinion is decisive. This 'is understandable considering that children above the age of twelve may be influenced and be incapable of independently seeing what is in their interests.'[10]

The Court may vary the right of contact and a contact arrangement made by the parents on the basis of a change of circumstances since the decision or agreement was made, or on the basis that the decision was taken based on incorrect or incomplete information.[11] This provision also applies in respect of parents who exercise joint parental authority.[12] Dutch law consequently does not provide a

9 ASSER-DE BOER, 2006, supra, p. 826-827. See further p. 827-828 for a substantiation of the individual reasons for a discharge.
10 Rechtbank 's-Gravenhage 02.02.2007 annotated by IJ. Pieters, *FJR*, 2007, 63.
11 Art. 377e(1), DCC.
12 Art. 377h(e), DCC. In respect of contact there is consequently a limitation on the parents' right to bring a dispute to court pursuant to Art. 253a, DCC.

general right to have the situation reassessed, for example, in the situation where the parent has been discharged of the right to contact.[13]

The pending proposal on 'Continued Parenting' has several consequences for the law on contact as deliberated in Chapter II.[14] Two aspects of this proposal – the use of the term contact and the obligation of the parent to have contact – warrant specific mention. In the first place, the proposal contains a shift in terminology with respect to the contact rights of parents who exercise joint parental authority. Contact in respect of these parents becomes part of the '*division of care and responsibilities*' between the parents, perhaps indicative of a preference for shared residence.[15] The term contact is thus reserved for parents who do not exercise parental authority. The Council of State has criticised this change of terminology considering two perspectives.[16] The '*division of care and responsibilities*' does not reflect the most common situation where one parent is the resident parent and the other has limited contact. Further, that the use of the term contact or contact right corresponds with the use in several international conventions and instruments. The Council of State thus recommends that the term contact be preserved.[17] This criticism has not led to an amendment of the proposal, however.[18]

In the second place, the proposal on 'Continued Parenting' contains an enforceable obligation of the parent who does not exercise parental authority to have contact with the child. This part of the proposal has also been criticised by the Council of State from the point of view that the obligation only explicitly encompasses the parent who does not exercise parental authority. The proposal has not been changed to accommodate this criticism. The Minister of Justice considers the obligation of the parent who exercises parental authority to be inherent in the right and duty to raise the child, which is contained in the present Article 247(1) of the Dutch Civil Code.[19] The lower courts have already

---

13 J. De Boer questions this result on the basis of the decision of the ECtHR in Nekvedavicious v. Germany, 19.06.2003, 46165/1999 and considers that a change of circumstances must be viewed in the context of the criteria contained in Art. 377a, ASSER-DE BOER, 2006, supra, p. 835.

14 Section II.2.6.2.

15 See further Chapter VI, Section VI.3.1.

16 The Raad van State (Council of State), amongst others, advises the Dutch government and parliament on legislation.

17 Parliamentary proceedings 2004/2005 (*Kamerstukken*), 30 145, No. 4, p. 6.

18 Pertaining to the proposed Art. 253a(2) as contained in the pending proposal, Parliamentary proceedings 2006/2007 (*Kamerstukken*), 30 145, No. A.

19 Parliamentary proceedings 2004/2005 (*Kamerstukken*), 30 145, No. 4, p. 5.

established an obligation to have contact, in one case 'anticipating' the proposal on 'Continued parenting.[20]

VIII.2.1.2. Denmark

In Danish law, the contact rights of parents have been seen not as a right inherent in the concept of parental authority, nor as a modification thereto, but as a correlation of the concept of parental authority.[21] Pursuant to Article 18(1) of the Act on Parental Responsibility, the child's connection with both parents is maintained through the right to contact with the parent with whom the child does not reside. The possibility to obtain a decision on contact is reserved for legal parents who do not reside with the child and is thus not dependent upon the holding of parental authority.[22] The fact that a parent holds joint parental authority also does not alter the possibility to reject or annul a contact decision.[23]

Since the 2007 Act, the right to contact is construed as the child's right to contact. It is nonetheless the parent with whom the child does not reside who may apply for a decision on contact. Further, the parent with whom the child resides can, in situations where there is no contact or only very limited contact between the child and the other parent, request the regional state administration to summon the other parent for a meeting concerning contact.[24] The other parent is not obliged to participate in such a meeting and the state administration cannot issue a contact order if this parent objects. While contact is construed as a right of the child, this right has a moral rather than a legal character. The aim, according to the notes to the Act, is to stress the point that it is the child's interests in the contact which are central.[25]

---

20 Rechtbank Groningen (District Court) 07.02.2006, LJN AV4849. See further; Rechtbank Amsterdam (District Court) 12.07.2007, LJN BA9482.

21 J. Graversen, *Fælles forældremyndighed efter separation og skilsmisse og andre forældremyndighedsproblemer*, Copenhagen: Socialforskningsinstituttet, 1984, p. 40.

22 The parent holding sole parental authority cannot request a decision on contact if, for example, the child has taken up residence with the other parent, Commission report No. 1279/1994, p. 192.

23 However, it has been envisaged in the Explanatory notes to the 2007 Act that joint parental authority will not be established against the wishes of the other parent, if the parent is in a position where contact may be rejected or annulled, Chapter V, Section V.4.6.2.

24 Art. 18(4), Act on Parental Responsibility.

25 Lov 133, Comments to § 18.

Both parents are responsible for the child's contact with the other parent.[26] If the parents disagree on the content or exercise of contact, a decision can, at the request of a parent, be taken by the regional state administration, or, if a case on parental authority is pending before the court, by the court.[27] The relevant criterion is the general best interests criterion contained in Article 4 of the Act on Parental Responsibility.

The establishment of contact may be rejected and an agreement or previous decision may be annulled.[28] Further, an agreement on contact or a decision can be changed.[29] The Regional State Administration can reject a request for a change to a contact decision or agreement if circumstances have not considerably changed.[30]

The text of this last-mentioned provision has been changed in the 2007 Act to specifically provide for the possibility of rejecting a request also in a situation where circumstances have changed.[31] It had already been attempted to provide the previous provision with an understanding which would grant the regional state administration the possibility of rejecting a request for a change in connection with the Rule Simplification Reform (2005).[32] The previous provision had provided parents with the possibility to repeatedly request changes concerning minor differences, for example concerning the clothes that the child should bring, the food it should eat and TV viewing habits. Further, the regional state administration often came to serve as a 'post office' for parents who could not communicate by exchanging messages, letters and presents between themselves. Finally, parents sought ad hoc changes in connection with participation in particular events, such as a family weddings or birthdays, and replaced contact (*erstatningssamvær*) in cases where contact had not taken place.[33]

With the 2007 Act[34] the aim has been to change the existing practice on contact concerning both *a reduction of parental rights* and *an increase in parental rights.*

---

26 Art. 18(1), Act on Parental Responsibility.

27 Arts 20 and 35, Act on Parental Responsibility.

28 Art. 20(3), Act on Parental Responsibility.

29 Art.20(2), Act on Parental Responsibility. Prior to the 2007 Act it was only possible to reject contact or to annul an agreement or prior decision if this was necessary in the interest of of the child, Art. 17(3) repealed the Act on Parental Authority, Act. No. 39 of 15.01.2007.

30 Art. 36, Act on Parental Responsibility.

31 Lov 133, Comments to § 36 and § 20.

32 See generally on this reform, Chapter II, Section II.3.2.1.

33 *Regelforenkling på det familieretlige område*, Ministry of Justice, December 2003, p. 29-31.

34 Lov 133, Comments to § 20.

In the first place, it is aimed to ease the practice relating to the possibility of rejecting or annulling a previous decision or agreement, so that a rejection or annulment may take place at an earlier stage than was previously the case.[35] This is to be implemented through the enhancement of the 'child's perspective' and a strengthening of the interdisciplinary approach between the regional state administrations and the social services. In this respect, it has been specified that documented violence against the child should always result in a rejection or annulment of contact.[36] In the second place, it is aimed to provide increased possibilities in respect of contact with very young children. Finally, the scope for establishing replaced contact is increased in cases where the other parent has obstructed contact.[37]

VIII.2.1.3. The CEFL principles

In the CEFL principles, contact between the child and the holder of parental responsibilities is a right which is inherent in the concept of parental responsibilities, as this concept includes the right 'to maintain personal relationships'. It is, however, also construed as an independent right and an obligation of the legal parent as well as a right of the child based upon established parentage.[38] Moreover, the possibility to restrict, terminate or make the contact conditional in cases where 'the best interests of the child so require' is also possible in situations where the parent holds parental responsibilities.[39]

VIII.2.1.4. Comparison: Parent-child

The right to contact between the parent and child is construed as a mutual right in Dutch and Danish law and in the CEFL principles. In Danish law and Dutch law (at least formally), this right does not confer an actual obligation upon the parent as provided for in the CEFL principles.

In Dutch law a distinction is made between the parent who exercises parental authority and the parent who does not do so. This distinction is relevant with regard to the possibility of discharging a parent's right to contact. This distinc-

---

35 It is generally acknowledged that practices in contact cases had reached a level where contact decisions could be viewed as being damaging to children see Chapter IV, Section IV.3.3.

36 Violence against the other parent and/or the other parent's family may also have the same consequences, depending on the seriousness thereof, L 133, Comments to § 20.

37 As opposed to the general limitation concerning replaced contact, see above.

38 Principles, principle 3:25(1), p. 164 and Comments 1, p. 173, 3, p. 173 and 4, p. 174.

39 Principles, principle 3:28, p. 185.

tion is not made in Danish law or the CEFL principles, although the CEFL principles also view the right to contact as being inherent in the concept of parental responsibilities.

In Dutch law, a decision by the court may discharge a parent of the right to contact, while in Danish law a decision may be rejected or annulled. It is consequently not *the right as such* which is discharged in Danish law. The CEFL principles also provide for a termination of the contact rather than a discharge.

VIII.2.2. CONTENT, RESTRICTIONS AND CONDITIONS

VIII.2.2.1. The Netherlands

Contact encompasses direct personal contact where the child visits the parent and other forms of contact such as through letters or telephone conversations. The court may determine the concrete circumstances of the contact arrangement, such as the duration and the supervision of contact, if the parents cannot agree on contact.[40] A standard contact arrangement is considered to encompass a weekend every two weeks and a part of the holiday period; but more extensive contact arrangements are also possible.[41]

The supervision of contact has no legislative basis in Dutch law. The Child Protection Board can, in its advisory function to the Court, commence a contact arrangement which may be supervised in order to monitor the contact parent's interaction with the child. The Court cannot, however, request the Board to supervise contact following a contact order.[42] There have been and are certain private projects offering supervised contact in 'contact houses' and the Dutch Child Protection Board has regional projects offering supervised contact. The lack of a general possibility to provide for supervised contact is considered to be a problem in the Dutch literature.[43]

---

40 Art. 377a, DCC and Nieuwenhuis et al., 2004, supra, p. 439 and p. 441.

41 M.J.C. Koens and C.G.M. van Wamelen, *Kind en Scheiding*, the Hague: Koninklijke Vermande, 2001, p. 85. For very young children contact is often established more frequently for shorter periods, for example, for one day per week. See also Chapter VI, Section VI.3.1. concerning shared residence.

42 Hoge Raad (Supreme Court) 29.06.2001, *NJ* 2001, 598 deliberated in Chapter III, Section III.7.4.

43 B. Chin-A-Fat and C. van Rooijen, 'Oplossingen voor omgangsproblematiek', *FJR*, 2004, p. 226-230.

The duty to provide important information concerning the child to the other parent rests primarily with the parent who exercises sole parental authority. The parent who exercises sole parental authority further has a duty to consult the other parent on important matters.[44] A decision on the provision of information may also be given in respect of the non-resident parent who exercises parental authority.[45] The right to information or consultation may be excluded where the best interests of the child so require.[46] It is not possible to exclude the right to information with respect to a parent who exercises parental authority.

Furthermore, the parent who does not exercise parental authority may request information from third parties such as teachers, social workers and doctors when they have information with regard to important facts and circumstances concerning the child or its care and upbringing.[47] This right is inherent in the concept of parental authority for the parent who exercises parental authority.

VIII.2.2.2. Denmark

Contact encompasses direct personal contact where the child visits the parent and may *exceptionally* encompass other forms of contact such as through letters, by telephone, electronic mail or the provision of photographs and the like.[48]

If the parents cannot reach an agreement on contact, the regional state administration will decide thereon. The amount of contact depends upon an individual assessment and may encompass half an hour a week to seven days out of fourteen.[49]

The possibility of placing conditions for and restrictions on the contact arrangement is extensively regulated in the Contact Guideline. The regulation concerns matters such as transportation and the costs related to transportation, passport agreements and the possibility to travel outside the jurisdiction during contact.[50]

---

44 Article 377b(1), DCC.
45 Art. 377h, DCC.
46 Art. 377b(2), DCC.
47 Article 377c(1), DCC.
48 Art. 21, Act on Parental Responsibility.
49 Detailed descriptions of different contact arrangements may be found in the Guidelines on Contact; Section 5, Vejledning om samvær, No. 9860 of 06.09.2007.
50 Sections 5 and 6, Guidelines on contact.

Supervised contact is a measure which must be available when it is deemed necessary in concrete cases. The regional state administration must provide the supervision. The supervision of contact may only be ordered where unsupervised contact is not possible and should only be used where it is necessary for the child and, if possible, in surroundings known to the child, for example, with the assistance of family members. In most cases supervised contact does, however, take place at the state administration. Generally, four types of supervision are possible:

1. Protected contact is the most intense form of supervision as the contact is constantly monitored. This form is typically used when there has been no contact for a long time and if it is uncertain whether the contact parent can care for the child, for example because of substance abuse. It is also used when there is a suspicion of abuse or a risk of abduction.
2. Observed contact is used in the process of gathering further information about the child and/or the parent as part of the child expert report or as an alternative.
3. Supported contact is used in cases where the contact parent is young, immature or not used to caring for a child or the child is young or handicapped, so that it is ensured that the contact parent gradually adapts to and learns how to care for the child. Further, it may be used in cases where the conflict level is high and where a neutral person may assist with picking up or returning the child.
4. Supervised contact is used where there is a need for a neutral person, for example because of a high conflict level. It may also be used in the case of 'getting to know contact' (*kendekontakt*). 'Getting to know contact' is infrequent contact, for example, every six months and may also be used when the contact parent is in prison. Supervised contact may also be used to make the arrangement for picking -up and returning the child work in practice, for example by providing a neutral pick-up place.[51]

A parent who does not hold parental authority has the right to receive information from third parties, for example, from school personnel and doctors and has a right to receive relevant documents concerning the child from schools and day-care facilities and so forth. The parent who does not hold parental authority further has a right to request information about social activities taking place at

[51] Art. 13(1), Bekendtgørelse om forældremyndighed, barnets bopæl og samvær m.v., No. 1071 of 06.09.2007 (Ministerial decree on parental authority, residence and contact) and Section 6.2., Guidelines on Contact.

the child's school or day-care facility and to participate in such activities. The parent who holds sole parental authority has no duty to provide information.[52]

VIII.2.2.3. The CEFL principles

Principle 3:26 provides that the content of contact encompasses that the child stays with or meets the parent with whom he/she does not normally reside and any other form of communication such as by phone, letter, mail or fax between the child and the parent.[53] The parent further has a right to information from the resident parent. The question whether information can be claimed from third persons is left to national law.[54]

Contact may be restricted or made subject to conditions if the best interests of the child so require. The CEFL principles mention the use of supervised contact but further leave this matter to national law considering the complexity of the matter.[55]

VIII.2.2.4. Comparison: Content, restrictions and conditions

The content of contact encompasses direct personal contact and other forms of contact in Dutch and Danish law and in the CEFL principles. The duty to provide information to the non-resident parent rests primarily with the resident parent in Dutch law and the CEFL principles while in Danish law this duty rests upon third persons only.

The possibility to restrict or place conditions upon contact is regulated in more detail in Danish law than in Dutch law and the CEFL principles. It is only in Danish law that supervised contact has a legislative basis.

---

52 Art. 22(1) and (2), Act on Parental Responsibility.

53 Principles, principle 3:26, p. 176 and Comment 2, p. 178.

54 Principle, principle 3:29, p. 194, Comment 3, p. 196.

55 Principle, principle 3:28, p. 185, Comment 4, p. 192-193. The question whether parental agreements should be subject to scrutiny is left to national law, principle 3:27(2), p. 180, Comment 5, p. 184. In the case of divorce by mutual consent the Principles provide for scrutiny, Comment 4, p. 184.

VIII.3. PROCEDURES

VIII.3.1. PROCEDURES: THE NETHERLANDS

VIII.3.1.1. A court-based system

The district courts have sole competence in divorce cases and cases concerning parental authority and contact.[56] Legal representation is generally required.

A little more than half of all divorce cases are based upon a joint petition. In principle, the divorce procedure consists of a written phase and subsequently a hearing. In cases where the parties have submitted an agreement covering the consequences of divorce and the court does not render a decision on parental authority or contact or hear minor children, the divorce may be granted without a hearing.[57]

Procedures involving children are presided over by the juvenile court judge (*kinderrechter*). The court may in the course of the procedure, if requested, provide a temporary decision, for example, entrusting the child to one parent or providing a decision on contact. An interim decision cannot, in principle, be appealed but can be changed by the court.[58] The reason for this is to avoid unnecessary delays.

Decisions on parental authority and contact may be appealed to the Court of Appeal and further may be appealed in cassation to the Supreme Court. The Supreme Court will only review the case if it concerns a matter of law. The Supreme Court may clarify a point of law without actually reviewing the case. In cases where a review leads to cassation, the case will most often be remitted to a Court of Appeal which then renders a new decision.

The introduction of an administrative divorce procedure has been debated in the Netherlands for a considerable length of time as illustrated in Chapter II.[59] The

---

56 The possibility still exists to convert a marriage into a registered partnership and thereby to dissolve this partnership in a non-judicial procedure. This possibility is likely to be repealed with the pending proposal concerning 'Continued Parenting', Parliamentary proceedings (*Kamerstukken I*), 30 145, No. A.

57 See extensively; L. Coenraad, 'Afdoening zonder mondelinge behandeling', *FJR*, 2004, p. 2-10.

58 Art. 824, Civil Procedural Code. The only exception is an appeal in cassation in the interest of the Act.

59 Section III.2.6.

recent proposal aiming to introduce an administrative divorce procedure was only adopted by Parliament after spouses with children had been excluded from this proposed procedure.[60] The court-based system could be viewed as providing a protective role with respect to children under Dutch law.

VIII.3.1.2. The use of child expertise

The public organisation called the Dutch Child Protection Board has an advisory function in cases concerning minors. In most court jurisdictions an employee[61] of the Board is present in cases where there are disputes concerning parental authority or contact. If the dispute cannot be settled and/or the judge feels that more information is necessary, the judge can order the Board to make an investigation into the relationship between the parents and the child.[62]

The investigation takes place at the Board's office and results in a report which contains advice for the judge. An investigation by the Board begins by interviewing both parents and the child (aged twelve or above).[63]

VIII.3.1.3. Alternative dispute resolution

Alternative dispute resolution in the form of mediation or other forms is currently not specifically provided for in Dutch law. The proposal on 'Continued Parenting' contains the possibility for the court to defer parents to mediation and provides a temporary financial incentive.[64]

However, mediation has already been incorporated into court procedures in various ways. In the first place the Dutch Child Protection Board has adopted a mediation approach in its investigation on behalf of the court. This mediation approach is not separated from the advisory function of the Board, in other words, the mediator who prepares the advice for the Court may be the same person who has failed in the attempted mediation.

---

60 Section III.2.6. The proposal was finally rejected by the Dutch Parliament's First Chamber.

61 These employees usually have a university or higher technical background in areas such as psychology, social work or similar and receive further education arranged by the Board.

62 The judge may find that an extended psychological investigation is necessary. Such an investigation may be carried out by an external bureau such as the FORA. The result of such an investigation is incorporated in the Board's report. The judge may, at the request of a parent, allow conflicting expertise, Article 810a, Civil Procedural Code.

63 *Normen 2000*, Raad voor de kinderbescherming.

64 Chapter II, Section II.2.6.2.

In the second place, the Dutch Ministry of Justice started two mediation experiments in 1999, one for divorce, which could include a conflict concerning contact, and one for contact. These experiments were evaluated and were generally found to be successful, but less so for contact cases. The divorce mediation experiment resulted in approximately 75% of cases reaching an agreement and the contact experiment resulted in approximately 50% of cases reaching an agreement.[65] Mediation was voluntary albeit that in contact cases mediation occurred normally upon the referral of the Court where the Court used its authority to convince the parents of the usefulness of mediation.

Finally, the courts have on several occasions obliged parents to participate in forensic mediation (*forensische bemiddeling*). In such cases the court appoints the mediator who is to report to the court. The mediation is consequently not confidential or separated from the judicial procedure.[66]

VIII.3.2. PROCEDURES: DENMARK

VIII.3.2.1. Courts and administrative authorities

A distinctive feature of Danish family law is the use of administrative procedures. While, traditionally, administrative procedures were reserved for non-contentious cases,[67] a recent reform of the family law procedures has provided that the state administration is to be the administrative portal to divorce procedures as well as to procedures concerning parental authority, residence and contact.[68]

---

65 B.E.S. Chin-A-Fat, M.J. Stekete, *Bemiddeling in uitvoering*, Utrecht: Verwey Jonker Instituut, 2001, p. 12 and p. 16.

66 For example, Gerechtshof, The Hague (Court of Appeal) 04.08.2004, LJN AQ6572. See also E. Spruijt, M. Mallens, M.M. Mos, G. Topper, R. Vugt and C. van Leuven, 'Onderzoek naar effecten van vrijwillige en forensische scheidingsbemiddeling', *EB*, 2004, p. 37-40. B.E.S. Chin-a-Fat is critical of the 'institutionalised' approach where mediation is incorporated into the judicial procedure and thereby becomes obligatory and not confidential; B.E.S. Chin-A-Fat, *Scheiden terechter zonder rechter*, Doctoral thesis (PhD), The Hague: Sdu uitgevers bv, p. 383-386.

67 Save for contact cases where the administrative authorities used to have sole competence.

68 The regional state administration continues to be competent in cases that only concern contact. The court can render a decision on contact as an ancillary decision in a case concerning parental authority, if requested by one of the parties, Art. 35(2), Act on Parental Responsibility. See further on the previous system; C. Jeppesen de Boer, 'Administrative echtscheiding in Denemarken', *FJR*, 2005, p. 231-235.

A case on parental authority, residence and contact as an ancillary matter may only be submitted to the district court *by* the regional state administration if the parents have participated in a meeting at the state administration and request that the case is submitted to the court. If one parent does not attend the meeting *only* the other parent may request that the case be submitted to the court.[69] The purpose of the meeting is to provide the parents with guidance and to offer them counselling and mediation. Further, the regional state administration may initiate a child expert investigation on a voluntary basis. If an investigation is initiated it must be completed and it may be used in the court procedure.[70]

It is possible to obtain a judicial separation and divorce on a written basis without attending a meeting at the state administration. This is also possible when there are children involved and the parents have made an agreement on the allocation of parental authority or when joint parental authority continues.[71]

The regional state administration has the primary competence to decide on contact. The regional state administration cannot render a final decision on parental authority and residence but may render an interim decision during the procedure. The decision of the regional state administration may be appealed to the Family Agency.[72]

If the case is submitted to court, the court can render or change an interim decision of the state administration. Interim decisions and final decisions of the court may be appealed to the High Court but only to the Supreme Court if permission is granted from the Appeals Permission Board.

VIII.3.2.2. The use of child expertise

Both the regional state administration and the courts can make use of child expertise.[73] The state administration generally has 'in-house' specialists while the courts make use of private practising psychologists and psychiatrists.

69 Art. 37, Act on Parental Responsibility. In special cases the regional state administration can submit the case to the court directly.
70 Art. 30, Act on Parental Responsibility.
71 See for this procedure, C. Jeppesen de Boer, 2005, supra, p. 233-234.
72 Arts 23 and 38, Act on Parental Responsibility.
73 Art. 30, Act on Parental Responsibility.

The use of child expertise both in court and at the state administration is to be increased since the entry into force of the Act on Parental Responsibility and only qualified psychologists and psychiatrists may provide the expertise.[74]

A full investigation generally requires the expert to observe the parents' interaction with the child individually in the home setting and requires the expert to have a separate conversation with the child. The expert's role is also to act as the child's 'mouthpiece'. The expert should not try to mediate or conciliate the parents as this would compromise his or her tasks.[75]

VIII.3.2.3. Alternative dispute resolution

The regional state administration provides the administrative portal for procedures regarding divorce, parental authority, residence and contact in order to endorse negotiated solutions in an informal setting.[76] The possibility to advise parents and make use of child experts is inherent in the construction of an 'administrative portal'. The administrative procedures are generally free of charge.

The regional state administration must offer parents and children counselling by 'child experts' (*børnesagkyndig rådgivning*) in cases involving a dispute on parental authority, residence or contact and can offer counselling in other situations if there is a special need for this.[77] The offer is directed towards parents and children. It is not a condition that both parents and/or the child participate. Counselling may take place with one parent and/or the child alone. Counselling takes place at the state administration office.[78] The offer can be made during divorce proceedings or in a procedure concerning parental authority, residence and contact. Open counselling, that is when there is no official case,[79] is also

---

74 L 133, Comments to § 30.

75 Commission report No. 1275/2006, Annex A, Vejledende retningslinier for børnesagkyndige undersøgelser og erklæringer.

76 Mediation and other conciliatory measures may also be available at a later stage, if the case has been submitted to the court. The general intention, however, is that the negotiated solution is reached at the administrative level.

77 Art. 32, Act on Parental Responsibility.

78 The counsellors will have special expertise regarding children. Counsellors are most often psychologists or social workers.

79 Recently the regional state administrations have, as an experiment, started to offer partner counselling for parents who wish to prevent a divorce or a breakup or wish to settle their differences amicably.

possible. While it is not obligatory to participate in counselling, the parents will be summoned if one parent requests counselling.[80]

Counselling sessions, principally independent of the legal case, falls within the decision-making competence of the state administration. In principle, only the result of the counselling is reported to the legal case officer unless the parents agree otherwise or the case officer has participated in the counselling at the request of the parents.[81]

From 2001 mediation has been offered as an alternative to counselling. Mediation requires that both parents voluntarily participate and that a case concerning contact has been closed before mediation takes place.

A new method is used in complicated contact cases involving, for example, violence or substance abuse: *interdisciplinary meetings*, which may involve elements of counselling and mediation (*tværfagligt samarbejde*). KRONBORG provides an example from a concrete case. In this case, the father had been criminally convicted of violence against the mother and the mother had left the home with the children. The police had imposed a restriction order on the father compelling him to stay away from the mother. The Regional State Administration had made an interim decision on contact and summoned the parents to an interdisciplinary meeting. A letter to the father, a copy of which was sent to the mother, contained the following passage:

> 'The purpose of interdisciplinary meetings is to maintain that it is the parents' responsibility that contact takes place in the best possible manner for the child. The child's welfare depends upon the parents' co-operation. Interdisciplinary meetings may be used as an alternative to child expert counselling or mediation so that mediation and counselling is integrated in the meeting. Interdisciplinary meetings are typically used when communication between the parties is difficult. (...) The purpose of the meeting is to talk about contact and in particular to restore the confidence between you and the mother after the incidents where the mother *has felt threatened or attacked by you* and particularly after the last

---

80 Child expert counselling is regulated in detail in the Contact Guide.

81 A. Kronborg, 'Forvaltning af familieretligt samvær', *Juristen* No 9, 2000, p. 325-333 points out that the fact that the counselling takes place at the administrative authority means that parents do not experience a separation between counselling and their case in which a judicial decision must be made. The counsellors and the case officers are colleagues and the case may contain a memo indicating whether the parents have agreed to counselling.

violent episode which resulted in your conviction for violence against the mother. The focus of this conversation is the needs of the children.' (Emphasis added).

KRONBORG considers that the approach provides an example of how the state administration overrates the possibility of providing co-operation between parents and how they further fail to provide a protective role in respect of a mother who should be supported in her role as a mother rather than being burdened with procedures.[82]

VIII.3.3. PROCEDURES: THE CEFL PRINCIPLES

VIII.3.3.1. A competent authority

The CEFL principles provide that decisions on parental responsibilities should be taken by the competent authority which can be either a judicial or an administrative body.[83]

VIII.3.3.2. The use of child expertise

The CEFL principles provide that the competent authority should appoint any suitable person or body to investigate the child's circumstances where necessary.[84] This principle lays down a minimum requirement leaving it to national law to provide more extensively for the use of child expertise.[85]

VIII.3.3.3. Alternative dispute resolution

Alternative dispute resolution should be available in all disputes regarding parental responsibilities according to principle 3:36.[86]

The CEFL considers that the best interests of children require that the parents have the best possible relationship and that alternative dispute resolution is the best way to achieve this goal at all stages in the procedures, including enforce-

---

82 A. Kronborg, *Forældremyndighed og menneskelig integritet*, Copenhagen, Jurist- og Økonomforbundets Forlag, 2007, p. 205-206.

83 Principles, principle 3:35(1), p. 224.

84 Principles, principle 3:35(2), p. 224.

85 Principles, principle 3:35, Comment 4, p. 229.

86 Principles, p. 231.

ment procedures. Further, the CEFL considers that the child should be informed and consulted in this process.[87]

The CEFL has not commented upon the use of alternative dispute settlement in particular cases, for example, involving violence, drugs or alcohol abuse.

Alternative dispute resolution is not compulsory in the CEFL principles. Rather, the matter is left to national law recognising that alternative dispute resolution is compulsory in some countries.[88]

VIII.3.4. COMPARISON: PROCEDURES

Procedures in Dutch and Danish law differ considerably because of the use of administrative procedures in Danish law. Further, there is a stronger emphasis on (free of charge) counselling and mediation in Danish law than in Dutch law. The CEFL principles provide that both administrative and judicial procedures are possible.

It is a common feature that the competent authorities require parental co-operation and that the use of alternative dispute resolution is acquiring an increasingly obligatory nature.

VIII.4. THE CHILD'S PROCEDURAL POSITION

A child or young person is generally represented by his or her parent in Dutch and Danish law and in the CEFL principles.[89] The child's position in procedures concerning divorce, parental authority and contact has received special attention in both Dutch and Danish law.

VIII.4.1. DUTCH LAW

Dutch law provides the child with three main ways to participate in a procedure concerning parental authority and contact: the child may be heard in a procedure, the child may informally approach the court and a special guardian (*bijzondere curator*) can, in principle, be appointed to represent the child.

[87] Principles, principle 3:36, Comments 1 and 3, p. 237.
[88] Principles, principle 3:36, Comment 4, p. 238.
[89] Chapter VII, Section VII.2.2.

The Dutch Civil Procedural Code contains a general provision on the hearing of children in matters that concern them.[90] Before a decision on parental authority or contact is taken, the court should give a child or young person who has reached the age of twelve or above the opportunity to express his or her views unless it clearly concerns a case of minor importance. The court may provide the same possibility in respect of a child under the age of twelve.

It has been assumed that the continuation of joint parental authority does not constitute a decision and that therefore the child does not need to be heard in the procedure. Nonetheless, some Dutch courts do provide this opportunity also when joint parental authority continues automatically after divorce.[91]

Dutch courts generally provide the opportunity for children aged twelve or above to express their views by means of a letter addressed to the child, providing an invitation to appear before the court with the stated alternative to submit his or her views in writing. Children below the age of twelve may also be provided with an invitation to appear before the court or to state their views in writing. Generally, children are heard from the age of ten to twelve depending upon the court in question.[92]

The Dutch approach, consequently, does not necessarily involve a formal hearing of the child. Children often choose to submit their views in writing.[93] The question whether or not the views and information provided by the child is confidential is still uncertain in Dutch law.[94]

A child or younger person who is twelve years or older, or a younger child with sufficient maturity can informally approach the court in the divorce procedure. The court can thereafter make a decision on the allocation of sole parental authority *ex officio*. This informal access to the court was laid down in the 1998 reform so as to provide a means to prevent the automatic continuation of joint parental authority.[95] The informal access to the court does not seem to have been used in accordance with its purpose. Rather, the scope of the provision has been interpreted broadly and has served to provide children with a means to request

90 Art. 809(1).
91 A. van Triest, 'Het kinderverhoor in het resort Den Bosch onder de loep', *FJR*, 2004, p. 16-26.
92 Different courts follow different procedures, see further; A. van Triest, 2004, supra.
93 A. van Triest, 2004, supra.
94 P.A.J.Th. van Teffelen, 'Vertrouwelijk of geheim kinderverhoor', *EB*, 2007, p. 83-87.
95 Art. 251a, DCC and J.H. Nieuwenhuis a.o., 2004, supra, p. 300.

a reallocation of parental authority, for example, in a case where the child had moved from one parent to the other parent.[96]

A child or young person who has reached the age of twelve or above or a younger child with sufficient maturity can also informally approach the court in matters concerning contact. The court may then *ex officio* give a decision[97] on contact or change a contact decision. This provision does not seem to be often used.[98]

The court can appoint a special guardian when there is a conflict of interests between the parent(s) and the child. The appointment of a special guardian in a procedure concerning divorce, parental authority or contact, or, extrajudicially, probably rarely takes place.[99] The Sub-District Court of Arnhem rejected a request from a child, aged approximately thirteen, to appoint a special guardian to represent him extrajudicially concerning differences with respect to his care, which were a result of the parents' divorce. The Court rejected the appointment considering that the parents were close to reaching agreement and that it was their task to reach an agreement. Further, the Court considered that:

> 'It is undesirable that the child is further involved in the parents' legal proceedings and that the legal proceedings become further strained with the addition of a third intervening party, the special guardian, whereby the possibility exists that the (...) relationship between the parents and the minor is further legalised.[100]

VIII.4.2. DANISH LAW

Danish law provides the child or young person with a right to be heard and, since 2007, with an informal access to the regional state administration in matters concerning parental authority, residence and contact. The use of a legal representative is possible, but is reserved for exceptional situations and probably

---

96 Rechtbank Zutpen (District Court) 02.07.2003, LJN AH9200.The Rechtbank Roermond (District Court) had rejected such a request in its decision of 29.03.2001, LJN AB1868.

97 Art. 377g, DCC.

98 In a decision by the District Court of 's-Hertogenbosch, the court rejected a request from two children to establish a shared residence, Rechtbank 's-Hertogenbosch 11.07.2006, LJN AY6483.

99 See also: Chapter VII, Section VII.2.2.1.

100 Sector Canton Rechtbank Arnhem 12.01.2005, LJN AS3527.

rarely takes place.[101] It is common that a special representative from the Social Services is present in enforcement procedures.

The new Act on Parental Responsibility is deemed to implement a 'child's perspective'. This has several consequences. In the first place Article 31 of the Act now provides that the child must be involved in a case concerning parental authority, residence or contact so that the child's perspective and views are brought to light. This Article must be read in conjunction with Article 5 of the Act according to which the child's views must be taken into consideration in all matters depending upon his/her age and maturity.

The involvement is voluntary for the child and may be implemented through a conversation with the child, through the use of a 'child expert' or in another way. A conversation will normally take place with a child aged seven or older, while the views of younger children will be brought to light through the use of child experts. At the regional state administration, only child experts such as psychologists and psychiatrists can hear a child irrespective of the child's age. In court, the judge can hear the child, but the judge has the option of requesting that a child expert participates in the conversation.[102]

Children are generally not heard when the parents are in agreement. The Explanatory notes consider that the hearing of children should take place at an early stage if there are disagreements, for example, before or in connection with mediation or counselling so that the involvement of the child 'will contribute to maintaining focus on the child's needs and allow the parents to see new perspectives concerning the ability to safeguard their child's needs in the best possible way.'[103]

A child does not need to be directly involved, if being involved is damaging to the child, or if it is unnecessary due to the circumstances of the case, for example, if it concerns only minor matters such as transportation in connection with contact.[104] A child must always be offered counselling when a conversation takes place.[105]

---

101 Art. 450d, Procedural Act. See also Chapter VII, Section VII.2.2.2.
102 L 133, Comments to § 31.
103 L 133, Comment to § 31.
104 Art. 31(2), Act on Parental Responsibility and L 133, Comments to § 31.
105 L 133, p. 16.

Parents or legal representatives do not attend the conversation that takes place with the child. Currently, the rules concerning the parents' possibility to gain an insight into the child's views in the administrative procedure are under consideration. There are no clear rules concerning the confidentiality of children's views in court proceedings, although the content of the conversation tends to be kept secret. In the case law of the High Courts it is often stated 'that the parents have agreed not to participate in the conversation and not to receive information with respect to the child's views'.[106] DANIELSEN considers that this secrecy cannot be maintained.[107]

Since 2007, a child aged ten or older has been given informal access to the regional state administration on matters concerning parental authority, residence or contact. If a child contacts the regional state administration, it can summon the parents to a meeting and may offer the child and/or the parents mediation or counselling. The state administration cannot oblige the parents to attend a meeting or make a decision *ex officio*. The child also does not formally become a party in the procedure and cannot, for example, appeal against a decision (if a decision has been requested by one of the parents). The reason for this is that it is not considered desirable that children initiate proceedings against their parents. This access is considered to provide children with a 'lifeline' and support in the formulation of views so as to make the parents aware of the child's perspective.[108]

VIII.4.3. THE CEFL PRINCIPLES

The CEFL principles provide the child with the right to be heard in a procedure concerning parental responsibilities and contact. Further, the Principles provide that a special representative for the child should be appointed *ex officio* where there could be a serious conflict of interests between the child and the holders of parental responsibilities or in other situations where the welfare of the child is at risk.[109]

Principle 3:37(1) provides that the competent authority should hear the child in all proceedings concerning parental responsibilities, but if it decides not to do so it should give specific reasons.[110] This principle should be read in conjunction

106 S. Danielsen, 'Børns rolle under forældremyndighedstvister', *TFA*, 2004, p. 271-281.

107 S. Danielsen, 2004, supra, p. 280.

108 L 133, p. 17.

109 Principles, principle 3:37, p. 239 and principle 3:37, p. 253 with comment 3, p. 258.

110 Principles, p. 239. The child should also be heard when the parents agree; Comment 1, p. 250.

with principle 3:6 according to which the child should have the right to be informed, consulted and to express his or her opinion in all matters concerning the child, with due weight being given to the views expressed by him or her. Regard must be had to the child's age and maturity.

Further, the hearing may take place either directly before the competent authority or indirectly through a person or body appointed by the competent authority and the child must be heard in a manner which is appropriate to him or her.[111]

The Principles do not contain a specific age requirement but depend upon the circumstances of the case and the age and maturity of the child in order to determine whether the child should be heard.[112] The hearing must take place ex officio and a decision not to hear the child must be reasoned so that the child's right to be heard is ensured and arbitrary refusals are avoided.[113]

Finally, the CEFL considers that parents or other concerned persons should not be present during the hearing to avoid undue influence being exerted. The CEFL recommends that a record of the child's opinion is kept but reserves the question whether parents should have access to the opinion to national law. The principle of a fair trial as contained in Article 6 of the ECHR should be observed, however.

VIII.4.4. COMPARISON: PROCEDURAL POSITION

Both Dutch and Danish law and the CEFL principles provide for a hearing of the child and, in principle, for the appointment of a special representative/guardian. Only Dutch and Danish law provide explicitly for informal access to the court/administrative authority.

The hearing of children is regulated differently. Only Danish law and the CEFL principles provide for a right to be heard without a specified age requirement. The CEFL principles provide that the child should be heard in all cases, also when the parents agree, while Danish law provides this right only when there is a disagreement between the parents. In Dutch law the matter is unsettled. The Danish approach to hearing children may be viewed as a new approach since the children come to play a role in the parents' negotiations at the state authority.

---

111 Principles, principle 3:37(2) and (3), p. 239.

112 Principles, principle 3:37, Comment 2, p. 251.

113 Principles, principle 3:37, Comment 3, p. 251.

The possibility to appoint a special guardian or representative has a broader scope in Dutch law and the CEFL principles than in Danish law. This possibility is, not frequently used in Dutch law, however.

Informal access to the court provides the Dutch courts with the possibility to render a decision *ex officio* while this is not possible in Danish law.

VIII.5. ENFORCEMENT

The enforcement of parental authority, (the main) residence and contact is discussed separately for Dutch and Danish law and the CEFL principles. While the enforcement of contact is possible both in Dutch and Danish law, it is characteristic of Dutch law that the enforcement of contact has been seen as being ineffective. The enforcement of contact has been an important issue in the parliamentary debates in the pending Dutch reform on 'Continued Parenting'.[114]

VIII.5.1. THE NETHERLANDS

VIII.5.1.1. Enforcement of parental authority and residence

Article 812 of the Dutch Code of Civil Procedure provides that every decision (both temporary and final decisions) concerning the exercise of parental authority gives the person who is entrusted with the child the right *ex lege* to have the child handed over, if necessary with the use of force.

While this provision does not mention a decision on the main residence, there is a link between the ancillary provisions, which can be decided in the course of the divorce procedure, and the enforcement of the exercise of parental authority.[115] The establishment of the main residence belongs to the ancillary provisions, although it is not explicitly mentioned in the relevant Article.[116] Consequently, it must be assumed that both decisions on sole parental authority and decisions on the main residence, whether they have been made in the course of a divorce procedure or in a procedure concerning parental authority, for

---

114 Chapter II, Section II.2.6.2.

115 Art. 827(1)c and 827(2), Dutch Code of Civil Procedure.

116 Pursuant to the decision of the Dutch Supreme Court; Hoge Raad, *NJ* 2001, 123 annotated by S.F.M. Wortmann mentioned in Chapter VI, Section VI.2.1.

example, in respect of unmarried parents, are directly enforceable, if necessary with the use of force.[117]

The request to have the child handed over must be directed to the Public Prosecution Service (*Het Openbare Ministerie*), which will assign police officers who will assist with the handing over of the child.[118] The police are not obliged to assist without being assigned to do so by the Public Prosecution Service.[119]

Additionally, a request for the handing over of the child can be made to the court, if a procedure is pending, or to the President of the court. The court or the President can, in that case, decide that the child should be handed over using the enforcement measure of a single or accumulating fine, if the child is not handed over voluntarily.

VIII.5.1.2 Enforcement of contact

Dutch law does not provide specific measures for the enforcement of a decision on contact. It is an open question whether the abovementioned right to have the child handed over *ex lege* with the assistance of the police applies in cases concerning the enforcement of a contact decision.[120]

A commonly used enforcement measure is the fining (*dwangsom*) of the parent who violates the other parent's, or, in principle, a third person's right to contact.[121] A fine may be single or accumulating and may be imposed prior to an actual violation.[122] The imposed fine belongs to the wronged parent and if the other parent has no means, it may in fact be futile to impose it. The fine can, however, be set off against debts such as against a property claim in the divorce

117 Although the situation with respect to a decision on the main residence concerning unmarried parents is less clear considering that Art. 827(1)c and 827(2) of the Procedural Code does not apply in this situation. A main residence agreed upon by the parents in the course of the divorce procedure by means of a covenant probably does not constitute a 'decision' and the effect of such an agreement may be considered to be uncertain, even if it has been adopted in the dictum, see also Chapter VI, Section VI.2.1.

118 Art. 813(1)c, Civil Procedural Code.

119 C.J.J.C. van Nispen, A.I.M. van Mierlo and M.V. Polak, *Burgelijke Rechtsvordering, Tekst & Commentaar*, Deventer: Kluwer, 2002, p. 1015. This also applies when the court has ordered that the child be handed over.

120 Art. 812 and 813, Civil Procedural Code, above Section VIII.5.1.1. The question is if a decision on contact may be viewed as a temporary decision entrusting the child with the contact parent. This has been assumed by the lower courts, see further ASSER-DE BOER, 2006, supra, p. 832.

121 Third persons' right to contact will probably seldom justify enforcement.

122 M.J.C. Koens, C.G.M. van Wamelen, 2001, supra, p. 105.

settlement, but only with limited effect against a claim on maintenance and probably not against child maintenance.[123]

Furthermore, it is not entirely impossible that the incarceration of the parent violating the contact decision may be used to enforce contact, although such a measure will rarely be compatible with the parent caring for the child.[124]

It is also possible that the court will use child protection measures to enforce contact. Child protection measures may only be used if the court clearly justifies the need for such a measure.[125] The placement of the child under supervision is considered to be a mild child protection measure[126] entailing a duty for the resident parent to consult with and seek support from the appointed guardian on matters concerning the contact arrangement. The child will normally remain living at home. A child may only be placed under supervision where the lack of contact forms a threat to the moral or mental needs of the child and where other means have failed or are expected to fail.[127]

Further, it is in principle possible that a special guardian is appointed to represent the child where there is a conflict of interests between the parent(s) and the child relating to contact. The special guardian will have the task assigned by the court, for example, to try to reconcile the parties or assist with the factual implementation of the contact.

Finally, measures such as the reallocation of parental authority, or changes in the child's main residence, mediation and supervised contact are considered in the context of enforcement in Dutch law.

VIII.5.1.3. Enforcement of other decisions

The enforcement of other decisions, for example, a decision concerning the exercise of parental authority pursuant to Article 253a of the Dutch Civil Code is also possible. An accumulating fine was, for example, imposed upon the

123 ASSER-DE BOER, 2006, supra, p. 832-833.

124 ASSER-DE BOER, 2006, supra, p. 833.

125 Hoge Raad (Dutch Supreme Court) 13.04.2001, *NJ* 2002, 4.

126 M.J.C. Koens, C.G.M. van Wamelen, C., 2001, supra, p.107.

127 The Hoge Raad (Dutch Supreme Court) found in its decision of 13.04.2001, *NJ* 2002, 4 that the mere possibility that a lack of contact is harmful or detrimental to the child, or brings about the risk that the child is placed in a conflict of loyalty situation, provided an insufficient reason for the child to be placed under supervision.

mother in the case referred to in Chapter VII concerning the duty to have the children vaccinated in accordance with the decision of the court.[128]

VIII.5.1.4. Criminal law

The enforcement of parental authority and contact in the Netherlands is, in principle, not regulated in the context of criminal law. There are, however, developments in the case law which may increase the use of the Penal Code in respect of enforcement.

Article 279 of the Penal Code[129] provides that it is a criminal offence to intentionally withdraw a child from the holder(s) of custody (parental authority) or from the supervision of the person who legally exercises custody, punishable with up to nine years imprisonment or a fine. It has been assumed that this provision did not apply to the parent who exercised joint parental authority.[130] In a recent decision, however, a father who exercised parental authority and who had retained the child beyond the time allowed by the contact arrangement (for approximately 20 days) in a place unknown to the mother was convicted pursuant to Art. 279.[131] It is an open question if this provision also applies to the resident parent who frustrates the other parent's contact rights (as laid down in a judicial decision).

VIII.5.2. DENMARK

VIII.5.2.1. General

In Denmark, a special division of the district court, the enforcement court (*fogedretten*), is charged with enforcement. The enforcement of parental authority, residence and contact is regulated separately in Chapter 48a of the Proce-

128 Rechtbank Haarlem (District Court) 15.04.2005, LJN AT4422 and Chapter VII, Section VII.4.3.1.

129 Wetboek van Strafrecht, Act of 03.03.1881 with later amendments.

130 Hoge Raad (Supreme Court), *NJ* 1954, 478. This provision had, however, been applied in respect of a temporary entrustment to the mother in the course of a divorce procedure, Hoge Raad (Supreme Court), *NJ* 1970, 266.

131 Hoge Raad (Supreme Court) 15.02.2005, LJN AR8250.

dural Act.[132] Decisions of the enforcement court may be appealed to the High Court.[133]

The enforcement court is not bound by the parties' request for a particular means of enforcement and the enforcement court may also allow for a short stay in respect of the child's return or before the contact is enforced.[134] While it is not the intention that the enforcement court should review the foundation for the claim, it may, in a case of doubt, require a child expert's opinion and it should hear a child who is old enough to form his or her own opinion (in the presence of a child expert or a representative from the social services) before enforcement measures are taken.[135]

The enforcement court's practices were reviewed by the Ministry of Justice's Research Unit in 2004.[136] The majority of enforcement procedures concerned the enforcement of contact.[137]

The average age of the child in enforcement proceedings was 6-7 years. Only a limited number of cases concerned very young children under the age of two and children older than eleven.[138] Almost two thirds of the cases were settled at the meeting in the enforcement court.[139] It should be noted that the perception of a settlement also concerned cases where the parents settled the matter only to avoid the enforcement and thus concerned all cases where no decision was taken by the enforcement court.[140]

---

132 Retsplejeloven, Act No. 1001 of 05.10.2006 with later amendments, amongst others, the changes made in connection with the Act on Parental Responsibility, Act No. 500 of 06.06.2007.

133 Art. 394, Procedural Act. An appeal does not stay the enforcement proceedings unless the judge so decides, Art. 395. An appeal to the Supreme Court is only possible if the case involves a matter of principle and permission is granted by the Appeals Permission Board.

134 Art. 537(1) and (3)3rd sentence, Procedural Act.

135 Art. 537(2)2nd sentence and 537(3).

136 Fogedretternes praksis i samværs- of forældremyndighedssager, May 2004 available at www.justitsministeriet.dk/fileadmin/downloads/Forskning_og_dokumentation/fogedretternes_praksis.pdf. The review concerned all cases which had been initiated in 2002 and which had been concluded by August 2003.

137 The report concerned a total amount of 1224 cases. 72.5% of the cases concerned contact, 13.6% concerned parental authority and 13.9% were unspecified. The enforcement of residence decisions has only been possible since 01.10.2007.

138 5.6% concerned children under the age of two and 11% concerned children older than 11.

139 61.5%. Further 22.6% of the cases were retracted before a meeting had taken place.

140 Supra, p. 4-7 and p. 11.

VIII.5.2.2. Enforcement of parental authority and residence

The following decisions serve as a foundation for direct enforcement: court decisions on (sole) parental authority and residence; agreements on parental authority notified to or approved by the state administration or the court; agreements on the child's residence entered into at the state administration; and *private agreements* on residence explicitly stating that they may serve as a foundation for enforcement.[141]

The enforcement of parental authority and residence is possible by means of daily or weekly (accumulating) fine,[142] the use of direct force involving the physical fetching of the child and, in principle, the incarceration of the parent.[143]

If a request is made for the enforcement of parental authority or residence, the parties will generally be summoned to a meeting within seven days. This meeting will be presided over by a judge who will try to reconcile the parents. The use of direct force without prior notice is, however, possible in exceptional cases, for example, when there is a risk of abduction. The use of direct force, the psychical fetching of the child, is generally used at an earlier stage in cases concerning parental authority and residence compared with cases concerning contact.[144]

If the enforcement court decides to use direct force, involving the physical fetching of the child, it is the enforcement court (the judge) who with the assistance of the police, a child expert and a representative from the social services collects the child from where it is staying, for example, in the home of the non-resident parent, in a day-care facility or at school. Enforcement is not possible if the physical or mental health of the child is *seriously* endangered.[145]

VIII.5.2.3. Enforcement of contact

Decisions on contact, agreements entered into at the state administration or in court as well as *private agreements* explicitly stating that they may serve as a foundation for enforcement, serve as a foundation for the direct enforcement of contact.[146] Enforcement is possible only in respect of decisions or agreements

141 Art. 537(1), Procedural Act.
142 Such fines go to the State and if they are not paid, they may be converted into detention.
143 Art. 537(1), Procedural Act.
144 Fogedretternes praksis i samværs- of forældremyndighedssager, May 2004, supra, p. 4.
145 Art. 537(5) and 537(6), Procedural Act.
146 Art. 478(1), No. 1 and 3, Procedural Act.

which have been violated. It is not possible to use measures in anticipation of a violation.

The enforcement measure most often used in contact cases is the use of an (accumulating) or a single fine.[147] Contact in respect of third persons (non-parents) may only be enforced by means of a fine.[148] The physical fetching of the child or, in principle, the incarceration of the parent is also possible, although such measures are generally used at a later stage in the enforcement of contact than in the enforcement of parental authority.[149] The procedures at the enforcement court and the procedures pertaining to the physical fetching of the child, if employed, are the same as deliberated above concerning the enforcement of parental authority and residence. While the physical fetching of the child does not occur frequently and is supposed to be handled with care, incidents do happen.[150]

The enforcement court may adapt the content of the contact decision or agreement as well as the timing and conditions thereof, if this is necessary for the enforcement, and it may also decide on 'replaced contact' (*erstatningssamvær*) to replace contact which has not taken place.[151]

VIII.5.2.4. Criminal law

In principle, the enforcement of parental authority, residence and contact is not regulated in the context of criminal law. However, it is a criminal offence, which may be punished with a custodial sentence of up to 4 years, to retain a child from the holder(s) of parental authority.[152] This provision applies to the illegal retention of the child by any person including the parent who does not hold parental

---

147 Fogedretternes praksis i samværs- of forældremyndighedssager, May 2004, supra, p. 4.

148 Art. 537(1)2nd sentence, Procedural Act.

149 Art. 537(1), Procedural Act. Fogedretternes praksis i samværs- of forældremyndighedssager, May 2004, supra, p. 4.

150 For example, involving the retention of the child by force in the mother's car, decision mentioned in: I. Lund-Andersen, N. Munck, I. Nørgaard, *Familieret*, Copenhagen: Jurist- og Økonomforbundets Forlag, 2003, p. 95.

151 Art. 537(7) and 537(8), Procedural Act. Adaptation is possible, for example, in relation to the manner in which the child is picked up and returned, the change of contact from one weekend to another weekend, conditions pertaining to the place where contact is to take place and the requirements for depositing a passport. It is not the intention that the enforcement court should regulate contact decided by the state administration or the courts, L 134, Comments to § 537.

152 Art. 215 and 261, Straffeloven (Penal Act), consolidated Act No. 1000 of 05.10.2006 with later amendments.

authority. The provision does not apply to the parent holding parental authority. This also applies in situations where residence has been established with the other parent.[153]

However, bringing or retaining the child outside the territory of Denmark, without the consent of the other holder of joint parental authority, is a criminal offence in situations where the parents disagree on the allocation of parental authority (unless a decision on the child's residence or a decision allowing the parent to travel with the child has been rendered).[154] This provision was enacted in support of the provisions concerning child abduction. The provision may also apply in other situations, for example, with respect to a planned holiday.[155]

VIII.5.3. THE CEFL PRINCIPLES

Principle 3:39 provides that, failing voluntary compliance, enforceable decisions and agreements should be enforced without undue delay. Enforcement should not take place if it is manifestly contrary to the best interests of the child.[156]

The CEFL principles leave the choice of 'coercive measures' to national law; however, they consider that criminal sanctions do not seem to be the most appropriate solution.[157]

While enforcement must generally take place and the exception of 'manifestly contrary to the best interests of the child' is narrow, the CEFL considers that the enforcement of parental responsibilities, residence and contact must not take place against the wishes of the child, subject to the condition that the child has sufficient understanding *since the use of force against the child should be avoided.*[158] It is not entirely clear if this would apply to all coercive measures, for example, directed at the parent or whether it only refers to measures directed at the child. Since the CEFL has not mentioned particular enforcement measures, it must be assumed to apply to all measures.

---

153 This provision has not been amended in connection with the 2007 Act on Parental Responsibility.

154 Art. 3(2), Act on Parental Responsibility and Art. 215(2), Penal Act. See further; Chapter VII, Section VII.

155 See further; Chapter VII, Section VII.4.5.2.

156 Principles, p. 259.

157 Principles, principle 3:39, Comment 1, p. 272.

158 Principles, principle 3.39, Comment 3, p. 273.

VIII.5.4. COMPARISON: ENFORCEMENT

The Danish enforcement system is intrinsically linked to the types of decisions which can be made: the decision on parental authority, residence and contact and the measures that can be used are clearly defined in the Act. The Dutch law on enforcement is of a more unsettled and developing nature. It is, however, a common feature that the use of direct force against the child is possible and that a parent, in principle, may be incarcerated while the most frequently used enforcement measure in contact cases is the use of a fine.

The CEFL principles leave the choice of measures to national law, although *the use of force against the child* should be avoided.

PART III
DEVELOPMENT

CHAPTER IX
MAIN CONCLUSIONS AND CRITICAL ASSESSMENT

IX.1. INTRODUCTION

This study was based on the notion that the law concerning the continuation of joint parental authority after divorce and the breakup of a relationship in Dutch and Danish law was based upon national developments, which due to similarity in form, content and timing, provided a *qualified tertium comparationis* to justify the purpose of providing a critical assessment of these developments.

The study has confirmed this notion to some extent, but has also revealed that there are underlying differences which have been associated with the level of individualisation, the relevance or validation of the institution of marriage in relation to the allocation of parental authority and the perceived role of the State in the procedures concerning the allocation of parental authority.

This final Chapter will integrate some of the main comparative conclusions and thereafter proceed to an analysis and a critical assessment.

IX.2. MAIN COMPARATIVE CONCLUSIONS

This Section integrates the main comparative conclusions based upon a selection of the most important features of the law to be derived from Chapters V-VIII.

IX.2.1. THE FRAMEWORK: CONCEPT OF PARENTAL AUTHORITY

The concept of parental authority/responsibilities in Dutch and Danish law and in the CEFL principles is not identical. This is not surprising considering that the Dutch and Danish concepts have developed over time without fully discarding their historic roots and the CEFL concept is a new construction. There are several differences in the framework. Viewed in the context of the subject-matter of this study, the most notable framework differences are:

1. the distinction between holding and exercising parental authority/responsibilities which is only made in Dutch law and in the CEFL principles; and
2. the possibility to discharge a parent of parental authority/responsibilities as a child protection measure which is only possible in Dutch law and the CEFL principles.

While the distinction in the CEFL principles between *holding and exercising* is made in order to provide a comprehensive and modern conceptual framework, the origins of such a distinction in Dutch and *previously* in Danish law seem to be related to the subservient position of the mother who previously yielded the exercise of parental authority to the father.

The distinction between holding and exercising in the CEFL principles allows for the attribution of the exercise of this authority to third persons in addition to parents. Further, the distinction allows for a division of powers and duties on more levels: the discharge of parental responsibilities (wholly or partly) and the division of the exercise. The distinction in Dutch law is not made with the purpose of a division at more levels, yet the pending proposal on 'Continued Parenting' could be seen as pointing in this direction.[1]

The distinction between holding and exercising is probably common to many European countries, although it is not relevant to all European countries. While the distinction is reasoned differently, the distinction may also be viewed as harbouring the notion that parental authority/responsibilities have a symbolic value even without exercise.[2]

The possibility to *discharge* a parent of parental authority/responsibilities is possible in Dutch law and in the CEFL principles, but not in Danish law. The discharge is a child protection measure, but is regulated in the context of private law. This private law approach is shared by many continental civil law countries in Europe.[3]

1 Chapter VII, Section VII.3.2.1.

2 With respect to Dutch law, it has been considered that there seemed to be an underlying understanding of the value of retaining some formal position since the lack of parental authority has been seen to constitute '*ontoudering*' (lack of parentage), Chapter II, Section II.4.3.

3 K. Schweppe, 'Child Protection in Europe: Different Systems – Common Challenges', *German Law Journal*, Vol. 3, No. 10, 2002.

Child protection measures in Dutch law are generally regulated in a private law context yet they also have a distinctive public law character. In Danish law parental authority may be viewed as a means to regulate the private law relationship between the parent and the child. The possibility of the state intervening is regulated in the context of public (social) law.[4]

The distinction made in Danish law and the lack of a clear distinction in Dutch law is relevant for the regulation of parental authority and contact after divorce and the breakup of a relationship, since it is clear that child protection measures may become relevant in a procedure concerning parental authority or contact in the Netherlands, for example, in the context of the enforcement of contact while this is not possible in Denmark. It should, however, be noted that the distinction in Danish law cannot be viewed as necessarily providing a non-interventionist approach.[5]

IX.2.2. THE ALLOCATION OF PARENTAL AUTHORITY

IX.2.2.1. The initial allocation

The main difference concerning the *initial* allocation of parental authority between Dutch and Danish law and the CEFL principles concerns the allocation of parental authority to the unmarried father. The CEFL principles provide for an allocation *ex lege* which is not provided in either Dutch or Danish law. Danish law does, however, provide the unmarried father, who cohabits with the mother, with parental authority *ex lege*, while Dutch law gives the father the possibility to register an agreement together with the mother or access to a court for an individual assessment.

The difference is indicative of a stronger validation of the formal relationship status in the Netherlands than in Denmark and consequently of a less individualistic approach.[6]

---

4 The CEFL principles consider that the relations between parent and child are private and public and should be accessible to public scrutiny. However, it should be noted that the fact that an obligation of a public law nature exists to protect the child cannot be viewed as necessarily implicating the concept of parental authority, Principles, Introduction p. 22.

5 See further Chapter V, Section V.2.3. and Chapter VIII, Section VIII.2.2. and VIII.3.2.

6 It may also be noted that at the empirical level the number of children born outside marriage in the Netherlands has reached the Danish level in 1981 where the unmarried father in Danish law also depended upon an agreement with the mother, Chapter I, Section I.4.2.

IX.2.2.2. Divorce and the breakup of a relationship

The general rule is that joint parental authority/responsibilities continue after divorce and the breakup of a relationship in Dutch and Danish law and the CEFL principles. While the CEFL principles provide that parental responsibilities are *unaffected*, both Dutch and Danish law provide for the possibility of an allocation of sole parental authority based, however, upon strict criteria, which seem to be particularly related to the parent's level of misbehaviour.

It would thus seem that Dutch and Danish law, while in principle allowing for the allocation of sole parental authority upon divorce or the breakup of the relationship, come close to the solution contained in the CEFL principles where a parent may only be discharged of parental responsibilities in exceptional cases.

IX.2.2.3. The substantive legal norm: joint parental authority

A substantive difference concerns the possibility for parents who do not live together to make agreements on the allocation of (sole/joint) parental authority, which is only possible in Danish law. Joint parental authority is the *predefined substantive legal norm* in Dutch law and the CEFL principles, but not in Danish law.

The freedom of parents to make agreements on the allocation of parental authority (sole/joint), which become valid upon notification, has been a gradual process in Danish law, which may be associated with a high level of individualisation based upon a notion of equality and self-determination and a receding role for the State. The role of the State in private law matters is limited to situations involving a dispute.

In the Netherlands the State continues to assume a protective and authoritative role. Parents are not free to agree upon the allocation of parental authority. Joint parental authority is the given substantive legal norm and the courts have the authority to enforce this norm. Marriage, the family and the family members are, as expressed by the Dutch Minister of Justice, *a concern of the state*.

The CEFL principles do not provide for the possibility of making agreements on parental responsibilities.[7] Parents cannot 'rid themselves of the complete package of rights and duties'. Viewed in the context of Dutch and Danish law, parental

---

7 As opposed to agreements on the exercise which are endorsed, Chapter V, Section V.9.

rights and duties cannot be viewed as being only inherent in the concept of parental authority since rights, such as contact rights, and duties, such as maintenance obligations, are also based upon legal parentage. The Principles seem to give the concept of parental responsibilities a certain symbolism resembling the unchangeable nature of parentage.[8]

IX.2.3. RESIDENCE, RELOCATION AND EXERCISE

IX.2.3.1. Parental authority: a fragmented concept

The construction joint parental authority, both after divorce and after the breakup of a relationship, in Dutch and Danish law has developed from a consensus-based construction with limited legal regulation into a fragmented legal construction. This construction can only be understood in relation to its deconstruction into legal sub-forms, such as the establishment of a (main) residence and increasing access to dispute settlement procedures. The increasing focus upon the internal and external competence of the holders concerning matters relating to the child's person is however also relevant for the understanding of this construction.

The choices made by the CEFL reflect this development. The Principles provide for an explicitly fragmented concept with a distinct possibility for decisions and agreements at the level of *exercising* this authority.

One of the main differences between Dutch law and the CEFL principles, on the one hand, and Danish law, on the other, is that the fragmented construction of joint parental authority in Danish law is based upon two main types of decisions concerning residence and relocation, while Dutch law and the CEFL principles rely upon a general access to dispute settlement involving judicial discretion.[9] The judicial discretion of the Dutch judiciary is further underlined by the fact that the judiciary participates in the conceptual development, which has as a consequence that the content of rights and duties remains open to assessment in individual cases.

---

8 This, however, has also been observed in respect of Dutch law, supra note 2.

9 The CEFL principles also rely upon the discretion of the national legislature to choose between two different solutions: dividing the exercise and deciding the dispute. The CEFL principles do, however, consider that there should be general access to dispute settlement.

IX.2.3.2. Substantive features

A decision on (the main) *residence* in Dutch law and in the CEFL principles is a decision concerning the *exercise* of parental authority/responsibilities. As such, it is the general dispute settlement provision which regulates the determination of (the main) residence and a later change thereof when there is a dispute.[10] In Danish law it is a new separate type of decision. The consequence is that the substantive implications of such a decision are clearer in Danish law than in Dutch law and the CEFL principles.[11]

Shared residence is possible both in Danish and Dutch law and in the CEFL principles based upon agreement. The establishment of a shared residence when a parent resists this by a decision of the court is *perhaps* possible in Dutch law. The CEFL principles provide for this possibility, while simultaneously expressing concern in respect of such a division.

A decision on *relocation* in Dutch law is a decision concerning the *exercise* of parental authority regulated by the general dispute settlement provision. The CEFL principles and Danish law provide for a decision on relocation. In Danish law this decision only concerns relocation outside the jurisdiction since the resident parent has an inherent right to relocate within the jurisdiction.[12] Danish law may be regarded as giving the relocation rights of the resident parent a stronger starting point than both Dutch law and the CEFL principles.

The main difference with respect to *access to dispute settlement* procedures is that Dutch law and the CEFL principles provide for general access, involving judicial discretion, while Danish law relies upon different types of decisions. At the practical level this difference becomes relevant with respect to more immaterial disputes such as disputes concerning medical treatment and educational choices.

IX.2.4. PROCEDURAL PERSPECTIVES

Dutch and Danish family law procedures differ considerably, primarily because of the widespread use of administrative procures in Danish law. The CEFL principles allow for both a judicial and an administrative procedure.

---

10 The CEFL principles alternatively provide for the possibility of dividing the exercise.

11 Chapter VI, Section VI.2.4.

12 The distinction between relocation within and outside the jurisdiction is relevant to both Dutch and Danish law, but not to the CEFL principles.

It is evident, however, that the common trend is the emphasis upon parents' own responsibility and the incorporation of alternative dispute resolution in the judicial procedure. Dispute resolution is not only endorsed, but may also be viewed as increasingly becoming an obligation for the parents. In the Netherlands the courts have placed parents under a duty to participate in mediation, while in Denmark the administrative portal to procedures concerning divorce and parental authority can be viewed as a means to oblige the parents to seek a negotiated solution.

Dutch and Danish law and the CEFL principles each follow a separate path on the question of reviewing a parental agreement concerning parental authority/ responsibilities. The Dutch approach provides for a certain level of judicial review in proceedings concerning parental authority and divorce, also when parents agree. This review will probably increase if the present pending proposal on 'Continued Parenting' is adopted. The approach could be viewed as being consistent with the fact that joint parental authority is the predefined substantive legal norm.

The CEFL principles draw a distinction between the holding of parental responsibilities and the exercise thereof and provide for the possibility of agreements between the parents only with respect to this exercise. Such agreements must be reviewed in certain cases, for example in cases of divorce by mutual consent and with respect to agreements on shared residence, while in other cases the matter is left to national law.

It is only in Danish law that parental agreements are no longer subject to a review but become valid upon notification, because joint parental authority is not the substantive legal norm.

IX.3. ANALYSIS

The regulation of parental authority after divorce or after the breakup of a relationship may be viewed as involving a choice between different types of regulation each providing both advantages and disadvantages.

The developments which have constituted joint parental authority as a strong legal norm may be argued on the basis of human rights principles such as those contained in the ECHR and the CRC. However, these international conventions cannot yet be viewed as requiring that joint parental authority after divorce and the breakup of a relationship should be possible, needless to say that it should be a strong legal norm.[13]

The available choice of regulation may prescribe an allocation of sole parental authority, a type of regulation which provides a clear legal regulation of the subsequent exercise of parental authority. It may require that parents agree to an allocation of joint parental authority or provide for an automatic continuation of joint parental authority unless a parent requests an allocation of sole parental authority. While this type of regulation does not provide a clear legal regulation in situations where disputes subsequently arise, it does provide for the construction of joint parental authority, at least formally, to be consensus-based. Finally, it may provide joint parental authority as a strong legal norm which may also be enforced upon parents who resist such an allocation. In this latter case, the joint exercise of parental authority acquires a different form necessitating a more intense regulation of the exercise.

On the basis of the development in Dutch and Danish law the choice which may be considered relevant is a choice between a regulation which is deemed to secure a proper exercise of parental authority, for example, by requiring that parents agree upon joint exercise and a regulation that is aimed at securing the legal norm of joint parental authority.

The analysis will be devoted to three aspects, which can be regarded as being central to the development of joint parental authority. In the first place this concerns two ideals which have been actively pursued in recent and pending Dutch and Danish reforms: the endorsement of *equality* between the parents and the endorsement of *parental co-operation*. The third aspect concerns the *child protection function*. In the context of this analysis, which focuses upon a choice between different types of regulation, the child protection function reflects a choice between an effective exercise of parental authority or an effective intervention remedying a dysfunctional exercise of parental authority.

Finally, the relevance of the CEFL principles to Dutch and Danish law will be reviewed.

---

13 Chapter III, Sections III.2.2 and III.6.1.

IX.3.1. EQUALITY

The development in joint parental authority can be viewed as representing an endorsement of an ideal concerning equality between fathers and mothers. The endorsement of this ideal in a legal regulation may take various forms. The most direct form is the substantive legal norm providing for joint parental authority and a more equal access to the child, for example, through the establishment of a shared residence. A more indirect procedural form promotes equality by placing the parents in a position where they must negotiate their own position.

Both Dutch and Danish law may be viewed to have strengthened a substantive norm favouring a more equal access to the child in recent and pending reforms. The pending Dutch reform on 'Continued Parenting' contains an equality norm which points in the direction of a more equal position of the parents. The new Danish Act on Parental Responsibility introduces the possibility of establishing a contact arrangement amounting to a shared residence which is also applicable in situations where a parent resists.

The procedural form involving parental negotiation may be viewed as being highly developed in Danish law where the administrative portal to divorce procedures and procedures on parental authority and contact places the parents in a situation where they must negotiate concerning their own position. The pending Dutch reform on 'Continued Parenting' may be viewed as adopting a similar approach through the requirement that a 'parenting plan' must be submitted with the divorce petition.

The procedural form can be viewed as representing an independent ideal favouring parental co-operation. This form may, however, also be viewed as preparation for or a corollary to a substantive equality norm where the parents negotiate in the shadow of the law.

IX.3.2. PARENTAL CO-OPERATION

Parental co-operation can be viewed as being either an independent ideal or being ingrained in the equality ideal.

In discussing this question it is interesting to recall FLENDT'S analytical description of Danish law. In her view joint parental authority should be viewed in the context of the shift from the 1986 reform to the 1996 reform, as involving a shift from an *is* construction to an *ought to* construction.[14] The 1986 reform provided joint parental authority as a positive choice for parents who agreed upon all aspects concerning the child. As a result, joint parental authority was not the preferred construction.

The 1996 reform continued to be based upon a notion of co-operation maintaining the right of one parent to request the termination of joint parental authority, yet the preference for joint parental authority was clear.[15] FLENDT considered that:

> 'It is evident that divorces would have a different reputation if all parents were able to work intensively on the cause and themselves. It was and is to a certain degree the ideal on which the invention of the construction of joint parental authority is based. Time has shown, however, that parents cannot live up to this ideal; rather, they exercise varied forms of separated family forms where only a quarter of parents exercise something which can be understood as joint parenting.
>
> The fact that the legislature places such emphasis upon joint parental authority, amongst other things, by making it extremely easy to obtain joint parental authority and by removing a critical decision from the parents and giving it to the authorities[16] in order to prevent parents from requesting the termination of joint parental authority (...) can no longer be defended based upon the previous aims concerning responsibility and co-operation. Rather, the answer lies in the fact that there has been a tendency for many years to promote the idea that children's welfare benefits from contact with both biological parents.'[17]

The general development in Danish law providing for an automatic continuation of joint parental authority in 2002 and for the possibility of establishing joint

---

14 H. Flendt, *Fælles forældremyndighed i praksis*, Copenhagen: Jurist- og Økonomforbundets Forlag, 1999, p. 63. This book was based upon empirical research.

15 Chapter II, Section II.3.2. See also; A. Kronborg, *Forældremyndighed og Menneskelig Integritet*, Copenhagen: Jurist- og Økonomforbundets Forlag, 2007, p. 88-89 who places the development in the context of a return to marital norms, which, however, were based upon duty and fault rather than the best interests principle, furthermore considering that legislation, which does not set boundaries, acquires a moralising character and places the authorities in a position where they must discipline the parents into normality.

16 A decision on contact, Chapter II, Section II.3.2.2.

17 The term biological parent should be taken to mean legal parent.

parental authority against the wishes of one parent in 2007 has confirmed this development.[18]

The change from an *is* construction to an *ought to* construction is also visible in Dutch law although it is characteristic of Dutch law that it was a gradual process which is difficult to link to a particular moment in time since the relevance of the notion of a 'good mutual understanding' was central throughout two legislative reforms with inherently different starting points.[19] Furthermore, it is characteristic of Dutch law that *ought to* became relevant with respect to the termination of joint parental authority before it was relevant to the establishment of joint parental authority. Dutch law could be regarded as having placed a greater emphasis on the legal relationship, which had already been established, than upon the premise 'good mutual understanding' for its continuation than was the case in Danish law.[20]

Moreover, competing legal discourses have been relevant for Dutch developments, for example, the notion that a care relationship deserves recognition[21] and the notion that there is a 'right to exercise parental authority' based upon the ECHR.[22] It is perhaps the influence of different legal discourses and the interaction between the legislature and the judiciary in the creation of law which best explain why legal concepts and provisions often have an unsettled nature in Dutch law.

It is, however, also distinctive of Dutch case law on joint parental authority, at least until recently, that the allocation of joint parental authority has often been

18 The co-operation norm also came to support the obligation of parents to co-operate, Chapter V, Section V.6.2.

19 The 1995 and 1998 reforms; Chapter II, Section II.2.2.2.

20 This assertion continues to be true with respect to residence. Dutch case law often relies upon maintaining the status quo, for example, maintaining an established shared residence or not allowing a parent to relocate while Danish law provides that a shared residence cannot be maintained against the wishes of one parent and provides more explicitly for relocation rights; Chapter VI.

21 In the landmark decision of the Dutch Supreme Court in 1984 which allowed two divorcing parents to continue exercising parental authority after divorce, the Supreme Court considered that the *de facto* enjoyment of family life (co-parenting) deserved legal recognition; Chapter II, Section II.2.2. Van Wamelen has argued that the *de facto* care relationship involving a shared residence and not the agreement on the exercise of joint parental authority should be the foundation for joint parental authority; C. van Wamelen, De eerbiediging van een zorgrelatie, *NEMESIS*, 1996, No. 3, p. 76-82. However, factual care never became relevant for the allocation of joint parental authority in Dutch law.

22 Chapter III, Section III.3.

viewed as providing a 'rag to wipe off the blood' since *some* decisions maintaining joint parental authority informally, may be viewed as involving nothing more than the toleration of the other parent's *holding* of parental authority.[23] It is perhaps in this light that the aim of the pending proposal on 'Continued Parenting' must be understood as providing a distinctive 'ought to' factor for the concrete exercising of joint parenting within the concept of joint parental authority.

The *ought to* construction may imply a belief in the normative powers of legal regulation and a belief in the 'makeability' of joint parenting and parental co-operation. The increasingly obligatory nature of alternative dispute resolution and other procedural means such as the Dutch 'parenting plan' support the notion that joint parenting is possible. It is, however, also a fact recognised by the national legislatures that this approach will not work in all post-divorce families.[24] In these cases, the *ought to* construction will become a burden which weighs down the family under a plethora of processes.[25]

It should also be noted that the increasing importance attached to parental co-operation, which in Danish law has been described as the co-operation norm, means that parental co-operation gains importance as a *regulatory means* between the parents which is relevant for the allocation or reallocation of parental authority or the establishment of residence.[26] A parent viewed to be lacking in co-operation potential may 'lose' a case concerning the allocation of parental authority or the child's residence.[27] In this respect it is worth noting that parents do not always enjoy an equal position in relation to this norm.[28]

IX.3.3. CHILD PROTECTION

The regulation of parental authority is a complex matter involving a triangular construction between parents, the child and the State where the State has a particular responsibility towards the weaker party – the child.

---

23 Chapter II, Section II.2.2.2. and Chapter V, Section V.4.5.

24 Chapter I, Section I.2.2.

25 The term processes is to be understood broadly as encompassing legal procedures and disputes which, for example, come to involve third parties such as the child's school or medical practitioners.

26 Chapter V, Section V.6. and Chapter VI.

27 In the Netherlands, as yet, only the formal holding of parental authority, Chapter V, Section V.6.1.2.

28 Chapter V.6.2.1. with reference to the Danish case: Højesteret (Supreme Court) 28.10.2004, *UFR* 2005.363H and A. Kronborg, 2007, supra, p. 143-144.

Historically, the general boundary for state intervention was limited to the possibility of intervening through child protection measures. In the case of divorce the role of the State was principally to provide *a dispute settlement function* involving a choice between two parents, a solution which may be viewed as providing an effective exercise of parental authority. It is common to the development of both Dutch and Danish law that the regulation of parental authority increasingly comes to reflect a *child-protection function* setting boundaries for acceptable parental behaviour.[29] This latter type of regulation implies that there must be effective intervention to remedy a dysfunctional exercise of parental authority.

The child-protection function in procedures concerning parental authority may be viewed as having greater importance in Dutch law than in Danish law. The Dutch courts have jurisdiction in both civil cases and cases concerning child protection, while the separation of these types of cases is not always distinct.[30] The role of the courts in civil cases is further considered to be important[31] and the courts have the competence to intervene on behalf of the child also when parents agree.[32] In Danish law the child-protection function in a procedure concerning parental authority or contact is limited to situations where there is a dispute. Parents are free to agree on a division of parental authority.

The substantive element of the Dutch courts' role in the procedures has, however, been based upon changing perceptions. It was not evident that the courts had a role to play after the 1998 Act when joint parental authority was continued after divorce or that a parental agreement on the allocation of sole parental authority should be subject to a substantive review considering that the 1998 reform provided a non-interventionist approach based upon Art. 8 of the ECHR. Nonetheless, subsequent developments provided that the courts have come to hear children in the procedure also when joint parental authority continues and have provided joint parental authority as the predefined substantive legal norm also when parents agree upon an allocation of sole parental

29 See further for the definition of the child protection function in this respect, Chapter I, Section I.2.1.

30 Chapter V, Section V.2.3.

31 The proposal concerning an administrative divorce passed through the Dutch Parliament's Second Chamber only after spouses with children had been excluded from the administrative procedure. This proposal was finally rejected by the Dutch Parliament's First Chamber, Chapter II, Section II.2.6.2.

32 Chapter VIII, Section VIII.4.1.

authority. It is perhaps inherent in Dutch law that there are tensions between interventionist and non-interventionist discourses.[33]

While child protection can be viewed as being more important in Dutch law than in Danish law, this study provides little evidence to substantiate that this actually results in more protection in situations where the exercise of parental authority can be viewed as being dysfunctional. Adherence to the substantive legal norm of joint parental authority seems to take precedence.

IX.3.4. THE RELEVANCE OF THE CEFL PRINCIPLES

The CEFL has provided a set of principles which it considers to be suitable for the harmonisation of parental responsibilities and which will promote the free movement of persons in Europe. The Principles also aim, however, to contribute to common European values regarding the child's rights and welfare.

The CEFL principles on parental responsibilities provide a concept of parental responsibilities, which in the framework probably reflect a common core in many European jurisdictions. This framework containing a distinction between holding and exercising and the possibility of discharging parental responsibilities caters much more for Dutch law than Danish law. Furthermore, the general access to dispute settlement procedures and the reliance upon judicial discretion better fit Dutch law than Danish law. Finally, the Principles, just as Dutch law, provide for a more substantive review of parental agreements than Danish law.

The allocation of parental responsibilities *ex lege* when parentage has been established would, however, require a substantive change to both Dutch and Danish law.[34]

While the Principles in many ways may be viewed as generally reflecting national developments in Dutch and Danish law providing for a fragmented

---

33 Above Section IX.3.1. M. Antokolskaia points to the contradictory elements of both the liberal and interventionist nature of the Luchtenveld proposal on an administrative divorce procedure; M. Antokolskaia, 'De voorstellen tot hervorming van het echtscheidingsrecht naar de vorm modern, naar de inhoud een stap terug', *WPNR*, 2005, p. 737-744.

34 Although Danish law provides for an *ex lege* allocation for cohabiting parents covering the vast majority of parents, the compulsory establishment of paternity could be viewed as a major obstacle to an allocation *ex lege*. For Dutch law the allocation of parental authority *ex lege* pursuant to voluntary acknowledgement (excluding judicial establishment) has been considered to be going too far; see further Chapter II.2.4.1. and Chapter V, Section V.3.2.1.

concept of parental authority, it is also clear that they address issues which are central to Dutch and Danish law in a general manner.[35]

The Principles may, for example, be regarded as providing joint parental authority as a substantive legal norm, yet they seem to provide the possibility for a division at the level of exercising parental authority based upon the criterion of best interests. The best interests criterion in the CEFL principles is the *paramount consideration*. This criterion, however, is an open one which provides little guidance. The Principles consequently could be viewed as providing for joint exercise or joint parenting as the general norm, but with little substantiation of the concrete scope in comparison to Dutch and Danish law.

The Principles provide for compulsory scrutiny in some situations and leave the matter to national law in others. It is not entirely clear why public scrutiny is necessary in respect of parental responsibilities, but unnecessary with respect to the concrete division of care and why scrutiny is necessary in one particular event: divorce by mutual consent, but not required in all other cases, for example, involving unmarried parents considering that the CEFL generally provide that parental responsibilities belong to parents *ex lege* and are *unaffected by divorce*.

The child's protection, participation and autonomy rights are broadly formulated in the CEFL principles and may be viewed as providing the child with a more general autonomous position as provided for in Dutch and Danish law. The Principles, however, do not address the actual content of these rights, for example, stating whether the child is a party to the legal procedures and whether the child or a young person may initiate such procedures also against the parents. The Principles could thus be viewed as promoting children's rights yet providing limited guidance with respect to the concrete scope and implementation of children's rights.

While the Principles aim to promote the free movement of persons, the right to relocation depends upon a balancing of interests rather than providing a general starting point. This solution would perhaps provide limited harmonisation concerning a matter with specific relevance for the free movement of persons.

35 The general manner may be seen as being consistent with the status of *principles*.

IX.4. CRITICAL ASSESSMENT

The current discourse in both Dutch and Danish law underpinning the law on parental authority and contact is the understanding that parent-child relationships should not be affected by divorce or the breakup of a relationship. The ideal of the amicable post-divorce family and the 'child's right to two parents' have provided the main rule favouring the continuation of parental authority and a narrow exception, which point in the direction that an allocation of sole parental authority is associated with the level of the parent's misbehaviour rather than with an assessment of the risks or benefits involved for the individual child.

IX.4.1. THE SOCIO-LEGAL CONTEXT

Research does not prove that joint parenting, joint parental authority or even contact benefit children independently of the parents' ability and willingness to co-operate. The most important factors for children's well-being in the post-divorce family seem to be related to the parenting potential of the resident parent and a lack of parental conflict.

Dutch research has clearly shown that the changes pursuant to the 1998 reform, which provided for the automatic continuation of parental authority and soon developed into the strong legal norm, led to substantively increased conflict levels.

On the other hand, Danish research clearly indicates that the foundations for joint parenting after divorce and after the breakup of a relationship depend upon the parents' relationship with each other, with the understanding that the foundations for joint parenting are connected to circumstances which were already present at the child's birth. Further Danish research provides the insight that a lack of ability or the potential to co-operate is often associated with other social vulnerability factors such as being connected to violence within the relationship and substance abuse, giving rise to the understanding that the parent-child relationship affected by conflicts after divorce is a vulnerable construction due to factors other than the divorce itself.[36]

---

36 This has also been observed in a legal perspective with respect to Dutch law, E.C.C. Punselie, 'Geen verantwoordelijkheid nemen, dan geen gezag!', *FJR*, 2005, p. 161.

IX.4.2. THE LEGAL CONTEXT

The legal regulation of joint parental authority after divorce and after the breakup of a relationship can be viewed as involving a choice between different types of regulation. The present regulation is often viewed or criticised within the context that, on the one hand, joint parental authority should not be dependent upon parental agreement, while, on the other, it should not be enforced upon parents who have serious conflicts or when there are other contrary indications.

The Danish 2006 Commission had suggested a 'light version' concerning the possibility of establishing joint parental authority against the wishes of one parent in situations where the parent could be viewed as having 'no good reasons' for wishing an allocation of sole parental authority'.[37] VAN ROOIJEN recently found that the continuation of joint parental authority in Dutch law was a positive development considering the normative effect upon parents, yet simultaneously finding that case law went too far in individual complicated cases and, furthermore, considering that it should be a requirement that the parents continue to be involved in the child's life. VAN ROOIJEN suggested the adoption of legal criteria based upon criteria with an inherent pedagogical or psychological nature to provide guidance to the court in the choice between sole and joint parental authority.[38]

The question is whether such an approach, involving detailed criteria of a psychological or pedagogical nature, is a feasible approach in law. The decisions of the Dutch Supreme Court in 1986 provided the possibility for joint parental authority (then joint parental power) outside of marriage. Parental agreement was not sufficient for such an allocation according to the Supreme Court. The court should also have been satisfied that there was a 'good mutual understand-

---

[37] Chapter II, Section II.3.2.2.

[38] C. Van Rooijen, *Scheiden zonder vrijheid, Is gezamenlijk ouderlijk gezag na echtscheiding in het belang van het kind?*, Nijmegen: Wolf Legal Publishers, 2007, p. 254, p. 258, p. 274 and p. 279-281. The criteria are derived from the book M. Kalverboer and E. Zijlstra, *Het belang van het kind in het Nederlands recht, voorwaarden voor ontwikkeling vanuit een pedagogisch perspectief*, Amsterdam: SWP, 2006 and concern family-based development conditions such as: 'Physical well-being' involving adequate care and a safe and close environment; 'upbringing' involving an affective climate, a supportive and a flexible structure; 'parents as adequate role models' and interests; and, finally, 'past and future' involving continuity in caring and nurturing and future prospects. The criteria concerning the: 'Community-based development conditions' are not deliberated here considering that van Rooijen places less emphasis on these criteria.

ing' between the parents and ascertain that the best interests of the child were not contrary to this allocation. Although the criteria laid down by the Supreme Court required the court to make an assessment for the future, the courts soon came to rely upon something more concrete; a joint request being viewed as evidence of a 'good mutual understanding'. Furthermore, while a 'good mutual understanding' continued to play a role in the parliamentary debates prior to the 1998 Act concerning the continuation of joint parental authority, the positive requirement of a 'good mutual understanding' soon became irrelevant for the continuation of joint parental authority.

These developments give rise to the question whether the courts are willing or able to make such welfare assessments concerning the future. It may be suggested that the law tends to rely upon more concrete facts such as a joint request or ascertainable misbehaviour on the part of one parent. Furthermore, it is worth considering whether a procedural approach aiming to retain the normative values of joint parental authority and contact, often involving lengthy procedures before an allocation of sole parental authority or a discharge of contact rights will (perhaps) eventually take place, does not represent 'blindness to the damage, which the procedures in themselves may inflict.'[39] It seems inherent in both Dutch and Danish law that, save in exceptional cases, an allocation of sole parental authority (in Dutch law) and the discharge of contact rights are subject to lengthy procedures, which may continue for years and even extend throughout the child's entire childhood.

It is a pertinent question whether the aim of promoting the amicable post-divorce family and the child's right or obligation to have two parents does not harm children in families where this aim is unattainable and where the concrete result is that the family become embroiled in legal procedures for many years to come. Furthermore, it is worth posing the question whether it is possible to compel parents to co-operate in pursuit of an ideal and to protect vulnerable family life at the same time.

In answering these questions the bottom-line should be that the choice of a certain form of regulation will determine the level of processes involving children in post-divorce families. The price for the present type of regulation is to be paid by children who come from families where the aim of promoting the

39 A. Kronborg, 2007, p. 202. The procedural approach can be considered to give rise to the understanding that the assessment of the best interest of the child in individual cases cannot be granted more scope than allowing for a public administration of individual rights in the family.

amicable post-divorce family is unattainable. Research shows that this often encompasses children in families where there are other social vulnerability factors such as violence or substance abuse indicating that there is a special need for protection. Compelling parents to co-operate in these situations may prolong the procedures unnecessarily and may even prove to threaten the safety of certain family members. These circumstances are to be taken into account when considering the role of the State. Would it not be more appropriate for the State to adopt a protective role aiming to prevent distress through the requirement that joint parental authority is based upon the parents' request and a continued ability to hold parental authority jointly?

According to this author's view, a feasible approach which will limit the amount of processes is to base the allocation of joint parental authority after divorce and after the breakup of a relationship upon the parents' (continued) willingness to hold joint parental authority. This implies a return to the joint request procedure for married parents.[40] The advantage of this approach is that it provides an unambiguous legal regulation of the allocation of parental authority while being amenable to parents who can agree on joint parental authority. This approach strengthens the effective exercise of parental authority and reduces the need for a detailed regulation.

40 For unmarried parents parental authority will continue unless a request for sole parental authority is made.

BIBLIOGRAPHY

Albæk Jensen, J., 2001, 'Human Rights in Danish Law', *European Public Law*, Volume 7, No. 1, p. 1-10

Amato, P.R., 2001, 'Children of divorce in the 1990s: An Update of the Amato and Keith (1991) Meta-Analysis', *Journal of Family Psychology*, No. 15, p. 355-370

Anders Scheiden, Rapport van de Commissie Herzienning scheidingsprocedure, 02.10.1996

Andersen, J., 1999, *Rapport fra Folketingets konference om behovet for en grundlovsrevision*, to be found on www.folketinget.dk

Antokolskaia, M., (Ed.), 2006, *Herziening van het echtscheidingsrecht, Administratieve echtscheiding, mediation, voortgezet ouderschap*, Amsterdam: SWP

Antokolskaia, M., 2006, 'Administratieve echtscheiding vanuit national en international perspectief' in: Antokolskaia, M. (Ed.), *Herzienning van het echtscheidingsrecht*, Amsterdam: SWP

Antokolskaia, M., 2006, *Harmonisation of Family Law in Europe: A historical perspective*, Antwerp-Oxford: Intersentia

Antokolskaia, M., 2005, 'De voorstellen tot hervorming van het echtscheidingsrecht naar de vorm modern, naar de inhoud een stap terug', *WPNR*, p. 737-744

Antokolskaia, M., 2004, 'Human Rights as a basis for the Harmonisation of Family Law?' in: Lødrup, P., Modvar, E. (Eds.), *Family Law and Human Rights*, Oslo: Gyldendal Norsk Forlag A/S

Antokolskaia, M., 2002, 'The Recent Developments in Dutch Filiation, Adoption and Joint Custody Law', *Rivista di Diritto della familia e della Successioni in Europa*, No. 3, p. 791-804

Benen, E., Vlaardingerbroek, P., 2004, 'Doorlopend ouderlijk gezag in de praktijk', *FJR*, p. 36-40

Benzon, V., 1926, *Familieretten II, Ægteskabets retsvirkninger*, Copenhagen, G.E.C. Gad

Benzon, V., 1924, *Familieretten*, Copenhagen, C.E.G. Gad

Bille, A., 1997, 'Samvær og forældremyndighed i historisk belysning', *UFR*, Section B, p. 408-413

Bjerg, O., 2005, 'Er kønsmæssig diskrimination i forældremyndighedssager en – myte ej?', *TFA*, p. 277-279

Boele-Woelki, K., Ferrand, F., González Beilfuss, C., Jänterä-Jareborg, M., Lowe, N., Martiny, D. Pintens, W., 2007, *Principles of European Family Law Regarding Parental Responsibilties*, Antwerp-Oxford: Intersentia

Boele-Woelki, K., Curry-Sumner, I., Jansen, M., *Schrama, W.,* 2007, *Huwelijk of Geregistreerd Partnerschap?*, Deventer: Kluwer

Boele-Woelki, K., Braat, B., Curry-Sumner, I. (Eds), 2005, *European Family Law in Action, Volume III: Parental Responsibilities*, Antwerp-Oxford: Intersentia

Boele-Woelki, K., 2005, 'The working method of the Commission on European Family law', in: Boele-Woelki, K. (Ed.): *Common Core and Better law in European Family law*, Antwerp-Oxford: Intersentia

Boele-Woelki, K., Ferrand, F., González Beilfuss, C., Jäntera-Jareborg, M., Lowe, N., Martiny, D., Pintens, W., 2004, *Principles of European Family Law Regarding Divorce and Maintenance Between Former Spouses*, Antwerp-Oxford: Intersentia

Boele-Woelki, K., Braat, B., Sumner, I. (Eds.), 2003, *European Family Law in Action, Volume I: Grounds for Divorce*, Antwerp-Oxford-New York: Intersentia

de Boer, J. (ASSER- DE BOER), 2006, *Asser's Handleiding tot de beoefening van het Nederlands Burgerlijk Recht, Personen- en Familierecht*, Deventer: Kluwer, 2006

de Boer, J. (ASSER-DE-BOER), 2002, *Handleiding tot de beoefening van het Nederlands burgerlijk recht*, part 1, Zwolle: Tjeenk-Willink

de Boer, J., 1982, 'Omgangsrecht als mensenrecht', *NJB*, p. 1125-1134

Bondesen, U. (Ed.), 2006, *Law and Morality*, Copenhagen: Forlaget Thomsen

Boserup, B., Hansen, H.R., 2003, *Samværsklemmen*, Copenhagen: Gyldendal

Braun, M., 1992, *De prijs van de liefde, De eerste feministische golf, het huwelijksrecht en de vaderlandse geschiedenis*, Amsterdam: Het Spinhuis

Brenninkmeijer, A.F.M., 2006, 'Judicial Organization', in: Chorus, J., Gerver, P., Hondius, E., *Introduction to Dutch law*', Alphen aan den Rijn: Kluwer

de Bruijn Lückers, M.L.C.C., Punselie, E.C.C., 2004, 'Medisch handelen en kinderbescherming', *Tijdschrift voor gezondheidsrecht*, No. 28, p. 578-591

de Bruijn-Lückers, M.L.C.C., 1994, '*EVRM, minderjarigheid en ouderlijk gezag, A whole code of juvenile law?*', Deventer: Kluwer

Burkens, M.C.B., 1982, 'The Complete Revision of the Dutch Constitution', *Netherlands International Law Review*, p. 323-336

Cantwell, N., 2007, 'An uncharacteristically concise comment' in: '*Liber Amicorum*', Defence for Children International

Caspersen, E., 1995, 'Børnekonventionen og dens efterlevelse i Danmark', *Juristen*, No. 6, p. 275-283

Chin-A-Fat, B., 2004, *Scheiden terechter zonder rechter*, the Hague: Sdu Uitgevers bv

Chin-A-Fat, B., van Rooijen, C., 2004, 'Oplossingen voor omgangsproblematiek', *FJR*, p. 226-232

Chin-A-Fat, B.E.S, Stekete, M.J., 2001, *Bemiddeling in uitvoering*, Utrecht: Verwey-Jonker Instituut

Christoffersen, J., 2006, 'Den danske debat om den internationale menneskeret', *Nordisk Tidsskrift for Menneskerettigheder*, p. 97-114

Christoffersen, J., 2002, 'Højesterets prøvelse af folkeretlige diskriminationsforbud', *UFR*, p. 407-410

Christoffersen, J., 2000, 'Højesteret og Den Europæiske Menneskerettighedskonvention', *UFR*, p. 593-598

Coenraad, L. M., 2006, 'Procederen over het voortgezet ouderschap', in: Antokolskaia, M. (Ed.), 2006, *Herziening van het echtscheidingsrecht, Administratieve echtscheiding, mediation, voortgezet ouderschap*, Amsterdam: SWP

Coenraad, L., 2004, 'Afdoening zonder mondelinge behandeling', *FJR*, p. 2-10

Combrink-Kuiters, L., 1997, 'Gelet op de feiten; een analyse van 50 rechtbankdossiers inzake voogdijwijziging', *EB*, p. 6-9

Coppens, H.P., 2002, 'Is door huwelijk gezamenlijk gezag ontstaan?', *EB*, No. 7-8, p. 103-105

Curry-Sumner, I., 2005, *All's well that ends registered? The substantive and private international law aspects of non-marital registered relationships in Europe*, Antwerp-Oxford: Intersentia

Danielsen, S., 2007, 'Foreløbig forældremyndighed', *TFA*, p. 5-13

Danielsen, S., 2004, 'Børns rolle under forældremyndighedstvister', *TFA*, p. 271-281

Danielsen, S., 2003, *Nordisk Børneret II*, Copenhagen: Nord

Danielsen, S., 1997, *Lov om forældremyndighed og samvær med kommentarer*, Copenhagen: Jurist og Økonomforbundets Forlag

David, R., 1974, *Les Grands systēmes de droit contemporains*, Paris: Dalloz

Delfos, G., Doek, J., 1974, *Kinderrecht, Civilrechterlijk deel*, Zwolle: Tjeenk Willink

Deuntzer, I.H., 1878, *Den Nordiske familie- og arveret*, Copenhagen: Gyldendalske Boghandels Forlag

Doek, J.E., 1984, *Omgangsrecht*, 's-Gravenhage: VUGA

Espersen, O., 1970, *Indgåelse og opfyldelse af traktater*, Copenhagen: Juristforbundets Forlag

Esping-Andersen, G., 1990, *The Three Worlds of Welfare Capitalism*, Princeton, Princeton University Press

Evald, J., 2002, 'Om forholdets natur', *Rettid*, p. 100-111

Fischer, T., 2004, 'Onderwijsachterstand door echtscheiding?', *Demos*, No. 8, p. 61-63

Flendt, H., 1999, *Fælles forældremyndighed i praksis*, Copenhagen: Jurist- og Økonomforbundets Forlag

Fogedretternes praksis i samværs- of forældremyndighedssager, 2004, Justitsministeriet, May 2004 available on www.justitsministeriet.dk

Foighel, I., 1997, 'Gælder menneskerettighederne', *UFR*, p .1-4

Forder, C.J., 1995, '*Legal Establishment of the Parent Child Relationship, Principles*', Maastricht: University Press

Forsøgsprojekt om øget samarbejde mellem Kommune og Statsamt i sociale og familieretlige sager, February 2004

Franken, H., 1995, (a.o.), *Inleiden tot de Rechtswetenschap*, Arnhem: Gouda Quint

Franken, J.B.M., 2005, *Mr. C. Asser's Handleiding tot de Beoefening van het Nederlands Burgerlijk Recht, Algemeen Deel, Een Vervolg*, Deventer: Kluwer

Frost, L, 2003, 'Ændring af forældremyndighedsdomme og –aftaler efter forældremyndighedsloven §13', *TFA*, p. 351-362

Frost, L, 1997, *Samspillet mellem forældremyndighedslovens og bistandslovens regler om samvær og anden kontakt*, Skarrildhus, 27.10.1997

Garde, J., Hansen Jensen, M., 2002, 'Den Europæiske Menneskerettighedsdomstols praksis', *Juristen*, p. 76-82

Gerads, J., 2005, 'Protocol No. 12 – The Dutch Debate', in: Lagoutte, S. (Ed.), *Prohibition of Discrimination in the Nordic Countries: The Complicated fate of Protocol No. 12 to the European Convention on Human Rights*, The Danish Institute for Human Rights

Gerritse, J., 2007, 'Blijft co-ouderschap na echtscheiding een uitzondering?', in: Boele-Woelki, K. (Ed.), *Actuele ontwikkelingen in het familierecht*, UCERF, Nijmegen: Ars Aequi Libri

van Gestel, S., 1998, 'Beëindiging gezamenlijk gezag', *Advocatenblad*, p. 899-900

de Graaf, A., 2005, 'Scheiden: motieven, verhuisgedrag en aard van de contacten', Voorburg: CBS, Bevolkingstrends 53

de Graaf, A., 2001, 'Onder moeders paraplu. Ervaringen van kinderen met relaties na echtscheiding', *Demos*, No. 17, p. 33-37

Graversen, J., 1984, 'Fælles forældremyndighed ved separation og skilsmisse', Copenhagen: Socialforskningsinstituttet, No. 43

Graversen, J., Beck, S., Munck, N., Højgaard Pedersen, M., Vesterdorf, P., 1986, *Familieret*, Copenhagen: Juristforbundets Forlag

Graversen, J., 1988, 'Familieret som afspejling af familieideologien', in: Graversen, J. (Ed.), *Familieretspolitik*, Copenhagen: CARNET

de Groot, B.E.L.A.M., 1999, 'Ex-partner, maar niet ex-ouder', *FJR*, p. 90-96

van Grunderbeeck, D., 2003, *Beginselen van personen- en familierecht, Een mensenrechtelijke benardering*, Antwerpen: Intersentia

Harck, S., Palmer Olsen, H., 1999, 'Decision concerning the Maastricht Treaty', *The American Journal of International Law*, p. 209-214.

Harris, D.J., O'Boyle, M., Warbrick, C., 1995, *Law of the European Convention on Human Rights*, London: Butterworths

Heida, A., 2000, 'Gezamenlijk ouderlijk gezag na scheiding', *EB*, No. 7/8, p. 1-6.

Heide Ottosen, M., 2004, *Samvær til barnets bedste*, Copenhagen: Socialforskningsinstituttet

Heide Ottosen, M, 2004, *Samvær og børns trivsel*, Copenhagen: Socialforskningsinstituttet

Heide Ottosen, M., 2000, *Samboskab, Ægteskab og Forældrebrud*, Copenhagen: Socialforskningsinstituttet

Henstra, A., 1998, 'Kroniek van het personen- en familierecht', *NEMESIS*, No. 6, p. 181-189

Holtrust, N., de Hondt, I., 1985, 'Gezamenlijk ouderlijk gezag', *NEMESIS*, No. 5, p. 241-246

Husa, J., 2004, 'Classification of Legal Families Today – Is It Time for a Memorial Hymn?' *Revue Internationale de Droit Comparé*, p. 11-38

Højgaard Pedersen, M., 2002, 'Når den fælles forældremyndighed skal ophøre', *TFA*, p. 81-83

Illum, K., 1932, 'Skyld og Skilsmisse', *UFR*, p. 274

Jansen, S. ,2003, 'Gezamenlijk gezag moet, en omgang niet minder', in: de Bruijn-Lückers, M.L.C.C., Giele, J.F.M., Heida, A., Kraan, C.A., Zonnenberg, Vos, M.J., (Eds.), *EB Klassiek*, Deventer: Kluwer

Jansen, S., 2002, 'Gezamenlijk gezag na scheiding: over een dubieuze voorwaarde', *FJR*, p. 109-111

Jensen, T., 1990, 'Domstolenes retsskabende, retsudfyldende og responderende virksomhed', *UFR*, p. 441-448

Jeppesen, C., Kronborg, A., 2007, 'Danish Regulation of the Parent-Child Relationship', in: Schwenzer, I. (Ed.), *Tensions Between Legal, Biological and Social Conceptions of Parentage*, Antwerp-Oxford: Intersentia

Jeppesen, C., 2006, 'Administratieve echtscheiding in Denemarken' in: M.V. Antokolskaia, *Herziennning van het echtscheidingsrecht*, Amsterdam: SWP

Jeppesen de Boer, C.G., 2005, 'Administratieve Ectscheiding in Denemarken, *FJR*, p. 231-235

Jeppesen, C., 2002, 'Moeder- en Vaderschap in Denemarken: de nieuwe Deense kinderwet gezien vanuit een Nederlands perspectief', *FJR*, p. 174-181

Jeugdbeschermingsrecht, Commission Wiarda, 26.01.1971

Kaganas, F., Piper, C., 2001, 'Grandparents and Contact: 'Rights v Welfare' revisited', *International Journal of Law, Policy and the Family*, Volume 15, No. 2, p. 250-275

Kalverboer, M., Zijlstra, E., 2006, *Het belang van het kind in het Nederlands recht, voorwaarden voor ontwikkeling vanuit een pedagogisch perspectief*, Amsterdam: SWP

Kjølbro, J.F., 2005, *Den Europæiske Menneskerettighedskonvention*, Copenhagen: Jurist- og Økonomforbundets Forlag

Kleijkamp, A, 1998, '*Family life and family interests*', Utrecht

Knijn, T., 2002, 'Social and Family Policy, the case of the Netherlands,' available on www.york.ac.uk

Koens, M.J.C., van Wamelen, C.G.M., 2001, *Kind en scheiding*, the Hague: Koninklijke Vermande

Kok, J., 2006, 'Gelijkwardig ouderschap, een nieuwe norm in het scheidingsrecht', in: Antokolskaia, M.V. (Ed.), *Herzienning van het ectscheidingsrecht*, Amsterdam: SWP

Kokkini-Iatridou, D., 1988, *Een inleiding tot het rechtvergelijkende onderzoek*, Deventer: Kluwer

Kokkini-Iatridou, D., 1986, 'Some methodological aspects of comparative law', *NILR*, p. 143-194

Kronborg, A, *Forældremyndighed og Menneskelig Integritet*, 2007, Copenhagen: Jurist- og Økonomforbundets Forlag

Kronborg, A., 2000, 'Forvaltning af familieretligt samvær', *Juristen*, No. 9, p. 325-333

Kweens, W.J.P., 1998, 'Nieuwe wetgeving inzake het ouderlijk gezag na echtscheiding', *FJR*, p. 278-284

Lagoutte, S. (Ed.), 2004, '*Prohibition of Discrimination in the Nordic Countries: The Complicated fate of Protocol No. 12 to the European Convention on Human Rights*', Copenhagen: The Danish Institute for Human Rights

Lenters, H., 1993, *De rol van de rechter in de echtscheidingsprocedure*, Arnhem: Gouda Quint

van Leuven, C.A.R.M, 1998, 'De verblijfplaats van het kind na echtscheiding', *EB*, p. 1-5

van Leuven, C.A.R.M., 1998, 'Het gezamenlijk gezag van ouders na scheiding, een praktijkmodel', *EB*, No. 10, p. 1-4

van der Lippe, T., Dijk, L., 2002, 'Comparative Research on Women's Employment', *Annual Review of Sociology*, No. 28, p. 221-241

Lookovsky, J., 2006, 'Precedent and the law in Denmark', to be found on http: //cisgw3.law.pace.edu/cisg/biblio/lookovsky15.html

Luijten, E.A.A., 1997, *Het Nederlandse personen- en familierecht*, part 1, Deventer: W.E.J. Tjeenk Willink

Lund-Andersen, I., Munck, N., Nørgaard, I., 2003, *Familieret*, Copenhagen: Jurist- og Økonomforbundets Forlag

Lünnemann, K., Steketee, M., Annuska, M., Overgaag, M., 2003, *Minderjarigen als procespartij*, Utrecht: Verwey-Jonker Instituut

Maris, C.W., Jacobs, F.C.L.M., 2001, *Rechtsvinding en de Grondslagen van het Recht*, Assen: Van Gorcum

Mertz, E.M., Schultze, H.J., 2007, 'Relatie gescheiden ouders en hun kinderen', *Demos*, No. 5, p. 6-8

Meyer, S., 2004, 'Nye regler er hul i hovedet', *Dagens medicin*, 19.11.2004

Mnookin, R.H., 1975, 'Child Custody Adjudication: Judicial functions in the Face of Indeterminacy', *Law and Contemporary Problems*, No. 39, 1975, p. 226-293

van Moorsel, M., 2000, *Gezamenlijk Gezag: Een onderzoek naar de positie van de zorgouder na echtscheiding*, Utrecht: Wetenschapswinkel Rechten

van Moorsel, M., 2000, 'Het gezamenlijk gezag na echtscheiding', *Rechtshulp*, No. 3, p. 1-10

Nicolai, E., 2002, 'Bij gezamenlijk gezag geen ontzegging van omgang', *Perspectief*, No. 5, p. 17

Nicolai, E.J., 1998, 'De juridische positie van de niet-verzorgende ouder na echtscheiding', *NJB*, p. 695-699

Nielsen, L., Vorstrup Rasmussen, 2001, *Familieretten*, Copenhagen: GadJura

Nieuwenhuis, H, Stolker, C.J.J.M., Valk, W.L., Koens, M.J.C., Vonken, A.P.M.J., 2004, *Personen- en Familierecht, Tekst en Commentaar*, Deventer: Kluwer

van Nispen, C.J.J.C., van Mierlo, A.I.M., Polak, M.V., 2002, *Burgelijke Rechtsvordering, Tekst & Commentaar*, Deventer: Kluwer

Normen 2000, Raad voor de kinderbescherming

Orloff, A.S., 2002, 'Women's Employment and Welfare Regimes: Globalization, Export Orientation and Social Policy in Europe and North America', Social Policy and Development Programme, Geneva: United Nations Research Institute for Social Development, Paper No. 12

Polak, M.V., Polak, J.M., 1986, 'Faux pas ou pas de deux? Recent developments in the relationship between the legislature and the judiciary in the Netherlands', *Netherlands International Law Review*, p. 371-411

Punselie, E.C.C., 2007, 'Artsen let op!', *FJR*, No. 57, p. 133

Punselie, E.C.C., 2005, 'Geen verantwoordelijkheid nemen, dan geen gezag!', *FJR*, p. 161

Punselie, E.C.C., 2001, 'Gezamenlijk gezag', *FJR*, p. 313

Rafffnsøe, S., 2002, *Sameksistens uden common sense. En elliptisk arabesk*, Volume I-III, Copenhagen: Akademisk Forlag A/S

Reece, H., 1996, 'The Paramountcy Principle, Consensus or Construct', *Current Legal Problems*, p. 267-304

Regelforenkling på det familieretlige område, 2003, Copenhagen: Justitsministeriet, December 2003

Reinhartz, B.E., 2000, 'Afstamming' in: *De familie geregeld*, Lelystad: Koninklijke Vermande

van Rooijen, C., 2007, *Scheiden zonder vrijheid, Is gezamenlijk ouderlijk gezag na echtscheiding in het belang van het kind?*, Nijmegen: Wolf Legal Publishers

Rood-De-Boer, M., 1986, 'Duidelijkheid en Zekerheid', *NJB*, p. 601-603

Rood-de Boer, M., 1962, *Ouders en Kinderen, aspecten van het familierecht*, Amsterdam: Becht

Ross, A., 1953, *Om ret og retfærdighed*, Copenhagen: Nyt Nordisk Forlag

Ruitenberg, G.C.A.M., 2003 *Het Internationaal Kinderrechtenverdrag in de Nederlandse rechtspraak*, Amsterdam: SWP

Rytter, J. E., 2003, *Den Europæiske Menneskerettighedskonvention – og dansk ret*, Copenhagen: Forlaget Thomson, Gad Jura

Schols, F.W.J.M., 1998, 'Gezamenlijk gezag en gezamenlijke voogdij, een goed begin van het nieuwe jaar', *WPNR*, p. 1-5

Scholten, P., 1974, *Mr. C. Assers Handleiding tot de beoefening van het Nederlandse Burgerlijk Recht, Algemeen deel*, Zwolle: Tjeenk Willenk

Schrama, M.H., 2007, 'Is het Nederlandse afstammingsrecht in strijd met het gelijkheidsbeginsel? Over kinderen en badwater', *RM Themis*, No. 3, p. 86-94

Schweppe, K, 2002, 'Child protection in Europe: Different Systems – Common Challenges', *German Law Journal*, Vol. 3, No. 10

Smith, C.E., 2005, *Regels van Rechtsvinding*, the Hague: Boom Juridische uitgevers

Spiermann, O., 2006, 'Lovgivnings tilsidesættelse og det retlige grundlag herfor: Grundlov – menneskerettighedskonvention – traktat', *UFR*, p. 187-192

Spiermann, O., 2002, 'Tilbageholdenhed i anvendelsen af internationale menneskerettighedskonventioner', UFR, p. 412-418

Spruijt, E., 2007, *Scheidingskinderen*, Amsterdam: SWP

Spruijt, E., Mallens, M., Mos, M.M., Topper, G., Vugt, R., van Leuven, C., 2004, 'Onderzoek naar effecten van vrijwillige en forensische scheidingsbemiddeling', *EB*, p. 37-40

Spruijt, E., 2002, *Het verdeelde kind*, Utrecht

Sumner, I., Forder, C., 2006, 'The Dutch Family Law Chronicles: Constituted Parenthood notwithstanding divorce', in: Bainham, A. (Ed.), *The International Survey of Family Law*, Briston: Jordan Publishing Limited

Sumner, I., Warendorf, H., 2003, *Family Law Legislation of the Netherlands, A translation including Book 1 of the Dutch Civil Code procedural and transitional provisions and private international law legislation*, Antwerp-Oxford-New York: Intersentia

Tak, P.J.P., Fiselier, J.P.S., 2004, *Denemarken – Nederland, De rechtspleging vergeleken*, Nijmegen: Wolf Legal Publishers

van Teffelen, P.A.J.Th., 2007, 'Vertrouwelijk of geheim kinderverhoor', *EB*, No. 7, p. 83-87

van Teffelen, P.: 'Gezamenlijke gezag na scheiding: tijdbom, lege huls of groeimodel', *FJR* 2000, p. 26-29

van Triest, A., 2004, 'Het kinderverhoor in het resort Den Bosch onder de loep', *FJR*, p. 16-26

Tuinstra, R.M.H.H., 2006, 'Ontzegging omgang aan gezagouder via achterdeur van art. 1:253a BW', *EB*, p. 64-66

Tøgersen, L., Fogt-Nielsen, C, 2007, 'Aftaler om børnebidrag og ægtefællebidrag – en gennemgang af regler og praksis' *TFA*, p. 35-40

Vlaardingerbroek, P., 2006, 'Echtscheiding, ouderschap en voortgezet gezag', in: Antokolskaia, M., '*Herzienning van het echtscheidingsrecht*', Amsterdam: SWP

Vlaardingerbroek, P., 2006, in: Chorus, J., Gerver, P., Hondius, E., *Introduction to Dutch law*, Alphen aan den Rijn: Kluwer Law International

Vlaardingerbroek, P., Blankman, K., van der Linden, A.P., Punselie, E.C.C., van Wamelen, C.G.M., 2002, *Het hedendaagse personen- en familierecht*, Deventer: Tjeenk Willink

Vonk, M., 2007, *Children and their Parents, A comparative study of the legal position of children with regard to their intentional and biological parents in English and Dutch law*, Antwerp-Oxford: Intersentia

Vonk, M, 2006, 'Voorkinderen en gezamenlijk gezag door huwelijk', *WPNR*, No. 6671, p. 457-459

Vonk, M., 2005, 'Enige overdenkingen bij de voorgestelde wijziging van art. 1:253o en de positie van de opvoeder niet-ouder', *FJR*, p. 34-39

Vranken, J.B.M., 2005, *Mr. C. Asser's Handleiding tot de beoefening van het Nederlands Burgelijk Recht, Algemeen deel, een vervolg*, Deventer: Kluwer

de Vries, A.D.W., van Tricht, F.J.G., 1910, *Geschiedenis der wet op de ouderlijke macht en de voogdij*, part I, Haarlem: Tjeenk Willink & Zoon

de Vries, A.D.W., van Tricht, F.J.G., 1905, *Geschiedenis der wet op de ouderlijke macht en de voogdij*, part II, Groningen: J.B. Wolters

de Vries, L., 1986, 'De Hoge Raad als pseudo-wetgever', *NJB*, p. 1117-1119

van Wamelen, C., 2000, 'Eenhoofdig gezag na scheiding', *NEMESIS*, p. 58-63

van Wamelen, C.G.M., 1997, 'Nieuw Gezagsrecht', *FJR*, p. 264-274

van Wamelen, C., 1996, 'De eerbiediging van een zorgrelatie', *NEMESIS*, p. 76-82

van Wamelen, C., 1984, '*Ouderschap en ouderlijke gezag na scheiding: voorstellen tot wetgeving op basis van art. 8 EVRM, de Recommendation on parental responsibilties van de Raad van Europa (1984) en empirisch onderzoek naar opvattingen van kinderen over gezin en echtscheiding*', Zwolle: W.E.J. Tjeenk Willink

Webner, C., Abrahamson, P., 'Individualisation of family life and family discourses', 2004, ESPAnet conference, Oxford available on www.apsoc.ox.ac.uk

Wiarda, G.J., 1988, *3 typen van Rechtsvinding*, Zwolle: W.E.J. Tjeenk Willink

Wiarda, J. (ASSER-WIARDA), 1957, *Handleiding tot de beoefening van het Nederlands burgerlijk recht*, part 1, Zwolle: Tjeenk-Willink

Willems, A.W.M., 1986, 'Ouderlijke macht van ongehuwden', *NJB*, p. 604-607

Wortmann, S.F.M., 2002, 'Bij gezamenlijk gezag kan rechter toch omgang met kind ontzeggen', *Perspectief*, No. 4, p. 26

Wortmann, S.F.M., 1998, *Als een eigen kind*, the Hague

Wortmann, S., 1996, 'Duidelijkheid en Zekerheid', *NJB*, p. 603-603

Zahle, H., 2003, *Menneskerettigheder*, Copenhagen: Christian Ejlers Forlag

Zahle, H., 2003, *Omsorg for retfærdighed*, Copenhagen: Gyldendal

Zahle, H., 2001, *Dansk Forfatningsret 2*, Copenhagen: Christian Ejlers Forlag

Zahle, H., 1987, *Dansk Forfatningsret 4*, København: Christian Ejlers Forlag

Zweigert, K., Kötz, H.,1995, *An introduction to Comparative Law*, Oxford: Clarington Press

Danish Commission reports:

Udkast til lov om ægteskabs indgåelse og opløsning, 1913

Commission report No. 369/1964

Commission report 4, No. 719/1974

Commission report 7, No. 796/1977

Commission report 8, No. 9157/1980

Commission report No. 918/1981

Commission Report No. 985/1983

Commission report No. 1220/1991, Betænkning om den Europæiske menneskerettighedskonvention og dansk ret

Commission report No. 1279/1994, Fælles forældremyndighed, samværsvanskeligheder, børnesagkyndig rådgivning

Commission report No. 1350/1997, Betænkning om børns retsstilling

Commission report No. 1407/2001, Betænkning om inkorporering af menneskerettighedskonventioner

Commission report No. 1475/2006 Barnets perspektiv, Forældremyndighed, Barnets bopæl, Samvær, Tvangsfuldbyrdelse

TABLE OF CASES

I. The Netherlands

Hoge Raad (Supreme Court):

Hoge Raad 28.08.1939, *NJ* 1939, 948 annotated by P. Scholten
Hoge Raad 04.02.1983, *NJ* 1983, 527 annotated by E.A.A. Luijten
Hoge Raad 04.05.1984, *NJ* 1985, 510, annotated by E.A.A. Luijten, E.A. Alkema.
Hoge Raad 21.03.1986, *NJ* 1986, 585 annotated by E.A.A. Luijten and E.A. Alkema
Hoge Raad 21.03.1986, *NJ* 1986, 586 annotated by E.A.A. Luijten and E.A. Alkema
Hoge Raad 21.03.1986, *NJ* 1986, 587 annotated by E.A.A. Luijten and E.A. Alkema
Hoge Raad 21.03.1986, *NJ* 1986, 588, annotated by E.A.A. Luijten and E.A. Alkema
Hoge Raad 14.04.1989, *NJ* 1989, 469
Hoge Raad 25.05.1990, *NJ* 1991, 267 annotated by E.A.A. Luijten
Hoge Raad 19.11.1993, *NJ* 1994, 241, annotated by W. Hammerstein-Schoonderwoerd
Hoge Raad 21.11.1997, *NJ* 1998, 164
Hoge Raad 10.09.1999, *NJ* 2000, 20 annotated by S.F.M. Wortmann
Hoge Raad 10.09.1999, *NJ* 2000, 167 annotated by S.F.M. Wortmann
Hoge Raad 19.11.1999, *NJ* 2001, 214 annotated by Th.M. de Bolkenstein Boer
Hoge Raad 15.12.2000, *NJ* 2001, 123 annotated by S.F.M. Wortmann
Hoge Raad 15.12.2000, *NJ* 2001, 710 annotated by S.F.M. Wortmann
Hoge Raad 13.04.2001, *NJ* 2002, 4
Hoge Raad 29.06.2001, *NJ* 2001, 598
Hoge Raad 10.08.2001, *NJ* 2002, 278, annotated by J. De Boer
Hoge Raad 05.04.2002, LJN AD9142
Hoge Raad 19.04.2002, *NJ* 2002, 458.
Hoge Raad 07.02.2003, LJN AF0892
Hoge Raad 28.03.2003, *NJ* 2003, 359 annotated by S.F.M. Woortmann
Hoge Raad 13.07.2004, LJN ZC3639
Hoge Raad, 29.10.2004, LJN AR1213
Hoge Raad 18.03.2005, LJN AS8525
Hoge Raad 27.05.2005, *NJ* 2005, 485 annotated by J. de Boer
Hoge Raad 27.05.2005, LJN AS7054
Hoge Raad 18.11.2005, *NJ* 2005, 574 annotated by S.F.M. Wortmann
Hoge Raad 31.03.2006, *NJ* 2006, 392 annotated by S.F.M. Wortmann
Hoge Raad 31.03.2006, LJN AV2863

Hoge Raad 28.04.2006, *NJ* 2006, 284
Hoge Raad 10.11.2006, LJN AY8773
Hoge Raad 23.03.2007 LJN AZ5443
Hoge Raad 14.09.2007, LJN BA5198

Hoven (Appeal Courts):
Gerechtshof 's-Hertogenbosch 28.06.1973, *NJ* 1974, 6
Gerechtshof Amsterdam 07.01.1999, *FJR* 1999 No. 12, p. 259
Gerechtshof 's-Hertogenbosch 07.07.1999, *Nemesis*, No. 1271
Gerechtshof Amsterdam 20.09.2001, *FJR* 2001, p. 342/343 annotated by P. Dorhout
Gerechtshof 's-Gravenhage 13.02.2002, LJN AE2305
Gerechtshof's-Hertogenbosch 04.06.2002, LJN AE4053
Gerechtshof 's-Gravenhagen 03.07.2002, LJN AE8529
Gerechtshof 's-Hertogenbosch 26.11.2002, LJN AF2955
Gerechtshof Leeuwarden 05.02.2003, *NJ* 2003, 352
Gerechtshof 's-Gravenhage 05.03.2003, LJN AG1643
Gerechtshof 's-Gravenhage 27.08.2003, LJN AI1828
Gerechtshof 's-Gravenhage 03.09.2003, LJN AL8181
Gerechtshof Amsterdam 07.01.2004, LJN AO5637
Gerechtshof 's-Hertogenbosch 15.04.2004, LJN AO7714
Gerechtshof 's-Gravenhage 12.05.2004, LJN: AP0510
Gerechtshof Arnhem 08.06.2004, LJN: AQ5059
Gerechtshof 's-Gravenhage 04.08.2004, LJN AQ6572
Gerechtshof 's-Hertogenbosch 09.09.2004, LJN AR5959
Gerechtshof Arnhem 16.11.2004, LJN AR8769
Gerechtshof 's-Hertogenbosch 15.12.2004, LJN AS2646
Gerechtshof 's-Hertogenbosch, 13.01.2005, LJN AS2624
Gerechtshof Amsterdam 27.01.2005, LJN AS6020
Gerechtshof Amsterdam 17.02.2005, LJN: AT2891
Gerechtshof Arnhem 22.03.2005, LJN: AT2560
Gerechtshof Amsterdam, 07.07.2005, LJN AY3928
Gerechtshof 's-Gravenhage 31.08.2005, LJN AS6020
Gerechtshof 's-Gravenhage 21.09.2005, LJN AU3030
Gerechtshof 's-Gravenhage 22.03.2006, LJN AX7311
Gerechtshof 's-Hertogenbosch 30.03.2006, LJN AX9618
Gerechtshof Amsterdam, 06.07.2006, LJN AY3929
Gerechtshof Arnhem 29.08.2006, LJN AZ5530
Gerechtshof 's-Hertogenbosch 31.08.2006, LJN AZ2571
Gerechtshof''s-Hertogenbosch 11.10.2006, LJN AZ3900
Gerechtshof 's-Gravenhage 18.10.2006, LJN AZ2072
Gerechtshof 's-Hertogenbosch 26.02.2007 LJN BA1915
Gerechtshof 's-Gravenhage 06.06.2007, LJN BA9040

Gerechtshof 's-Hertogenbosch 11.06.2007, LJN BB1534
Gerechtshof 's-Hertogenbosch 09.07.2007, LJN BB1541
Gerechtshof Leeuwarden 01.08.2007, LJN BB1198

Rechtbanken (District Courts):
Rechtbank Roermond 11.02.1999, *Nemesis*, No. 1038, p. 17
Rechtbank Roermond 29.03.2001, LJN AB1868
Rechtbank Zutpen 02.07.2003, LJN AH9200
Rechtbank Maastricht 18.11.2003, LJN AN8695
Sector kanton Rechtbank Zwolle, 09.02.2004, LJN: AO3270
Rechtbank Utrecht, 28.07.2004, LJN: AQ9901
Rechtbank Zwolle 19.08.2004, LJN ATAQ7125
Rechtbank Roermond 10.11.2004, LJN AR5891
Rechtbank Zutphen, 10.11.2004, LJN: AR5611
Rechtbank Haarlem, 02.12.2004, LJN: AR5017
Rechtbank Arnhem 12.01.2005, LJN AS3527
Rechtbank Utrecht 26.01.2005, LJN AS6703
Rechtbank Zwolle, 24.02.2005, LJN: AS7567
Rechtbank Haarlem 15.04.2005, LJN AT4422
Rechtbank Haarlem 26.07.2005, LJN AU0323
Rechtbank Rotterdam 11.10.2005, LJN AU 4409
Rechtbank 's-Gravenhage 21.11.2005, LJN AU8801
Rechtbank Groningen 07.02.2006, LJN AV4849
Rechtbank Leeuwarden 15.02.2006, LJN AV5268
Rechtbank Alkmaar 16.02.2006, LJN AV2146
Rechtbank Alkmaar 05.04.2006, LJN 8683 XX
Rechtbank Utrecht 12.04.2006, LJN AZ1191
Rechtbank 's-Hertogenbosch 11.07.2006, LJN AY6483
Rechtbank Utrecht 18.08.2006, LJN AZ1192
Rechtbank 's-Gravenhage 02.02.2007, *FJR* 2007, 63 annotated by IJ. Pieters
Rechtbank Haarlem 06.02.2007, LJN AZ9643
Rechtbank Haarlem 06.02.2007, LJN AZ9635
Rechtbank Haarlem 27.02.2007, LJN BA1742
Rechtbank Haarlem 20.03.2007, LJN BA1738
Rechtbank Amsterdam 12.07.2007, LJN BA9482
Rechtbank Rotterdam 23.07.2007, LJN BB0581
Rechtbank Haarlem 14.08.2007, LJN BB1817
Rechtbank Roermond 12.09.2007, LJN BB3532

Others:

Centrale Raad van Beroep 22.06.1999, *RSV* 1999, 235
Centraal Tuchtcollege voor de Gezondheidszorg 23.11.2006, *Tijdschrift voor Gezondheidsrecht*, 2007, No. 31, p. 161-165
Regionaal Tuchtcollege voor de Gezondheidszorg te Eindhoven 01.02.2007, *Tijdschrift voor Gezondheidsrecht*, 2007, No. 31, p. 321-324

II. Denmark

Højesteret (Supreme Court):

Højesteret 12.08.1996, *UFR* 1996.1300H
Højesteret 06.04.1998, *UFR* 1998.800H
Højesteret 30.10.2000, *UFR* 2001.153H
Højesteret 25.09.2001, *UFR* 2001.2518H
Højesteret 21.05.2002, *UFR* 2002.1789H
Højesteret 03.11.2003, *UFR* 2004.296H
Højesteret 28.10.2004, *UFR* 2005.363H
Højesteret 24.08.2007, case No. 82/2007 as yet unpublished

Landsretter (High Courts)

Vestre Landsret 15.11.1991, *UFR* 1992.186V
Vestre Landsret 15.12.1994, *UFR* 1995.249V
Vestre Landsret 01.12.1995, *UFR* 1996.428V
Østre Landsret 29.08.1996, *TFA* 1997.181Ø
Vestre Landsret 14.12.2001, *TFA* 2002.144V
Østre Landsret 28.01.2002, *TFA* 2002.938Ø
Østre Landsret 28.05.2003, *TFA* 2003.392Ø
Vestre Landsret 04.06.2003, *TFA* 2003.395V
Vestre Landsret 28.11.2003, *TFA* 2004.139V
Vestre Landsret 24.08.2004, *TFA* 2004.535V
Østre Landsret 15.09.2005, *TFA* 2006.450Ø
Østre Landsret 14.02.2006, *TFA* 2006.227Ø
Østre Landsret 16.02.2006, *TFA* 2006.238Ø
Østre Landsret 21.02.2006, *TFA* 2006.250Ø
Østre Landsret 24.02.2006, *UFR* 2006.1623Ø
Østre Landsret 27.03.2006, *UFR* 2006.1959Ø
Østre Landsret 28.06.2006, *UFR* 2006.2816Ø
Vestre Landsret 28.09.2006, *UFR* 2007.92V
Østre Landsret 01.11.2006, *UFR* 2007.673Ø
Østre Landsret 19.12.2006, *TFA* 2007.267Ø

Familiestyrelsen (Family Agency):
Familiestyrelsen, *TFA* 2006.356CS

III. ECtHR

ECtHR 13.06.1979 Paula Marcx v. Belgium
ECtHR 28.11.1984 Rasmussen v. Denmark, 8777/79
ECtHR 08.07.1987 R. v. UK, 10496/83
ECtHR 28.11.1988 Nielsen v. Denmark, 10929/84
ECtHR 24.05.1989 Hauschildt v. Denmark, 10486/83
ECtHR 23.06.1993 Hoffmann v Austria, 12875/87
ECtHR 28.02.1994 Boyle v. the UK, 16580/90
ECtHR 26.05.1994 Keegan v. Ireland, 16969/90
ECtHR 27.10.1994 Kroon v. the Netherlands, 18535/91
ECtHR 09.06.1998 Bronda v. Italy, 22430/93
ECtHR 21.12.1999 Salgueiro da Silva Mouta v. Portugal, 33290/96
ECtHR 11.07.2000 Cernecki v. Austria, 31061/96
ECtHR 13.07.2000 Scozzari and Giunta v. Italy, 39221/98, 41963/98
ECtHR 19.06.2003 Nekvedavicious v. Germany, 46165/1999
ECtHR 12.02.2004 Perez v. France, 47287/99
ECtHR 01.06.2004 Lebbinck v. The Netherlands, 45582/99.
ECtHR 22.11.2001 R.W. and C.T.G.-W v. Austria, 36222/97

IV. European Commission on Human Rights

BN v. Denmark, 09.10.1989, 13557/88.
18.05.1999 Wolff Metternich v. the Netherlands, 45908/99.

CURRICULUM VITAE

Christina Gyldenløve Jeppesen de Boer was born on 19 December 1968 in Copenhagen. She studied law at the University of Copenhagen and the University of Edinburgh and graduated with a master's degree from the University of Copenhagen in 1994. In the period 1994-1999 she worked as a lawyer in Copenhagen, simoultaneously tutoring family and inheritance law at the University of Copenhagen. In 1998 she was admitted to the Danish Bar Association. After relocating to the Netherlands in 1999 she worked briefly in the field of international tax advice before starting to work on this PHD thesis in 2001 at the University of Utrecht's Molengraaff Institute for Private Law.

EUROPEAN FAMILY LAW SERIES

1. Legal Recognition of Same-Sex Couples in Europe, K. Boele-Woelki and A. Fuchs (eds.)
2. European Family Law in Action Volume I: Grounds for divorce, K. Boele-Woelki, B. Braat and I. Sumner (eds.)
3. European Family Law in Action Volume II: Maintenance Between Former Spouses, K. Boele-Woelki, B. Braat and I. Sumner (eds.)
4. Perspectives for the Unification and Harmonisation of Family Law in Europe, K. Boele-Woelki (ed.)
5. Family Law Legislation of the Netherlands, I. Sumner and H. Warendorf
6. Indépendance et interdépendance patrimoniales des époux dans le régime matrimonial légal des droits néerlandais, français et suisse, B. Braat
7. Principles of European Family Law Regarding Divorce and Maintenance Between Former Spouses, K. Boele-Woelki, F. Ferrand, C. González Beilfuss, M. Jänterä-Jareborg, N. Lowe, D. Martiny and W. Pintens
8. Inheritance Law Legislation of the Netherlands, I. Sumner and H. Warendorf
9. European Family Law in Action Volume III: Parental Responsibilities, K. Boele-Woelki, B. Braat and I. Curry-Sumner (eds.)
10. Common Core and Better Law in European Family Law, K. Boele-Woelki (ed.)
11. All's well that ends registered?, I. Curry-Sumner (ed.)
12. Model Family Code – From a global perspective, I. Schwenzer and M. Dimsey
13. Harmonisation of Family Law in Europe. A Historical Perspective, M. Antokolskaia
14. Brussels II bis: Its Impact and Application in the Member States, Katharina Boele-Woelki and Cristina González Beilfuss (eds.)
15. Tensions between Legal, Biological and Social Conceptions of Parentage, I. Schwenzer (ed.)
16. Principles of European Family Law Regarding Parental Responsibilities, K. Boele-Woelki, F. Ferrand, C. González Beilfuss, M. Jänterä-Jareborg, N. Lowe, D. Martiny and W. Pintens (eds.)
17. Juxtaposing Legal Systems and the Principles of European Family Law on Divorce and Maintenance, E. Örücü and J. Mair (eds.)
18. Convergence and Divergence of Family Law in Europe, M. Antokolskaia (ed.)
19. European Challenges in Contemporary Family Law, K. Boele-Woelki and T. Sverdrup (eds.)
20. Children and their parents, M. Vonk
21. La capacité de l'enfant dans les droits français, anglais et écossais, L. Francoz-Terminal
22. Joint parental authority, C.G. Jeppesen de Boer